The Apostles

The Apostles

Donald Guthrie

ZONDERVAN
PUBLISHING HOUSE
OF THE ZONDERVAN CORPORATION
GRAND RAPIDS, MICHIGAN 49506

THE APOSTLES

Copyright © 1975 by The Zondervan Corporation

Library of Congress Catalog Card Number 74-11856
ISBN 0-310-25421-3

Printed in the United States of America

83 84 85 86 87 88 — 10 9 8 7

Contents

7

THE END OF A MISSION AND ITS SEQUEL   104

8

A NEW CHARTER OF FREEDOM   115

9

PRACTICAL ADVICE AND PROGRESSIVE ADVENTURE   129

10

FROM PHILIPPI TO CORINTH   142

11

LETTERS TO THESSALONICA   157

12

FROM CORINTH TO EPHESUS   168

13

COMMENTS FOR CORINTH   179

21

A PERSONAL NOTE AND A GENERAL LETTER   313

22

LETTERS TO TWO FRIENDS   329

23

A WORD OF CONSOLATION   345

24

PETER TAKES TO WRITING   364

25

BRIEF LETTERS FROM JOHN   378

26

A GLIMPSE INTO THE FUTURE   387

List of Illustrations

Preface

The deeds and words of the apostles dominate the books of the New Testament outside the gospels. These books expound apostolic practice and doctrine. They are essentially a continuation of the life of Jesus. In this sense the present volume is a companion to my *Jesus the Messiah*. It is arranged on a similar pattern and aims both to present the New Testament information about the apostles and to set their writings in the context of early Christian history.

In this way it is hoped that a better appreciation of the origin and contents of the letters and of the Book of Revelation will be gained, together with an insight into the close connection between these books and the Book of Acts. It is recognized that some scholars maintain a different point of view regarding the historical reliability of many of the New Testament books from that adopted in this volume, which has been based on the dependability of the records. No discussion has been included of the various theories to the contrary, since these have been set out in detail and examined in my *New Testament Introduction*.

It is hoped that this book, like its companion volume, will inspire many to a more diligent study of the New Testament itself. For this reason it is arranged, like its predecessor, in convenient sections to provide a basis, if desired, for daily studies over a period of six months. The relevant New Testament passages are noted in each section.

The Apostles

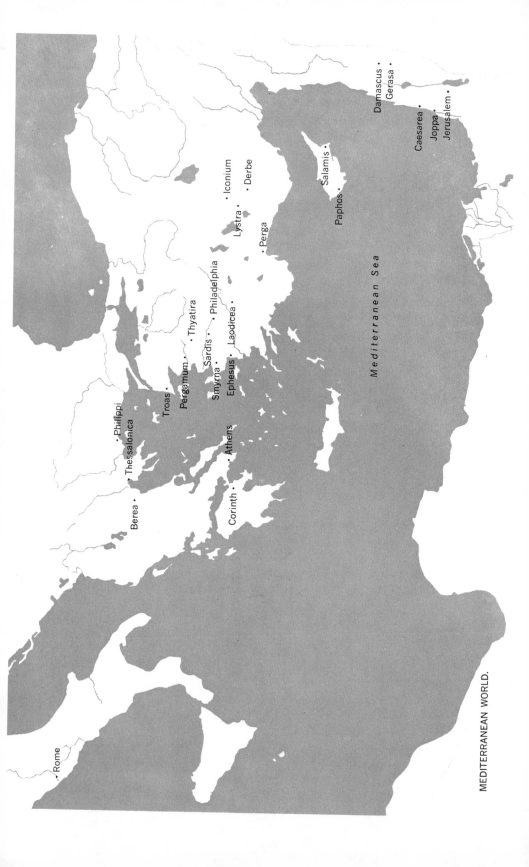

MEDITERRANEAN WORLD.

1

Beginnings

1. *Prologue to the Age of the Apostles*
(Acts 1:1-5)

The passion of Jesus was now over. What had appeared at first to the disciples to be a disaster had become the prelude of greater things to come. It was like the sudden bursting of dawn after a series of nightmares. The disciples now knew that Jesus was risen from the dead. That was the turning point in their spiritual experience. It opened up vistas of opportunities of which they had never dreamed. Their limited horizons were suddenly enlarged in a way which developed into a world mission. The account of how this happened is of abiding interest. It was this that led men to write down something of the events which had significance (the Book of Acts) and something of the Christian approach to the developing situation within the Church (the epistles).

We are indebted to Luke for giving us an insight into early Christianity. We must not suppose that he intended to write an exhaustive account. He has clearly been selective. But his introduction is worth pondering for its sets the scene for the whole book. It is addressed to Theophilus, which at once links it to Luke's gospel. It is of small importance who this Theophilus was, for the books which were addressed to him were clearly intended for a wider audience. No doubt Luke himself never thought that his book would become the only narrative of early Church history.

He reminds us that Jesus showed Himself alive to His disciples over a period of forty days. He had no doubt about the reality of the resurrection. He speaks of proofs, which rules out the view that the disciples were suffering from hallucinations. They did not convince themselves of the resurrection, because they needed to find some way of explaining the disaster of the crucifixion. The account which Luke gives us is solidly based on an unshakeable conviction that Jesus was alive and had continued His communication with men. The subsequent account of the activity of the apostles is unintelligible apart from this assumption. It is worth noting that the subject of the risen Lord's communication was the kingdom of God, a theme much spoken about by Jesus during His ministry, as Luke shows in his gospel (in common with Matthew and Mark). As the apostles preached the Gospel this kingdom theme did not find so much prominence, but there is no doubt that Luke recognized that the preaching of the apostles had as its basis the teaching of Jesus.

It was not an easy matter for men who had accompanied Jesus during His ministry to adjust themselves to the entirely new situation now that He had died and then had risen from death. Indeed it was impossible for them to adjust themselves. They were wholly unequipped to do so. The risen Lord had, however, anticipated this and had commanded them to wait for spiritual power. They needed the baptism of the Holy Spirit before the Christian Church could get off the ground. As Luke's narrative proceeds one is impressed by the number of times that he mentions the Spirit as the dynamic force behind the development of the Church. It is not without strong grounds that it has been suggested that a good name for his book would be the Acts of the Holy Spirit.

It is worth noting that Luke attaches importance to the command to the disciples to stay in Jerusalem. He can, of course, see the relevance of this as he looks back to the beginnings. But in his gospel he also shows special interest in Jesus' connection with Jerusalem. More than half the gospel describes Jesus moving toward Jerusalem, while all the resurrection appearances which Luke mentions are set in Jerusalem. It was the city which had rejected its Messiah. It was also the city which would witness the beginning of a movement which was to spread beyond the borders of Judaism to the whole world.

2. The Ascension of Jesus
(Acts 1:6-11)

None of the evangelists except Luke mentions the ascension. In his gospel the mention is very brief but he comes back to a

The Place of the Ascension of Jesus on the Mount of Olives.

fuller description of it here. Before he began the account of the development of the Church, it was essential for his readers to know that the missionary activity of the Church was the parting command of the risen Lord. He needed to show that the forty days of appearances were temporary and unrepeatable. The Church did not begin until after the final departure of Jesus, but He was still to be with His people in His Spirit.

It is understandable that the disciples had not as yet grasped the spiritual nature of the kingdom of God. Their minds were conditioned to thinking in material terms. They all came from a Jewish background, which means that they expected that when the Messiah came he would establish the kingdom of Israel. It is against this background that the disciples' question ("Lord, will you at this time restore the kingdom to Israel?"), put to the risen Lord just before His ascension, must be understood. The restoration of Israel was not, however, the mission of Jesus, not at any rate in the sense in which it was currently understood. The minds of the disciples were moving on the wrong plane. They were in fact asking the wrong question. They were prying into the future, into an area which God the Father had reserved for His own authority. The disciples' responsibility was in the present, not the future. Luke's story would never have been written had they continued to be preoccupied with future events. Although the teaching of Jesus about the future was important, He had warned His disciples against being obsessed with times and seasons.

The risen Lord's positive injunction has been the charter of the missionary Church ever since. All that was needed was a general directive. Matthew records the words of the great commission to go and make disciples of all nations, but Luke here shows a more specific approach. He shows that the development — Jerusalem, Judaea, Samaria, the end of the earth — had the sanction of the Lord Himself. This may be taken as the key to His plan. The subsequent course of events shows the spread of the Gospel from Jerusalem to Rome, from the center of the Jewish world to the center of the Gentile world. It is a reminder that Christian testimony must begin at home and spread outward.

The comprehensive character of the disciples' mission demanded a source of power beyond themselves. Luke adds a second promise from the Lord regarding the Spirit. There was no possibility that the disciples could witness to Jesus Christ in their own strength. They had not as yet fully grasped the significance of the resurrection and this was to be the main theme of the apostolic preaching. They desperately needed further illumination. But the promise of the Spirit was specific. It was not a pious hope, but a firm assurance. It is to be noted that one of the special functions of the Spirit in the promises given to the disciples by Jesus in the upper room (as John records them) was to bear testimony to Jesus. The New Testament idea of witness is inseparable from the idea of Christian believers. The promise was not given to some with special qualities, but to all committed to the Gospel. Spirit-filled men cannot absolve themselves from the Spirit's task of witness.

It was immediately after giving this specific commission that Jesus ascended. The disciples remembered seeing Him disappear into a cloud. There is no need to theorize about the location or direction. The finality of the disappearance is the most impressive feature. Luke knew, as they all knew, that after that day Jesus would never again appear as He had done over the past forty days. Luke would later record an appearance to Saul of Tarsus, but this was in a category of its own. The Church was to be launched by the Spirit, not by the Son. There was in fact to be a brief interval between the ascension and the coming of the Spirit at Pentecost to highlight this fact. The era of the Christian Church was to be distinguished from the time of the ministry of Jesus, although there was a continuity between them.

It is not surprising that the ascension left the disciples nonplussed. They indulged in momentary stargazing as if they were not sure what had happened. Or perhaps they were expecting Jesus to reappear. They had not grasped the finality of the event. They needed some further supernatural interpretation, which Luke describes in terms of a vision of two white-clad men giving a message about the future. Jesus would return in some such way as they had seen Him go, but the implication is that the time is not ripe. If the disciples had stood waiting for it to happen, no history of the Church would have been written. The little community would have died on its feet. But God had greater and better plans. Multitudes were yet to hear the Gospel before Jesus returned. The age of opportunity is still present and no one knows how much longer it will last. The whole matter is in the Father's hands. The Church's task is to witness.

3. *Days of Waiting*
(Acts 1:12-14)

It is impossible to say what was in the minds of the disciples as they crossed the valley from the Mount of Olives, where Jesus had given His final message to them, and entered again into Jerusalem. It was not a long journey, but their conversation must have been on the immediate future. How would they set about the task of witnessing in Jerusalem? It was only a few weeks since the Jews had crucified their Master. It was not likely that any of the disciples had any delusions about the probable hostility of the authorities toward a group of people who proclaimed their faith in a Jesus who had been crucified. As Jews the disciples would know full well that the religious authorities would regard a crucified man as cursed. It would make no sense to them that a group of his disciples were asserting that he had come to life again. In spite of the assurances of Jesus, these very human men must have been acutely aware of the formidable character of their task.

They were moving back to the upper room. It was there that Jesus had given such astonishing promises about the Spirit. They probably wondered what He meant when He had spoken about the Spirit coming upon them in His farewell words. To one versed in the Old Testament the idea would be linked with the prophetic commissions. Maybe the disciples reflected on the reluctance of men like Isaiah or Jeremiah and the need for repeated assurance that their commissions were from God. They would be surprised by the extent of the power when it came, but at this stage they could only conjecture.

On arriving at the upper room which was at present serving as their headquarters, they were in complete agreement about the best way of spending the time. Some of them, like Peter, may well have found it irksome to wait. Activist as he was, he agreed with the others that the Lord's command to wait must be obeyed. They would devote themselves to prayer. This exercise did much to prepare their minds for the Spirit's coming. It encouraged an attitude of dependence upon God apart from which the Spirit's activity would be impeded. The waiting period served to remind them that the initiative was with God and not with them. The Spirit's coming was to be a sovereign operation. The conditions of His coming have never changed. In the analogy used by Jesus

He comes as wind, invisible and unpredictable. If He is to visit His people today as He did in the beginnings, a similar attitude of humble dependence is indispensable.

Luke gives a list of the most notable people present in the upper room. Eleven of the disciples called by Jesus to be apostles are specifically named. Of these Peter is mentioned first, as he is in all the lists included in the gospels. There was no debate about the leadership. Those whom Jesus had appointed apostles were clearly at once acknowledged. The resurrection had not altered this. The apostolic office was the key to early Christian procedure.

But the apostles were accompanied by a considerable number of other disciples. Luke mentions that there were about 120 in all, but he only singles out Mary the mother of Jesus to refer to by name, although he does allude to the women, presumably those who had constantly ministered to the needs of Jesus during His public work. Perhaps the most significant inclusion in Luke's note is his mention of the brothers of Jesus. These had been hostile until now. The events of the passion and resurrection of Jesus had clearly effected a transformation. They are numbered among the "brethren," which shows that they were now identifying themselves with the disciples. Those sessions of prayer must have been sessions of revelation to those men who had had family connections with Jesus in the days of His flesh, but now found themselves thinking of Him in an entirely new way. They too were waiting for the Spirit so as to become witnesses to Him whom they had previously ridiculed.

4. *A Day of Decision*

(Acts 1:15-26)

Of the days that the disciples spent waiting and praying the most notable was when the apostles filled the vacancy in their number. (The vacancy had occurred through the defection of Judas.) It was Peter who broached the subject and his manner of doing so is worth noting because it shows the apostles' views about their own office. The apostolic office was of such importance that significance was attached to the original number chosen by Jesus. Being Jews the disciples may have seen some symbolic importance in the number twelve, corresponding to the twelve tribes of Israel. The nonconformist Jewish sect at Qumran in the Judaean desert also had a council of twelve. But the most probable reason why the apostles wanted to keep the complement of twelve was because of the importance which the authority of Jesus had given to it. Jesus' authority, however, had been disregarded by Judas. All the evangelists lay stress on the betrayal of Jesus by this man. It no doubt had a profound effect on the apostles. Luke records that Peter, in referring to the incident, specifically mentions that Judas was one of them and had had a share in their ministry with Jesus. That one of their own number would do such treachery as Judas was distressing for them all.

Luke sees the need for including a reference to Judas' untimely end, presumably because his readers might not know about it. He omits reference to it in his gospel, although Matthew mentions it in his. Both accounts agree that Judas committed suicide, although Matthew mentions hanging as the means while Luke suggests a headlong fall. Luke is less concerned with the details than with the fact of Judas' self-destruction. He does not mention, as Matthew does, the remorse of Judas. Nor does he mention that the chief priests bought the field with the betrayal money which Judas returned to them. For him it was enough that Judas himself was finally responsible. He remembers the name of the field, the field of blood, and knows that the place became well-known under that name in Jerusalem.

The most significant thing about Luke's reference to Judas' fate is that he records Peter's appeal to Scripture as a warrant for his suggestion that Judas' place should be filled. Peter recognized that what Scripture says is what the Spirit speaks. He referred to two Psalms (69 and 109), both of which are ascribed in their titles to David, but he regarded them as the voice of the Spirit. This high view of Old Testament Scriptures is reflected elsewhere in Luke's narrative. It was clearly assumed by the earliest Christians. The two Psalms do not, of course, refer to Judas, but since David was a type of the Messiah, his enemies were regarded as typical of the enemies of Jesus. The principle is the same and so justifies the appeal to Scripture. So deeply conscious were the apostles of the importance of the fulfillment of Scripture that even in the matters of an election for their own office they considered it to be imperative to appeal to Scripture, which also shows how important they considered the apostolic office to be.

The question of eligibility for the apostolic office is of great importance. Having been led to propose the appointment of a replacement for Judas on the basis of Scripture, they were at once faced with the problem of essential qualifications. They had never had to appoint an apostle. Jesus had done that. Perhaps they tried to think back to the reason why Jesus chose any one of them. The only obvious qualifications as far as they could see was the fact that all of them had followed Jesus from the earliest days of the preaching of John the Baptist till the day they saw Him ascend. Peter reasoned that the same qualification must hold for a replacement. It is obvious that this requirement would severely limit their range of choice. It involved a firm conviction that Jesus had risen from the dead, for the apostles' special task was to bear witness to this fact.

Two men met the requirements — Joseph Barsabbas and Matthias. Some method of choosing between them was therefore necessary. They at once acknowledged that the appointment of an apostle was God's task not men's and therefore committed the whole procedure to God in prayer. They were sincere in wanting God's choice and believed that He would answer the prayer through the casting of lots. The procedure raises problems. How could they be sure that the method used met with the divine approval? They could, of course, appeal to an Old Testament instance where the casting of lots revealed the divine will (Prov. 16:33). But it is significant that the early Church did not continue the practice. At least the Book of Acts mentions it only here. Perhaps the apostles soon learned that the Christian era would possess a better counterpart to the Old Testament Urim and Thummin (cf. 1 Sam. 14:41). The Christian era was the age of the Spirit whom Jesus had Himself promised as an infallible Guide.

Some have supposed that the apostles acted prematurely in the appointment of Matthias in view of the later calling of Paul to be an apostle. We do not hear any more of Matthias by name, and his enrollment among the twelve does not appear to have achieved anything, as far as Luke is concerned. Perhaps the apostles should have waited until after the gift of the Spirit at Pentecost. Who can say? One thing that is clear is that the casting of lots was firmly believed to have indicated the divine choice of Matthias. By the time of Saul of Tarsus, God used other ways of appointing men of His choice to the apostolic office.

5. The Descent of the Spirit

(Acts 2:1-4)

It was not an accident that the promised gift of the Spirit came on a festival day in the Jewish calendar. The feast of Pentecost was a joyous feast. It was originally the festival of firstfruits. Because of the gift of the Spirit on that day it has become as important in the Christian calendar as it was in the Jewish. The occasion had such widespread repercussions that it was well for the early Christians to be reminded of it and there was no more effective way than by replacing the Jewish with a Christian festival. The day on which it all happened was seven weeks after the Passover, and therefore after the crucifixion of Jesus. Enough time had elapsed to prepare the minds of the disciples for the gift they were told to expect.

All the followers of Jesus were assembled in one place. Luke does not tell us where. It was sufficiently spacious for a considerable crowd of people to meet. The size of the company of followers is indicated by the 120 people in the upper room during the period of waiting. The assembling together of such a group of people would in itself be sufficient to arouse considerable curiosity.

From what Luke says it is clear that the disciples were not expecting the Spirit to come as He did. The suddenness is vividly brought out in Luke's narrative. It was another evidence of the sovereignty of the Spirit. This inaugural coming could never have been engineered. It did not belong to the normal phenomena of history. It was supernatural and mysterious. The external accompaniments were intended to make this clear. The apostles themselves must have described what they saw and the information came into the hands of Luke. At least it is possible that the metaphors used by Luke were those reported to him. But words are poor channels for describing divine actions. They can only approximate the reality.

Luke speaks of a sound like a great rushing wind — a kind of thunderous tornado. The metaphor may have been suggested by the Old Testament use of wind to describe the activity of the Spirit (e.g., Ezek. 37). Jesus had Himself used wind to illustrate the Spirit (John 3:8). But if the wind itself was metaphorical, the sound certainly was not. Everyone heard it in the house where they were. Moreover crowds heard it outside. The tongues like fire are in a similar category. Although fire was metaphorical, symbolic of purity, something objective came to each one of them in turn. Luke narrates the occasion in deeply impressive terms. The sound and the sight must have contributed to a sense of awe. Because the Spirit's coming was a unique occasion — the launching of the Christian Church as a real community — it was fitting that supernatural signs should accompany the event. As the sequel shows, the uninitiated interpreted the signs quite differently.

The filling with the Spirit marks the fulfillment of the predictions of Jesus. It is characteristic in Luke's narrative for him to note when men are in a special way filled with the Spirit. The fact that he speaks of fullness is another instance where human language is stretched to describe the richness of Christian experience. Fullness suggests an absence of limit — a complete and satisfying experience. God does not give the Spirit by measure, as Jesus pointed out on one occasion (John 3:34). There is no niggardliness with Him.

The immediate sequel of the fullness was that the believers spoke in other tongues, that is in languages different from their own. Speaking in tongues is also mentioned by Paul in 1 Corinthians. There are two schools of interpretation of this phenomenon. Some think that the Acts happening concerned known foreign languages whereas the phenomenon in 1 Corinthians did not necessarily. Others consider that both Acts and 1 Corinthians refer to the same phenomenon, which was a normal accompaniment of early Christian experience. Luke's description of the effects (see next section) makes quite clear that intelligible languages were involved which needed no interpreter, whereas Paul says much about the gift of interpretation. What is of most interest here is the question why this phenomenon occurred at all at this initial stage in the development of the Christian Church. It is only possible to conjecture. But the universality of the Christian faith was by this means supernaturally demonstrated. The one basic message was to be translated into hundreds of languages as later the missionary activity of the Church developed. The many tongues were a sign that language was to be no barrier in the spread of the Gospel.

6. Popular Reactions to the Spirit's Working

(Acts 2:5-13)

Whenever God works in a manner outside man's normal experience, popular opinion will attempt a rationalization. Minds which are conditioned to think in material terms are completely baffled in the presence of the supernatural. A new dimension confronts them which is no part of their normal way of thinking. This happened on the day of Pentecost and Luke records the crowd's reactions, presumably because these were to be typical of what the developing Church would face.

Since it was festival time in Jerusalem the city was thronged with visitors from various parts of the ancient world who had come from the diaspora (the Jewish dispersion throughout Gentile countries) to worship. The Temple worship in Jerusalem was a great draw for Jews outside Palestine. It served as the symbol of unity for the Jewish people. Annual pilgrimages attracted great numbers. Luke mentions some of the areas from which pilgrims had come and his list covers many parts of Asia Minor, Arabia, North Africa, and Rome. Jerusalem had a cosmopolitan influx on these occasions. It included not only Jews but Gentile proselytes who had submitted to initiation into the Jewish faith. This initiation involved among other requirements circumcision.

It was when the people outside the house where the disciples were meeting heard the considerable noise accompanying the descent of the Spirit that their curiosity was aroused. It was so clearly abnormal that immediate investigation was natural. They were astonished at hearing the babel of voices, and even more astonished at hearing Palestinian Jews speaking in other languages which various people in the crowd recognized as their native tongue. There was evidently still enough of the Galilean inflection to enable the hearers to know at once the part of Palestine from which they came. As evidence increased through the recognition of more and more languages, the extraordinary character of the phenomenon impressed itself upon them. It was disturbing because inexplicable.

What they heard was the mighty works of God. That is how Luke reports the popular summary of the apostles' words. We are left to conjecture the precise contents of the message. We cannot suppose that the apostles omitted to mention the mightiest work of all, that of the redemption of man through Jesus Christ.

Luke does not even say whether the Christians were conscious of what they were saying. Their minds had been dwelling on God's activity and the descent of the Spirit in power was God's confirmation that they were to see that activity through their own witness to Jesus Christ.

There were two main attitudes which people adopted in the face of this inexplicable phenomenon. One was more realistic than the other. Many were so confused about the abnormal happenings that they could only ask, "What does this mean?" Of course, even this question may have various implications according to the tone of voice in which it is asked. It may include a genuine note of enquiry or it may be an expression of incredulity. Serious enquiry into spiritual phenomena is found all too seldom in popular reactions. When the human mind is confronted with abnormal happenings it more often dismisses them as unintelligible. The approach is — "We see no meaning in this; therefore it has no meaning." Where God still acts in a mighty way the same approach is to be found.

The other attitude seen in the Jerusalem crowd was the rationalistic. It is characteristic of some types of minds that all phenomena must be interpreted in terms of their own rationale. Such exuberance as the disciples were showing could be interpreted in spiritual terms only by those who are spiritually attuned. The rationalistic explanation was a surfeit of new wine. The people were drunk. Hasty popular rationalizations are basically uncritical. Whoever proposed this solution should have known that it was too early in the day for too much wine to have been consumed, as Peter points out in his address. But popular opinion rarely keeps an open mind in face of perplexing phenomenon. It is less disturbing to accept a wholly unlikely rational explanation than to leave open the possibility of spiritual forces of which the mind is ignorant.

7. The First Christian Sermon

(Acts 2:14-36)

One thing is certain about Peter's speech at Pentecost. It was not premeditated. It was not a conscious sermon at all. No rules of rhetoric hampered its spontaneity. It happened in response to a specific situation. The people's attitude toward the disciples demanded some comment. Conscious as he was of the infilling of the Spirit, Peter could not allow the new-wine rationalization to pass unchallenged. A spiritual explanation must be given of the spiritual phenomenon. Many of the considerable crowd which had now assembled were genuinely wanting some better explanation than the facile one which had been proposed.

Fishermen on the Sea of Galilee.

In his introductory remarks Peter gives a considerable quotation from Joel 2:28-32. In its original context the passage accompanies a call to repentance and a promise of forgiveness. These are the themes with which Peter ends (cf. Acts 2:38). The use of the Old Testament in early Christian preaching is brought out clearly in all the evangelistic sermons in Acts. The Old Testament was regarded as the Christian Scriptures. Both Jews and Christians accepted it as inspired and authoritative. As an informed Jew Peter would at least be conscious of the importance of scriptural testimony. The fulfillment of scripture in the events of the ministry of Jesus is stressed by all the evangelists, particularly by Matthew. And this idea of the foreshadowing in the old era of the major events of the new is carried over into the Acts narrative. Peter was addressing a Jewish audience which would be impressed by the witness of Scripture to contemporary happenings. A spiritual explanation which was based on a right understanding of Scripture would be the soundest approach to an audience such as Peter had. Indeed it is a sign of the authenticity of the Acts account that all the sermons are adapted to audiences of the most primitive stage in early Christian development. Joel's words had relevance for an age later than his own. The outpouring of the Spirit was to give spiritual vision to people in all stages of life. It was to be accompanied by signs in the natural world and by the offer of salvation in the spiritual world. The prophecy mixes mercy with judgment.

The second part of Peter's speech (2:22-36) is mainly historical although interspersed with scriptural quotations. The historical facts of Jesus' death and resurrection form the core of the sermon. But it is not a mere recital of facts. Peter sees the events from a theological point of view. The crucifixion was not merely seen as a criminal act of the Jewish authorities, but as part of the purpose of God. It is astonishing that so few weeks after the profound shock that the crucifixion brought to the disciples, it had dawned on the apostles that it was part of a definite divine plan. In Peter's approach there is an important connection between the historical Jesus, whose mighty works were known to his audience, and the exalted Christ. He insists that it was God who raised Him from the dead, backing His claim from the testimony of David in Psalm 16:8-11. For Peter the resurrection of Christ was the central feature of the Christian faith. Christians were promulgating a faith which had as its basis an event which strictly does not belong to the sphere of history. No one saw God raising Jesus from the dead, nor God exalting Him to His right hand. But Peter has no doubt about either proposition. He claims that all the Christians are witnesses to this fact. Yet it required an act of faith on his part to come to a theological interpretation of this, and would similarly demand an act of faith on the part of his hearers. Another Psalm (110:1) comes to Peter's mind as he affirms that God has made Lord and Messiah the man whom they had crucified. The directness of his statement is provocative. He makes no distinction between the Jewish public and their leaders. Indeed he assumes that the people must accept responsibility for what their leaders had done. This is particularly striking in view of the fact that many of Peter's hearers were probably not present in Jerusalem when the crucifixion took place.

It is instructive to note certain features about this sermon insofar as it can serve as a pattern. It at once introduces the hearers to the historic facts about Jesus of Nazareth and then proceeds to show a more than human view of Him. Although there is no attempt to bring out the depth of the Christian view of Jesus Christ, the two titles Lord and Christ contain in embryo much of what the Christian Church came to understand of the exalted nature of Jesus, especially as seen in the theology of Paul. Both titles must be seen against a Jewish background. The former was an accepted title for God in Old Testament times and the latter a title for the widely expected leader who was to come for the deliverance of Israel. The fact that the latter was usually conceived of in a political sense does not detract from the remarkable nature of Peter's announcement. This man who was crucified seven weeks ago was God's Messiah. Peter does not waste words on platitudes. He gets to the main point: who Jesus was. If the arrangement of the sermon cannot be regarded as a model, its theological purpose cannot be improved. Another feature is the strong scriptural basis which in modern times should be even more strengthened in view of the existence of the New Testament.

8. Audience Reaction

(Acts 2:37-41)

Since God has chosen to reveal Himself both in the acts of history and in the words of men, a study of audience reaction is of vital importance. Luke is careful to give specific information about the impact of this first Christian sermon. Peter's forthright style in laying the blame for the crucifixion fairly and squarely on the whole house of Israel (i.e., the Jewish nation) at once stung many in the audience into a willingness to respond. When Luke says that they were cut to the heart he means that they were profoundly disturbed by the challenge which Peter had put to them. They clearly had a conscience about their responsibility for rejecting Jesus as the Messiah. The preacher's shafts had struck home.

The question, "What shall we do?" is a considerable advance on the earlier question, "What does this mean?" The challenge is no longer abstract but personal. When conscience pricks there is an immediate urge to do something to alleviate the discomfort it brings. Nevertheless the question is wrongly phrased. It reflects too much the typical Jewish idea of salvation by merit. But it is not exclusively Jewish. Most men have the hope of gaining restitution with God. It is basic to all religions which rest on works. Doing is always easier than being. Peter's answer shows that Christianity is a matter of attitude rather than action.

The call to repentance reverberates throughout the New Testament. John the Baptist called for it. Jesus continued it in the first recorded words of His public ministry. Here in the first Christian sermon Peter calls for it, and later in the epistles the same theme is echoed. Repentance is both an acknowledgment of sin and a desire to be freed from its consequences. To repent involves a change of attitude, an act of humiliation before God. When this is done forgiveness is available, of which baptism is an outward symbol. It is important to note that Peter never said in answer to the question, "What must we do?", "Be baptized and that is all that is needed." To submit to any outward rite is simple compared with the spiritual revolution needed before a man can truly repent. It is also important to note that Peter's reference to baptism is in the name of Jesus. This at once distinguished it from the various other types of baptism being practiced in the contemporary world of the first century. Christian baptism in Jesus' name involved an identifying of oneself in Him. It was full of profound significance and must never be thought of as a liturgical formula. Peter's application of his appeal was on the broadest basis — "all that are far off." That was of wider application than Peter then knew, for it was wide enough to include Gentiles as well as Jews. But the Jerusalem apostles were not yet conditioned to the revolutionary idea that Christian salvation would overleap the deeply seated Jewish-Gentile barrier. All who responded would receive the gift of the Spirit, which implies that the gift was simultaneous with the act of faith.

Luke obviously could not report all that Peter said in his sermon. He speaks of "many other words," but gives only one example — "Save yourselves from this crooked generation." That command must have impressed him forcibly. It at once draws a clear line of distinction between the believers and their environment. It implies that faith in Christ is the one antidote to corruptness in contemporary society. Peter's expression is in full agreement with the approach of Jesus, who spoke of His own contemporaries as an evil generation.

The response to Peter's appeal was unbelievably great. Three thousand baptized must be regarded as a round figure, but it is most impressive. The sheer administration, of however primitive a kind, for coping with such a massive response can hardly be imagined. Luke does not say whether all the people were baptized on the same day. Such a detail is immaterial. They all came to identify themselves with the group of people who believed in Jesus and whose leaders were the apostles. It is easy to dismiss the massiveness of the response as exceptional in which case it cannot serve as a pattern for contemporary preachers. But there is no basic reason why similar responses should not occur. A danger which is ever present, however, is to imagine that the Spirit of God will repeat His activities in the same way.

2

Fellowship and Opposition

9. *Early Christian Fellowship*

(Acts 2:42-47)

When people have undergone a spiritual revolution, a new way
of life opens before them like an unexpected vista. It is not a
time for carefully calculated rules. It is rather a time for rejoicing
over present experiences and future prospects. The first impulse
is to enjoy the company of others of like mind. The considerable
number of converts from Peter's sermon must have made it difficult for all to be involved in Christian fellowship. But this is
precisely what Luke says they did.

It is important to notice the order in which he mentions the
various expressions of their common faith. The apostles' doctrine
comes first. Christian faith involves more than an initial response.
It involves a progressive understanding of Christian teaching.
That the apostles appear as the custodians of the authentic teaching is both natural and significant. It means that a norm exists
against which wrong teaching might be gauged. It means also
that the new converts had much on which to stretch the mind.
It is not impossible that Christians followed the Jewish practice
of committing their sacred traditions to memory. Prominent
among the themes in the apostles' doctrine must have been the
teaching of Jesus. This would have followed from obedience to
the great commission recorded in Matthew's gospel. The teaching
they were to hand on was what Jesus had commanded. This was
the basis of the apostles' doctrine. As they recalled, through the
Spirit's aid, the events and teaching of Jesus they laid the foundation of the Christian oral tradition from which the earliest
Christian manuscripts were composed.

The Christians' fellowship was based on a common interest in the apostles' teaching. It was no sentimental get-togetherness. They had fellowship because they wanted to share the teaching. This rich idea of fellowship is very different from many modern uses of the term. It has a theological aspect which is all too often lacking. It is an idea which finds many other echoes in the New Testament. The Christian Church at its beginnings was in essence a company of believers who shared a common doctrine.

The breaking of bread must be viewed against the background of the doctrine and the fellowship. The account of the institution of the Last Supper would be an important part of the doctrine. It was observed in an informal way in the homes of believers, which was no doubt how Jesus intended it to be. The apostles would instruct the believers how Jesus had commanded the observance of the simple ordinance as a memorial feast. It was simple enough to require only the minimal amount of preparation. The emerging Christian community moved straight into it.

The other feature which marked this earliest community was prayer. The apostles had already set the pattern as they waited for the gift of the Spirit. Prayer was to become a characteristic of Christian life, both individual and corporate. Both the Book of Acts and the epistles frequently mention the prayer life of the believers. The community, although living its life on earth, maintained close contact with God, who had brought it into being. It proved a source of incomparable strength to the first Christian groups facing the task of witnessing in the very city which had crucified Jesus.

When people are motivated by intense seriousness of purpose, things begin to happen. The apostles themselves had power to perform signs. Luke gives no details of what these were. For him their importance lay in the fact that they testified to God's approval of the new group. Throughout his book he draws attention to various occasions when signs confirmed God's hand upon His people.

These early believers at once inaugurated a system of communal living. The impulse behind this seems to have been an overwhelming desire to share with others of like mind. It was not the result of a carefully worked out theory of socialism. It was entirely spontaneous. It does not appear to have been the result of reaction against the existing social order. Material possessions ceased to have importance except to provide the necessary maintenance. A similar urge toward communal living has been the spontaneous expression of new life in Christ in other instances, the most recent of which is the Jesus revolution which began in California. The mode of living which the Christians chose enabled them to worship together both in the Temple and in various homes, to share fellowship over common meals, and to engage in corporate praise to God. This sudden movement caused a stir among the populace, who could not fail to be impressed by the sheer exuberance of the believers. It speaks much for the open-mindedness of the popular approach toward them that, as Luke says, they had favor with all the people. It is not surprising that the community rapidly expanded. But as Luke is careful to note it was the Lord who was adding to their number. He makes no mention of human personalities.

10. *A Lame Man Healed*
(Acts 3:1-10)

Among the early signs performed by the apostles, Luke singles out one of special importance because of the clash with the authorities which resulted from it. It concerned the healing of

Egyptian, apparently a victim of infantile paralysis, with his family, brings an offering to a Syrian shrine.

a man who had never walked, but all his life had been dependent on others to carry him. He could pursue no normal occupation and was forced to beg as his only means of livelihood. He was a pathetic figure, typical of many to whom nature has given a crippling disability. Such people excite pity from all who have a spark of humanity, and more especially from the followers of Jesus, who had Himself been so frequently moved with compassion. The Temple gates, which normally were crowded with beggars, became the daily destination of this lame man.

To him all the worshipers in the Temple were potential benefactors. He had no power to discern one from another. It is improbable that he would have known that the two men who were about to enter the Temple were followers of Jesus. They mixed with the other worshipers at the hour of prayer. He asked alms of them as he would of any who came toward him, but he could not have anticipated the remarkable sequel to his routine act of begging.

Peter, having shared his possessions with the others, was not in a position to give alms, but gave the man something infinitely better. It was a critical test of Peter's own faith. His first reaction was to get the man to look at him, no doubt to assist his powers of concentration in responding to a challenge which involved an act of will on his part. The command came abruptly — "In the name of Jesus of Nazareth, walk." There was no mention of faith, but walking could not be contemplated by any other means than a supernatural act. The miracle cannot be explained away. Even if the complaint was psychosomatic or psychophysiological (new Amer. Psych. Assoc. term), a man lame from birth could never be stirred to walk unless by miraculous means. It is worth noting that the name of Jesus was invoked. What Peter did was merely a continuation of what Jesus had done. Such miracles occurred for a time, but when the developing Church became more established the accompaniment of supernatural signs gradually reduced.

Luke specially mentions the strengthening of the ankles and feet. As a doctor these features would especially impress him. It is no wonder that the temple crowds were astonished. The man had no doubt achieved a kind of notoriety by his constant begging. He was a familiar figure as his friends daily pushed him through the crowds to his begging place. When the same man was seen leaping about and shouting praise to God, the transformation was unmistakable. His sheer joy can be imagined as he experienced for the first time independence of movement. He was not content merely to walk. Luke says he leapt, as if he were determined to put his new powers to the fullest test.

The audience reaction in this case was wonder and amazement, which suggests that they were nonplused to explain the phenomenon. It is characteristic of those who are not acquainted with the power of God to marvel. What really astonished the observers were the men who had apparently been responsible for the healing. They were men of the sea, from the despised northern district of Galilee. They had none of the culture of the city men. Yet they had performed a notable miracle. It is not without significance that God used men at the earliest stages of the Christian Church who were not recognized in the religious world. Not for the first time God was acting mightily out of the conventional run of religious organizations. In this case it was inevitable. The religious leaders had been directly responsible for the crucifixion, which the apostles were now declaring to have saving value. The phenomenon of healing had not only raised popular curiosity, but demanded an adequate explanation, which gave Peter his opportunity for another sermon.

11. *Another Sermon by Peter*

(Acts 3:11-26)

Peter had a flair for seizing opportunities. His second address, like his first, was in response to audience perplexity. This gave him a good start, as it would any preacher. He at once disclaimed that it was by any human ingenuity that the man was healed. It was all bound up with God's activity in Christ. Peter feels that he cannot explain the miracle without first stating the historic facts about Jesus Christ. His hearers needed to be reminded that it was the same God who had healed the lame man who had raised Jesus. Peter bluntly lays the responsibility for the arrest and trial of Jesus on his audience. Again the idea of solidarity is being assumed. What the leaders in fact had done must be accepted as the responsibility of the populace. Peter speaks almost apologetically of Pilate. The Jewish people had actually resisted Pilate's desire to release Him. They had denied the Holy One. They had preferred a murderer. It was all very vivid to Peter as he recalled the sequence of events. The Jews had not realized the character of the One they had killed. Not only was He holy and righteous and therefore without any cause for the criminal proceedings which had been enacted against Him, but He was the Author of life. It was the supreme paradox of history that men thought they could destroy the giver of life. They never reckoned that God would raise Him from the dead. They thought only in categories of death and destruction. They did not understand the real meaning of life.

Behind Peter's claim, "We are witnesses" (i.e., of the resurrection) lay the astonishing revelations of the risen Christ. He was sure of this and this assurance gave him confidence in the face of the lame man's challenge. He told the crowd that faith in this name had healed the man. What they saw before them was indisputable evidence that the one they had killed was still working in mighty power.

Having stated the facts of the death and resurrection of Jesus, Peter moves on to mention that things had happened in fulfillment of the prophetic Scriptures. The idea of a suffering Messiah had escaped the Jewish people. Indeed it was abhorrent to them. They could not imagine that God could deliver His people that way. But Peter is bold to show that their own prophets had predicted it. This leads him to a direct appeal. The same exhortation which closed the first sermon recurs in this — "Repent and turn." Sins may be obliterated and spiritual refreshment obtained. God has acted on behalf of His people. He has shown Jesus to be the Messiah, although His final revelation on earth is not yet. Peter's words suggest that we have only the faintest indication of God's plan for the future, for He is more urgently concerned with the present.

A prophetic utterance of Moses backs up Peter's point. The lawgiver had predicted that God would raise up a "prophet" (Deut. 18:15, 16). Although the prediction was centuries before, the Jews believed that that "prophet" was still to come. Peter sees the prediction as fulfilled in Jesus Christ. In an incredibly short time, through the Spirit's guidance, the apostles had learned that the happenings of the present were the subject of prophetic predictions from the times of Samuel. They had learned something of the unity of God's dealing with His people. The span of years was irrelevant. What God had revealed in the past had found its perfect fulfillment in Christ. In this sermon as in his first, Peter is laying a solid foundation for the Christian interpretation of the Old Testament. His remarks carry with them the same authority which the Scriptures themselves convey.

Peter's closing appeal to his hearers is suitably clad in typically Jewish terms. His audience were sons of the prophets and men of the covenant. They regarded themselves as superior on that account. But Peter turns this sense of privilege into a challenge. With such a heritage his hearers ought to listen to the voices of the past which spoke of Christ. He reminds them of their great privilege that God had chosen to send His Servant Jesus to Israel first. His purpose in doing this had been wholly spiritual, i.e., to turn men from wicked ways.

Many would not consider the technique of Peter's sermon to be appropriate as a pattern for modern practice. But insofar as the preacher aimed his remarks at the needs of the audience his method cannot be improved upon. And insofar as it was essentially based on Scripture, this too cannot be dispensed with. Moreover, its forthright challenge contrasts strikingly with an attitude of mind which utters platitudes for fear of offending. It is less wonder that the Spirit blessed Peter's robust approach than that he ever blesses those who never speak of sin and wickedness.

12. First Opposition

(Acts 4:1-12)

Opposition was bound to come. Officialdom was unlikely to take no action against the strange new sect which was making such an impact at the expense of orthodoxy. It was embarrassing for the hierarchy, having engineered the crucifixion of Jesus because Jesus was considered to be a threat to their political status, to discover that His disciples were not dispersed as a result of the execution of their leader. The religious authorities must have had some misgivings that their plot had misfired. None of the enemies of Jesus believed the resurrection reports which were circulating in Jerusalem. They probably regarded the reports as pure imagination, although they had had a nasty shock over the empty tomb. They knew very well that their own story about the disciples having stolen the body was a fabrication and all the reports they were now receiving showed clearly enough that their propaganda scheme had been ineffective. Large numbers of people were believing that Jesus had risen from the dead. They may well have had misgivings that they were now faced with a worse threat than when Jesus Himself was alive.

The resurrection was a theme that completely upset their calculations. The Sadducees, who were the ruling party, were angry about this resurrection theme because they repudiated the idea of resurrection altogether. Their minds were therefore completely closed to the possibility of Jesus having risen from the dead. To them this was a sheer impossibility. They could think of no other way of dealing with the problem than to arrest the men involved. This is exactly what they had done with Jesus. They no doubt thought the movement would die down if the leaders were given a strong enough caution. Their very anger was evidence enough of their acute embarrassment that Jesus, though dead, was still speaking through His followers. In the meantime the number was increasing. It had now reached 5,000. At that rate of growth the Christian Church would soon make a considerable impact on the contemporary Jewish religious world.

It was the first occasion when disciples were brought before rulers to answer for their faith. Jesus had predicted that this would happen and that the Spirit would give wisdom in such circumstances. Peter and John were challenged to give the authority by which the healing of the cripple was accomplished. It has always been the concern of officialdom to check on authority. Anything outside the authorized circle is at once suspect.

Peter seizes the opportunity to testify. The form of the question invited a reference to Jesus Christ of Nazareth, but Peter brings the same forthright accusation against the leaders as he had brought against his first audience on the day of Pentecost (cf. Acts 2:36 with 4:10). He could have answered the question without making the accusation. But he was too deeply aware of their complicity in the crucifixion. He never supposed that some weeks after denying Jesus during His trial he would be able to level an accusing finger against those same official leaders whom he had seen inciting the crowds to demand the crucifixion of Jesus. As always in Acts the crucifixion was at once linked with the resurrection. Peter insists that it was God's doing. The Jesus whose name had healed the cripple was the same Jesus who had been raised from the dead. At this point Peter uses a figure of speech, which Jesus had himself used. It had earlier been employed in Psalm 118:22. Jesus saw Himself as the rejected Stone which finally became the chief stone in the building. Peter's hearers would not have been unfamiliar with the metaphor, but would certainly not have identified the Stone as the Jesus they had crucified. Peter later once again echoes the same imagery in his epistle (1 Pet. 2:7). It was a figure which drew attention not only to the rejection of the Messiah, but also to His exaltation. Because of this it made a strong appeal to the early Christians.

Peter added to the Stone imagery a statement which claims uniqueness for Christ. He alone is the means of salvation. All other means are excluded. Such an exclusive approach as this must have astonished the religious leaders who were examining the two apostles. It hit at the very foundations of the Jewish system. It was firmly believed that merit had much to do with a man's standing before God. The idea of salvation solely through the name of one who had so recently been crucified was inconceivable. But the fact that men like Peter and John were actually proclaiming it was disturbing to the minds of the leaders. They could not deny that a great many people were believing it and that some extraordinary things were happening as a result. They no doubt dismissed the whole matter as mass delusion. They were not to know that they were witnessing the beginnings of a movement which was to encompass the world. The exclusiveness which Peter claimed in those early days has never been shaken. The Christian faith firmly maintains that only in Christ is there hope for mankind.

13.   A Religious Dilemma

(Acts 4:13-22)

It is always difficult for established institutions to recognize the claims of others who do not conform. This was the case with the religious authorities in Jerusalem. There were accepted schools for the training of religious teachers, and it was not considered desirable for any teaching to be done outside those schools. The training involved the committing to memory of considerable quantities of oral tradition, which formed the basis of all judgments made on religious or ethical issues. In the Jewish world of that time the trained religious teachers accordingly held a privileged position, which generally led them to regard others as inferior. This will explain the official attitude toward Peter and John.

These men were essentially laymen. Luke calls them "uneducated, common men," which would be a fair description of what the privileged class would think about the nonprivileged. These were men without formal religious education and yet they were pronouncing on the essentially religious theme of salvation. Naturally the orthodox were reluctant to attach any importance to pronouncements made by unqualified men. But they could not deny their boldness. It made them perplexed. Some of them recalled having seen them with Jesus. But they had no real grounds for opposing them in view of the fact that the crippled man was standing beside them. Matters of education became distinctly secondary in face of the indisputable evidence of a man whose whole life-history had become changed.

In face of the problem the officials decided to discuss the matter among themselves. Reports of this must have reached the apostles later, probably through sympathizers who were present at the time. The leaders were perplexed over what action to take. It was useless to hush up the miracle. It was being talked about all over Jerusalem. It was too late to put out counter explanations. They had to recognize that a miracle had happened. The best they could do was to try to stop this kind of thing from spreading. There was apparently no desire to see a repetition of the healing ministry, no urge to aid other cripples to become mobile. Their horizon was too prescribed for that. Authoritarian considerations were of greater concern than humanitarian. They supposed that a warning from them would stop further preaching in this name.

The response of Peter and John to the threat is typical of the earliest Christian resolve to proclaim the message at all costs. They at once recognized a cleavage between the command of God and the command of the religious leaders. It was a question of conscience. When conscience clashes with authority, the latter, however formidable, must take second place. The apostles appear to have had no hesitation in refusing to heed the threat. There was a divine compulsion upon them. This is clear from their comment, "We cannot but speak of what we have seen and heard." What they spoke was the result of personal experience so real that they could not keep it to themselves. The name of Jesus may well have carried an anathema in the minds of the religious leaders. They could not appreciate the sacredness of that name in the minds of the believers. They might as well command the apostles not to breathe as to command them not to speak about that name.

The religious leaders' dilemma was made more acute when their resort to intimidation failed. They dared not take more forceful action because of popular opinion. Luke's narrative suggests that punishment had been discussed. There was an obvious desire to make a more powerful display of authority. It was not the only time that public opinion restrained tyrannical action. The official support for the crucifixion of Jesus had looked as if it were backfiring because of popular opinion. The religious leaders could not at this stage risk a direct clash with the popular front and could think of no other recourse than further threatenings. They were in fact clearly out of step with the widespread recognition that the healing was a work of God.

Luke adds a note that the healed man was forty years old. As a physician he would appreciate all the more the powerful healing that could make a man so set in his ways begin at once to walk. But even the layman could not fail to be impressed by the remarkable evidence. All Jerusalem was talking about it.

14.   *Return to a Prayer Meeting*

(Acts 4:23-31)

Immediately following their release, Peter and John sought out their friends. No doubt with considerable eagerness and no small alarm, the friends listened to the apostles' report of their brush with the authorities. Their response was spontaneous. They at once turned to God and prayed. The prayers of the New Testament make a valuable study. This one is of special value because Luke gives the gist of it in some detail. It is valuable as a pattern for similar situations. The first real test for the growing community was facing them. They had some grounds for misgivings in view of what the authorities had done to Jesus. Could His disciples really expect any better treatment?

The prayer first concentrates on the character of God. He is called Sovereign and Creator. Against this magnificent canvas the present crisis is considered. The sovereignty of God has always been a tower of strength to His people. It enables the most powerful opposition to be seen in its true perspective.

Next comes an appeal to Scripture. Psalm 2 is seen to be relevant. The Gentile nations raging against the Lord's Anointed were considered typical of the religious authorities' opposition to the name of Christ. The psalm was regarded as foreshadowing the Messiah and could legitimately be applied to the present situation. Luke somehow received the report of this prayer and specially notes the fulfillment of this Old Testament passage. The kings of the earth setting themselves in array against the Lord are illustrative of the recent events in the city when both civil and religious authorities opposed Jesus. As the disciples come to God they call to mind that Jesus was anointed by God. He had come to fulfill the ancient predictions concerning the Servant of the Lord. They were placing their prayer to God on a sound basis by assuming the fulfillment of prophecy. A God who had brought such prediction to fruition was more than a match for Pilate or the Jewish authorities.

These early believers had progressed a long way in grasping the divine plan in the events of the Passion Week. These events were predestined. In the ultimate analysis men had done what God had predicted. This does not absolve the men from complicity or responsibility. It rather shows a strong conviction that a divine plan was behind the events. Peter had already stated this belief in his Pentecost sermon (cf. Acts 2:23). The early Church could not have been unaware of the theological mystery involved. Yet they were convinced that the crucifixion was no accident. It follows from this that any action against the disciples could not be accidental.

The specific request at the conclusion of the prayer is highly instructive. It displays no trace of malice or peevishness. The disciples were prepared to leave the issue with God. "Look upon their threats" is suggestive, for the threats are distinguished from the people. This is a vivid way of seeking help in face of the possible consequences of the threats. But they did not pray for deliverance from the threats. In a remarkably brief period they had grown to sufficient maturity to place the main burden of their prayer on a request for boldness. There is no question of being intimidated. They do not consider retreat or modification of their methods. They must speak the message of God. Threats merely mean the greater need for courage, which God can amply provide.

Moreover having already seen one remarkable instance of divine healing they are expectant of others to follow. The name which could heal a cripple could heal others. They felt it to be right to pray for a continuation of God's power. The disciples had grasped something of the powerful character of the Gospel, although they may have been too specific in their idea of how the power was to be expressed. The sequel shows a powerful testimony with no mention of healings (see verse 33).

The prayer for boldness was immediately answered by an infilling of the Spirit which at once gave remarkable liberty in speaking the Word of God. This characteristic of the Spirit is evident throughout the Book of Acts. The Spirit's main work is testimony.

3

Early Problems

15. *Early Christian Communism*
(Acts 4:32-35)

The earliest experiment in communism in the Christian Church is significant for a variety of reasons. We may inquire what its motive was, what form it took, and why it disappeared. Its development seems to have been spontaneous. The believers were one in heart and mind, and when this occurs there are bound to be spontaneous expressions of that unity. Indeed the urge to share had arisen immediately after Peter's sermon on the day of Pentecost (cf. Acts 2:44). The believers ate together with typical oriental generosity (Acts 2:46). The sharing of other possessions was but a short step from this. A spontaneous communism was born. What is most significant about this phenomenon is the complete absence of any theorizing concerning it. This at once marks it out from political communism, which although showing certain common features, lacks the motive power which compelled the early Christians to embark on the experiment. The idea of having all things common is meaningful only if those sharing have a deeper basis of unity than the fact of sharing itself.

The form which early Christian communism took was of the simplest kind, involving a pooling of possessions, which appears to have been quite voluntary. It was an expression of Christian fellowship. There was no organization behind it. It was simply a matter of meeting each need as it arose. Why did material considerations of this kind spring from the spiritual challenges of early Christianity? The answer must be found in the spiritual impulse which sprang from the apostolic preaching. The resurrection was the main theme of the preaching and this set a high spiritual tone. It was probably the corporate desire of believers to give a consolidated testimony to this spiritual truth which had revolutionized their lives that prompted a communal way of life. They were united on the basis of their common resurrection faith.

There is no suggestion in the record that their communal policy was in any sense a reaction against the society in which they lived. They were not prompted by a monastic ideal. Their desire to share was so real that possessions were at once sold and the proceeds put into the common exchequer. But because the action of these early Christians was entirely voluntary there was no question of communal living becoming an indispensable part of Christianity. It was only natural, however, that those whose devotion had led them to a whole-hearted desire to share would be marked out from those who had retained their possessions. It is clear that the communal idea had the backing of the apostles, who acted as custodians of the contributions. The whole procedure was a remarkable demonstration of Christian unity.

The further question of the extent to which this early experiment can be regarded as a pattern is relevant. It seems clear from the rest of the New Testament that the experiment was not continued elsewhere. There is no hint that any Gentile church adopted a communal basis of living. Why not, if the Jerusalem believers were prompted by a spontaneous desire to share? It is not without some significance that from the Pauline letters it becomes clear that the Judaean churches were poverty stricken and needed contributions to be sent for their relief from Gentile churches. The Jewish-Gentile church at Antioch began such a relief scheme as a result of the prophecy of Agabus that a famine would soon affect the world (cf. Acts 11:27 ff.). The Antioch church must have known that the Judaean believers were in no financial position to withstand a famine. Was the communal experiment, even at this early stage, known to have landed the Christians in financial difficulties? This seems the most likely explanation. Nevertheless the strength of Christian love which this experiment demonstrated far outlasted the experiment itself.

16. *Barnabas, Ananias, and Sapphira*

(Acts 4:36 – 5:11)

A bare statement about communal living is less pointed than the mention of specific people involved in it. Luke refers to only three people by name, Joseph Barnabas, Ananias, and his wife Sapphira. His choice provides a study in contrasts, for the latter pair not only reacted differently from the former, but brought the first major tragedy to the early Church.

Barnabas was a notable character in the early period. He had come from Cyprus but had relatives in Jerusalem, for it was at his cousin's home that many of the first Christian meetings were held. He must have been well versed in the procedures of Temple worship, for he was a Levite and would have taken his turn to perform certain functions. His functions would have been inferior to those of the priests. The fact that Barnabas had property to sell shows that by this time the Mosaic restriction on priests and Levites owning possessions was not enforced. Luke specially notes the meaning of the name, Barnabas, given to him by the apostles, i.e., Son of Consolation. No doubt he recognized the name as being particularly appropriate in view of the generosity of Barnabas. This reflects the greater significance of names in those times, compared with modern times.

The case of Ananias and Sapphira involved a double tragedy, which proved a profound shock to the Christian Church. Both husband and wife were clearly desirous of making a contribution to the common exchequer, which stood in their favor. But they decided between them to retain some of the proceeds for themselves. There was no reason why they should not have done this, for contributions were purely voluntary and no one had decreed that the whole amount must be given. But they were evidently concerned about their status among other Christians. When a man like Barnabas had given everything, Ananias and Sapphira presumably had no desire to appear inferior by announcing that part had been withheld. They decided to say nothing about the amount withheld, but this amounted to a deception, which proved to be their undoing. They could not have the credit of giving all, while at the same time retaining part.

Peter at once detected the deception. He must have been sensitive to the Spirit's revelation. Perhaps there was something in Ananias' manner which showed an uneasy conscience. Peter did not hesitate to condemn. He attributed the deception to Satan, declaring that Ananias had lied to God, not simply to the apostles. The effect on Ananias was dramatic. His instantaneous death caused great fear to come upon all who heard. The cause can only be conjectured. Was the shock of discovering that his deception was exposed so great that Ananias died from fright? Or was this an altogether exceptional act of divine judgment especially given to impress on the growing Church the need for moral purity? It seems a drastic measure, but moral purity in a world of low moral standards was of particular importance at a stage when believers were having to forge out their Christian approach to so many ethical problems.

The case of Sapphira was even sadder. Unaware of the tragic death of her husband, she was confronted by a challenge from Peter to declare the amount obtained from the sale of the property. Out of her own mouth she condemned herself as she corroborated her husband's lie. Peter's words to her are challenging in the extreme. Their united deception amounted to a tempting or testing of the Spirit of the Lord. He predicted the same fate for her as had overtaken her husband. At once she collapsed and died. The shock of detection in addition to the sudden revelation of her husband's death proved too great. The whole Church saw it as an act of God and was impressed with the awesome character of it. The fear they experienced was no craven fear, but a reverential awe over God's dealings with His people. The group of Christians could not ignore this demonstration of God's judgment. It reminded them of their calling into the service of a holy God.

17. Signs and Wonders

(Acts 5:12-16)

On several occasions in the book of Acts, Luke mentions that signs and wonders were performed. It has raised the problem whether his idea of Christianity was too much bound up with a wonder-working performance. In modern times, when miracles are often considered to be impossible in a scientific approach to the world, it is not surprising that some have seen fit to dispute Luke's narrative. They do not necessarily think of Luke as intentionally misrepresenting the early history of the Church, but simply as reflecting his own non-scientific and somewhat magical interpretation. It is suggested that what appeared to him as historical must now be regarded as myth. But this is to make Luke rather naive. His linking of "signs" with "wonders" shows clearly that for him the wonders were not important for their own sake, but only because of the truths to which they pointed. In this the apostles were only following in the steps of the Master, whose miracles were described by John as "signs." The people of Jerusalem had ample demonstration of the power of God working through the apostles. Luke had correctly interpreted the unusual acts of the apostles as acts of God. If the Book of Acts were stripped of its miracles, the remarkable development of the Christian Church would in any case demand some miraculous power to account for it. The "signs" are but confirmations of what would need to be inferred.

The "togetherness" of the believers is another often-repeated theme in Acts. It is another aspect of early Christianity which impressed Luke. He notes especially that the believers congregated in Solomon's portico, which was a large section of the Temple area where people could meet and discuss. These meetings of Christians would soon have been noted by others, but the unbelieving onlookers dared not join them. Perhaps they were afraid to join a group from among whose members two had already mysteriously dropped dead. These hesitant onlookers contrast with the many more who were joining the company. Luke characteristically explains that they were "added to the Lord." The growth rate moreover was phenomenal — not one or two at a time, but multitudes. Such development is a remarkable testimony to the sincerity and clear testimony of the earliest believers.

The healing ministry played an important part in early Church life and this must be regarded as an integral part of the growth. As in the case of Jesus, so with the disciples, healing miracles preponderated. Peter was at the center of the activity. Multitudes of sick people placed in the narrow streets of Jerusalem would have caused traffic problems of considerable proportions. But there was no restraining people with sick relatives from bringing them into the streets in the hope of receiving healing. In our modern age, even in societies which offer all the advantages of a Welfare State, there would still be the same eager quest for healing. Some in Jerusalem were content simply to come under Peter's shadow, in the belief that this would suffice to heal them. Although the method smacks of superstition, it witnesses to the strong belief in the power of the apostles.

The congestion in the city was intensified by the swelling of the numbers by people from outlying towns. Along the routes into the city were clusters of people carrying their sick and leading their demon-possessed relatives and friends. The preaching of the kingdom was bringing new hope to multitudes of people. The prince of the power of the air was being overthrown. Those who entered the city with ailments or who were under Satan's power went home completely healed. The spectacular impact on Jewish society which the Christian movement was having once again became a matter of concern to the religious authorities.

18. *Another Arrest*

(Acts 5:17-32)

It took little to stir the Jewish high priest to jealousy. The Jewish officials recognized that the remarkable growth of the company of Christian believers was a potential threat to their own position. Those who had responded to the challenge of the Gospel were Jews and the hierarchy were fearful lest their own authority over so many was being undermined. They had threatened two of the apostles apparently without effect. They decided on firmer suppression. Not only the two, but all the apostles were arrested. The ruling party, being Sadducees, were particularly hostile to the new movement, because it was based on belief in the resurrection. Sadducees denied the possibility of resurrection and would see no reason to make an exception in the case of Jesus.

The officials never bargained for the subsequent events. The doors of the prison were miraculously opened the same night and the apostles escaped. Luke mentions an angel and there is much to be said for the view that when he refers to the "angel of the Lord," he means to denote the direct intervention of God. The command to the apostles was specific. They were to continue witnessing not only in the city but in the Temple itself. In no more vivid way could the superiority of the authority of God over the authority of the Temple officials be demonstrated. The apostles were to act with courageous defiance. They immediately obeyed next morning at dawn. They were so convinced of their divine guidance that they did not adopt the more prudent course of leaving Jerusalem while the opportunity existed.

It must have been a considerable shock to the Sanhedrin to be told that the apostles had escaped. The prison officers were clearly in a dilemma. They had to report that the prison was locked but the prisoners had gone. It would not have been surprising had the hierarchy refused to believe them and had condemned them for negligence. But the various reports of extra-ordinary happenings performed through the apostles had apparently conditioned them to accept at least the possibility of an inexplicable escape. They were more inclined to fear that worse problems lay ahead of them. A further report that the apostles were publicly teaching in the temple only confirmed their fears. They decided to arrest them again, but were bothered about the reaction of the crowds. They knew very well that popular reaction to the apostles differed greatly from their own. Those who have seen remarkable healings among their families or friends or neighbors would be well disposed toward the healers and totally unaffected by the political problems of the rulers.

The high priest's approach when the apostles appeared before him the second time is essentially defensive. He interpreted their continued teaching in defiance of official threats as an intention to bring the blood of Jesus on his own head. By this time, not so many weeks after the crucifixion, he is certainly perplexed, but nevertheless in no mood to reconsider his own responsibility. Far from any sense of regret, the authorities were rather the more enraged that their plan to stamp out Jesus and his movement was failing to achieve its end. Their anger was intensified by the approach of Peter and the other apostles. It was one thing for Peter to claim that he must obey God rather than men, but the high priest regarded himself as the official mouthpiece of God among the Jews. Officialdom never takes kindly to unofficial "authorities" and when supposedly "ignorant" men claim access to their own revelation of God's will, it is not surprising that the official line is antagonistic. This is doubly so when the unofficial charges the official with responsibility for a crime which God was using for the salvation of His people. The mention of God raising up Jesus incensed the Sadducees still more.

Peter made the bold claim that God had made Jesus Leader and Savior, but it would have been beyond the comprehension of orthodox Jewish interpreters for a crucified man to be a Savior. The Jewish rabbis talked of repentance and forgiveness but not in the way that Peter did. They could not divorce these things from human merit, whereas Peter declared them to be a divine gift. To the merit-conscious official Jews, Peter's speech must have seemed wholly incredible. Moreover it was a bold step for Peter to link the apostles' witness with the Spirit's witness. This was an unmistakable claim to the inner witness of the Spirit which those devoted to formal religion have never understood. This second brush with officialdom on the part of the apostles shows how great was the rift between official Judaism and Christianity, even at its beginnings.

19. *Gamaliel*

(*Acts* 5:33-42)

Among most social groups there is usually one, at least, who stands out as being more moderate than the rest. In the Jewish Sanhedrin that man was Gamaliel. The rest were violent types who could only think in terms of killing. They had thought to do away with Jesus by that means, but God had turned their intentions to fit in with His own purposes. The Jewish leaders had not learned the lesson. Death could not stop the mission of Jesus. Did they seriously think that a spate of killing was going to stop the progress of the Gospel? Anger which is engendered by frustration over thwarted plans is always the most unreasonable. But Gamaliel alone seemed capable of taking an objective view of things. Lone protest voices are frequently swamped, but no one dared to ignore the advice of a man like Gamaliel. He had a massive reputation for learning, and popular Jewish opinion held famous rabbis in high regard. The lone voice on this occasion was a voice to be reckoned with.

The apostles at Gamaliel's request were ordered out of the Council chamber. Someone on the Council must later have reported what happened, for Luke records Gamaliel's speech to his fellow members. He first appealed to fairly recent history. Two uprisings which had gained considerable support had come to nothing. The first mentioned, led by a man named Theudas, has led to difficulties. The Jewish historian Josephus mentions such a rising as occurring in the time of the procurator Cuspius Fadis (A.D. 44-46), whereas Gamaliel's speech occurred some years earlier. In view of Josephus' occasional aptitude for historical discrepancies it would be unsafe to suppose that he is right and that Luke is wrong. If both are correct it is most likely that there was an earlier rising under another Theudas which Josephus does not mention. The name was common in those days.

The other uprising referred to by Gamaliel, occurring under Judas and the Galilean, is also mentioned by Josephus. It occurred during Quirinius' census in A.D. 6. Many Jews were angered by the census because they anticipated that it would lead to a further restriction of their freedom. Judas had led a revolt against the census, but his revolt had come to nothing. It had been essentially a religious revolutionary movement. Although that movement had fizzled out, the further movement of the Zealots emerged from it and this became powerful prior to the fall of Jerusalem about thirty years after Gamaliel's speech. Gamaliel's main point was, nevertheless, that history had recently shown that these revolutionary movements were not of God because they had failed. He advised that the Council should do nothing lest they be found to fight against God. It is surprising to find such advice coming from within the same council which had that year condemned Jesus. Why did Gamaliel not raise his voice in protest then? Had he by this time had second thoughts about the Sanhedrin's action in plotting against Jesus? There is no knowing, but in spite of his sound advice, he gives no indication of having been influenced by the Christian movement. His cautious approach was possibly dictated by political expediency.

Gamaliel's dictum — "if it is of God, you will not be able to overthrow them" — is worth pondering. It is a fitting commentary on the whole history of the Christian Church. Many tyrants have tried to overthrow the Christian Church. All persecutions, stretching from the earliest to modern times, have been based on the assumption that violence and death are effective methods against a movement which is essentially spiritual. But men in successive generations have failed to note the basic principle which Gamaliel, a man not committed to the Christian mission, so clearly enunciated. Modern anti-God movements will be no more successful than ancient movements.

It is to the credit of the rest of the Jewish Council that they accepted Gamaliel's advice. At least they partially did so. They dropped their plan to kill, but did not leave the apostles alone as Gamaliel had suggested. They ordered a beating, presumably supposing that this would bolster their authority. To send them out free would look too much like a capitulation. But an authority which needs barbarous methods for its support is already cracking. The beatings were unlikely to intimidate the apostles to refrain from preaching in the name of Jesus.

In spite of physical violence inflicted upon them, the apostles still rejoiced. Luke records the fact as if it were no more than might be expected. He knew, of course, that Jesus had told the apostles that they would suffer for His sake. The present incident strikingly showed the contrast between the angry and violent leaders and the triumphant though suffering apostles. The bleeding backs of the latter were nothing compared with the religious animosity of the former. Long after the physical wounds had healed, the mental hatred still festered until it broke out like an ugly gangrene to destroy what religious feeling the leaders still had. The apostles went back to their preaching stand in the temple courtyard and many more heard that Jesus was the Messiah. Persecution had merely succeeded in intensifying the testimony.

20. *The Seven*

(Acts 6:1-7)

At first, the Christian Church showed little concern for organization. There was no immediate appointment of Church officers. The apostles were the acknowledged leaders. They had been careful to complete their number with the addition of Mathias. But the remarkable and rapid expansion of the Church was bound to pose problems. The apostles were regarded as responsible for everything. Proceeds from property sales following the policy of communal living had been brought to them. The distribution of food was a major task of organization. Moreover there were other problems which arose over personalities. An early problem concerned the Hellenists and the Hebrews because the former felt that their widows were not receiving a fair deal. It was a problem which arose from the fact that the administrators were all Hebrews, which gave the Hellenists some grounds for fearing discrimination against them.

The apostles wisely brought the matter into the open by summoning the whole body of disciples to discuss it. They at once proposed a delegation of duties. The practical duties of operating the communal scheme were jeopardizing the spiritual ministry of the apostles. Clearly the question of priorities at once arose. Which was the more important? Having decided that the vocation of the apostles was to prayer and ministry, it was obvious that the practical duties had to be delegated. It is worth noting that the proposition that others should be appointed for the ministry while the apostles devoted themselves to practical duties does not appear to have arisen. It was automatically accepted that the apostles were custodians of the Christian doctrine. This is of great importance when considering the developments of Christian theology. So vital a task as ministering the Word needed authority behind it. It could not be left to any unspecified eye-witness. The witnesses were authorized men who were set aside for the purpose. It is for this reason that the later developing Church was concerned to claim apostolic authority for the writings which came to be collected into the New Testament.

The advice given to the Christian body of disciples is also significant. The apostles, although appointed by Jesus (except for Matthias), were not inclined to regard themselves as an authoritarian hierarchy. They might well have argued this way, but in fact they proposed an essentially communal method. The choice of other officials was to be in the hands of the whole company . This may be termed democratic, although it must be recognized that there is a real difference between political government by the people and Christian government within the Church by the people. Unlike the former the Christian Church is a body dominated by a common bond — their allegiance to Christ — and their communal choice, if rightly made, reflects the will of the Church's Lord. It is theocratic rather than democratic.

The apostles, moreover, were specific in the direction they gave to the whole body of believers. They had calculated the need and suggested that a group of seven men would be sufficient. They evidently did not attach any significance to the number twelve. Moreover the men chosen had to qualify on the following grounds. They were to be full of the Spirit and of wisdom. The growing Church was essentially a Church of the Spirit. What had begun in the Spirit must continue in the same way. Even mundane duties must not be done by mundane men but by spiritual men. The requirement of wisdom is an obvious choice. Personality clashes and national differences require the wisdom of a Solomon and it speaks much for the growing Church that there were seven men who could fulfill this requirement. Those chosen were also to be men of repute whom the whole body would acknowledge as men of integrity. Such a requirement, had it been acted on more often in Christian history, would often have preserved Christian unity where it was shattered.

Of the men chosen that day we hear nothing further except for Stephen and Philip. The former is described by Luke as a man full of faith and of the Holy Spirit. No doubt his special interest in Stephen led him to make this comment. Stephen had impressed Luke with the fact that he was a "full" man, mature in every way. It is not without some significance that both the men of whom more is heard became renowned as preachers. The Spirit later directed these men into channels different from those chosen by the Church. In all good faith they were assigned to serve tables with the other five, and to this end the apostles laid hands on them, but the sequel shows that God had designed a wider ministry for them.

Luke at this point in his narrative adds another summary of progress. He notes that the Word of God increased, which is his picturesque way of describing the spread of effective preaching. It was as if each new hearer who responded to the Word strengthened the Word. Not only was the Word multiplied, but also the disciples. A special note is made of the high proportion of priests who were among the converts. Those who had had much to do with official worship were perhaps most conscious of its weaknesses and most ready to acknowledge the superiority of the Christian faith.

Ruins of the Synagogue at Capernaum in Galilee, typical of the structures in the days of the apostles.

4

Stephen, Philip, and Saul

21. *Opposition to Stephen*
(Acts 6:8 – 7:1)

Stephen seems to have been the kind of man who could not escape notice. Luke again draws attention to his fullness, this time fullness of grace and power. It is not often an abundance of both qualities is united in one man. Powerful men are not usually gracious and men of grace do not usually impress with their power. But Stephen was no ordinary man. Being a Christian the grace he showed was a reflection of the grace of God and the power he showed was a reflection of the power of God. A man whose qualities are derived from such a source can hold a position of strength without overpowering others. He was the sort of man who could be trusted to perform signs and wonders — the very thing the apostles had already done.

Stephen not only performed remarkable signs; he also preached in the synagogue. Luke's record is not clear as to whether there were several synagogues he visited or only one. But several groups of people are mentioned, including freedmen. It is most likely that at one synagogue there were freedmen from the districts of Cyrene, Alexandria, Cilicia, and Asia. Here particularly Hellenistic Jews engaged in dispute with Stephen over his doctrine. Stephen, however, was endowed with special wisdom by the Holy Spirit and none of his opposers were a match for him. It was naturally a blow to their pride to discover such depth of insight in a man who made fantastic claims about Jesus of Nazareth who had been crucified. The main problem was Stephen's approach to Judaism. He spoke in such a way that his hearers could only conclude that he was blaspheming the Mosaic law and therefore God Himself. This kind of reasoning is intelligible, but false. The Christian faith was not based, as Judaism was, on minute observance of the Mosaic law as the means of salvation, but on faith in a resurrected Christ. It was sometime later that the Apostle Paul came to recognize the true relation between faith and the law. But in his pre-conversion approach he considered obedience to Moses an indispensable requirement in a man's approach to God. Paul, then Saul, probably belonged to this synagogue where Stephen was being opposed.

Opposition and persecution again darken the horizon. These Hellenistic Jews hatched a plot against Stephen. Luke does not say who instigated the opposition, but it may be reasonably conjectured that Saul had something to do with it. Although he was a Diaspora Jew his approach was in sharp contrast to the more moderate approach of most Hellenists in that he had been educated under the famous Gamaliel and had a strongly orthodox approach. Stephen, on the other hand, sat more lightly on Jewish tradition and the effort required for him to orientate himself to a Christian view of the Mosaic law would have been much less than for Saul. It is worth noting, however, that Saul took a more violent approach than his famous teacher recommended. He may have been disappointed over Gamaliel's approach and decided to resort to more violent methods. A bigot like Saul would not find it difficult to turn people against Stephen if he spread a report about his "blasphemy." The signs and wonders would soon be forgotten in face of a serious religious threat. Having conditioned the populace, it was an easy matter for his opponents to arrest Stephen and bring him before the Jewish Council. But what charges could be cited against him? The reports of blasphemy were good enough for propaganda purposes, but further evidence was needed to substantiate them before the Council.

There seems to be a remarkable parallel between the trial of Stephen and the trial of Jesus. In both, false witnesses had to be deliberately briefed and in both the charge was a distortion of words that had been said. In the case of Stephen, Luke does not say what his statements were. But being a Hellenistic Jew he would give less importance to the centrality of the temple than the Jerusalem Jews. He found sympathy with the statement of Jesus that He would destroy the temple (meaning His body), but his opponents would have misunderstood this as the enemies of Jesus had done. Moreover the revolutionary nature of the mission of Jesus would appear to involve a change in the whole

Mosaic system. Such a charge would naturally meet with deep concern among those whose religious system was wholly bound up with the Mosaic law.

Luke was impressed by one feature of the report which he had received of Stephen's trial. It concerned Stephen's appearance. Even before he began his defense, his personal presence impressed itself on his hostile audience. Everyone noticed that his face was like an angel's face. This must have been talked about afterward, even by those whose indignation drove them to cast stones at him. Men like angels make other men feel uncomfortable. The contrast between Stephen and the official leaders was too marked to be tolerated. The "angel" face of the defendant did not lead his accusers to listen more tolerantly. The trial was in no sense a model of justice.

22. *Stephen's Defense and Martyrdom*

(Acts 7:2 – 8:1a)

Stephen's opponents had brought two main charges against him. One concerned the law of Moses, the other concerned the temple. He was assumed to be against both. The charges were not original, for similar charges had been brought against Jesus. In Stephen's case he was given the opportunity to answer the charges, and Luke who evidently regarded his defense as important, gives in fair detail a resumé of his speech.

It was historically based. Stephen was addressing an audience which was proud of its heritage. To begin by speaking of "our father Abraham" would at once gain approval. Indeed as Stephen made much of the covenant given to Abraham, no Jewish hearer would have objected. This naturally led on to the patriarchs.

The story of God's dealings with Joseph in Egypt was a highlight in Jewish history. For Stephen, as for all Jews, the Exodus was no accident of history but a divinely overruled event. It was a part of the fulfillment of the promise given to Abraham that God would make of his seed a great nation. After Abraham Moses was the great hero in Jewish minds. Under God he had not only delivered the people from bondage, but had given the law. Stephen goes into considerable detail regarding Moses. He mentions his upbringing in the Pharoah's house and his development into a powerful figure in Egyptian life. He reminds his hearers of the events which led to his exile and to the remarkable revelation of God in the burning bush. He makes much of the fact that God reversed the decision of the Hebrews when they rejected Moses and made him a ruler over them. The same Moses had predicted a "prophet" to come. Stephen did not at this point press home that that "prophet" had now come in Jesus Christ. He chose rather to deal with the temple charge.

What is particularly brought out in the next part of the speech is the wrong attitude of the Israelites at almost every stage of God's dealing with them. Their idolatry under Aaron especially illustrated this point. A prophet like Amos had had to remind the people of his time about the Israelites' failure in the wilderness and about the continued failure of their descendants, which later culminated in the exile. But it was the antecedents of the temple which particularly interested Stephen. The tabernacle under Moses, the continuation of it under Joshua, the desire of David to construct a more permanent dwelling and the building of the Temple of Solomon.

Of course there was nothing new in Stephen's speech up to this point. All in his audience who knew anything about Israel's history would know that Stephen's historical account was correct. His further point that the Most High does not dwell in humanly constructed temples had the support both of Solomon the great temple builder (1 Kings 6) and also of the prophet Isaiah (Isa. 66:1, 2). Stephen's aim is clearly to imply that the Jewish officials of his day were placing more stress than was justified on the magnificent temple which Herod had built for them. He may have been thinking also that in the Christian Church the concept of the temple had been transformed into something spiritual.

At this point Stephen makes a decided attack on the hearers. He does not mince his words. He is courageous almost to the point of being blunt. He calls them "stiff-necked," a description in line with frequent prophetical denunciations of their ancestors. The present generation was no different from the past. They were resisting the Holy Spirit. Their opposition to Stephen and to the Christian preachers was placed squarely in the same class as the persecution of the ancient prophets who had foretold the coming of Jesus Christ.

The effect of Stephen's accusation was electric. Anger rose to fever pitch. Hostility showed in the baring of teeth. Responsible officials were reducing themselves to uncontrolled behavior like animals. Their animosity showed up all the more violently against the calm statement of Stephen that he saw Jesus standing at the right hand of God. Men in a fury are not impartial judges. There was no question of calm deliberation to determine the truth of the words they heard. On the contrary the audience became an uncontrolled mob which took into its own hands the responsibility of executing judgment. They resorted to "lynch law" by stoning, a highly irregular procedure, but angry mobs never stop to submit to normal procedures. Stephen died as stones hailed upon him, the first martyr in a long succession of men and women who have died for their faith. Before he died he uttered a prayer which was loud enough for all his accusers to hear — "Lord, do not hold this sin against them." There must have been some who heard that prayer who remembered that Jesus had uttered a similar prayer when men were crucifying Him. Indeed Stephen may have learned it from such a source.

His enemies thought that Stephen was effectively silenced. His influence, however, lived on, for at least one of them probably never forgot the way he died. Saul, the pupil of Gamaliel, staunchest advocate of Moses and the temple, and in full agreement with the violence against Stephen, later came to think differently about Jesus Christ. Was he secretly impressed by the spirit of the victim as he guarded the clothes of the self-appointed executioners? If so, it did not show itself at once. Rather the reverse was true.

23. Organized Persecution

(Acts 8:1b-3)

It is clear that Saul was more than a caretaker of clothes in the whole operation of Stephen's death. He immediately becomes the main spearhead of a deliberate and intense hostility against the Christian church in Jerusalem. Luke's account suggests that Stephen's martyrdom sparked off a whole series of hostile actions. But he does not fill in the details. He leaves much to the imagination and makes no attempt to analyze motives as modern historians would. He almost treats the development of persecution as a matter of course.

It may be supposed that the arrest of Stephen had not been contemplated in isolation. The Jewish authorities probably compiled a list of wanted men, for they immediately instituted an

all-out onslaught against the members of the church. Luke merely says that the members of the Jerusalem church were scattered
throughout Judaea and Samaria, with the exception of the apostles. The exception is surprising. Now that Stephen had been
disposed of, it would have been natural for the Jewish leaders to
make a direct attack on the apostles. Why did they not follow
this procedure? It is possible that the apostles were more prepared and took steps to conceal themselves, but this seems completely out of character with their previous boldness. It is more
probable that the officials decided as a matter of policy to refrain
from arresting the apostles again in view of the earlier failure to
silence them by this means. They presumably thought that a
more effective method would be the scattering of the rank and
file members. Leaders without followers could be reduced to
ineffectiveness. They little realized that the policy adopted
would actually lead to the more rapid spreading of the Church.

Luke introduces a remarkable contrast into his narrative. The
devout men who buried Stephen are set over against the man
who had consented to his death and was now laying waste the
Church. Stephen was highly respected by his fellow Christians.
In view of his magnificent testimony, his loss was a great blow
to the young Church. The Christians' lamentation over him can
be imagined. They could ill afford to lose a man so full of the
power of the Spirit. Yet God had allowed it. Moreover Saul was
on the rampage. It was no time for extensive lamentation.

Saul's fury is described by Luke as "laying waste." He uses
a word which was especially used of the ravaging of a victim
by a wild beast. Although he knew when he wrote that the same
man was to become the apostle to the Gentiles, he did not spare
to describe the crude nature of his persecuting zeal. His faithfulness in doing so has enabled his readers to form a truer
assessment of the remarkable transformation effected at Saul's
conversion. The idea seems to be that he was like a wild beast
tearing apart the Church as a body until nothing recognizable
would remain of it.

The thoroughness of Saul's efforts is seen in his house by house
method. Presumably each household was questioned to discover
who were members of the Church and who were not. Luke
passes over without comment the many human problems this
presented. There were possibly some who chose to protect themselves by dissociating from the Church to avoid the fury of Saul's

persecution. But the early Christians, unlike those of a subsequent age, were not obsessed with the problem of distinguishing those who suffered from those who avoided suffering. The fight for survival was too intense. Many at least were dragged away to prison. Saul did not restrict himself to the men. He also dragged away the women. What happened to those who were imprisoned is not clear, but many others fled from Jerusalem into the surrounding districts where Saul's hostility could not so easily be directed against them. If Saul, presumably acting with the full support of the Jerusalem hierarchy, imagined that his persecution was achieving his aim of eliminating the Christian Church, he was badly mistaken. All he succeeded in doing was to fill the Jerusalem dungeons with people who would rather die than renounce their faith and to plant innumerable witnesses to the Gospel throughout Judaea and Samaria. This earliest persecution is typical of all. Saul would have done better to heed the advice of his tutor Gamaliel. If God is in any movement, no amount of fury can overthrow it.

24. *Stirrings in Samaria*

(Acts 8:4-13)

One of those who decided to move out from Jerusalem was Philip. His special task of serving tables had come to an abrupt end with the scattering of so many of the disciples, but together with the others who were scattered he seized the opportunity of preaching. In doing so he discovered a real gift for it. Soon multitudes were hanging on his words. He concentrated on the city of Samaria and preached Christ there. The persecutors had silenced one of the deacons in Jerusalem but another, equally gifted as an exponent of the Gospel, became more active in Samaria. Moreover Philip, like Stephen, accompanied his words with signs. Demon possession was rife in the world at that time, but many possessed people were being restored to their right minds. The city echoed with the sounds of final paroxysms as healing was being completed. In addition many paralytics were healed and people once lame were walking the streets. It is no wonder that Luke comments that there was much joy in the city. The dispersed who had left Jerusalem in sadness and who had probably regarded the ravaging of the church as a tragedy must soon have changed their minds on discovering that God was as active in Samaria as in Jerusalem. Christian action was not to be confined to any one place, a principle which was none too easy for Jews to accept with their strong Jerusalem-centered tradition.

The response of the Samaritans must be assessed against the background of the contemporary scene. These people were gullible. They had been dazzled by the magic and arrogant claims of a man named Simon. He was an impressive figure who appealed to all sections of Samaritan society from the least to the greatest. His magic was evidently convincing, for the people were certain that there was a divine quality about it. They identified him as the "power of God which is called Great." It is not certain what this means, but it is clear that Simon's source of power was thought to be from the supreme God. But when they listened to Philip's preaching and saw his signs they recognized a superior power operating through him. They heard him explain the kingdom of God and the name of Jesus Christ. When they compared it with Simon's magic, they believed the Gospel.

Simon himself recognized the inferiority of his own magic and possibly urged on by the defection of his supporters decided to throw in his lot with Philip. He joined a multitude who were baptized by Philip. His conversion seemed a remarkable trophy for the Gospel in Samaria. Nevertheless a man steeped in magic does not easily shake it off. He seems to have regarded the signs and miracles as no more than superior displays of magic. He had yet to learn that the miracles were signs of the dawning of a new spiritual kingdom under the direction of the Spirit of God. Simon is typical of many who have been intrigued by the miraculous achievements of Christianity into a kind of superstitious regard for it without appreciating its spiritual basis.

Because of the preponderance of miracles in Luke's narratives of early Christian developments, some have questioned their historical validity. It is suggested that he attributed miracles to the apostles and others as a way of describing divine action in human life; but that in modern society, in which miracles are rejected as scientifically untenable, the miraculous element must be excluded from our understanding of early Christian history. But such a view is based on the assumption that what does not happen now could not have happened then. It would seem reasonable to suppose, however, that the beginnings of the Christian movement were attended by some supernatural intervention in view of the divine intervention into human history that occurred both at the incarnation and at the resurrection. It is worth noting that Jesus himself recognized that some who would not believe His words would nevertheless believe because of His works. The rest of the New Testament is sufficient proof that Christian theology was not based on magical performances, but on the conviction that God had revealed Himself in the acts of history.

25. Peter and John in Samaria

(Acts 8:14-25)

Reports of the way the Samaritans received the Christian faith soon reached Jerusalem. The apostles discussed what should be done and decided that Peter and John should be sent to investigate. On arrival the two apostles inquired about what had happened and learned that many had been baptized but had not yet received the Holy Spirit. This lack was made the immediate burden of their prayers. They decided to lay hands upon the Samaritans, as a result of which they received the Spirit. Luke's first mention of the practice of laying on of hands deals with the seven who were set aside for serving at table (Acts 6:6). It was on that occasion a symbol of being set aside for a specific task (cf. also Acts 13:3). On this occasion, however, it symbolized the reception of a specific gift (see also Acts 19:6). A similar use occurred when Ananias laid his hands on Saul, who at once received his sight to the accompaniment of a prayer that he should be filled with the Spirit. Peter clearly saw in the Samaritan Christians the lack of spiritual power.

Simon, the one-time magician, had watched the transformation which the gift of the Spirit effected, and coveted not the gift itself but the authority to bestow it. He was one of those people who could never take a secondary place. He was smarting under his loss of authority since the Christians arrived in Samaria. But his own interest in Christianity was entirely self-centered. He was still materially minded. He considered it to be worth paying for the authority to bestow the Holy Spirit probably because he could then satisfy his lust for greatness. But his reasoning was sadly wrong. Spiritual gifts cannot be gained by bribes. Indeed the idea that spiritual authority can be purchased with money shows a lamentable lack of a basic understanding of the Gospel.

Ruins of Herod's Augustan Temple in Samaria.

THE DISTANCE FROM DAMASCUS TO JERUSALEM.

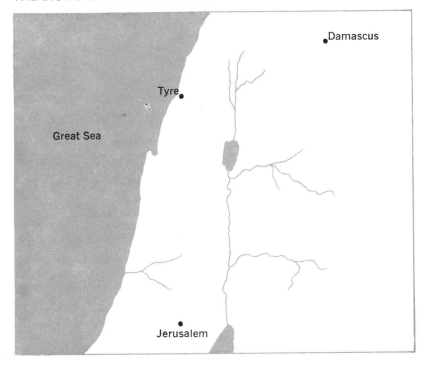

Damascus

Tyre

Great Sea

Jerusalem

No wonder Peter was severe with Simon. The money he had offered was no bait to the apostles. They were not in this for gain. But in any case the notion of buying a gift of God is so incredible that Peter declares that Simon's heart is not right before God. A Christian does not desire to lord it over others. It is basically alien to the pattern of Jesus Christ. The Christian way is a path of humility, not of arrogance. Simon needed a change of heart.

When a man's heart is not right with God, there is only one way to deal with the problem. Peter urges repentance. Both John the Baptist and Jesus had called on men to repent. The first Christian sermon had ended in a call to repentance and no Christian preaching which omits this demand is worthy of the name. There was hope yet for Simon provided he first acknowledged his wickedness and was truly sorry for it. Then and then only could he pray for forgiveness.

It may be asked why Peter considered that Simon's sin was so serious as to make him describe Simon as in the gall of bitterness and in the bond of iniquity. It was strong medicine, but this was the first case in a long line of such cases within Christian history where men have imagined that money has given them special privileges in spiritual matters. Simon's approach was so alien to the operation of the Holy Spirit that Peter reflected intense opposition to it. Simon's response was typical. He did not trust his own prayer, but asked Peter to pray for him. But no one can repent for another. That responsibility Simon had to bear for himself.

It is worth noting that Simon became a notable character in later Church history as the first heretic, an advocate of Gnosticism. He was depicted as the adversary of the apostle Peter. This tradition may be founded on historic fact, in which case Simon's love of power proved greater than his desire for repentance. It is improbable in that case that Simon ever came to a real experience of Jesus Christ.

The apostles returned to Jerusalem taking the opportunity of preaching the Gospel en route in the villages of Samaria. They must have come across many of the dispersed Jerusalem disciples in those villages. They would certainly be constantly reminded that Jerusalem was a dangerous place to be in, but they did not hesitate to go back. Saul's threatenings had not intimidated them.

26. *Philip and the Ethiopian*

(Acts 8:26-40)

Philip was a man sensitive to the Spirit's leading. He had stood aside while Peter and John took over the situation in Samaria. He was ready for further directions from the Spirit. He was directed by an angel of the Lord to journey south to meet the junction with the Jerusalem Gaza road. He was in no doubt regarding the directions. Although angel communications do not still occur, there is no reason to question the reality of the communication to Philip. God has many means for the directing of His servants. Philip might well have marvelled at the details. The spot indicated was desert. What purpose could there be in going to such an isolated spot? But Philip went.

It was not a coincidence that he did not find himself alone at that junction. A traveler was passing from Jerusalem to Gaza. If his guidance had been right so far, Philip could hardly doubt that the traveler approaching in his chariot must be connected with the purpose of his journey. Indeed the Spirit who had directed him to this spot also directed him to join the chariot. The traveler turned out to be an important man, a court official of the Candace or Queen of the Ethiopians. This queen was probably the queen mother, but was nevertheless the real head of the government. The official was a eunuch. Oriental monarchs often used eunuchs as officials of state and in this case he was the keeper of the queen's treasure.

The man, although an Ethiopian, was an adherent of the Jewish faith. This was the reason for his visit to Jerusalem. He was evidently of devout mind for he spent his traveling time studying the Hebrew Scriptures. He possessed a scroll of Isaiah which he may well have purchased in Jerusalem. He had reached Isaiah 53 and was reading it aloud in accordance with the universal practice in ancient times. Philip's heart must have warmed as he heard the passage being read. At least the man had a real interest in the Word of God, an inestimable advantage to anyone approaching him in Christ's name. Philip possibly ran beside the chariot as he asked whether the Ethiopian understood the passage he was reading. The courtier did not regard the question as an insult to his intelligence. He welcomed the opportunity for further guidance.

The conversation between the Ethiopian and Philip illustrates one successful method of approach. Most people in endeavoring to understand the Scriptures are conscious of the need for guidance. Not all are as fortunate as the Ethiopian in having so acomplished an expositor near at hand. It may be that more perplexity would be removed if more who possessed the gift were as sensitive to the Spirit's leading as Philip.

The preacher did not disdain an audience of one. He based his remarks on the passage that the eunuch was reading. It was one of the best places in the Old Testament from which to speak about Christ. Isaiah's lamb was none other than Jesus the Messiah. His humiliation was interpreted in terms of a crucifixion in Jerusalem. From this point Philip could explain all that had happened since, how that Jesus had risen from the dead. It is not impossible that the Ethiopian had already heard about Jesus in Jerusalem. While he was there the commotion instigated by Saul was still going on. Whatever his previous knowledge, the man came to see the real meaning of Christianity while still traveling toward Gaza with Philip as his guide.

Philip had evidently told him about Christian baptism, for he expressed the desire for baptism at the first opportunity. At the sight of water the chariot was stopped and the baptizing was performed. Mysteriously Philip vanished after the service. Luke says that the Spirit of the Lord caught him up and that he was found at Azotus. Luke seems to have regarded it as a miraculous event. He is deeply convinced that God was intervening in the lives of communities and individuals alike. Philip continued his preaching work and the eunuch his journey. Nothing more is known of him, but it is highly probable that this first African Christian had a personal hand in planting Christianity in his own country. It is known that the church in Ethiopia has an ancient past, although there are no records of its beginnings. God has strange ways of evangelizing areas where people are ignorant of the Gospel. His timings are perfect. The crossing of Philip's and the eunuch's paths was no coincidence. It was all in the plan of God.

27. A Divine Revelation to Saul

(Acts 9:1-9)

The most unlikely person ever to become a Christian in those early days was Saul of Tarsus. He was not merely unaffected by the Christian message, but was positively hostile. He was not content with hounding out the Jerusalem Christians. He had a murderous intention toward them. He was determined to outshine all other Pharisees in his persecuting zeal. He was the sort of man who would stop at nothing, made worse by the fact that he was convinced he was doing God's work. Violence in the cause of God is always the most tragic, for it reveals a totally wrong idea of God. Granted the fact that Saul sincerely believed that the Christian Church was a scourge which must at all costs be stamped out, it is difficult to conceive how a man as devout as he could stoop to such inhuman methods of doing it. Yet so it has been in all the long history of religious persecutions. A blind devotion to orthodoxy has not infrequently led to a blind opposition to humanity itself. So strong was Saul's crusading zeal that he wished to extend his sphere of operation from Jerusalem to Damascus.

It may be wondered why he chose Damascus. He must have known that there were many Christian believers there. Undoubtedly some of the dispersed from Jerusalem had traveled north and had settled there. Perhaps they thought they would be at a safe distance from Saul's persecution. Why Saul chose Damascus rather than Samaria, which was so much nearer, is puzzling.

The Abana River in Damascus.

Perhaps it was a determination on his part to show the Christians that he was prepared to go considerable distances to prevent the spread of what he believed to be a dangerous heresy. Yet this distance was nothing compared with the journeys he would make in the cause of the One he was now persecuting by pursuing His followers. To achieve his end in Damascus he needed authority from the chief priest, because those who were the objects of his hostility were Jews who would be connected with the synagogues there. He wanted to arrest them and bring them bound to Jerusalem. Since the high priest's authority would be acknowledged throughout Judaism he would have no difficulty in securing their extradition.

Without his knowing it Saul's own soul was darkened, until he met the unparalleled brilliance of light which struck out his physical sight on his way to Damascus. He became sightless through excess of light. But God intended it that way. Saul was at once reduced to helplessness. All he could do was listen. At last it had become possible for him to tune in to the divine voice, which now came through to him undistorted. It was startlingly direct and personal. "Saul, Saul, why do you persecute me?" He reported later that the language was Hebrew (Acts 26:14). He never forgot the sound of that sudden arresting challenge. His first impulse was to ask who was speaking. He could hardly have had any doubt that the implication was that it was Jesus of Nazareth whom he had been persecuting. It was Jesus Himself against whom his fury was directed. He was the great stumbling block. Whether Saul had had misgivings it is difficult to say, but crises do not usually occur abruptly. When reporting the matter himself he noted that the voice had referred to his kicking against the goads (Acts 26:14), as if the pricking of conscience had many times been stifled. Or it may be the goads were all those God-appointed influences which challenged him. Perhaps each time he recalled the face of Stephen he smothered his nobler thoughts in an ever more intense whirl of persecuting activity. His very fury suggests an intense instability.

The heavenly voice directed him to proceed into Damascus, where he would receive further instructions. Those traveling with Saul, oblivious to the spiritual revolution occurring in the man's mind and unaware that the noise they had heard was a divine voice, no doubt concluded that he had some form of sunstroke from the excessive brilliance of the light which they had all seen. They had to lead the great persecuting crusader by the hand into the city. Did they commiserate with him on the unfortunate calamity which would now prevent him from carrying out the mission on which he had set his heart? And did he tell them of the voice? Even if he had told them they would probably have attributed that also to a touch of the sun.

They led him to the house of Judas, one of Saul's contacts in Damascus. Not only was Saul sightless, but in no fit state even to eat or drink. Judas must have wondered what had arrived. Was this the envoy of the high priest? There could have been no greater humiliation for the proud Pharisee than to be reduced to this. As his host watched him for three days, he could have had no idea what a revolution had taken place in the soul of Saul. As yet nobody realized this, not even Saul himself in any clear sense. He could only pray to God for more light.

28. *A Special Mission for Ananias*

(Acts 9:10-19)

The church at Damascus had heard reports that Saul was on the way. It was no pleasant prospect. They faced the possibility of dispersal as the Christians at Jerusalem. Some may have had the impulse to clear out of Damascus. Others could only wait in suspense. No one knew what had happened just outside the city. They had no idea that Saul had already arrived, although a very different Saul from the man they expected. One of them, Ananias, a Jew of considerable repute in Damascus as a devout man (cf. Acts 22:12), received a vision which landed him with the key role in the conversion of Saul.

Ananias' vision is instructive because it is both human and specific. He was first invited to respond to a personal appeal. Then he was given directions which frightened him. He was to go to Judas' house in Straight Street, Damascus, to ask for a man named Saul who was praying there. Moreover, Saul had seen someone named Ananias coming to lay hands on him to restore his sight. At this Ananias protested. He could not credit the truth of his own vision. All the reports he had heard about Saul of Tarsus had shown him to be an evil man utterly hostile to the believers in Jerusalem and with authority to be equally hostile at Damascus. It seemed incredible that such a man should be praying. Ananias was furiously questioning his guidance. He had stayed in Damascus to await the persecuting lion, but had never bargained for putting his head in the lion's mouth. Surely something must be wrong with the vision? Ananias was not the first to be misguided by reputation and authority. They are sufficient to strike terror into most men. But God's dealing with Saul of Tarsus shows. His power to annul both in the pursuance of His purpose. Nevertheless no one who attempts to visualize the reactions of Ananias can fail to appreciate his deep apprehension.

The Lord simply said to him, "Go," and it speaks much for his spiritual maturity that he made no further protest. His was to be the privilege of being the Lord's messenger to the man who, more than any other, was responsible for molding the early history of Gentile Christianity. It was an activity, however, which called for considerable courage. A message was given to Ananias about Saul's future which opened up a wide vista of possibilities. "A chosen instrument" — who would have thought it? God's choices fall on many unexpected people, and none more unexpected than Saul. His main task was to witness and to suffer. It is strange to think of the persecutor persecuted, of Saul being dosed with his own medicine. But subsequent history abundantly bears testimony to the accuracy of that prediction.

Ananias found Saul precisely as the vision had said. As he laid hands on him and a scaly substance fell from his eyes, his sight was restored again as the vision had said. He did not hesitate to address this erstwhile persecutor as a brother in Christ. Moreover he had the joy of seeing the man filled with the Spirit. Luke says that Saul arose and was baptized, which presumably means that Ananias took him to some place where water was found. He also saw to it that Saul had a good meal. Luke does not say what Judas' reactions were to these extraordinary happenings. Whether he followed his notorious guest in becoming a Christian is not known. All that Luke records is that Saul remained with the disciples at Damascus.

Little is known of the community of Christians at Damascus. It was not one of the foremost churches of the early period. But the Damascus disciples are to be commended for the way in which they at once received the converted persecutor. Their warm welcome contrasts strongly with the approach of the Jerusalem church people, who were afraid of him. The Damascus Christians could have imagined that Saul's profession of faith was a subterfuge to enable him to discover who the Christians were and where they met. But they were presumably completely disarmed by Ananias, who must have related in detail his divinely directed visit to Saul. Because of his devoutness, his opinion would be highly respected. He had been present when the Holy Spirit came upon Saul and he was not the kind of man to be deceived. The whole church at Damascus stood behind him in receiving Saul as a true disciple of Christ.

29. *Saul at Damascus, Jerusalem, and Tarsus*

(Acts 9:20-31)

Saul was not the kind of man to keep quiet. He could have had little time to sort out his newfound faith before he began proclaiming Jesus as Son of God. Probably some interval elapsed which Luke does not record. When writing to the Galatians, Paul mentions a period he spent in Arabia immediately following his conversion (Gal. 1:17) and it is reasonable to suppose that this preceded any period of public preaching. The area of Arabia to which he refers was no doubt the part inland from Damascus, where Saul would have had the opportunity to think out the theological implications of his conversion experience. He at once recognized that Jesus was no mere man. He soon came to the conclusion that Jesus was not only the Son of God, but was also the long awaited Messiah. How long he spent in Arabia he does not say, but it is probable that the period was not prolonged. He was bursting to declare what had been revealed to him. He soon returned to Damascus to begin to preach.

He went straight to the synagogues. The Jews there were astonished that the man who was said to have letters from the Jerusalem high priest to arrest the Christians was now preaching about Jesus. Many of them began contending with him. Saul had himself used the same arguments that they were now using, only more vehemently. He had nevertheless thought out the answers to his own former position so effectively that no opponent could stand up to his reasoning. It was clear at this early stage that the Christian Church had gained in Saul a powerful intellect. His subsequent letters show how profoundly he followed out the implications of his faith.

It is not surprising that opposition arose against so powerful an advocate of the Christian position. The Jews at once turned against him and determined to kill him. The Damascus Jews were no more enlightened than their Jerusalem brethren in resorting to violent methods for disposing of unwelcome opponents. Hostility is moreover never more intense than when directed against a renegade supporter. The governor's consent was obtained. Paul, in later reporting this (2 Cor. 11:32), does not say on what grounds. A guard was set on all the gates to prevent Saul's escape, but somehow news of the plot reached the apostle. Using a basket, the Christians lowered him by night from a window in the wall and enabled him to escape. He was experiencing the first dose of the receiving end of the kind of persecution he had himself administered.

His escape from Damascus posed a problem. Where should he go? He decided to return to Jerusalem, an action of considerable courage, for the Jerusalem Jews would certainly not be amenable to the man who had let them down in Damascus. His intention was to associate with the church there. But even this nearly misfired. He had obviously assumed that the Jerusalem Christians would treat him as warmly as those at Damascus. But they were understandably suspicious. There was no Ananias to pave the way, so they had no guarantee that he was a true disciple. One man at Jerusalem, however, stands out for his Christian charity and understanding. He was Barnabas, who had already impressed the believers with his generosity. He listened to Saul's story and believed it. He then reported the story to the apostles, informing them of Saul's courageous preaching at Damascus. By this time the apostles were prepared for reports of preaching by those outside their own number. Stephen and Philip had forged the way. Luke does not say whether the apostles encouraged Saul to preach in Jerusalem, but he mentions the boldness of his preaching there. As Stephen had done, he found a ready hearing among the Hellenists, but found them equally intractable. Another plot was hatched, but once again the Christians knew about it and decided to send Saul away. He went back home to Tarsus via Caesarea. His early preaching appears to have been explosive in character and he may well have been considered an embarrassment to the apostles. Some time was to elapse before he would be properly fitted for his role as missionary to the Gentiles.

Back at Tarsus Saul's movements are shrouded in obscurity. The only hint of activity is in the Galatian letter, where he speaks of visiting the regions of Syria and Cilicia (Gal. 1:21). No mention is made of preaching, but it is a reasonable assumption that he took the opportunity to proclaim the Gospel in districts near his home town of Tarsus. What is surprising is that several years were to pass before anything else was heard of him. During those years his increasing grasp of the Christian faith and his meditation on Christian theology were part of his preparation for more extensive work in the future.

Paul probably traveled through this valley which lies between Tarsus and the Cilician Gates.

5

Peter Launches Out

30. *Peter at Lydda and Joppa*
(Acts 9:31-43)

Before switching from the story of Saul back to the Apostle Peter, Luke inserts another of his brief summaries. It would appear that the conversion of Saul had removed the chief source of opposition among the churches generally. The persecution collapsed through lack of a dynamic leader. In Judaea, Galilee, and Samaria there was no hostility, which gave opportunity for the building up of the Church. Luke accounts for the continued spread of the Church by the life of the Christians. They showed such piety and spiritual concern that a real work of God was evident.

The narrative focuses again on Peter, whose ministry appears at this period to have been of an itinerary kind. In the course of his travels he arrived at Lydda, an inland town some ten miles southeast of the harbor town of Joppa, the modern Jaffa. The most notable event that happened there was the healing of a man named Aeneas. He was paralyzed, having been bedridden for eight years. The cure of an apparently incurable invalid was bound to create a stir. It was performed with utmost simplicity. Peter commanded the man in Christ's name to rise and make his bed (or get ready to eat, as the words might be rendered). As in so many other instances the miracle of healing was the occasion for many turning to the Lord, not only at Lydda but throughout the Vale of Sharon, which stretched along the coast from Lydda to Mount Carmel. Luke's words suggest that considerable numbers of people became Christians as a result.

Reports reached Joppa of what had been happening in Lydda. One of the best-loved Christians in Joppa had died. Many in the place were grateful to her for her charitable works. Her name was Tabitha (Dorcas in the Greek). She had been prepared for burial, when some of the disciples wondered whether Peter might be able to do anything. They must have had considerable faith even to consider the possibility that he could. It was one thing to restore a paralytic at Lydda. It was quite another to raise a person from the dead. None of the apostles had ever done this. Yet it was considered worth trying. Two men were sent to press Peter to come immediately. It says much for Peter's faith that he was prepared to respond to such an impossible situation. But his faith was in process of maturing.

On arrival he soon discovered what a remarkable person Dorcas was and why there was such sorrow over her death. In the upper room where the body had been laid, weeping widows were lamenting. They paused in their weeping to show the apostle garments which Dorcas had made. The woman had clearly lived an unselfish existence, considering others rather than herself. Peter at once assessed the situation. Everyone was excluded from the upper room while he stayed there to pray. He felt constrained to address the body and command the woman to rise. Maybe he remembered the occasions when Jesus had restored people to life. God honored his faith and the woman revived. In such exceptional circumstances it is impossible to conceive the reactions of either the woman or Peter. The apostle made no comment as far as we know. Luke simply says that he presented her alive to the saints and widows. It was the most remarkable event that had yet happened. The whole town soon heard of it. An event like that could hardly be kept a secret. Those who had received gifts from the benefactress would be overjoyed at her restoration and would not be slow to spread the news.

As for Peter, he stayed on for some time in Joppa, where his host was a local tanner. The tanner's home was to be the setting for a remarkable vision destined to play a significant part in the progress of the Gospel.

31. *Cornelius' Vision*

(Acts 10:1-8)

So far the Christian Church had been a wholly Jewish affair. It was bound to happen sooner or later that Gentiles would become interested in the Gospel. The Gentile world had little to offer those who desired a religion of high moral standards. Most of the Gentile proselytes were attracted to Judaism because of the contrast with the corruption and immorality rife among the Gentile nations. These proselytes and others who had not formally aligned themselves with Judaism were among those most ready to turn to the Christian faith with its high moral standards, linked with universal appeal.

In Caesarea one of the officers of the Roman army was notable for his piety and good works. Cornelius was a generous man whose home was a model of God-fearing religion. His way of life could not have been bettered by any pious Jew. Nevertheless he had a sense of need. There had been prayer offered for more satisfaction, although he probably had little idea what form it should take. He was the kind of man who was open to religious inquiry and wanted nothing less than the best.

In view of his constant prayer life, it is not surprising that Cornelius had a vision. Luke actually mentions the time of the vision, which suggests that his narrative is probably based on information derived from Cornelius himself. Each time he recalled the vision, he would remember that mid-afternoon. It was about 3 P.M. when an angel of God appeared to him. In Luke's narrative angelic agency has already been responsible for Peter's release from prison (Acts 5:19) and for directing Philip (Acts 8:26). And there are other instances yet to come. In the present case it is clear that God was communicating with Cornelius.

The nature of the vision follows the pattern of others. A direct address to Cornelius by name is followed by a reaction of fright. The Lord's answer is specific. Cornelius is commended for his prayer life and his generosity. His religious devotion is seen as an acceptable sacrifice which ascends to God. Then follow the directions to send for Simon Peter at Simon's house in Joppa. It is significant that in this vision, as in that to Ananias, the directions include specific details regarding location. The guidance of God in the developing period of the Church was more specific than many moderns would consider possible. In those days there was no room for vagueness regarding God's intentions.

Cornelius did not hesitate to act at once on the angel's directions. Two servants and a trusted and devout military man were immediately sent to Joppa. These men were told the whole vision. They probably shared something of Cornelius' piety since they went on what might otherwise have appeared a fool's errand.

There is no knowing whether Cornelius had previously heard of the Apostle Peter. If he had not done so he may well have wondered at the mysterious character of the command. But if he had heard of him he might have been excused for declining to act on the vision, for he would have known only too well that Jews were not partial to crossing the threshold of Gentile homes with a view to social fellowship. It was a real barrier in the world of that time and would not be easily overcome. The messengers would go to Simon's house in Joppa with some reservations, but spurred on by the vision given to their master.

32. *Peter's Vision*

(Acts 10:9-23a)

In the house at Joppa, Peter was still harboring his ingrained Jewish prejudices. In spite of what Jesus had told the disciples about preaching to all nations, traditions die hard. It had probably never occurred to Peter that the Christian faith would require the abolition of the prejudice about Jews going to Gentile homes. He was convinced that Gentile homes were ritually unclean. The Gospel had not as yet penetrated that far.

It was noonday and Peter was praying. He was using the time profitably while waiting for a meal to be made ready. As guest at the home of Simon he would occupy the guest room on the roof of the house. In the sultry midday heat he had a dream. Subconsciously his sense of hunger contributed to the shape of the dream, for it centered on food.

A descending sheet held by its four corners was seen to contain a wide variety of animals, reptiles, and birds. The character of the dream was fantastic but the message was clear. As a Jew aware of his present hunger, Peter looked for some clean animal such as the law permitted an orthodox Jew to eat. But all the animals he saw were considered to be ritually unclean and therefore impossible to use as food. The strong Jewish prejudice against eating with Gentiles arose because the latter ate food which in Jewish eyes was unclean. It was more important to the Jew to maintain his taboos than to cultivate good human relationships with people of other nations.

The command to Peter to rise, kill, and eat touched him on a sensitive spot, and caused him to protest that his lifelong practice had been abstinence from common or unclean meat. It was natural enough, for it was not merely a religious convention but a deep conviction. Nevertheless it was not easy to dispose of the message of the dream. A voice reminded him that what God

Herod's fortress at Caesarea.

JOPPA IN RELATION TO CAESAREA.

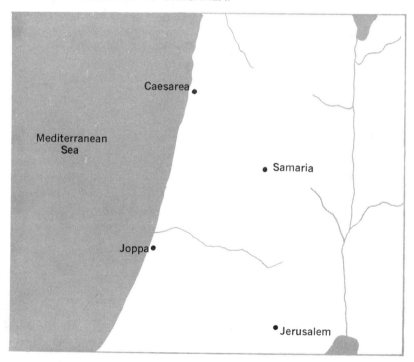

Caesarea

Mediterranean Sea

Samaria

Joppa

Jerusalem

had cleansed, no one should call common. Although he was perplexed at the meaning of this message, he was not permitted to ignore it. It was repeated three times. A threefold message impresses itself more vividly than a single message. Maybe Peter was more disposed to listen the third time. Maybe he had reached the point of examining himself to discover the application of the dream.

One point of detail is worth noting and that is the remarkable timing of God's communications. Peter's dream, through which God was undoubtedly preparing him, was at midday just as Cornelius' servants were nearing the city. This was some twenty-one hours after Cornelius' own vision. Had Peter had the dream earlier he would not so easily have understood the application. But with Gentiles on the point of knocking at the door, the perfect timing of the various events is at once apparent.

Cornelius' men had found their way to Simon's house at the precise time of Peter's perplexity over the vision. Still in a condition of reflection Peter heard the men inquiring for him. He no doubt realized they were Gentiles, but the Spirit gave him specific instructions to accompany them. The timing was perfect. Luke notes that the Spirit revealed that he had sent them. In no clearer way could the synchronizing of the two visions be indicated.

Peter was obedient to the Spirit's leading. The Book of Acts is studded with instances of this kind. In conversation with the men he discovered the reason for their visit to him. It is noteworthy that Cornelius is described as an "upright and God-fearing man," a high testimony from his own servants. Moreover, his reputation among the Jews is mentioned and this must be regarded as more than a policy comment to commend him to Peter. In the midst of the general hatred and antipathy among the Jews toward the Roman occupying forces, any instance of Jewish regard for a Roman officer stands out the more notably. Peter made an immediate start on the process of reorientation, by entertaining the three Gentile men as his guests.

33. *Peter at Cornelius' House*
(Acts 10:23b-48)

The day after Peter's vision he set off with Cornelius' servants to Caesarea. Other Christians who had heard about Peter's mission decided to accompany them. There were evidently six of these (cf. Acts 11:12), making a traveling party of ten. The party took longer than the three servants had taken on the forward journey and they did not arrive until the next day, that is four days after Cornelius had sent his men to Joppa.

Cornelius must have calculated fairly accurately the time of their arrival, for not only was he expecting them but he had gathered others into his home to meet with Peter. The first act of the pious centurion was to offer homage to Peter as if he stood in some awe of a man to whom he had been directed by an angel. Peter at once rejected such action. The Christian Church was not to be built on obeisance to personalities. Whenever this happens, it must be regarded as a deviation.

The conversation which ensued between Peter and Cornelius reiterated the events of the past few days. Peter announced to the whole company the sweeping away of his objections to associating with Gentiles which must have put him in rapport with his audience at once. They would know that a Jew admitting this would be an unusual character. Cornelius repeated his reason for sending for Peter, which the apostle had in fact already heard. The whole company was ready to listen to Peter, or rather to what God had to say through him. Cornelius had grasped with remarkable clarity that Peter, rough fisherman as he was, was nevertheless the mouthpiece of God.

Peter's address that day, reported in summary form by Luke, is notable as the first Christian proclamation to a Gentile audience. The preacher began by recognizing a basic principle in God's dealings with men, which shows the revolution which had occurred in his Jewish mode of thinking. God makes no distinction among nations — Jews and Gentiles are on the same basis. There were to be further difficulties in the outworking of this in Peter's mind, as Galatians 2:11 ff. shows, but faced with the fact of God's obvious leading of Cornelius he could not deny the universal application of the Gospel. He went on to explain what the Gospel is by an account of the historical facts about Jesus. Luke gives the bare bones — the preaching of Jesus, the baptism of John the Baptist, the anointing of Jesus of Nazareth with the Holy Spirit, His acts of healing and exorcisms of demons. Peter reminded his hearers that he was an eyewitness to these things. He then spoke of the crucifixion and the resurrection of Jesus on the third day. In relating these events he again appealed to the fact that he was among the eyewitnesses specially chosen by God.

He recalled the occasions when he and others had shared meals with the resurrected Lord. He could speak vividly of these occasions. He related how the resurrected Lord had left them a command to preach. They were to declare Him to be the Judge of the living and the dead. Peter could hardly have spoken in these terms without enlarging considerably upon them. As at Pentecost he must have linked judgment with a call to repentance before giving the offer of forgiveness. Luke relates Peter's statement that all the prophets had testified that faith would bring forgiveness through Messiah's name.

What else Peter intended saying is not clear, for his sermon was unfinished, interrupted by the direct activity of the Holy Spirit on the audience. The most astonished were Peter's six Jewish traveling companions. They had never imagined that the gift of the Spirit was to be poured out equally on Jews and Gentiles. Jewish superiority was demolished at one sweep. The Gospel was opening up remarkable possibilities for a better understanding between different racial groups. With the gift of the Spirit came also the gift of tongues, which at once placed the experience of these Gentiles on a level with the Jewish audience at the feast of Pentecost. It was a notable landmark in the development of Christianity.

The baptismal service at which the Gentile believers confessed their faith in Jesus Christ must have been a moving occasion as the Jewish Christians witnessed the baptizing of their first Gentile brethren in the name of Jesus Christ. In view of the remarkable significance of Peter's visit to Cornelius it is not surprising that the arrangements for it were overruled by God. In His infinite wisdom He had superintended by means of visions a major breakthrough which not only transformed the Christian Church, but also transformed man's relationship with his fellow men.

34. *Peter Defends His Action*

(Acts 11:1-18)

Not all criticism is harmful. Nevertheless, the Christian Church has always found ready critics when some new development takes place. Traditionalists have often been both the most sincere and the most critical in assessing new movements. Gentile admission into the Church was a case of serious deviation from tradition. The circumcision party in the Jerusalem church, who had not yet been able to escape from the narrow nationalistic mould in which they had been reared, were worried because it appeared that the new departure was an infringement of orthodoxy. Their anxiety, it is only fair to say, was based on reports, which no doubt did not give the whole story. They had to await the return of Peter from Caesarea to Jerusalem. They were ready with their criticisms, and their question to Peter regarding his visiting and eating with uncircumcised people implied a censure before Peter was given the opportunity to speak. But this kind of attitude is typical of critics who speak from a strongly traditional point of view.

Peter's explanation consisted of a recital of events which led to his visit to Cornelius' house. The details of the vision evidently made a deep impression on Peter's mind, especially the words addressed to him. He told his critics how the Spirit had commanded him to go. His action was therefore in obedience to the Spirit and was not a decision of his own. Moreover he showed how Cornelius' vision dovetailed with his own. The occasion in Cornelius' household was clearly prepared by God.

The climax of Peter's explanation was when he related the descent of the Spirit on those Gentiles and compared this precisely with what had happened when the first Jews believed at the beginning of the Christian Church. This must have been the most powerful point that Peter could make in answering the criticism leveled against him. At this stage he recalled what the Lord had said about his disciples being baptized with the Holy Spirit. It is important to note the reminiscence. It was obvious that anything which Jesus had said possessed considerable importance and care would be taken to preserve such sayings. It is here an echo of the final advice given by the risen Lord before his ascension (Acts 1:5). Peter implies that what the Lord had promised has been fulfilled in a full measure with the inclusion of both Jews and Gentiles.

The account given to the criticizing Jews was building up in impressiveness and reached its climax when Peter asked the rhetorical question, "Who was I that I could withstand God?" Since God had made no line of distinction between Jews and Gentiles in His gift of the Holy Spirit, this seemed a conclusive argument to Peter. There could be no possibility that Peter had suffered from delusions, for there were six other Christians who could confirm that the Spirit had descended on a house full of

Gentiles. With great insight the apostle had been prepared to follow the dictates of the Spirit, even when to do so cut right across his national and religious prejudices. It may be that in modern times the processes of the Spirit will cut across other barriers which Christians have traditionally maintained, in which case real progress will be made only in so far as the Spirit's guidance is followed.

It is to the credit of the Jewish critics that they changed their tune after hearing what Peter had to say. There could be no denying that this was of God. Repentance which leads to life was possible for Gentiles also. The critics turned to glorifying God. Practical testimony concerning God's leading in the affairs of men proved a powerful antidote to genuine criticism and gave the best fuel for the praising of God. The strength of the Christian movement may be seen in the effectiveness with which it can remove deep-seated prejudices, and this early and basic example is an indisputable witness to such effectiveness.

35.   *Beginnings at Antioch*

(Acts 11:19-26)

The spreading of the Gospel as a result of Saul's persecution of the Church was extensive, including Phoenicia, the coastal strip which included the cities of Tyre and Sidon, the island of Cyprus, and Antioch, the capital city of the Roman province of Syria. The latter place held most interest for Luke. It was a city with a large number of Jews among its population. It was therefore one of the chief cities of the Jewish diaspora. Luke is particularly concerned to show that it became an important center of early Christianity.

The church there consisted of both Jews and Gentiles. There were in fact two parallel movements. One was aimed at the Jewish section and was the work of Jewish-Christians who had come from Jerusalem. The other was a Greek mission conducted by Hellenists from the islands of Cyprus and Crete. Both had the same purpose — to preach the Lord Jesus. When Luke records the results of the preaching he mentions no difficulties in the mixing of Jews and Gentiles. The two streams appear to have happily merged. Luke simply says that the hand of the Lord was with the preachers, showing once again his acute awareness that the progress of the church was the result of divine initiative. The remarkable growth at Antioch was achieved without the leadership of any apostles or well-known figures. The preachers remain anonymous.

Reports soon reached the Christian headquarters in Jerusalem. It was naturally of great interest to the church there to investigate these reports. Perhaps some questioned the validity of a work so independent of the Jerusalem church. Barnabas was sent to find out. His part in receiving the converted persecutor, Saul of Tarsus, has already been noted. He was clearly a liberally minded man, who had nevertheless won the confidence of the Jerusalem church.

He was a man of great perception, who at once saw the evidence of divine work in the lives of these people at Antioch. Luke characteristically says that Barnabas saw the grace of God, by which he evidently means the evidence of the work of God's grace in the transformation of the people and in the overcoming of racial barriers. For a spiritually minded man, there is no greater joy than to see God's grace at work. Barnabas was happy about all he saw among the believers at Antioch. There was no doubt in his mind that this was a real work of God. He felt it necessary simply to encourage them to continue as they had begun. The continual stability of newly converted Christians is the surest test of the true basis of any work. The Antioch church came through this test successfully, as the subsequent events show. Luke mentions that Barnabas was a man full of the Spirit and of faith, which is precisely the same description he gives of Stephen. Both were notable men in early Church history, although Barnabas' ministry turned out to be more widespread than Stephen's. After Barnabas' arrival, further crowds were added to the company of believers.

The rate of growth was so phenomenal that additional assistance was needed. Barnabas decided to obtain help, not from the Jerusalem apostles, but from Saul of Tarsus. Some time had elapsed since the latter's conversion and since his introduction to the Jerusalem church under Barnabas' recommendation. Whether or not there had been any communication between them since Saul's return to Tarsus is not known. Nor is it known why Barnabas suddenly decided that Saul was the man for Antioch. But he was clearly led of the Spirit, as subsequent events show. It is noteworthy that Barnabas took the trouble to go to find Saul himself. Perhaps he imagined Saul would need some persuading to come. But the combination of Barnabas with Saul was to prove significant for further developments.

Luke specially notes that the Antioch church was taught for a whole year by Barnabas and Saul. There is no need to inquire what was the main subject of their teaching for it must have centered on Christ. The believers so frequently had that name on their lips that they were dubbed Christ's men or "Christians" for the first time in that place. Little did the people of Antioch know that their nickname for believers would survive throughout history and become the commonly accepted term to describe adherents of Jesus Christ.

36. *Famine Relief for Judaea*

(Acts 11:27-30)

It speaks much for the church at Antioch that it was at once open to social concerns. The arrival of a prophet named Agabus found them prepared for social involvement. When through the Spirit he predicted there would be a worldwide dearth, the Antioch church knew what course to take. The major difficulty with any prophecy is to decide whether or not it is authentic, but in the case of Agabus' forecast the church at Antioch had no doubt. They recognized the evidence of the Spirit in the man. He was no charlatan, but a deeply sincere man with a special gift for predicting the future. Luke, ever anxious to demonstrate the many-sided nature of the Spirit's activity, comments in an aside that the famine took place in the time of Claudius. Although no worldwide famine occurred in Claudius' reign there is known to have been a great dearth at this time, according to Suetonius. Josephus mentions a famine during this period in Judaea.

The church at Antioch must be warmly commended for their immediate reaction. They might have been excused had they concentrated on their own coming needs if famine conditions were to affect them, but they did not do this. They were more concerned about Judaea. Barnabas had presumably told them about the conditions in the churches there and they at once desired to do something to assist. Maybe Barnabas, who had been intimately concerned in the communal experiment, had warned of the disaster to the scheme if famine conditions prevailed. Ignoring their own probable needs, the Antioch church made a collection to relieve the situation for their Palestinian brethren. All had a share in it. It was a different kind of communal effort. It was, in fact, the first joint Jewish-Gentile relief scheme.

When deciding who should take the contribution, the Antioch church did not hesitate to send its two most notable men, Barnabas and Saul. Any contribution sent through such men would be doubly welcome in Jerusalem, for both were well known there. The financial relief was delivered to the elders, who were presumably responsible for the financial arrangements.

It is important to note that Luke mentions only the elders and not the apostles. It would appear from this that the two delegates did not see the apostles. Some find it incredible that Barnabas and Saul could have delivered the money without contact with the apostles. Would they not want to know about the happenings at Antioch? But Saul especially would probably not want to stay long in Jerusalem in view of the hostility of the hierarchy.

The matter assumes some importance when Paul's statements in his letter to the Galatians are compared with Acts. Some consider that the famine relief visit is the same as that mentioned by Paul in Galatians 2, in which case Galatians could have been the earliest epistle written by the apostle.

The social concern of the Christian Church is a matter of deep interest. Some have taken the view that the Church's concern is to preach the Gospel, not to involve itself in relief schemes. Others have supposed that the Church's Gospel must mainly be expressed in terms of social reform and social relief. Neither view is in keeping with the New Testament Church, which as in this case did not ignore social responsibility, but regarded its main task as preaching the Word. What is specially impressive about the Antioch scheme is that it anticipated the famine. All too often the Christian Church has been slow to act after the need arose. To do so beforehand shows a high degree of understanding of the social implications of the Gospel.

6

Crises and Challenges

37. *Action Against James and Peter*

(Acts 12:1-11)

A clash between the new movement and the State had been
brewing for some time. There had already been two occasions
when apostles had been arrested and charged before the high
priest. In Palestine at that time the religious authorities had
considerable powers in secular affairs and it was inevitable that
opposition from the hierarchy would sooner or later spill over to
the secular authorities. King Herod, who did his best to keep
the right side of the Jews, was on occasions used by the hierarchy
to effect their designs. For some reason which Luke does not
mention Herod decided to take violent action against the Church.
His policy was dictated by a desire to maintain his position by
supporting at times schemes which met the approval of the Jews.
He had received reports that the apostles had angered the Jews
and saw an opportunity of appeasing them without harm to himself. This Herod, unlike his grandfather Herod the great, was
assiduous in observing Jewish customs and was consequently on
better terms with his subjects.

Why Herod killed the Apostle James is not known. It probably
did not matter to him so long as a blow was struck against the
apostles. The action immediately received the approbation of
the Jews and whetted the appetite of Herod for more. Some have
supposed that John was killed at the same time as James, on the
grounds of an edited text of Acts and the witness of some later
none-too-reliable historians. But this view runs counter to the
strong tradition of John's survival to a great old age in Ephesus.

Peter was Herod's next target. He was obviously a more prominent apostle and action against him would enable Herod to

ingratiate himself still more with the Jews. It was feast time in Jerusalem, approaching the Passover, which meant that the city was thronged with people. Herod would vividly remember the popular demand for the crucifixion of Jesus at an earlier Passover, stirred up by the priests. He had similar designs in publicly displaying Peter to the crowds after the Passover was over. In view of Peter's previous escape from prison, he decided to take no chances and appointed four squads to guard him. The apostle must have feared the worst in view of what had happened to his friend and fellow apostle James. He must have wondered why he had not been summarily executed as James had been. This was the most determined attack yet on the new faith.

Those Christians who still remained in Jerusalem were alert to pray. They could do nothing else. They were powerless in the face of the secular authority. But prayer was a force to be reckoned with. Even Peter, bound by chains and guarded by two soldiers, could not have foreseen what prayer would effect. It is worth noting that Herod Agrippa had himself been imprisoned in Rome by Tiberius and had been similarly chained. But he was evidently not intending to release Peter as Tiberius' successor Gaius had released him. The same night when Herod intended exhibiting Peter, an angel of the Lord took action on Peter's behalf. The incident as Luke records it is vividly portrayed. Peter needed speed, courage, and faith. It was only as he obeyed the summon to get up that the chains dropped off. He had other specific instructions to obey before he was able to escape.

Peter was in a daze as he followed the angel. It could easily have been a vision. He might have thought that his imagination was running away with him. But as they passed the second guard safely and had come to the outer iron gate, he could have had no further doubts as the massive gate opened of its own accord and he found himself in the street outside the prison. By some miracle he had actually escaped. This was the second time it had happened to Peter. It was clearly not the Lord's will that he should be murdered to satisfy the whim of an officious tyrant and some of his hostile subjects against the Christian Church. Such releases from prison were not to be the pattern for all servants of God caught up in the rush of violent hostility. This was an exceptional case. Iron gates of a different sort have often yielded in a miraculous way, but multitudes have followed in the steps of James and have died for their faith. The release from prison was a great boost to Peter's faith. He could not doubt that the hand of the Lord continued to be with him.

38. *The Effect of Peter's Release and the Death of a King*

(Acts 12:12-24)

Peter made straight for Mark's mother's house, which he was clearly used to visiting. It was the place where Christians met to pray. There were many urgent topics for prayer, among them the imprisonment of Peter. In their sessions the course of recent events would be vividly in their minds — the scattering of many of their number, the killing of James, the persistent hostility of the Jewish leaders, and now the arrest and threatened execution of Peter. They were still praying as Peter approached the house. Many of the Christians must have been in perplexity about the opposition. They probably wondered whether the whole Christian movement was destined to battle against impossible odds, but their hope was in God.

Luke specially records what happened when Peter arrived, perhaps because it struck him as an example of man's reluctance to accept the possibility of God doing the impossible. A maid named Rhoda answered Peter's knock and heard his voice. He presumably called out for security reasons. But Rhoda was too excited to open the door. She was in no doubt that it was Peter, but the others to whom she reported this were highly skeptical. Either Rhoda was mad or she was seeing things — what she had seen was probably Peter's angel who had appeared to her. Neither of these proposed alternatives to the simple truth was anywhere near as credible as Rhoda's report, but this kind of thing happens when men dismiss the possibility of a miracle. Those Christians should have known better. They had already seen many striking instances of the power of God in action. Nevertheless Herod and his four squads of soldiers, the chains and the iron gates certainly presented a very considerable challenge to the power of faith. The Christians' lack of readiness to expect a release was no doubt conditioned by what had happened to James. Could Peter expect any better treatment? They had in fact already given him up as lost. But they had reckoned without God.

Meanwhile Peter continued knocking. When at length the

door opened, they were amazed. For the second time Peter had escaped. He was obviously in a hurry to be gone, for it was not safe there. But the Christians ought to know what had happened. After a rapid report of what the Lord had done, he requested that James and the brethren should be told and then he vanished. This James must be James the Lord's brother, who is met with in the latter half of Acts as the leader of the Jerusalem church. It is extraordinary that he assumed leadership apparently in preference to any of the Twelve. Peter's singling out of James by name is evidence that he himself acknowledged James' importance. The Christians must have been somewhat frustrated when Peter so abruptly silenced their questions and, after telling them what God was doing, disappeared as quickly as he came. Luke gives no indication where he went. The view that he departed for Rome and founded the church there cannot be right in the light of Acts 15:1 ff., where he is present at the Council at Jerusalem.

The position of the guards who had allowed Peter to escape was precarious. It was assumed that any guards whose prisoner had escaped had neglected their duty, and punishment for this was severe. The soldiers were completely baffled. They could not conceive how the prisoner could have escaped. There was no rational explanation and Herod could not be expected to accept any less satisfactory explanation. Moreover, the king was not the kind of person to show mercy. Life was cheap in those days and a monarch's security and dignity more important than human lives. It made no difference whether he was disposing of an apostle who was proving to be a disturbing influence or sentries whose lapse of duty might undermine the loyalty of his own army. It is characteristic of tyrants, however petty, to use violence in preference to reason.

At that time a political crisis arose for Herod. His disagreement with the cities of Tyre and Sidon created a serious situation for those cities, for they depended on being on friendly relations for economic reasons. Not surprisingly, a petition was sent to Herod, who had now returned from Jerusalem to Caesarea. A considerable deputation brought the request for peace. No doubt in modern days a similar request would have taken the form of a protest march ending in a deputation. In the case of Tyre and Sidon, it is evident that the people were bypassing normal diplomatic channels. The king's chamberlain, a man named Blastus who is otherwise unknown, made arrangements for Herod to address the delegation. This the king did with suitable pomp, yet apparently in fairly conciliatory terms, since the people called him a god. No doubt in his speech he was playing to the gallery. The idea of being thought a god would greatly bolster his pride. Josephus records that divine honors were given to him at Caesarea just before he died. His sudden death appeared to Luke to be a divine judgment against him for not rebuking the people for worshiping him. The precise nature of the disease from which he died is not known. Josephus mentions that he had violent internal pains and died five days later.

Luke contrasts the miserable death of Herod, so soon after he had killed James and imprisoned Peter, with the continued growth of the Word of God. It seems that he wants to make clear that whatever happened in the secular world could not prevent the development of the Church. There is almost an air of inevitability about the way that God was giving the increase. He was persistently overruling the adverse designs of men.

39. *Barnabas and Saul Again*

(Acts 12:25 – 13:3)

The mission of mercy which Barnabas and Saul had carried out at Jerusalem was completed and they were now back in Antioch. The Christians there were a go-ahead group. They were men with vision. Among them were men of notability, for in addition to Barnabas and Saul, there was Simeon Niger, a man with both a Jewish and a Latin name (the Latin name suggests that he was an African for Niger means Black). There is a suggestion that this Simeon is to be identified with Simon of Cyrene, but there is no evidence either to prove or disprove this. Similarly some have supposed that Lucius of Cyrene, another of their number, was in fact the evangelist Luke, but no supporting evidence exists for this. The most notable of the prophets and teachers at Antioch, however, was Manaen who had been closely associated with the Court of Herod Antipas. It is probable that Luke's description of him as a member of the Court means that he was on terms of close friendship with the king. It is of some significance that Luke relates this man's interest in Christianity immediately after mentioning the death of Herod, the nephew of the man to whose court Manaen had belonged. The work of God was not to be barred even from king's courts. It would be interesting to know how Manaen became a Christian, but Luke does not say. He was probably the source of Luke's information about Herod Antipas.

The missionary movement had such world-shaking effects that it is well to note the simplicity of its birth. There was no general conference or special committee or publicity campaign. It happened when a group of men were worshiping and fasting. When Luke speaks of worship he means more than an organized worship service. For the early Christians, the whole of life was a service to God. Concentration on spiritual matters led to a self-denying attitude toward material things (as fasting must here be interpreted in its broadest sense). Whereas the denial aspect is not indispensable for God's communication with men, those who have received the clearest visions in the service of God have most often been those who practiced self-discipline.

Luke is specific that the impetus for the missionary task came from the Holy Spirit. However, the direction actually came from the people of Antioch who were in no doubt that the Spirit was leading them to set apart Barnabas and Saul for the purpose. Had it not been for this they might well have hesitated to send out the two preachers who had instructed them for a whole year. They would be sorely missed, but the Antioch church was outward looking. The secret strength of the Christian mission is groups of Christians who are more concerned about others than about themselves. The Spirit found a ready response to the proposition that Barnabas and Saul should be commissioned for God's work elsewhere.

The commissioning ceremony was simple. It consisted of prayer and fasting and laying on of hands. In the laying on of hands the church was identifying itself with the mission and in the former acts was pledging its prayer support. Although there was no organized missionary society behind the two workers, they had the backing of a church with wide horizons. There were historical reasons why Christian missions began at Antioch and not Jerusalem. It was at Antioch that the first real mixture of Jewish and Gentile believers occurred, and the possibilities of mission work among Gentiles were clearly seen. The Jerusalem church had difficulties in shedding its narrower viewpoint and God in His wisdom gave wider horizons to the Antioch community. It is significant that the two who were so closely associated in the first missionary tour from Antioch had first become associated at Jerusalem, where the Jewish Christians had even hesitated to receive Saul. The idea of commissioning him as apostle to the Gentiles did not occur to the Jerusalem apostles, although they were gracious enough to accept it later as an accomplished fact, as Paul shows in his Galatian letter.

40. *The Gospel in Cyprus*

(Acts 13:4-12)

Whereas the Spirit was specific about the men to be sent, nothing was said about their destination. This appears to have been left to their discretion, because these were men of the Spirit, sensitive to His leading.

It is reasonable to suppose that Barnabas at first acted as leader and in that capacity was responsible for choosing Cyprus. He was a native of the island, although he had been domiciled in Jerusalem. Moreover, there were many from Cyprus in the Antioch church, who had helped to found it by preaching among the Greeks. How those Cypriots heard the Gospel is not known,

PAUL'S FIRST MISSIONARY JOURNEY.

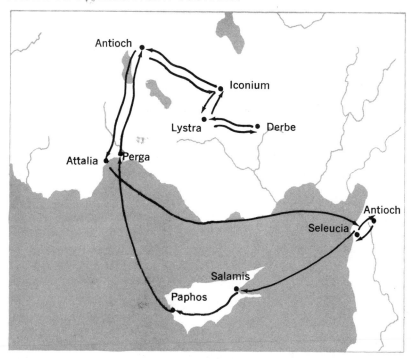

but some of the Jewish Christians scattered from Jerusalem went to Cyprus and must have instructed some of the Greeks there. In a short time both Jews and Greeks crossed to the mainland at Antioch. The Antioch church, with its strong links with the island, no doubt encouraged Barnabas and Saul to head for Cyprus. They had the company of John Mark, whom they had brought back to Antioch from Jerusalem. Their policy was to preach first in the synagogues, a procedure which Paul followed throughout his missionary work.

Luke relates one notable occurrence at Paphos, the official capital of the western part of the island. He may have had special interest in relating this because of its parallel with an incident which happened to Peter at Samaria. Both Peter and Paul had to deal with a magician. But Luke's interest here centers not so much on the magician as on the notable convert who was won as a result of the encounter. The magician, Bar-Jesus, who was of Jewish origin, had obtained favor in the eyes of the Roman proconsul, Sergius Paulus. Luke does not say how the proconsul knew about Barnabas and Saul. What he knew was enough to suggest to him that they were worth hearing. Luke specially notes that he was a man of intelligence. In that case it may seem surprising that he gave any heed at all to a man like Bar-Jesus (or Elymas as he was otherwise called). But he clearly had an inquiring mind and perhaps wished to compare the preaching of Barnabas or Paul (as Luke from this point calls him) with that of the magician. There was immediately a battle for the mind of the proconsul.

Elymas' tactic was to prevent a fair hearing and to attempt to prejudice the proconsul against the preachers. It was Paul who took the lead in dealing with the opposition He showed something of the fiery spirit which at times comes through his letters. He did not mince his words. He recognized at once that opposition to the Gospel could only ultimately be traced to the devil. He accused Elymas of being a son of the devil, an enemy of all righteousness. Paul was later to develop the theme of righteousness (as in Romans and Galatians), but even at this stage was hotly opposed to anything and to anyone who was an enemy of it. Not only so, but he sees Elymas as no more than a trickster, as if his magic was used with villainous intent. Paul had meditated enough on Christian truth to know that there are "straight paths of the Lord." It is essential to get clear the nature of truth before error can be defined. Deviations are meaningless unless some standard exists with which the deviations can be compared. Paul was illustrating his point from those straight highways for which the Romans were justly famous. They would not tolerate crookedness. And Paul sees the perversions of Elymas as nothing other than intentionally making crooked what God had made straight. There is a lesson here. Paul recognized that standards existed and was uncompromising toward those who opposed them, in marked contrast to those modern schools of thought which deny the possibility of absolute standards and which cannot in consequence speak with an authoritative voice against deviation.

It may seem surprising that Paul pronounced a judgment of blindness upon Elymas. It may be thought that this smacks of vindictiveness. But he was convinced that the hand of the Lord was active in the matter. Perhaps he recalled the dark blindness which came to him at his conversion. The blindness of Elymas was said to be temporary. Luke, a doctor, describes the stages of the blinding, mist being distinguished from darkness, a distinction between partial and total blindness. As Paul saw Elymas groping for guides to lead him, he must have remembered the day he was led by others into Damascus. As a result the proconsul believed. It must have been a real encouragement to the missionaries to find so notable a man among the first converts of their tour. However, as Paul was later to discover, not many noblemen would be won for Christ. Nevertheless the converted proconsul of Cyprus is evidence that Christianity was powerful enough to affect even the highest ranks of society.

41. *Paul at Pisidian Antioch*

(Acts 13:13-41)

Luke reports that "Paul and his company" left Cyprus, a sure evidence that Paul had now assumed the leadership. After the incident with Sergius Paulus this is not surprising. Whether Paul's leadership had anything to do with John Mark's returning to Jerusalem from Perga is not known. But a later comment by Luke suggests that Paul and Mark did not get on too well (cf. Acts 15:38). There were personality clashes in the earliest mission, preludes to many more in later Church history. What is important is not the differences between people, which will always exist, but the avoidance of resentment. But we know nothing about the spirit in which Mark here withdrew.

When Luke says that they came to Antioch of Pisidia, he means Pisidian Antioch as it was called, although it strictly was not in the district known as Pisidia. It was an important place, not only as the main center for that part of the provincial district, but because Augustus had made it a Roman colony. It was therefore a strategic place for the planting of the Gospel.

Paul and Barnabas made for the synagogue. It was customary, particularly in the Diaspora synagogues, for notable visitors to be given the opportunity of addressing the company at the appropriate time in the worship. This would be after the reading of the Scriptures, which generally took the form of a passage from the law and another from the prophets. At a later date there is evidence of a three-year lectionary cycle which may well have been observed as early as the first century. The rulers of the synagogue, who were responsible for the arrangements at public worship, would have authority to invite anyone in the congregation to participate.

When the two men were given such an invitation it was Paul who seized the opportunity. He had had previous experience of contending with Jewish synagogue audiences and was glad of this further opportunity. The main gist of his address will be noted, as it may be regarded as typical of Paul's synagogue speeches. It is important to bear in mind the nature of his audience. It was a group of Hellenistic Jews, the basis of whose Jewish faith was centered much more on the importance of the law and the prophets than on the Temple ritual at Jerusalem. It is for this reason that Paul takes a biblical approach, using the Scriptures to lead up to the main features of Christian history.

He began with the Exodus, moved on to the conquest, then to the judges until Samuel's time, and finally to the kingdom under Saul and David. No Jew would need any convincing about these details. Jews and Christians were agreed that God had established His people. But Paul concentrates on David, through whose ancestral line Jesus had been born. This gave him his point of contact. There was a general belief that the Messiah would come from the line of David. Paul himself mentions this when writing to the Romans (1:3), but he does not make anything of it in his other letters. Mention of the Messiah leads him to refer to the forerunner John the Baptist. Paul had been educated in Jerusalem under Gamaliel, and would have been well acquainted with the strange ministry of John, but it was not until he became a Christian that he realized the significance of his testimony. He reminded his synagogue audience that John had preached a baptism of repentance, that is a baptism which was a sign of an inward repentance. He also informed them of John's testimony to the "Coming One," in words which are paralleled in all the gospels. He had received authentic reports of John's testimony. He may even have heard John preach.

The next part of the address concerned the killing of Jesus. Paul does not hesitate to place the responsibility for the death of Jesus on the Jerusalem Jews, although he admits that they were oblivious to the fact that they were fulfilling prophecy concerning Jesus. The placing of the body of Jesus in a tomb and the resurrection appearances to many witnesses are stated as historic facts. These basic evidences are mentioned by Paul in 1 Corinthians 15:3 ff., in such a way as to suggest that he had received firsthand reports confirming them. In continuing his address he again returns to the testimony of Scripture, citing passages from Psalm 2, Isaiah 55, and Psalm 16. All these he sees as relating to the risen Christ. In maintaining the contrast between the incorruptible character of Jesus and the corruption of the body of David, Paul is demonstrating the superiority of Christ. At this point he applies his message, proclaiming forgiveness of sins through Christ for all who believe, which exceeds anything the law of Moses could offer. He pressed home his conclusion by a warning from Habakkuk 1:5.

A comparison between this mission sermon of Paul and the earlier sermons of Peter shows much in common, particularly the Old Testament basis, the historical facts about Jesus' death and resurrection, and the offer of forgiveness. It is evident therefore that Paul preached the same Gospel as the other apostles. The one development is the idea of justification through Christ rather than Moses, an idea which Paul greatly elaborates in his epistles.

42. *The Aftermath of a Sermon*

(Acts 13:42-52)

Not many sermons call for repetition, but Paul's audience at Antioch wanted to hear the same theme again the following sabbath. In addition there was a kind of after meeting in which many Jews and proselytes lobbied Paul and Barnabas, who at once told them more of the grace of God. It is a happy situation for any preacher when his words create an appetite for more. It is noticeable that the hearers were struck more by the subject matter of Paul than by his eloquence.

The synagogue audience effectively spread the news about the two visiting preachers for multitudes assembled the next week to hear them preach. There was clearly a real desire to hear the Word of the Lord, but a situation like this always presents a problem. Although the Jewish teachers faithfully expounded the Scriptures weekly to the best of their knowledge, they never made much impact on the multitudes. No sermon of theirs had ever brought the whole city to the synagogue doors. They might have rejoiced that many who had never heeded their teaching were hearing about God, but the ingredients were present for the development of an intense jealousy. They felt they must put a stop to what was so vividly showing up their own ineffectiveness. They decided on two lines of attack — contradiction and abuse. When the former fails to convince, the latter is an easy weapon to use. Nevertheless a cause which can only be sustained by abuse reveals at once an inherent weakness. The Christian mission which had at its center a Christ who, when He was reviled, reviled not again, was not likely to be impeded by the scornful language of jealous men. The attitude of the orthodox Jews is not unexpected, but what is surprising is that the opposition did not arise on the first occasion, but developed only when the astonishing draw of Paul's preaching became apparent.

Paul's answer was courageous and specific. The Jews as a matter of policy were the first to hear the Word of God, but their attitude in rejecting it showed them to be unworthy to receive it. It was as if Paul were demonstrating that those who refuse a rich treasure show themselves to be incapable of appreciating it. It was right that the treasure of the Gospel should be offered to the Gentiles. Paul quotes Isaiah 49:6 in support of this. Simeon made allusion to the same passage when he made his prophecy over the infant Jesus. In this passage God is addressing His Servant, and Christians soon came to recognize that the Servant was Christ. It was easier for Gentiles to appreciate the universal scope of what Jesus had done for men, for even the most enlightened Jews were too inclined to think that any benefits which Gentiles received would be no more than an overspill from Jewish privilege. But Christian preachers like Paul and Barnabas were proclaiming an equality of salvation for Jews and Gentiles. No wonder the Gentiles were glad as they listened to the message!

Luke makes another of his contrasts in commenting on the effects of the preaching. The Word of the Lord spread, but the Jews incited persecution against Christians. This was to show that in spite of determined opposition, nothing could prevent the spread. There was nothing magical about this. Wherever a widespread sense of need exists, the Word, which alone can satisfy the need, will spread accordingly. The most expansive periods of Church history have been preceded by widespread disillusionment, which have led to earnest seeking for the only true answer.

It is noticeable that the persecution which was stirred up against Paul was channeled through the most influential members of the community. These are always the most impervious to the Gospel, because their reliance on the status tends to crust over their sense of need. In this city of Antioch influential women occupied important positions, which could never have happened in a city like Athens. There were, in fact, few places in the ancient world where women had any public influence. In this case the noble women and the leading men formed a formidable bastion against the Gospel. They had power to drive Paul and Barnabas out of the district, and force is an easy instrument to use when backed by privilege. Yet even this did not impede the spread of the Word of God.

The action of Paul and Barnabas in shaking the dust off their feet on leaving the city was symbolic of rejection. They were doing, in fact, what Jesus had recommended his disciples to do (cf. Matt. 10:14; Mark 6:11; Luke 9:5, 10:11). The city authorities, by their action, had cut themselves off from communication with the messengers of God. Luke contrasts their approach with the great joy of the believers and with their being full of the Holy Spirit. The young Christian movement consisted of an exuberant and dynamic group of people, who were not intimidated by the opposition of the "authorities."

7

The End of a Mission and Its Sequel

43. *At Iconium and Lystra*

(Acts 14:1-18)

Iconium was a city in Phrygia Galatica, which since 25 B.C. had been part of the Roman province of Galatia. On arriving there from Antioch, Paul and Barnabas went straight to the synagogue. This was their policy. They were at once given the opportunity to preach and did so with great effectiveness. A large number of people believed, among them both Jews and Gentiles. The rapid success of this mission is notable, but it inevitably brought swift opposition in its wake.

It is highly probable that the Jews of Pisidian Antioch, who were instrumental in banishing Paul and Barnabas from their city, lost no time in advising their fellow Jews at Iconium against them, especially if a report had reached Antioch that the men were preaching in the Iconium synagogue. There were Jews in every synagogue who were hostile to the Gospel. They needed little incentive to stir up trouble. The Iconium Jews may well have agreed with the Antioch Jews to do everything possible to prevent the Gospel from spreading any further. According to Luke, Jewish opposition was remarkably ineffective. The Jews in Iconium planned to poison the minds of Gentile hearers against the apostles, thereby erecting a barrier of prejudice in their minds.

The apostles were certainly not intimidated by this anti-Christian propaganda. They went on preaching the Gospel and God honored their witness. The preaching was, moreover, supported by signs and wonders. The total testimony was having so powerful an impact that it gave rise to opposing opinions in the city. There were two main points of view, one for and the other against

104

the apostles. The opponents, comprising an uneasy partnership of Jews and Gentiles, determined to take the law into their own hands and decided by mob violence to stone the offending apostles This was the same kind of treatment that Paul himself had agreed to in the case of Stephen. But not wanting to risk martyrdom in Iconium, the apostles escaped from the place on learning of the plot. Nevertheless they left behind them a thriving community, which made their own continued presence there unimportant.

The next place was Lystra, another of the Roman colonies visited by Paul. Luke singles out a specific healing miracle which happened there, because of its effect on those who witnessed it. The subject was a man with deformed legs who had never walked. Not surprisingly, the healing of such a chronic case caused no little stir. The man, moreover, was one who had a sense of spiritual as well as physical need, for he listened intently while Paul spoke. His obvious interest led Paul to the conclusion that he was a man with the possibility of faith. It was an extreme challenge when he was commanded to stand, for he had never done so in his life. The faith of the apostle himself was notable, for he did not whisper the command as an experiment. Everyone in the vicinity heard him. There was no going back if the man did not respond. But he was miraculously strengthened not merely to stand, but to spring into action. A notable healing of this kind could not be explained by rational means. It was clearly a special instance of divine healing.

No doubt the apostles were taken aback at the immediate reaction of the crowds, who acknowledged at once the superhuman character of the healing and concluded that Paul and Barnabas must themselves be superhuman. Their logic was faulty, but to some extent understandable. In that district there was a cult which worshiped both Zeus and Hermes, which is testified to by evidence from inscriptions. In that case the belief that their special gods had come to visit then would be deeply impressive. They had no difficulty in deciding which was which. Since Paul was the more loquacious, he was identified with Hermes, and Barnabas was considered to be Zeus. The crowds holding this view had clearly not taken in much of Paul's preaching, for the Gospel was far removed from the worship of Zeus. But it needed only a section of the crowd to make the suggestion for the idea rapidly to spread. There is an inscription found near

Lystra which mentions priests of Zeus (dating from c. A.D. 250) and it is not surprising therefore that a priest of Zeus immediately began to organize suitable homage to Paul and Barnabas. There could hardly have been a stronger contrast between the reaction among the hostile Jews at Iconium and the totally undiscerning pagans at Lystra. The latter approach was in fact more dangerous than the former.

The apostles, immediately recognizing the danger, tore their garments as evidence of their humble position. Their extraordinary action in rushing madly among the multitude gave them an opportunity to make their point heard. The Gospel was giving the people good news. Their present style of worship was vain compared with the Christian belief in a God who was the creator of all things. Paul points out that God had allowed men to go their own ways — although all men shared in the benefits of creation. God makes no distinction as to who should receive the rains and the harvests. In all probability Paul never got to the main point of the Gospel. His energies were directed toward preventing the people from offering sacrifices to himself and Barnabas, which would have amounted to a complete reversal of all that they were preaching about the Gospel.

44. *The Conclusion of the First Mission Tour*

(Acts 14:19-28)

Mob opinions are notoriously fickle, because they are seldom based on conviction. The opinion that Paul and Barnabas were gods, having arisen spontaneously, as quickly vanished. Gods that can come and go in such a manner are certainly not worthy of worship. The cause of the change of climate for the apostles was once again the Jews. Why no Jews of Lystra took action is not known. Luke mentions that Jews from Antioch and Iconium descended on the city. They must have had some sort of espionage system which kept them alert to the movements of Paul and Barnabas. They were determined to stir up persecution against the apostles. Their procedure was once again to sow the seeds of hate by propaganda against them, and then to incite mob violence with the support of popular opinion.

In considering the extreme fickleness of the crowd, it must be remembered that a group of people who had been convinced that their two gods had visited them and had then made the rude discovery of their mistake would need some face-saving scapegoat, and who better than the apostles who had been the cause of their embarrassment? They needed little incitement from Jews from the neighboring cities. Stones were plentiful, and willing hands released a stream of them in the direction of the apostles. Paul was evidently hit and dragged out of the city to be left as dead. Barnabas seems to have escaped. Some of the Christians hastened to assist Paul, who revived sufficiently to accompany Barnabas to Derbe. He had tasted some of the medicine administered to Stephen, but God had other work for him yet to do.

It speaks much for the physical courage of the two apostles that they decided to revisit the troublespots of Lystra, Iconium, and Antioch. The determined opposition from Jewish sources which Luke highlights in his narrative was wholly incapable of silencing the powerful witness of the apostles. On these return visits, however, they concentrated on the building up of the disciples, especially impressing on them the need for persistence. They were to recognize that persecutions were unavoidable for those whose eyes were on the kingdom of God.

In his summary of the apostles' second visit to these towns, Luke mentions a significant decision affecting the organization of the churches. They appointed elders in every church. Some have maintained that this cannot be true because Paul does not show interest in Church officers in his epistles (except the pastoral epistles, which the same people reject as non-authentic). But it is reasonable to suppose that Paul would never have left a heterogeneous collection of newly converted Christians in any place without giving them some guidance about running their affairs. In any community, it would soon be apparent which men were spiritually and mentally equipped to understake the leadership. It is significant moreover that these early appointments were not made by democratic process. It was the apostles who appointed. Moreover the same kind of prayerful commissioning service was held for them as had been held for Paul and Barnabas when they were sent from the church at Antioch in Syria. These newly appointed elders were men of God whose task was as important as those with an itinerant ministry.

The apostles retraced their steps to Perga, where they preached the Gospel. Luke does not say whether they did so on the way out. Perhaps they were in a hurry to get to Pisidian Antioch. But Paul and Barnabas did not want to leave Perga without a witness.

The main port of Pamphylia was Attalia and they made for this to embark on a boat for the Syrian Antioch from which they had set out some two years earlier.

The return to Antioch was marked by a reports meeting. The apostles had no difficulty in gathering the church together. No doubt those who had commended the apostles to the work of the Gospel had been constant in prayer in their behalf and were keen to know what had happened. Paul and Barnabas related what God had done through them. It is characteristic of them that they claimed no credit for themselves. It was God who had opened a door for the Gentiles. This was a momentous discovery which the church at Antioch, in spite of its strong Jewish contingent, took in its stride. It speaks much for the spiritual maturity of the Antiochene church that it was more ready than the Jerusalem church to see the hand of God in Gentile evangelism. But the background problems for Jewish Christians must be given full weight in assessing the critical nature of the problem which led to a full discussion at the Council at Jerusalem.

45. A Church Council at Jerusalem

(Acts 15:1-12)

Church councils have not been the most exhilarating aspect of Church history, but there is no denying the great importance of the first occasion when the members of the Church met in session to decide a matter of policy. The whole issue was a crucial one for the future of the Church. It was handled in a most statesmanlike way by those who had no experience in such matters. The subsequent history of the Church could have been very different had this issue been bungled.

The problem centered around the Gentiles. The stricter Jewish party could not conceive of any true people of God who had not been circumcised. In orthodox Jewish minds the "uncircumcised" were castaways, an inferior breed. Conditioned as they were to think of circumcision as the sign of the covenant, they were incapable of conceiving the possibility of any uncircumcised person finding favor with God. Jewish Christians were not opposed to Gentile admission into the Church any more than orthodox Jews opposed the idea of Gentile proselytes to Judaism. But they insisted on circumcision. Those who came from Judaea to Antioch who were demanding this were undoubtedly sincere men. The issue was nevertheless controversial. Some wanted to know why Gentiles who had received the grace of God needed circumcision in addition. In their view Christianity was distinct from Judaism and what held for one need not hold for the other.

The Antioch church is to be commended for its foresight. In spite of the crucial nature of the issue and the depth of feelings about it, the church was not only able to debate the issue without causing a split, but decided on a course of action which showed considerable wisdom. They determined to consult with the Jerusalem officials to reach some agreement over it. Among the delegates appointed were Paul and Barnabas and some others. They all presumably went with a real desire to reach an amicable settlement.

Paul and Barnabas took the opportunity to hold report meetings on the way, both in Phoenicia and Samaria. There Paul would meet many who had been scattered to these parts from Jerusalem as a result of his earlier persecution before his conversion. He delighted to tell them of the expansion of the Gospel to the Gentiles. In these areas there was no carping criticism when they heard, only great rejoicing. The critics all seem to have stayed at Jerusalem or to have been sent to Antioch.

In Jerusalem the Antioch delegates were well received, not only by the apostles and elders, but also by the whole community. There seems to have been a spirit of Christian fellowship. But the critics were ready. They repeated the same demand for circumcision as the Antioch church had already heard. Clearly they were determined to pursue the matter. The apostles and elders agreed to consider the issue at once. Luke does not give any details of the debate. No doubt Paul contended with the group who wanted to impose circumcision on the Gentiles. But Luke takes up the matter toward the close of the debate. Peter's contribution is reported because of its great significance. As one of the Jewish apostles who had already been the mouthpiece for the Word of God to the Gentiles, he could speak from a position of authority. Peter makes the point that God had made no distinction between Jews and Gentiles in giving the Holy Spirit. Both were able to receive cleansing of heart through faith. It made no sense to impose another condition after such an experience as Peter had had. Moreover, he goes still further in pointing to circumcision and its implications as an unbearable yoke. All Jews would admit the yoke and would testify to its heavy load.

Peter, however, recognized the freedom of the Gospel. Salvation had come through grace for both Jew and Gentile. The apostle Paul must have said a hearty Amen to that sentiment, for it was this theme that formed the basis of some of his greatest theological expositions. Salvation by grace alone was not an exclusively Pauline concept, but was basic to the earliest theology of the Jerusalem apostles.

That speech of Peter's was the kind of key speech which left a hush upon the assembly. He had struck fundamental chords which could not be challenged. It was an opportunity for Barnabas and Paul to leave aside controversy and testify to what God had done through them among the Gentiles. There was a striking similarity between their reports and the main burden of Peter's speech. There could be no denying that God was acting in a big way on behalf of the Gentiles. This was more important than ritual procedure, however important the latter may be in the eyes of some. When God acts, highly prized traditions may have to be modified or even scrapped.

46. Critical Decisions

(Acts 15:13-29)

After Peter, Barnabas, and Paul had concluded their telling contributions to the conference, it was James who summed up. This was the James who was the brother of Jesus and who appears to have acted in the capacity of chairman. This is remarkable in view of the fact that he was not one of the original apostles. From Galatians 1:19, it seems highly likely that he came to be classed among the apostles. He would presumably have gained respect among early Christians because of his relationship to Jesus. It appears that he aligned himself with the stricter group of Jewish Christians, in view of which it is all the more significant that his summing up showed such liberal-mindedness. His opinion would clearly be respected by those opposing Paul's position, who must have awaited with considerable interest to hear what he had to say.

James takes as his starting point what Peter had said about God's dealing with the Gentiles. He finds support for this in certain Old Testament passages which he quotes. Most of it comes from Amos 9:11 ff. James sees "the dwelling of David," which is to be rebuilt, as a reference to the universal Church which is a development of the old idea of Israel. This is undoubtedly an extension of Amos' meaning, for he was thinking of the undivided kingdom of Israel as in the time of David. The main point is that the very Jewish James grasped that, even in the Old Testament, God had made provision for Gentiles to call on His name. With remarkable forbearance, he pronounced his conclusion that Gentiles should not be troubled with being circumcised. He suggested certain taboos simply to enable Jewish Christians, who had carried over into Christianity their Jewish scruples, to coexist with Gentiles. The latter would be expected to abstain from idolatry, fornication, and bloodshed, which Jews regarded as cardinal sins. But in addition Gentiles were requested to abstain from flesh with blood in it, presumably because not to do so would make fellowship at meals between Jews and Gentiles impossible. In other words Gentiles were asked to respect the scruples of their Jewish Christian brethren. It should be noted that the Gentile approach to sex relationships generally was much more lax than the Jewish and any marked differences among Christians was clearly undesirable. James concluded his remarks by pointing out that every city had its Jewish synagogue, implying that Gentiles would constantly have to contend with Jewish scruples.

It was a well-balanced speech. Not only the apostles and elders but the whole church were impressed by it and decided as a practical measure to send two delegates from their number with a letter showing their decision. Of the two men chosen nothing else is known of Judas Barsabbas, but Silas later became the special companion of Paul and is mentioned in some of his letters and also in Peter's first letter under the name of Silvanus, his Latin name as a Roman citizen. Both Judas and Silas possessed the prophetic gift which enabled them to proclaim authoritatively the Word of God. The Jerusalem church wisely selected men with real vision to represent its viewpoint to the Gentile churches.

It is usually supposed that James wrote the letter on behalf of the rest. His speech shows that he possessed in large measure the quality of tact and understanding so necessary for maintaining good human relationships. The letter was sent as from the officials, the apostles and elders, and was sent to all the brethren in Antioch, Syria, and Cilicia. Since Antioch was the chief town of the united province of Syria and Cilicia, it is clear that a directive sent to Antioch would be assumed to apply to all the Christian groups in the province. In point of fact the letter reached even further afield, for it was taken to the churches which Barnabas and Paul had visited in South Galatia on the first missionary journey (Acts 16:4).

The letter states some important principles. The critics were representing their own opinion as if it were the opinion of the whole Jerusalem church. Much harm has been done in the cause of Christ when minority views have been paraded as the orthodox line without the support or authority of the Church as a whole. The matter was delicate, but James dealt with it with commendable graciousness, not castigating the critics but firmly rejecting their claim to represent the authoritative line. The second point was a generous acknowledgment of the hazards endured by Barnabas and Paul in the interests of the Lord Jesus Christ and the obvious respect which this had earned them in the eyes of the Jerusalem brethren. This did much to cement solidarity of approach between the different groups. After mentioning the names of their representatives Judas and Silas, James goes on to describe the decision made as a decision of the Holy Spirit as well as of themselves. Then follow the taboos and the letter ends with the formal "Farewell." It is a highly desirable thing when Church decisions can honestly be described in this way. The Holy Spirit was not only guiding the messengers of the Gospel and blessing their ministry, but was showing the wisest course of action in crises over policy. This earliest corporate decision shows vividly the method of Church government which God richly blessed at the dawn of the Christian Church. In many subsequent church councils decisions have been reached without so much as a reference to the Spirit.

47. Back to Antioch

(Acts 15:30-41)

The scene in Antioch may be easily imagined. After the hot debates in which the stricter Jewish brethren contended with Paul and Barnabas, there must have been tension while all waited the return of the delegates. The Gentiles, who had already experienced the blessings of the Gospel, were in suspense as to whether their Christian experience was adequate apart from circumcision. They were not keen to identify themselves with the Jews if that meant accepting the yoke of the law. Yet there were many who feared that the Jewish claims over circumcision might be right.

On Paul's and Barnabas' return, the church at once assembled to hear the news. Judas and Silas were introduced and immediately delivered the letter, which was then read aloud for everyone to hear. The critics were put in their place. They were not representing the official Christian view. At news of this there was spontaneous rejoicing, which shows the essential oneness of the Jewish and Gentile Christians at the great-hearted church at Antioch.

The Antioch Christians had been well trained to listen, having been taught by Barnabas and Paul (then Saul) for a whole year. Judas and Silas both exercised their prophetical gift among them and found a ready response. These people were willing to be exhorted and for this reason could not fail to be strengthened. The two Christian prophets spent some time there admonishing the brethren.

After Judas and Silas returned to Jerusalem, Paul and Barnabas stayed on to minister the Word. There were also others at Antioch with the gift of ministry. Paul therefore soon after decided to revisit the churches founded on the first journey. It is surprising that he did not go back at once with the good news for the Gentile Christians, but it may be that he had already dealt with the problem in a letter of his own to those Galatian churches. It is not certain when his letter to those churches was written, since scholarly opinion is divided on the issue. Some think it was written before the church council at Jerusalem, in which case it was sent while Paul was at Antioch or else on his way from Antioch to Jerusalem. Others think that it was not written until after his second journey. It is impossible to be certain, but since the problems of Jewish-Gentile relations have just been considered, it will be most convenient at this stage to consider this epistle before going on to relate the second journey. Moreover, since James has come into the limelight at the Jerusalem Council, it will also be valuable at this stage to look at an epistle of his which has been included in our New Testament.

Before turning to these letters, the crisis which blew up between Barnabas and Paul must be mentioned. Luke did not gloss over it. Clashes between Christian ministers are regrettable, but this incident helps to remind us that even two such stalwart servants of God were not beyond serious disagreement. It was concerning the position of Mark, aggravated by the fact that he was a relative of Barnabas. Paul would not tolerate disloyalty and considered that Mark's action in going home from Perga on the first journey amounted to this. Barnabas was more lenient with his own relative. Feelings ran sufficiently high for Paul and Barnabas, who had been so closely associated in the work of the Gospel over some years, to separate and go their own ways. Barnabas headed for Cyprus with Mark, and Paul invited Silas, who had evidently returned to Antioch, to accompany him on his journey back to Galatia. In spite of the disagreement the Antioch church commended them both to the grace of the Lord. No doubt Paul had found Silas a congenial companion on his way back from Jerusalem to Antioch after the council and during the time that Silas had spent at Antioch prophesying and strengthening the church.

It is worthy of note that Paul seems to have had a particular capacity for attracting other men into his circle of workers. The Acts story does not mention them all. Some are known only through Paul's letters (as for instance Titus). Even the young Mark was later received back, Paul evidently revising his opinion of the man who had earlier let him down. In these initial stages of the Gentile mission Paul shows himself as an individualist, who is capable at the same time of drawing out the devotion of men of like mind. His strength of character is vividly reflected in the epistle to the Galatians, to which we next turn our attention.

8

A New Charter of Freedom

48. *Paul Battles for Freedom*

(Gal. 1)

Whatever the date of the epistle to the Galatians, it gives Paul's own view of the problem which led to the Jerusalem Council and is invaluable for its strong revelations of Paul's character. The same type of sincere but misguided Jews had reached the Galatian churches as had contended with Paul at Antioch. In these churches, however, many had been beguiled by the Jewish arguments to tie themselves to the Jewish yoke as something indispensable for salvation. Paul sees it as a direct challenge to the Gospel he has been preaching. He writes in a mood of intense feeling. He does not even include his usual courteous remarks commending his readers. In this letter alone, of all his letters, he hastens to the attack.

There are two things he intends to do. The first is to defend his apostolic authority and to establish his relationship with the Jerusalem apostles. The strong manner in which he does this suggests that the Jewish party was claiming to represent the Jerusalem apostles and were regarding Paul as no true apostle. In the second place he needs to defend his Gospel, because if it is true that salvation depends on circumcision, this would flatly contradict what he has been preaching.

In Galatians 1 he begins his defense of his apostleship. He says, in effect, "How dare you question my apostleship! Don't you know that God Himself appointed me an apostle? You have it all wrong if you think that apostles are men-appointed. You Galatians have in no time turned aside from the true Gospel." Again Paul clearly shows that he did not receive his Gospel from men. The fact is nobody did. It is God's Gospel, and is the same

Gospel whether preached by the Jerusalem apostles or by Paul. If anyone is telling the Galatians something which conflicts with the Gospel which Paul had already preached among them, he must have a curse upon him, even if he were an angel. This is strong language. Was it justified? Is the uniformity of the Gospel really so important? Wasn't Paul somewhat bigoted in the attitude he took? If he lived in the mid-twentieth century he would certainly be considered too narrow by many who call themselves Christians and yet whose idea of the Gospel is so broad that almost anything remotely Christian can come under its umbrella.

In thinking of the Gospel Paul naturally thinks of how the Gospel came to him. He indirectly refers to his Damascus road experience as a "revelation of Jesus Christ." Personal testimony is always effective in any presentation of the Gospel. For Paul it was a reality, for the contrast with his former life was particularly marked. He mentions his violent persecution of the Church and his personal zeal and ambitions. Yet as he looks back, he is convinced that God had him in mind before he was born. His strong conviction about God's sovereign purposes could not be more specifically stated. It was God who had called him for a twofold purpose — to reflect His Son and to preach to Gentiles.

So strong are the convictions that Paul states about his own calling as an apostle that it is clear that he has already arrived at an unshakable position. It is some years since his conversion during which time he has been preaching the Gospel. It is only in retrospect that he has come to the conclusion that the grace of God prepares a man from the time of his natural birth. Anyone with such a conviction is obviously not going to lay much store by the approval of men. Indeed he thinks the Galatians ought to know that he never even consulted the Jerusalem apostles about what he should preach. He beat a retreat from Damascus to Arabia, where he presumably sought an opportunity to be taught of the Spirit.

But why does he bother to tell the Galatians these historical details? He regards it of utmost importance that they should know, and it seems highly probable that someone had spread wrong ideas about him, in which case the facts become doubly important. It is for this reason that he goes to some lengths to mention contacts he had had with the Jerusalem apostles. The first time was three years after his conversion when he spent a fortnight with Peter in Jerusalem and at the same time saw

James, the Lord's brother. Paul gives no details of this visit, no
indication of the subject of discussion. It was apparently amicable. During this period Paul must have gleaned some historical
information about the deeds and words of Jesus. But when the
fortnight was up he went at once to Syria and Cilicia (Tarsus,
his home town, was in that province), not even delaying to visit
the Judaean churches. Nevertheless those churches knew about
the remarkable transformation which had happened to the
apostle.

49. *Paul Talks About the Jerusalem Apostles*

(Gal. 2)

Having mentioned his first private visit to the apostles, he
comes to the second occasion. He says this was after fourteen
years, but there is some uncertainty whether he means fourteen
following the three years mentioned in 1:18, or including the
three years. The latter is easier to fit into the general calendar
of Paul's life. There has been much debate about the second
visit, for some link this with the Council at Jerusalem (Acts 15)
and consider that the epistle was written after the Church had
made its decision about Gentile circumcision. Others, however,
think that the second visit is the same as the visit with famine
relief mentioned in Acts 11:29, in which case the letter could
have been sent before the Council. It is a difficult matter to settle,
but our decision will not greatly affect our understanding of what
Paul is saying. If the Council decision is a thing of the past Paul
does not bother to mention it, preferring to argue the matter
from first principles rather than cite an ecclesiastical decision.

He makes clear that on this second visit he informed the Jerusalem apostles about the Gospel he was preaching, and far from
imposing an additional condition of Gentile circumcision they
did not even insist on his Gentile companion Titus being circumcised. There were some people who wanted this as a matter of
policy, but Paul does not hesitate to call them "false brethren,"
and emphatically rejects any thought of yielding on inch to them.

When referring to the apostles, he describes them as "those
who were reputed to be something," as if he is quoting someone
else's description of them. Although he may appear to be speaking disparingly, his purpose is to correct the Judaizers' inflated
opinion of the Jerusalem apostles. In point of fact those apostles

were in complete agreement with Paul on the sphere of his service. He was to preach to the Gentiles and Peter to the Jews. The major apostles, Peter, James, and John, who were supposed to be the "pillars," established most cordial relationships with Paul and Barnabas. The one thing they insisted on was benevolence, for which Paul was wholly in support.

The solid front between the Jerusalem apostles and Paul and Barnabas was a direct refutation of the Judaizers' claims. Indeed their efforts to drive a wedge between Paul and the others could not be sustained. Nevertheless the Jerusalem church enjoyed a position of influence, and Paul remembers one occasion when Peter was at Antioch when he had to criticize his action before the whole church. It was over the question of Jews and Gentiles eating together. Peter, no doubt remembering what had happened in Cornelius' house, joined in fellowship with Gentiles when he first came to Antioch. When Jerusalem Jews arrived from James, Peter considered it politic to withdraw from eating with Gentiles for fear of offending the Jews. Even Barnabas did the same. Those Jerusalem Jews must certainly have been persuasive to mislead two such men. But Paul at once saw that a principle was at stake and challenged Peter on the grounds that his action was compromising the Gospel. When the Galatian Judaizers learned that the chief apostle had been rebuked by Paul, it must have come home to them forcibly that it was no use their appealing to the superiority of the Jerusalem apostles in seeking to discredit Paul. The incident is yet another example of the weakness of the men who founded the Christian Church. The man who could see three thousand at a time believe in Jesus Christ could nevertheless yield to inconsistency when too fearful for his reputation among the stricter Jews.

Paul has said enough about the Jerusalem apostles. He has answered the charge that he is not on the same footing as they. Although his Gospel has the divine stamp on it, it nevertheless agrees with what the Jerusalem apostles were saying. Paul has shown himself to be both independent of them and yet in harmony with them. He still has to show why he is so opposed to the idea of Gentile circumcision. He intends in the next part of his letter to establish the doctrine on which it is based.

It boils down to the basis of a man's justification. If a man has to be circumcised to be saved, he is committing himself to keeping the law, which was the rule of conduct for all circumcised people. This means that he would try to justify himself by the works of the law, that is by attempting to carry out what the law says. Paul has had experience of this and is utterly opposed to returning to it. It would be like reconstructing a building which has been pulled down because it was no use. Paul knows that he has died to the law as an effective means of salvation. Indeed, he sees himself as having died with Christ, which means that he has risen with Christ — and all this is by faith, not works. With such a wealth of Christian experience behind him, he could not possibly take up a position in which the grace of God was unnecessary, as it would be if a man could justify himself. It would in fact cancel out the purpose of the death of Christ. What Paul has to say on this matter affects the core of Christianity. It is no wonder that this epistle has been called the charter of Christian liberty.

50. *The Promise to Abraham*

(Gal. 3)

What Paul wants to do is to show the folly of relying on one's own efforts when all that is needed is faith. He makes much of the history of Abraham, but before doing so issues a direct challenge to the Galatians, who have fallen for the doctrine of salvation by works. Paul contrasts their beginnings as Christians with their present position. They came to believe in the crucified Christ, a truth which was so central that it was like a placard held up before them. They had received the Spirit by faith, not as the result of merit. What had made them now think that they needed to rely on their own efforts to obtain salvation? Paul can think of only one explanation — they must be bewitched, under some evil influence, which makes them act contrary to their best interests. In Paul's view they must be crazy.

To appeal to Abraham was a good move on Paul's part. He was revered by both Jewish and Gentile Christians alike. Any argument based on his case would be particularly telling. The key Old Testament statement about Abraham is that he believed God and as such was reckoned to be righteous. Moreover since God promised to make Abraham the father of many nations, what is valid for the father must be valid for the children. It is all a matter of faith.

In the contrast between faith and works, the former therefore has a formidable supporter in Abraham, and Paul has more to say in developing this theme. He maintains that works lead to a curse whereas faith leads to blessing. The problem about depending on fulfilling the law is that law is all demanding. It is not merely a question of doing the best we can. If we fail in any part of the law we incur the curse. Nevertheless curses can become blessings in God's hands. When Jesus died on a cross He became a curse for us but at the same time delivered us from the curse. Paul does not explain how the sinless Jesus could ever become a curse for us. Generations of theologians have puzzled over it without exhausting its meaning. Paul asserts that the blessing of Abraham has become possible through faith even to the Gentiles, because they were included in Abraham's promise.

Thinking of the "promise" leads Paul to use an illustration from everyday life. A man makes a will and his will is binding once it has been ratified. Or Paul may be thinking of a covenant, which once it is made can be annulled or modified only with the consent of both the parties involved. God's promise to Abraham He will keep. Almost as a side issue Paul points out that the promise was to Abraham and his offspring (singular) and not offsprings. The singular he applies to Christ as the seed of Abraham par excellence. He sees therefore some significance even in the grammar of Scripture although his method of argument is not appreciated by all modern exegetes.

If the promise holds, where does the law come in? This is not simply an academic question, but one which was vital to all in the early Church. Paul reminds the Galatian Christians that an interval of 430 years separated the law from the promise. When eventually the law was given, it did not affect the promise to Abraham, for promise by virtue of its greater antiquity takes precedence over law.

As he thinks aloud and reasons out his Christian assertions, Paul particularly wants to avoid the impression that law and promise are diametrically opposed to each other. He thinks of law as necessary to reveal transgressions, although it is not necessary for salvation. He makes another statement about the law which is worth pondering. Up till the coming of Christ the law had acted as "custodian." Paul uses a word which describes the function of one who watched over a schoolboy, escorting him to and from school and being responsible for his moral training. After the boy reached a certain age the custodian was no longer required. Paul draws out some of the implication of this in his next section. In Christ believers have become sons, a much superior status to slaves.

One tremendous advantage of the promise over the law is the fact that in Christ there are no distinctions. Jew and Gentile are on an equal footing. This means that Jews could no longer claim superiority. They are not only on an equal footing, but have become united in Christ, an even more striking idea in the ancient world. Moreover, the promise applies equally to slaves as to freemen, thus bridging another great divide in the ancient world. A considerable proportion of people at that time were slaves, which means that their social status was lower than the rest. Thus the Gospel, in offering unity between them, was leaping over a deeply ingrained barrier. Although centuries were to pass before the world was to be rid of the curse of slavery, the Gospel contained within it the principle of liberation. Similarly another great divide at that time was the disparity of status between male and female. In all but a few more enlightened areas in the ancient world (such as Macedonia) the woman was regarded as an inferior being. For the sexes to be regarded as equal was a revolutionary idea, but was inherent in the principles of the Gospel. That male and female could share in the fellowship of Christ on an equal footing showed the tremendous superiority of Christianity over Judaism, in which the woman was not allowed to have any part. The heirs of promise could be drawn from all nationalities, from all social classes, and from both sexes. The promise was wonderfully comprehensive.

51. *Arguments and Allegory*

(Gal. 4)

The comparison between the status of a slave and a freeman leads Paul to another analogy. A son before reaching the age of maturity is no better than a slave. Both are subject to the same discipline and the same restrictions. But at the time set by his father the situation changes and the son enters into his privileges. What legal system Paul has in mind is not clear, for in Roman law the time was set by someone else. But the point of the analogy is clear. God the Father appointed a time to send His Son to redeem men who were still under the restriction of the law, which would enable them to be adopted into His family as sons.

The analogy is a little mixed but the contrast between the old state of slavery and the new state of sonship is so remarkable that Paul's readers would surely be foolish to prefer the former to the latter.

But their policy of submitting to circumcision and salvation by works actually meant that they were going back from sonship to slavery. They were even tying themselves to the observance of festival days. No wonder Paul was disappointed with their retrograde policy. He decided to make an earnest personal appeal. He remembered his first visit to them, when he had a physical ailment that made him a liability to them. It is generally supposed that the apostle had some kind of eye disease. But Paul gratefully recalls their warm concern for him then, and now wonders what has happened to their willingness to do so much to assist him. They are treating him now as if he were an enemy. They have obviously been sadly misled by the Judaizers, who have set their minds against the apostle. When converts who had shown such promise suddenly step back and their friendship turns to hatred, it is deeply distressing. Paul compares his anxiety over them with a woman's labor pains, an astonishing but telling figure of speech. He thinks of himself as experiencing spiritual pains so that Christ might be formed in the Galatians. His readers might have objected that they were already Christians, but Paul knew that the course they were following would not lead to a Christ-like character. Religious systems which stress ritual observances are all too often neglectful of the quality of life. But any system which does not lead its members to become increasingly more like Jesus Christ is not fully Christian.

After these arguments Paul turns to allegory. His use of this method is rare, but he is not against using it if the occasion arises. In the present instance the allegory is not without difficulties, although its overall meaning is clear. Paul's mind goes back to Abraham and he remembers that there were two sons, Ishmael and Isaac, one born to a slave woman and the other to a free woman. He seizes on this as an illustration of his main point. Abraham had had no promise concerning Ishmael. He had conceived his own plan to produce seed by means of Hagar. The child born from such a union could never become the child of promise. God's plan was to provide an heir for Abraham through Sarah. Ishmael admirably represents all those who are attempting to obtain sonship through human effort, while Isaac represents the true child of promise. But Paul makes the allegory more complicated by identifying Hagar with the present Jerusalem, symbolic of the whole of Judaism. He can never forget the slavery from which he has himself been delivered.

When he quotes from Isaiah 54:1, he applies the words in a way which differs from what Isaiah had written. The barren one is clearly Sarah, who had no children until old age, when Isaac was born. Her children, however, outnumbered the children of Hagar, who, for the purpose of Paul's application of the passage, must be thought of as "she who has a husband." The analogy does not quite fit, but the blessings that followed through Isaac's seed would be acknowledged by every Jew who regarded himself as a son of Abraham.

It may be wondered if the Galatians would have followed Paul's type of reasoning. This passage is certainly not the easiest or clearest that Paul wrote. But the constantly repeated theme that Christians are children of promise could not be missed, even if many readers could not follow the whole argument. The apostle introduces another detail into the allegory which raised further problems. He speaks of Ishmael persecuting Isaac, of which there is no mention in the Old Testament story. He seems to be drawing his illustration from some other tradition, a kind of development of the Genesis reference to mocking. The main point is that Ishmael, not Isaac, was rejected, because he was not the child of promise.

In basing so much of his argument on the Old Testament, Paul is assuming that his readers will have a reasonable acquaintance with it even though they are Gentiles. Indeed, the fact that the Judaizers had such success with the Galatians suggests that they were people with a very real interest in the Jewish (and Christian) Scriptures. As is clear from the speeches in Acts, the early Christians assumed as axiomatic the continuity between the old order and the new. Unless that were so, Paul's argument from Abraham would make no sense.

52. *Christian Freedom*

(Gal. 5)

Having maintained the superiority of salvation by faith over salvation by works, Paul next shows what this means for practical Christian living. In Christ a man is meant to be a freeman not a slave. The Galatians were cutting themselves off from their freedom in Christ if they submitted to circumcision and so committed themselves to law-keeping as a way of life. Paul sums up the better Christian way as "faith working through love," and then makes another appeal to the readers to follow his view of things. He feels so strongly about this that he uses fierce words about those who were troubling the Galatians.

But what is this Christian freedom? Paul at once distinguishes freedom from license, a necessary distinction for Christians who had been reared in an atmosphere of moral slackness in the Gentile world. This Christian freedom involves love for one another. It also means a radical change of approach toward what Paul calls "works of the flesh," which is his name for moral and social sins. He quotes some samples, all of which were rife in the ancient world and are not alien to the modern world, especially in this permissive age. These are all utterly opposed to the new life in the Spirit.

It is especially valuable to note Paul's comments here about the Holy Spirit and the believer. We have already seen the activity of the Spirit in the Book of Acts controlling the developing Church. In this epistle we have a somewhat different insight into the Spirit's work in the details of the Christian life. Gentile Christians needed this specific teaching. Christianity involved a new walk guided by the Spirit. Those things which were normal for them in their pre-Christian days are now seen to be strongly opposed by the Spirit. Paul sees the Spirit and the flesh as continually at war against one another. The Christian life is no life of ease, but one of conflict. Nevertheless it is a conflict with the victorious Spirit on the Christian's side.

Permissiveness was a real problem in the Gentile world of the first century. Pagan society had low moral standards. Immoral relationships were regarded as a normal phenomenon. Moreover, they were an official part of much pagan worship and therefore had religious approval. At a time when public opinion was so heavily biased toward licentiousness, it was not easy for Christians to set a nobler standard. The rise of the modern cult of permissiveness is a similar critical challenge to the Christian Church, which will certainly not be met by a new morality which hesitates to class loose sexual relationships among sins of the flesh. Two problems which loomed large for Christians living in first century pagan society were idolatry and witchcraft. These could not be squared with life in the Spirit. It is worth noting that Paul had had personal experience in contending with a man whom Luke describes as a magician and who set himself in opposition to the Gospel (Acts 13:4).

Among the works of the flesh Paul names eight which may be described as social evils because they all affect other people. Some are sins of attitude like jealousy, anger, selfishness. Others are sins of antisocial behavior like drunkenness and carousing. These sins of intemperance were again sanctioned by much heathen worship and were in marked contrast to life in the Spirit. It was essential for Christians living in a pagan society to be clear about the conduct permissible in the kingdom of God. Many standards which were encouraged in pagan worship were wholly opposed to the standards of the Spirit of God. This becomes clear when the fruit of the Spirit is considered.

Paul's list of Christian graces is illuminating. The contrast with the activities of the "flesh" is striking. The apostle sees only one "fruit," with many aspects. The Christian does not take his pick. They are all essential. Moreover, fruit grows; it does not arrive through human effort. It is completely different from "works." Paul's list of nine aspects may again be roughly divided between individual and social kinds. Love, joy, and peace are so basic to Christian character it is no wonder that Paul places them first. The Acts story has already shown Christian love in action and has more than once mentioned great joy among Christians. The peace which existed among Christian churches is also noted. But the Spirit enables individual Christians to develop these qualities in an ever deepening way. Of the rest, some would have been regarded in contemporary society as signs of weakness, such as patience or kindness or gentleness. Christians who showed this kind of fruit would be blazing wholly new trails in the art of living. It would require something of a revolution for men to begin — something of a crucifixion of the flesh, an utter renunciation of the accepted standards of existing pagan society and the substitution of entirely new standards of value. Although Jewish ethics were of a considerably higher standard than pagan ethics, yet the fundamental difference between Christian and Jewish standards lies in the motive power behind them. The Christian is impelled by the Spirit of God in harmony with His own character, whereas the Jew was impelled by his own desire to win merit.

The Christian's quest is never finished. His life is a walk, in which each step requires the Spirit's guidance. No one can ever say he has arrived. This is why Paul urges the readers to have no self-conceit, no envy of one another. Life in the Spirit will never give anyone grounds for conceit over the amount of fruit he has produced, nor will it ever give anyone else real grounds for being envious. If this is what is meant by freedom in the Spirit, how foolish to go on living as slaves!

53. *Christian Responsibility*

(Gal. 6)

It is fundamental to the Christian way of life that no man live to himself. There is a corporate responsibility. Not everyone is strong enough to avoid the pitfalls of life in an adverse environment. Christians do fall into temptations and need to be helped by their Christian brethren when they do. The most spiritual will be the most help at such times, the men who have learned most about walking by the Spirit. There is no provision for censoriousness or carping criticism, for such attitudes do not appear among the fruit of the Spirit. The man of the Spirit is deeply aware that he too is subject to the possibility of falling into temptation.

Burden-bearing is inescapable for the Christian. If he is not bearing his own, there will be plenty of others to bear. It is part of the Christian's outlook to share. Paul thinks of it as the law of Christ — a very different kind of law from the one to which the Judaizers were wanting to subject the Galatians. It is a law that demands the sharing of loads, a true estimate of oneself and an objective examination of one's own work. This is down-to-earth advice on Christian relationships. There are certain burdens which cannot, of course, be shelved. The load of a man's conflicts with his nobler self cannot be pushed on to another. But those who have proved God's grace in bearing their own burdens are best able to bear the burdens of others.

Paul adds a brief note about pupils sharing with their teachers. He may have felt this was necessary because in the pagan world no provision was made for religious teachers to receive any financial support, and he considers it desirable that Christians should have a different standard. Or he may have been thinking of the need to encourage Christian learners and Christian teachers to have fellowship with each other.

In considering Christian action, Paul foresees there may well be a tendency to become discouraged. Perhaps this was a battle he had often needed to fight. His mind turns to the world of agriculture for an illustration. No farmer expects to reap anything different from what he sows, and Paul applies the same principle in the spiritual realm. Those whose sowing is in the sphere of the flesh cannot expect to reap spiritual benefits. There is all the more reason therefore to order one's whole life according to the Spirit. Reaping time may of course be delayed, in which case there is need for persistence in the present. Paul is not so spiritually superior as to be incapable of appreciating the temptation to lose heart. Once again the tremendous challenges of the Christian faith are placed before the readers. There is a special responsibility on Christians to do good to their fellow Christians, although other men are not to be excluded.

The conclusion to this letter is notable for various reasons. Paul specially mentions that he wrote the closing part with his own hand, which suggests that he did not do so for the earlier part of the letter. It was a frequent practice in the ancient world to use secretaries in the writing of letters, and this was certainly followed by Paul in many if not all of his letters. Another feature of his conclusion is that he comes back again to the main burden of his letter. He makes another criticism of the Judaizers — they thought that circumcision would insure them against persecution, and they found particular satisfaction in getting others circumcised. But Paul makes a statement about his own purpose, which might be treated as his motto — not to glory in anything but the cross of Christ. He is really saying again what he said in 2:20. He knows now that an entirely new mode of existence has opened up. He is a new creation. Yet he cannot refrain from a parting shot — he wants no one to trouble him — he has suffered already for Jesus Christ. He bears Christ's marks on his body.

It has been instructive to follow this epistle in some detail, for it presents an inside picture of the problems of the Galatian church and an insight into the mind and heart of the apostle. Our knowledge of the early Christian communities would be sadly deficient if the apostle Paul had not seen with remarkable clarity the value of semi-public letters for reproof and instruction. The Book of Acts cannot supply us with details of the inner working of any individual church, because Luke was strictly limited in his purpose. But the Book of Acts together with the epistles provide invaluable information about early developments.

Before returning to the narrative of Acts we shall consider briefly the letter of James. It may not be as early as this, although some consider it to be the earliest in the New Testament. It is quite different from Paul's letters, but there is one feature which it has in common with Galatians: the relationship between faith and works.

9

Practical Advice and Progressive Adventure

54.   *Practical Words From a Practical Man*

(James 1 and 3)

It is a good thing that there are some parts of the New Testament which are essentially practical. Although we could not do without great doctrinal passages, we need straightforward advice on everyday matters. Paul mixes the two, but James concentrates on the latter.

Although there are some scholars who would not agree that the writer was James, the Lord's brother, this seems to be the best view to account for all the evidence. It is not difficult to imagine this James, who soon sprang into the leadership of the Jerusalem church, as the author of this letter.

It is a practical letter, which is not notable for the systematic arrangement of its contents. It is rather a collection of reflections on a number of themes. James starts by giving advice about trials. Those early days were perilous days and the possibility was constant that believers would have to face trials. The best approach was to regard them as a testing of faith. Faith cannot fail to be strengthened as a result. Then there is the matter of wisdom. Many confuse cleverness or even knowledge with wisdom, but there is a wisdom which God alone can give. It can be had for the asking, provided the mind is not shaken with doubt. James cautions against any form of double-mindedness. Christians are people of a pure and single mind.

James adds a brief note about riches, a theme to which he returns later. Rich people (James is thinking in general terms) are like fading flowers. No doubt most of the early Christians were poor, and may well have cast envious eyes on the rich.

James' advice is simple — remember the transient character of material possessions.

His mind then returns to the subject of trials. He wants to make clear that God never tempts people. Temptation comes from within a person, from his own desire. One wonders whether James had the Lord's Prayer in mind — lead us not into temptation. It is important to notice this vital difference between trial and temptation. A right approach is necessary for Christians. Far from tempting men, God gives good gifts, which should give us great confidence. A right view of God would correct many wrong views of Christian behavior.

James next attacks anger, which is alien to the righteousness of God. He links with it filthiness and wickedness. Instead of these things, he urges meekness in receiving the Word. Moreover, receiving it is not enough. The Christian must *do* the Word he has received, otherwise he is like someone who notices what is wrong when he looks in a mirror, but does nothing about it.

Another brief comment characteristic of James is his definition of pure religion as ministry to those in need, such as orphans and widows. It is clear that James is not giving a full definition of religion. It is certainly more than almsgiving or keeping oneself from the stains of the world. What concerns James is that religion should extend to essentially practical issues.

Leaving aside for the moment James 2, which deals with a special theme, we note that James comes to the problems of the tongue. They are age-old problems, for the tongue is the most powerful means of communication. But it is also the most dangerous, for the same lips are capable of cursing as well as blessing. James emphasizes the great responsibility of keeping the tongue in check. This is especially so for any who want to teach others. The matter must have been a particular issue in the early Church. Those who occupy positions of leadership must clearly be even more guarded than others. The illustrations which James uses to press home his point are particularly vivid — bridled horses, ships, forest fires, the world of nature.

He has already said something about wisdom but he comes back to the theme. He wants to make clear that there are two kinds of wisdom — an earthly wisdom and a wisdom which comes from above. The fundamental difference between them is the quality of life which accompanies them. Any so-called wisdom which leads to selfish ambition or jealousy is no true wisdom.

James gives a striking list of qualities engendered by the higher type of wisdom, which bears some similarity with Paul's fruit of the Spirit. Purity, peaceableness, gentleness, reasonableness, mercy, and consistency are not the kind of qualities which come naturally to men. Unlike Paul, James does not enlarge on the source of these qualities. He assumes that his readers will know what he means by "wisdom from above."

55. *Against Partiality and Faith Without Works*

(James 2)

Favoritism of one kind or another is a hindrance in any community of people, but is wholly out of keeping in the Christian Church. The people for whom Christ died — the Lord of Glory, as James calls Him — are one family and are all on an equal footing in the sight of God. But James knows of some who were paying too much respect to those better off, as if material wealth gave them an advantage in the Christian Church. He describes a typical example of this. Two men come into the same assembly but differently clothed, one in rags, the other in rich raiment. The contrast is bound to be noticeable, but whenever difference of social standing determines difference of treatment within the Church, the action is open to criticism. It means that Christians are using wrong standards in judging others. James points out that God's choice is not based on such standards. More often than not it is the poor whom God chooses, whereas the rich are too often oppressors of the poor, who do not deserve excessive respect.

The fact that James makes so much of this suggests that the problem was a real one in the church or churches to which he writes. It shows moreover that there were some rich people who attended early Christian assemblies. It was important at the outset to give guidelines about this social problem. It would have been disastrous had it been supposed that material possessions gave a privileged position within the early community. Whenever this has happened, it has led to the dulling of the spiritual life of the community.

The real test is one's attitude to loving one's neighbor. This scriptural principal would at once banish partiality. Even if one adhered strictly to observing the law, this injunction to love must be included, for, as James says, anyone failing in one point of the law has failed to keep the whole. It may well have come as a shock to the Jewish Christians, who had great respect for the law, to note that partiality is against the requirements of that law. James is in agreement with Paul in insisting that anyone committed to observing the law is committed to observing the whole law, although they apply it in different ways. Indeed many think that James is at variance with Paul in the famous faith and works passage which follows. But a right understanding of both reveals no contradiction.

It is as well to be clear what kind of misconception James has in mind in his discussion. He is dealing with the man who says he has faith, but never shows any evidence of it in his actions. He is thinking of the kind of man who can send away a poor man or woman in need, even fellow Christians, and do nothing about food or clothing for them. Such a man may say that he has faith, but as far as James is concerned his faith is dead. Real faith cannot be oblivious to the needs of others.

James then proceeds to debate the relationship between faith and works. It is again needful to note the antithesis he is making. Someone is taking the view that faith and works are mutually exclusive. So James sets out to show that faith cannot exist without works. It is possible, of course, to have a theoretical belief, as for instance in the unity of God. But even the demons have belief of that kind, which is very different from a dynamic faith. Mere intellectual assent to a position is a sure way to barrenness.

It is strange that James introduces Abraham into his argument, just as Paul does in his Galatian letter. Both in fact quote the same verse from Genesis 15:6 about Abraham believing God and it being reckoned (credited) to him as righteousness. James sees this, however, as a combination of faith and works. He cites the case of Abraham's offering up Isaac. It was not enough for Abraham to say that he believed God. He had to be prepared to do as God commanded in offering up his son. James clearly means by works an acting upon a declared faith. It is because of this that he can speak of a man being justified by works. Rahab is another example of the same principle.

Since Paul rejects the idea of justification by works, is there a direct contradiction in James? We must note that when Paul speaks of works he is thinking of works of the law, that is, works done in an attempt to keep the law. But James is thinking of quite a different kind of works, more in the nature of social good works than legal good works. Indeed he is almost thinking of works as the necessary complement of faith. When he speaks of being justified by works, he is thinking of works as an expression of faith. There is no doubt that Paul would have agreed with this. He had a more specialized view of faith as a personal commitment to Jesus Christ, but never thought of it as an inactive assent. Although in his view a man is justified by faith alone, it is unthinkable that a vital faith like that should not express itself in good works. It is certain that James is not attacking the position taken up by Paul, but he may have been correcting a misunderstanding of him.

56. *Dangers*

(James 4 and 5)

The latter part of this epistle contains various practical injunctions. James concerns himself first with what might be summarized as friendship with the world. Wars, murders, covetousness are all part of the normal world order. But since these things are enemies of God, anyone who aligns himself too closely with them puts himself similarly at enmity with God.

A cardinal Christian characteristic is humility. This is not of course new to the New Testament, for the Old Testament contains similar exhortations to humility. Indeed James quotes an Old Testament passage to this effect. Humility begins before God, for those who submit to Him will not fall into violent collisions with others. James does not think of this as a purely passive submissiveness — it requires active resistance to the devil, a positive approach to God, a determination toward purity of action and purity of mind, and a real contriteness before God, which does not treat lightly matters which demand great seriousness.

He returns to an earlier theme when he comes to evil speaking, especially speaking against the law of God. This is wholly out of place since there is only one Judge and nobody but He has the right to judge other men. Once again it is plain that a right view of God leads to a right attitude toward our neighbors.

The will of God has always been a difficulty for Christians, and James is on a much recurring theme when he deals with it. The problem is that men are so used to making arrangements that they forget that there is an unknown factor in every program — the uncertainty of human life itself. James compares it with a mist, a telling illustration of transitoriness. What Christians ought to do in making arrangements is to acknowledge that they depend on the will of God. Christian living was very different from the pagan life style of that time, which saw life as dominated by evil spirits or ruled by an overhanging sense of fate. To the Christian, there is nothing impersonal about the will of God. What He wills is always perfect.

James has another go at rich people, but this time those not associated with the Church, whose whole life centers around their possessions. What is treasured becomes motheaten or rusted and wholly depreciates in value. Indeed, not only does it become worthless, but a positive hindrance, for it will cry out in judgment. Where possessions have been acquired by fraud, they will bear testimony against the rich. All those social evils which result from the extorting of the poor by the rich will rise up against them. It is not surprising that in modern times there has been such strong reaction against the wrongs of capitalist society, but it is not new. James condemned them long ago.

As far as Christians are concerned, the quality most needed is patience. The focal point for the future is the Lord's coming. The Christian lives in expectation of this. His conduct and attitude will be governed by this hope. Grumbling and criticism are out of place. Steadfastness in face of all situations, even suffering, is recommended. The well-known story of Job illustrates the point, especially as it shows the compassion of the Lord. Possibly James knows that some of these Christians have had to suffer for their faith and is anxious to encourage them.

This brief letter ends on the theme of prayer. It is reported that James himself was called "Camel-knees," because his knees had become hardened through his posture in prayer. In writing this note, he is no doubt speaking from his own experience. The major subject for prayer here is the healing of a sick person. The elders of the Church are to pray with the sick person and anoint him with oil. The prayer of faith has power to heal. James admits that sin must be confessed first, but there is a prominent Old Testament example of the power of prayer in Elijah's prayer for the ending of a three-year famine. There is no doubt that prayer played an essential part, not only in the development of the Christian community but also in the lives of individual believers.

The concluding exhortation of James about turning people from the errors of their ways shows his essentially pastoral concern. The Church was not a company of perfect people who were beyond succumbing to temptation, but a company of very human people who were not beyond wandering from the truth and who recognized the Christian's duty to restore any who did.

One of the values in examining this letter at this early stage in the history of Christian development is the help it gives in showing some of the human issues which had to be resolved according to Christian principles. Moreover, it gives further insight into the practical mind of a man who plays an important part in the Acts story. This letter and Luke's narrative enable us to estimate the kind of man James was.

57. *Timothy Joins the Team*
(Acts 16:1-5)

Paul was joined by Silas when the church of Antioch commissioned him on another missionary tour in Gentile territory. He is by now experienced, whereas Silas has known service only

PAUL'S SECOND MISSIONARY JOURNEY.

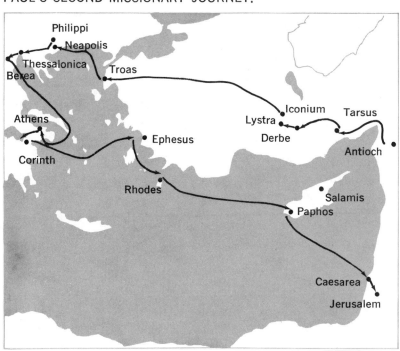

in Jerusalem and Antioch. They first went through Syria, and then through Cilicia, in which Paul's home town of Tarsus was situated. These two districts together formed one Roman province. There appear to have been many churches in these areas, and one wonders when they were founded. In his Galatian letter Paul mentions visiting these areas in between his Jerusalem visits, and it cannot be imagined that he visited without evangelizing. It must certainly have been a tower of strength to the believers in these churches to receive a return visit from the apostle, however fleeting.

After Cilicia, Paul retraced his steps to the Galatian towns where he had founded churches on his first journey. He went again to Derbe and then on to Lystra. It was there that he had been. left outside the city presumed dead. One of the Christians from that city had been deeply impressed by the apostle. He had not put off Christianity because of the threat of persecution. Timothy was young and the new faith had inspired him. He had had a Jewish upbringing, for his mother was Jewish, although his father was Greek. He had been well instructed in the Scriptures by Eunice his mother and Lois his grandmother (2 Tim. 1:5, 3:15). It seems highly probable that both these Jewesses had believed in Christ after hearing Paul on his first journey. Timothy had soon won the esteem of the brethren at both Lystra and the neighboring town of Iconium. This fact shows that there was close fellowship between the two churches and suggests that this was the pattern during the earliest period. It would explain how Paul could address a letter to a group of churches like the Galatian churches.

Not only had Timothy commended himself to his home churches, but he also caught the attention of the apostle. He was apparently willing to go with Paul and willing to submit to circumcision. It may seem surprising that Paul should insist on this after his great crusade against the circumcising of Gentiles. But in this case there is a different principle at stake. Timothy was not being circumcised as a contribution to his salvation, nor as an evidence of his obligation to keep the law. Since he was part Jew, he was not a pure Gentile. The problem was one of expediency. If Timothy remained uncircumcised it would be a hindrance when Paul was working among the Jews. But it was a different matter with Titus, who was a Gentile and who was not forced to be circumcised (Gal. 2:3).

The main business on this part of the second tour was to deliver the decisions which had been reached at Jerusalem. It is noticeable that James did not address the letter to these churches. But Paul evidently considered that there was some value in clarifying matters with the Galatian churches, especially as certain people purporting to come from James were deceiving them. The return visit to these churches was the occasion of much encouragement to the believers and of much further evangelizing activity, which was so successful that more were added daily to the Church.

58. *Moving on to Europe*

(Acts 16:6-15)

The early Christians were deeply sensitive to the leading of the Spirit. Each new move in the spreading progress of the Church was directed by God Himself through the Spirit. The missionary witnesses were convinced of this. There was no question of new developments being brought about by human ingenuity.

The province of Asia seemed a likely enough place for the Gospel. It was well populated and contained many important towns. Indeed, Paul later spent three years at Ephesus and during this time established many other churches in the province. Later still, seven churches in Asia were named in John's apocalypse. Yet for some reason the Spirit at this juncture forbade Paul to preach there. It is sufficient to reflect on the sovereign ways of God, who had a more urgent mission field in mind. Paul and his companions must have skirted around the borders of Asia, through the area where Phrygia adjoins the province of Galatia, until they reached the district in the north where the provinces of Asia and Bithynia join.

Paul supposed that Bithynia would make a profitable field of opportunity, but again he and his companions were prevented by the Spirit. This negative aspect of the Spirit's work is more important than is often realized. It is as much a part of his activity to close doors as to open them. The fact that Paul was twice forbidden of the Spirit before he really proceeded on his second tour shows his deep sensitivity to God's will. He might well have considered his long detour to have been a complete waste of time. But he plodded on without question. He was not to know God's purpose until reaching Troas, a harbor town on the northwestern coast of Asia.

Luke tells us how Paul obtained his next positive guidance by means of a vision. He records the gist of it in simple terms. A man of Macedonia beckons Paul to come over and help. Once again his sensitiveness to God's guidance comes vividly before us. A visit to Macedonia involved a sea voyage. It would certainly have been easier to go into Asia or Bithynia, but Paul is in no doubt that God's way is across the sea. It has been suggested that the man of Macedonia was Luke, since the narrative at this point uses the first person plural ("we sought to go"), although it had not done so earlier. The suggestion is attractive, but Luke's joining the party at this point need have nothing to do with the vision and in any case there is a strong alternative tradition that Luke was a man of Antioch. The most important feature in his narrative is the obedience with which Paul and his companions reacted to the vision. They at once made arrangements to go. It is small wonder their trip into Europe was so signally blessed of God.

From Troas they sailed to Neapolis, from which town they moved to Philippi. Paul's habit was to go straight to strategic centers. He might have delayed at the former town, but Philippi was considerably more important. It was the main city of Macedonia, which gave it special influence throughout the province. More important still, it was a Roman colony, which meant that it enjoyed special privileges. It obtained its name from Philip of Macedon, who had seized its gold mines, but it had been in the hands of the Romans since 168 B.C. It became a colony after Mark Anthony's veterans had been settled there. Colonists were exempt from certain taxes which were extracted from other subject peoples, and they were permitted to have similar administrative arrangements as the imperial city itself. For this reason colonists were proud of their privileges, and this must be borne in mind when considering Paul's strategy in selecting Philippi as his first base of operation in Europe.

He could hardly have questioned his guidance when in his initial work in Philippi he met Lydia by the riverside and found her open to the Gospel. She was not a native of Philippi, but came from Thyatira in the province of Asia. A business woman who traded in the famous purple dyes of her home district, she was also apparently a devout woman who had become acquainted with the Jewish faith in Asia. There was probably no synagogue in Philippi, and she and other devout women were in the habit of meeting for prayer by the riverside. Whether Paul had heard of this informal meeting is not clear, but Luke's narrative suggests that he and his companions expected to find some sort of gathering there. It was an excellent opportunity to expound the Gospel to the women. Lydia was probably the leader of the group. Indeed, she appears to have been the head of her household, in which case the others may have included her servants. It should be noted that Macedonia was more advanced than most areas in the ancient world in the respect given to women. Luke comments that the Lord had opened the heart of Lydia to give heed to Paul. It is one of his many incidental remarks which reveal his deep conviction about the sovereign operation of God. The passage under consideration is especially rich in such indications.

The first baptismal service in Europe was for a whole household. So was the second (see verse 33). God can do great things with Christian households, and in the case of Lydia there was an immediate offer of hospitality for the missionaries. This must have been the final seal on the divine leading through the vision of the man of Macedonia.

59. *The Fortune Teller*

(Acts 16:16-24)

Although Paul and his companions had the offer of hospitality in Lydia's house, they continued to frequent the place of prayer, no doubt in the hope of meeting with other devout people who would be open to the Gospel. On the way they met an altogether different challenge. A poor slave girl, who is said by Luke to possess "a spirit of Python," was being exploited by her owners. According to Plutarch, devotees of the Python were ventriloquists, whose words were out of the control of the person uttering them. At the famous shrine of Delphi in Greece, Apollo was believed to be embodied in a snake. In the case of this girl there was presumably some mystical value attached to what she was saying, which enabled her owners to make capital out of it.

It was startling when the girl declared that Paul and his companions were servants of the most high God who proclaimed salvation. It was totally unexpected that such testimony should come from such a source. Paul did not hesitate to act, for there was no question of his using such testimony to his own advantage. It could have been uttered only in ridicule and sarcasm. He did not conceal his anger. He at once rebuked the spirit in the name of Jesus. One of the constant activities of Jesus Himself was to cast out evil spirits, and it was also one of the activities of the disciples when they were commissioned by Him. The kingdom of darkness is bound to intensify its opposition when the Gospel is preached and its own hold is loosened. The clash between the slave girl and the apostle is typical of the constant clash between the forces of darkness and the forces of light.

Such transformation is bound to bring its repercussions. When vested interests are touched, all the machinery of opposition comes at once into play. A soothsaying girl who had become normal was a useless asset to her exploiters, who turned at once against Paul and Silas (Luke and the others were not included for some reason). They were brought before the magistrates in the marketplace. Luke describes these officials by the courtesy title allowed to the magistrates of a colony, but nowhere else except in Rome (i.e., praetors). The accusers were clearly astute men who in bringing their charge made no disclosure of their own vested interests. They fastened on public disorder, which would have been a matter of considerable concern to the magistrates. They pointed out that Paul and Silas were Jews and that their doctrines were not permitted among Romans. How they justified this latter charge, Luke does not say. They no doubt had only the vaguest notion of what Paul had in fact preached. But any insinuation of sedition provides a good springboard of attack on the part of unscrupulous men.

It is extraordinary how mob reaction works. There was no question of rejoicing because an enslaved girl had been liberated from spiritual chains. That was not the kind of event to whip up popular enthusiasm. What was of far greater consequence was that this Gospel of Paul's looked disturbing, as a threat to the status quo. Popular opinion is sensitive to this. Moreover, the Roman magistrates at Philippi do not show up today in a very good light. Their judgment that the missionaries should be beaten does not appear to have been reached after calm deliberation. It was easier to beat two unknown Jews than pacify a mob, and expediency was more important to them than strict justice. The violence with which the accused were treated seemed out of proportion to the supposed crime. They found themselves considerably battered and fastened in stocks in the inner jail. It was the kind of situation which Christians were to endure frequently for the cause of Christ. It was a painful reminder that the Gospel of salvation had to make its way in an intensely hostile world, that the message of love would constantly prove to be the object of hatred.

It is well to remember that the success or failure of any mission cannot be gauged by external circumstances, otherwise Paul and Silas might well have questioned God's guidance to this place. They were not at this juncture to know that God was to raise up in Philippi a strong body of believers who were to be a special source of joy to the Apostle Paul. Nor were the magistrates to know that their crude methods of violence would prove no match for the indomitable spirit of the apostles, nor would it deflect the mighty purposes of God. Never does the tyranny of man seem so futile as when it attempts to halt the progress of the Gospel by its own inhuman methods. The messengers of the crucified Christ were conditioned to expect suffering in His service, and some of the most heroic epics of Christian courage have come from prison cells. In the present case there was a remarkable sequel, as the next incident shows.

10

From Philippi to Corinth

60. *A Prison Shake-Up*
(Acts 16:25-34)

It would not be difficult to imagine what Paul and Silas might have thought as they nursed their considerable wounds with feet fastened in stocks. They might have indulged in self-pity. They might have discussed the possibilities of seeing again the light of day and enjoying the free air of Philippi. But their minds were concentrated on prayer. Humanly speaking, the situation looked grim, but God had not sent them for nothing. The more they prayed the more the spirit of praise filled their minds. They began spontaneously to sing. Being Jews used to singing psalms, they could without difficulty select those which encouraged faith in God in times of adversity. Or they may have known hymns about Jesus Christ. In his epistles Paul includes passages whose rhythmic character suggests that they were early hymns. One such possibility occurs in the letter he later sent to the church in this same city, where he was now singing in such adverse circumstances. It must be admitted that hymn singing in an unwelcome jail was hardly to be expected, especially at midnight. Other prisoners were startled enough to listen.

In a world in which violence and harsh treatment were normal and where jails were the meeting place of pitiable persons who had fallen afoul of the authorities, resentment and hatred were intense. The singing of hymns in a spirit of rejoicing introduced an element so alien that even the most hardened must have wondered at it. There was a nobility of spirit which marked Paul and Silas as men apart from the rest. It was not surprising that these men assumed moral leadership when an unexpected natural phenomenon threw the whole jail into confusion.

Earthquakes can be terrifying experiences. When not only the earth itself tremors, but substantial walls begin to move, it is enough to make the stoutest heart tremble in fear. Tremors which last only for seconds can cause considerable havoc. In the present case prison door latches were loosened and chains unlatched. After the initial shudder the prisoners realized their freedom from chains. The jailer imagined that all would rush for the doors. He seems to have been able to collect his wits more quickly than most of the prisoners. He thought only of his own responsibility to keep the prisoners safe, and being convinced that this was now no longer possible decided at once to commit suicide, as he would certainly have been executed when it was discovered that his prisoners had escaped. The whole scene is dramatic.

It was at this point that Paul's moral domination came to the fore. He prevented the suicide, having so impressed the rest of the prisoners that not one attempted to escape. This was remarkable. It may be that they were so intrigued by these unusual hymn-singing men that they wanted to stay and see what happened. They must have witnessed the conversation between Paul and the jailer after lights had been brought to dispel something of the dank darkness. Surrounded by the effects of the earthquake, they heard Paul exhort the jailer to believe in the Lord Jesus together with all his household. Paul then explained the way of salvation, which no doubt the hymns had already introduced. The fear which had made the man prostrate himself before Paul and Silas — strange reversal of the normal relation between warder and prisoners — had now vanished. He and his household had come to believe in the God who could fortify two men in the midst of suffering and terrifying natural phenomena.

The newly converted jailer saw his first duty to be a humanitarian act. He had been content to leave the prisoners with bleeding wounds to fend for themselves as best they could. It was no part of the rough execution of his duty to give any thought to the milk of humankindness. But the moment he believed in Christ, compassion was born in his soul. It took no time to incubate. The wounds became at once a challenge. He dressed and soothed them and only then did he submit to baptism. Moreover, after the baptism he gave them food, another act of practical Christianity which had not occurred to him before he became a believer.

This incident, set as it is against the harsh background of the ancient world and typical of the background of much of the modern, symbolizes the transforming power of the Gospel. Where fear and confusion are rife, the Gospel brings peace. Even in conditions of natural calamity, the messengers of the Gospel show themselves to be the real masters of the situation, the real leaders in the realm of the Spirit.

61.   *Dismissal From Philippi*

(Acts 16:35-40)

The magistrates meanwhile decided to release Paul and Silas. What caused them to choose leniency is not clear. Perhaps on reflection they realized they had acted with less than justice. Or perhaps the earthquake had given them second thoughts. Perhaps, indeed, it had caused more pressing social problems than those which two unknown Jews had caused by their preaching. Who knows? There was no delay in executing their decision. Darkness had hardly cleared before the police arrived giving the jailer instructions for the release. No doubt the jailer was overjoyed at being able to release his newfound friends and was hardly prepared for the response.

What possessed Paul to stand on his dignity is not stated by Luke, nor is it clear why he did not inform the magistrates the day before that he was a Roman citizen. But he considered it to be just that as the beating had been in public so should the vindication of the prisoners be public. It would clearly show that there was nothing criminal about the preaching of the Gospel. It was bold for Paul to request the magistrates themselves to escort them from the prison, but he knew well the power and privilege of Roman citizenship. This privilege was so highly prized that officials throughout the empire were sensitive lest they denied to any Roman citizen his rights. It was illegal in Roman law for such degrading forms of punishment as flogging to be inflicted on a Roman citizen. It is clear that the magistrates in the case of Paul and Silas had seriously exceeded their rights.

When the police reported Paul's demand to the magistrates they were afraid. Their own position could have been in jeopardy had it been generally known that they had acted against the law in publicly flogging Roman citizens. They recognized that they had no alternative but to concede to Paul's demand. In spite of the humiliation, they personally apologized. The public witnessed the ex-prisoners' unusual escort when making their way from the exit of the prison. When they requested them to leave, the magistrates no doubt thought that they had rid the city of a potential cause of disturbance, but they did not know that Paul and Silas would leave behind them the nucleus of a Christian church.

Before their departure they visited the home of Lydia. They met other believers there. Already Lydia's home had become the meeting place of the church. The jailer's was another Christian household. Whether the slave girl became a believer Luke does not say. It is reasonable to suppose that she did. Apart from these Luke mentions no others, but Paul in his later letter to the church at Philippi mentions a man named Clement and two women who are said to have worked side by side with him (Phil. 4:2, 3). These two, Euodia and Syntyche, must have belonged to the original church. They did not get on too well together, because Paul has to exhort them to agree in the Lord. Nevertheless, the Philippian church, in spite of the comparatively brief time that Paul and his companions spent there, was well and truly founded. It became one of Paul's best loved churches. It brought him more joy than any other.

For a study of Paul's general strategy, his experiences at Philippi are illuminating. More was achieved, it would appear, by the planting of the Christian faith in a few households than by widespread campaigns. The fact that the Church developed from such small beginnings is evidence of the activity of the Spirit. Paul had no option but to withdraw from the city. Left to his own decision, he may have acted otherwise, for it seemed that there were many in the city prepared to receive the Gospel. But it is the genius of the apostle that he never stayed to do what others could do. The Gospel developed in Philippi in spite of his withdrawal, and a similar pattern has occurred in many other places where official action has forced the withdrawal of God's messengers.

62. *Thessalonica*

(Acts 17:1-9)

The road that Paul and his party (which no longer included Luke) would take from Philippi would have been the famous highway known as the Via Egnatia. On all his missionary journeys Paul made the fullest use of the main highways constructed by the Romans to maintain communications between the provinces and the imperial city. These highways became to a remarkable extent arteries for the spreading of the Gospel.

Paul did not linger at Amphipolis or at Apollonia but pressed on to Thessalonica, another example of strategic choice, for the latter city was the provincial capital. In 42 B.C. it had been made a free city, a measure of its importance. As customary, Paul's party made for the synagogue, judging their first duty to preach to their Jewish compatriots. In any case, many interested Gentiles, fringe members of the synagogue, would be the most open to the Gospel. Moreover the synagogue audiences were used to expositions of Scripture and were in the habit of listening to visiting teachers. For this reason Paul had no difficulty in obtaining permission to speak. For three successive sabbaths he gave expository addresses which showed the necessity for the Messiah to suffer and rise from the dead and then made clear the identity of the Messiah as Jesus. Not surprisingly Paul's subject matter met with Jewish opposition, for the idea of a suffering Messiah was as inconceivable among the Jews of the Dispersion as it had been among the Jews of Jerusalem.

Nevertheless, the series of three expositions was not without considerable effect. While only a few of the Jews believed, a strong contingent of Gentiles, who had developed an interest in Judaism, found the new faith in Jesus Christ particularly satisfying. Surrounded by the widespread idolatry within paganism, the purer monotheism of Judaism made an appeal to the nobler pagans. There was much to appeal in the more exalted notion of Jehovah, especially the transcendental view of Him advocated by contemporary Jewish thought. Although the "otherness" of God meant that He had become far removed from man, this was preferable to the multiplication of pagan deities which had no standard of holiness. The nobler Gentile hunger for something better was partially, but only partially, satisfied by Jewish worship of the one true God. It left a void which Christianity was to fill, for it provided a perfect mediator between God and man and provided a way of faith as a better alternative to the Jewish demand for obedience to law. Another reason why these Gentiles turned so readily from Judaism was the general Gentile dislike of the narrowness of the Jewish outlook. There was little mixing between Jews and Gentiles, whereas in Christianity this barrier was overcome. In addition to the large number of these people, there were several of the leading women in the community who were attracted to Christianity. As at Philippi, the women had greater possibility of influence than in most of the Roman provincial towns. These women were also clearly searching for a satisfying faith, which they found in the Gospel.

In view of the greater number of fringe members of the Jewish synagogue who had turned to Christianity in a short time, it is small wonder that the Jewish authorities became alarmed. It is significant that these authorities in Thessalonica decided to employ very similar tactics to those adopted by the hierarchy in Jerusalem in their opposition to Jesus. They were not opposed to the use of mob tactics. It was not difficult to find a street mob thirsting for excitement. When once aroused, mobs usually act in the most irrational way. It required only a few loiterers to get things going, the sort of fellows who hang around the market-place looking for action to relieve the boredom. It mattered little to them who the victim of their gang warfare might be. If Paul and Silas were not in the house to which they were directed, they must seize someone, and the hospitable host Jason served as a suitable substitute, together with some of the brethren who happened to be in his house.

While the whole place was in an uproar they were dragged before the civil authorities. These officials are called "politarchs," a title known to have been used only in Macedonia and particularly in Thessalonica, a remarkable example of the accuracy of Luke's narrative. The charge against Jason and his companions was that they had harbored the men who had turned the world upside down. It was a striking tribute to the influence of Paul and Silas and to the whole Christian movement. Moreover, the missionaries were charged with sedition because they called Jesus a king. There is again a striking parallel with the charge leveled against Jesus. It is not surprising that the civil authorities were disturbed, for taken literally this might have led to an ugly political situation. It shows that other temporal authorities besides Pilate found it difficult to comprehend the spiritual kingship of Jesus. The officials were unable to take strong action against Paul and Silas, who were still at liberty, but they bound over Jason and the others to keep the peace.

63. Beroea

(Acts 17:10-15)

The Thessalonian Christians, realizing that Paul and Silas would be more a liability than an asset if they remained, decided to send them away secretly to avoid further trouble and to avoid further problems for Jason. Whether Paul and Silas stayed in Thessalonica for only three weeks it is difficult to say. Luke's narrative seems to support this, but Paul's first letter to the Thessalonians appears to require a rather longer stay, during which he could claim not to have been a burden to them, but to have worked night and day to maintain himself (1 Thess. 2:9). The suggestion that Luke concentrates on the brief Jewish mission, and by-passes the longer period of the Gentile mission, is not improbable. Our present interest is, however, in the sequel.

Beroea was not situated on the Via Egnatia and was less accessible than Thessalonica. This may have been the reason why the Thessalonians sent Paul and Silas there. They would know, moreover, that the Jews at Beroea were more open-minded. Paul and Silas were well received in the synagogue and found the Jews there ready to examine the Scriptures in a new way. With such an open approach to scriptural testimony it is not surprising that many believed. In addition, as at Thessalonica, the Gospel made a particular appeal to some of the influential Greek women. One of the features which appealed to them may well have been the principle of equality which existed between the sexes in Christianity, as compared with its absence from other ancient religious systems. Indeed, it must be noted as a special characteristic of the Christian faith.

Although Thessalonica was about sixty miles from Beroea, news of Paul's preaching at the latter city soon reached the Jews at the former. It was not long before a deputation arrived, intent on using the same method of mob incitement which had proved so successful at Thessalonica. The Jews again managed to cause a social problem, but the disciples did not wait for action to be taken against Paul. Having ascertained that he was the main object of attack, they decided to send him away at once by sea. No mob could pursue him aboard ship. Moreover, it speaks highly of the Beroean concern for Paul's safety that they sent men to escort him as far as Athens. The Beroean church is not as well known as many other early Christian communities, but we should be grateful to Luke for including this brief cameo of a people who were noted for their diligent study of Scripture. Their example has been the inspiration of many other groups who have sought out the biblical basis for their Christian faith.

While Paul has journeyed to Athens, Silas and Timothy remained at Beroea, and Paul now sends back with his Beroean brethren a message urging them to join him. This they apparently did while Paul was still at Athens. Luke does not record this, but Paul himself mentions it in his letter to the Thessalonians (1 Thess. 3:1). Timothy was then sent back to Thessalonica and Silas to some other place in Macedonia (cf. Acts 18:5). Paul then left Athens and moved to Corinth, where Timothy and Silas rejoined him. It will be seen that there are two journeys of Paul's companions which are omitted from Luke's story and this reminds us that the Acts is not a complete diary of events. It is only because this has not been recognized that it has been suggested by some that there are contradictions between Luke and Paul over Timothy's movements. The reconstruction suggested enables the historical allusions in Paul's epistles to be fitted into the Acts narrative. Luke at this juncture is more concerned about Paul's experience at Athens, to which we now turn.

64. *Paul at Athens*

(Acts 17:16-21)

When Paul arrived at Athens he waited for a time for the arrival of his companions. He probably felt the need of strong moral support in this city of ancient culture. But his impatience at last won through.

Athens had reason to be proud of its past. Some five centuries earlier it had attained its zenith as the leading city-state in Greece, and although twice defeated before the Romans conquered it, once by Sparta in the fifth century B.C. and again by Philip of Macedon in the fourth, it nevertheless retained much of its freedom. When Paul visited the city, the Athenians still maintained the intellectual leadership of Greece, although much of its classical glory had diminished. It had been the home of such giants as Socrates and Plato, Aristotle, Epicurus, and Zeno. It still retained magnificent evidence of the sculptor's art, and some of the buildings which stood in Paul's day are still sufficiently preserved today for an idea of their artistic proportions to be gauged. No one can stand on the Acropolis before the magnificent columns of the Temple of Athena without marveling at the ancient Greeks' mastery of the builder's art. In Paul's day the temple stood complete. There has been debate about his appreciation of artistic forms, since he never mentions such matters in his letters. But not even Paul could have been unimpressed by the cultural achievements of the city. In his letters, however, his mind dwells on spiritual matters.

Luke records in strong terms Paul's reaction to the Athenian scene as being one of distress, or rather of angry irritation. His strongly monotheistic faith reacted against the multitudinous idols. Some of these were works of exquisite art, but this made no difference to him. He was deeply concerned about the symbolic meaning behind the idols, and found himself in a wholly alien environment.

In view of this it is not surprising that he again turned his attention to the Jews in the synagogue, where he argued about the Christian faith. He seems to have had some hearing among the Gentile "fringe" at the synagogue, but he was irresistibly drawn into the marketplace, the agora, which formed the center

A portion of the panel on Mars Hill commemorating Paul's visit to Athens.

of Greek city life. It was a common feature for men to congregate to discuss topics, mainly of a philosophic character. It was inevitable that the serious-minded apostle, with his passion for imparting the Gospel, would have a confrontation with the more intellectual types in Athens.

Among the major philosophical schools were the Stoics and the Epicureans. The former were noted for their severity of self-discipline and the latter for their moral laxity. There were constant clashes between them, but they would be united in their rejection of the Gospel as Paul preached it. To them it was plain foolishness. The idea of a crucified Messiah would be wholly unintelligible. Moreover, the stress on faith would make no sense to those who believed that knowledge was everything and salvation a matter of knowing oneself. It is no wonder that the intelligentsia called Paul a babbler. There is an air of intellectual superiority in their remark that he appeared to be a preacher of foreign deities. Nevertheless they were curious to discover whether Paul had anything new to say. Luke remarks that the Athenians spent their time telling or listening to new doctrine. Their interest in Paul sprang mainly from curiosity.

The Athenians had a special council which possessed supreme authority in religious matters. It was of great antiquity and originally met on the Areopagus, a hill west of the Acropolis, which was nevertheless far less imposing than the much higher hill on which the Acropolis itself stood. In Paul's day the Council of the Areopagus probably met in the Council chamber which stood in the marketplace or agora, which was no great distance from the Areopagus hill. There is some dispute whether the Athenians took Paul to the hill and listened to him in the open air or whether they brought him before the official Council. Whichever it was, they appear to have adopted an attitude of intellectual superiority over him, which influenced the tenor of his speech before them. Luke records no other occasion on which the apostle presents the Gospel to an intellectual audience.

65. *Paul at the Areopagus*

(Acts 17:22-34)

There have been various opinions about the speech that Paul delivered at the Areopagus. His approach was quite different from his address at Pisidian Antioch (Acts 13). He made an effort to accommodate his hearers by the style of his address, which is more Greek than any of the Acts speeches, or for that matter than any other part of the New Testament. Opinions may vary as to the success of this approach, but the speech itself is a witness to Paul's conviction that the preacher of the Gospel must meet his audience on their own ground. It is probable that the speech was cut short, in which case there is no way of knowing how Paul intended to conclude.

He begins by mentioning what he had observed on entering Athens. He had passed an altar inscribed "To an unknown God." Although archaeological researches have uncovered many altars with varied inscriptions, there is none so far which corresponds to the altar seen by Paul. There is, however, some ancient literary evidence which associates altars to unknown gods (in the plural) with Athens, and there is no reason to exclude the possibility of the existence of an altar to an unknown god (in the singular). Such an inscription would form an admirable starting point for a Christian apologetic. At least the Athenians were religiously inclined, even if they were also superstitious. Paul at once chides them for their ignorance of their object of worship, and then proceeds to tell them about the Creator. He sees some value in the testimony of the natural creation. It is God who gives breath to every creature and He cannot therefore dwell in manmade shrines. Here Paul is knocking at the basis of paganism. Its view of its gods is wholly inadequate, because they can never rise above the level of created things. Of course the nobler pagan world have admitted this much, but Paul is dealing with the evidences of idolatry, which surrounded him in the Athens of his day.

His next point stresses that the God he worships is one who controls the destinies of men, of nations as well as of individuals. This at once puts his God beyond all local deities. He is the supreme and universal God. His omnipotent power is nevertheless not used in any tyrannical way, but that men might have a new relationship to Him, might seek Him and find Him. This seeking is, however, different from the intellectual pursuit of knowledge so characteristic of the Greeks and especially of the Stoics. Paul undoubtedly was using it in the Old Testament sense of seeking with a view to worship.

It is important to note that after speaking of the might and majesty of God, Paul went on to speak of His nearness, quoting from the Greek poets, Epimenides and Aratus, in support. It may be observed that Paul's knowledge of Greek literature, which obtrudes very little in his epistles, was nevertheless available at times when it could be usefully employed.

The idea of man being God's offspring is basic to the Old Testament, which even declares that man was made in God's image. Paul's aim at this juncture was to show his audience that even poets whom they respected had a view of God which undermined the idea of idols, however artistic their workmanship. Ignorance of the true God is now inexcusable. He has made Himself known and calls on men everywhere to repent. This exhortation to repent involves a radical change of mind not merely an intellectual adjustment. It is fully in line with the other addresses to non-Christians in Acts.

It was when Paul came to mention the resurrection that the crunch came. He introduced the idea of judgment which forms part of the divine plan. He implied that the Athenians' idolatry would come under that judgment. It might have been expected that he would make a direct reference to Jesus Christ, instead of which he refers to "a man whom he (i.e., God) has appointed." But when he declares that God had raised "this man" from the dead, he at once establishes his uniqueness. The "man" of whom Paul speaks is the "Son of man" as Jesus called Himself.

Mention of the resurrection evoked a mocking response from many of Paul's hearers. The Greeks, although accepting the immortality of the soul, had no time for the resurrection of the body. Some, however, were sufficiently interested to want to hear Paul again. And a few became believers, one of whom, Dionysius, was a man of considerable distinction, for he had the high honor of being a member of the Council of the Areopagus. With so distinguished a convert, it can hardly be said that Paul's Areopagus address was a failure. A tradition was preserved by Eusebius the Church historian that this Dionysius became the first bishop of Athens. The only other believer whom Luke mentions by name was Damaris, of whom nothing else is known. The tradition that she was Dionysius' wife, mentioned by Chrysostom, was probably no more than conjecture. It is worth noting that there is no other reference to a church at Athens in the early period, and Paul does not consider it a policy to spend much time there.

66. *Paul at Corinth*

(Acts 18:1-11)

Another important city in Southern Greece was Corinth, a commercial center which offered more varied opportunities than Athens for the preaching of the Gospel. It was admirably situated on the peninsula known as the Isthmus of Corinth, with two harbors, one on the eastern side of the peninsula and the other on the west. In modern times a shipping channel joins the two seas, but in Paul's time communcation between the two ports was overland. This meant that Corinth was strategically situated, since trade from east and west could pass through it, avoiding the treacherous sea route around the peninsula. Being on the main trade route, it became a cosmopolitan city. It had been completely destroyed by the Roman conquest of Greece, but had been restored by Julius Caesar less than a century before Paul's visit. Like Athens, its Acropolis stood high on a hill overlooking the city and dominated its marketplace or agora. Remains of this area still exist with various temple ruins in evidence. Corinth was noted for its Temple of Aphrodite, where the cult of Astarte practiced its immoral rituals. Indeed the whole city was noted for immorality and had the dubious distinction of giving its name to a new word in the Greek language. To Corinthianize meant to act immorally. In addition to all this there was some attempt to compete with the culture of Athens, although the latter with its antiquity overshadowed it. The pursuit of wisdom was not unknown in Corinth.

It was against such a background of cosmopolitan life with all its social problems of sinful living that Paul arrived in Corinth. To preach the Gospel there was a formidable task. But the apostle was not alone as he had been at Athens. He found two congenial companions who had not long been in Corinth. Aquila and his wife Priscilla (or as Paul always names her, Prisca) were Jews who had been exiled from Rome under an imperial decree of Claudius. The reason for such an anti-Jewish decree is not clear, but it is not impossible that there had been some kind of revolt which made their presence undesirable. If this edict is the same one that the historian Suetonius mentions over an uproar caused by one Chrestus, it may have been due to some clash between the orthodox Jews and the Christian Church. It is highly probable that Aquila and Priscilla were Christians before meeting

The ruins of the Temple of Apollo at Corinth.

THE ROUTE FROM ATHENS TO CORINTH.

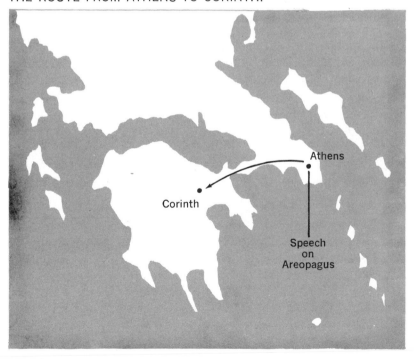

Athens

Corinth

Speech
on
Areopagus

with Paul, in which case they at once found a common basis for fellowship. In addition to this they plied the same trade as Paul. They were tentmakers, who had set up business in Corinth and established their home there. For some time they were to act as hosts to the apostle.

As usual Paul launched his mission at the synagogue and debated with both Jews and Greeks there. He had immediate success, for some were persuaded by his presentation of the Gospel.

At this point Silas and Timothy arrived from Macedonia. They were witnesses of the first opposition from the Corinthians. Once again this opposition came from Jews because Paul declared Jesus to be the Messiah. Having suffered their abuse, with a symbolic gesture he turned from them to the Gentiles. He clearly regarded preaching to the Jews first as a solemn responsibility. When they rejected the message he considered he was innocent regarding them. This is instructive for any assessment of Paul's approach to his missionary activity. He could accept no responsibility for the reception of the message, only for its proclamation.

It was ironical that the Gentile sympathizer, Titus Justus, who offered Paul the use of his house, lived next door to the synagogue, for the Jews had the chagrin of still observing the progress of the Gospel. It was even more ironical that Crispus, one of the synagogue officials, became a Christian with his whole household and went next door. The chagrin of the Jews increased as they saw many of the Christians believing and being baptized.

One wonders why in these circumstances Paul began to question whether he should stop preaching there. He actually needed a vision to reassure him. It was unlike Paul to be fearful, but when he was so close to the opposition, he no doubt felt the rising intensity of it. In the vision the Lord said, "I am with you," which is reminiscent of the final commission which Jesus gave to His disciples before departing from them (Matt. 28:20). Moreover, it was a real assurance for the apostle to know that God had many people in the city. The results of the work were in other hands than his. He was yet to see demonstrated before his eyes that God's power was great enough to win many believers even in the most infamous city in Greece. He stayed a year and a half to see it, during which many heard the Word of God. A strong church was established, although it turned out to be a church with many problems, as Paul's Corinthian letters show.

Two views of Corinth: Top: Looking north. Below: South Stoa, statue and ruins, looking southeast.

11

Letters to Thessalonica

67. *Paul Writes to the Thessalonians*

(1 Thess. 1:1 – 2:16)

While at Corinth Paul received a firsthand report of the progress of the Christians at Thessalonica from Silas and Timothy. It was most encouraging, although a few difficulties of a practical nature caused Paul some concern. He decided to write a letter, but since the work at Thessalonica had been a team effort, he would send it as from the three of them. When referring to Silas, Paul always gave the fuller name Silvanus, but it is the same person.

As is customary in most of his letters, Paul gives a prayer of thanksgiving after the opening greeting. In this way he reveals his great affection for the believers at Thessalonica. They had persisted in what he calls their "labour of love." He reminds them how they had received the Word in power and in the Spirit. He is a great believer in the value of recollection. They must remember their affliction when they received the Word. They could hardly forget what happened to Jason and the brethren. Paul rejoices that their stand has become an example throughout Macedonia and Achaia. No doubt he had himself told the Corinthians of his experiences at Thessalonica, but news of their example had spread in other ways. Many had heard how those believers had turned from idolatry to the worship of the true God, and were now living in the expectation of the return of Christ.

Evidently Silas and Timothy had reported that some of the Thessalonians were nevertheless critical of the apostle, for he makes a kind of apology for his actions. He finds it necessary to remind them of the sufferings of himself and his companions at

Philippi, which had not deterred them from boldly preaching at Thessalonica, in spite of the opposition there. Were some of the Thessalonians inferring that Paul and his companions were out to please men? He states most clearly that their aim was to please God. He despises the use of flattery and gives no place to greed. Both have spoiled the witness of the Christian Church many times since Paul's day, but he and his companions could not be charged with them. Indeed, they had acted independently of any support from the Thessalonians, although as apostles he considered that they had a right to expect it. Their work among them was a real share-out, not only of the Gospel but also of themselves. He speaks of their attitude toward the Thessalonians as a nurse's care for children.

In all this one can detect a mixture of tenderness and restrained indignation. It is as if Paul is amazed that anyone should charge them with self-seeking. They had worked for their living, even into the night hours, so that no one could charge them with feathering their own nests through preaching the Gospel. Moreover, Paul feels it is necessary to remind the Thessalonians of the missionaries' example among them. He is confident that no one could accuse them of inconsistent behavior, and that God will testify to that whatever men may say. He then uses another analogy to illustrate his concern — that of a father's attitude toward his children. The Thessalonians are told to remember the way that Paul and his party exhorted them to live a worthy life, and recognize that the whole purpose in their mission work was to glorify God's kingdom.

One thing that had particularly gladdened the missionaries was the way that the Thessalonians had recognized in their message the Word of God. Moreover, having become believers, they were prepared to suffer for their faith, precisely as the Judaean churches had done in the earlier persecutions. Paul does not mention, although he must have had in his mind, his own part in the persecution of those early Judaean Christians. He had carried on the same policy that had led to the death of Jesus. But now he is in the opposing camp, being hindered by the Jews in his work among the Gentiles. Whether he wrote this before or after his appearance before Gallio is not clear, but he knows of Jewish opposition in Corinth even as he writes. Because they are hindering God's work, he concludes that God's wrath must be upon them.

68.   *Present Relationships*

(1 Thess. 2:17 – 3:13)

After leaving Thessalonica, Paul had many times intended to pay a return visit to the Christians there, but had been prevented from doing so. He attributes the hindrance to Satan, although he does not say what form the hindrance took. It is important to note how conscious the apostle was of spiritual opposition. In the immoral city of Corinth he had ample opportunity to observe the activities of Satan. He was acutely aware that he was engaged in a spiritual warfare. Nevertheless he consoled himself with the thought that the Thessalonians were a great joy to them — he calls them their "crown of boasting." He remembered his stress at Athens when he decided to send off Timothy for further work in Thessalonica. This in itself was a testimony to his concern for them, especially as it meant that he was left at Athens alone. He vividly remembers his solitary experience there.

In this letter Paul reveals much of the feeling he had when he worked among the Thessalonians. He was experienced enough to know that he could not escape suffering in the cause of the Gospel. He had warned the Thessalonians that he and his companions would suffer and they should not have been surprised when the street mob caused the uproar that led to the hasty withdrawal of the missionaries. But with a natural concern, Paul had been wondering ever since whether their faith would stand firm. Again he recognizes that a spiritual opposition was at work. Would they fall prey to the tempter?

It is refreshing that Paul does not hesitate to tell his readers about his own fears for them, in spite of the fact that Timothy's report has confirmed that the fears were groundless. Indeed, what Timothy told him brought great encouragement to the apostle. We are grateful that this letter which sets out Paul's reactions has been preserved, for otherwise we should have had little idea of the thoughts of this restless apostle as he pressed on from Thessalonica, through Beroea to Athens and then to Corinth. Luke, who aimed to record the developing stages of the history of Christianity from Jerusalem to Rome, does not pause to give information of the most personal kind. But Paul's letters show the real man, a man capable of a variety of reactions, and by no means always confident and self-reliant.

Timothy had not only reported the Thessalonians' faith and

love, which greatly rejoiced Paul's heart, but had also told how deeply they were concerned about Paul, how they remembered him with kindness, and how they greatly desired to see him. This kind of news makes the hardships of any work for God worthwhile. Human fellowship and human encouragement mean much to all but the most stoical of men, and Paul was not that sort of man. As he thinks of his difficulties since leaving Thessalonica, few of which are mentioned by Luke, but many of which are later enumerated by Paul himself in 2 Corinthians 11, he is girded up by recalling the strong faith of his converts. It seems that at times he is tempted to wonder whether he is achieving anything. He fears that his labor may be in vain, but the report of believers standing fast provided a real tonic. It had filled his heart with joy and had driven him to pray constantly for some further opportunity to visit these people. Day and night it was in his mind. Whether such intensity of prayer for this purpose is in harmony with complete confidence in the Lord's leading is a relevant question. Paul almost seems to think that he is indispensable for the bringing of these Christians to mature faith. His intense prayers were not in fact answered, not at least for some considerable period of time and then only for a brief period. In the interim God had other ways of supplying what was missing in their faith, independent of the apostle's presence. Yet the desire to see these warmhearted Macedonians as soon as possible is perfectly understandable.

Paul's prayer for them was not simply concentrated on his own desire to see them. He makes clear that he wants to follow the Lord's direction. His main burden is that they should increase in love. However glowing the report that Timothy has brought, Paul knows there is room for more love, for love is the most expansive of all human qualities. It can never exhaust its opportunities. With the love there must also be holiness, which places the love which Paul prays for in a category of its own compared with all forms of natural love, since holy love comes only from God Himself. He closes this brief prayer with another reference to the second coming of Jesus.

69. *Practical Advice for Hard-Pressed Christians*
(1 Thess. 4 and 5)

It is time for Paul to give advice to the Thessalonians. Most of it is the kind of advice which would be relevant and valuable to

Christians in any church and in any age, which accounts for the ageless quality of Paul's letters. Nevertheless in order to appreciate the force of the words as he wrote them, their original relevance to the Thessalonians themselves must be kept before us.

He first deals with moral purity. The Thessalonians were living in a pagan environment. They had brought into Christianity that background of paganism. They needed to learn a new approach to moral purity. The pagans around them, their neighbors and acquaintances, exercised little restraint in the satisfying of their lusts. If Paul writes from the capital city of immorality, he knows well enough that all the Gentile cities presented much the same problems. Paganism had no established code of honor in sexual relationships, but Paul had already given instructions on a new level, based on the Lord Jesus. It was a matter of a believer's consecration that Christian marriage should be honorable. On no account must Christians wrong each other, for in doing so they would be wronging God. Such teaching as this presented a striking and courageous contrast to the prevailing pagan laxity. Paul would have had no patience with the modern permissive society. He would have no other word for it than "uncleanness," an affront to the Holy Spirit. Thessalonian Christians, in common with all other Gentile Christians in that contemporary world, would need to take a firm and "narrow" view in the matter of sex. This is one of the first of the challenges which came in the wake of the apostolic preaching of the Gospel.

Paul next returns to the theme of love. He must have felt strongly about it, for he again admits that the Thessalonians had shown evidence of it already. Indeed he notes their warm love for the brethren throughout Macedonia, presumably mainly those at Philippi and Beroea. But he encourages them to increase their love. Perhaps he is thinking of the need for the Corinthians to become objects of the Thessalonians' love. Christian love overleaps all provincial barriers. Paul is not only concerned with their relationships with other Christians, but also with those outside the Church. He establishes the principle that the behavior of Christians must command respect from non-Christians. Two particular matters are mentioned. Avoid interfering with other peoples' affairs and do an honest day's work. These are no doubt samples of what was pressing for the Thessalonians. The list might have been extended to include anything in the nature of practical living which lessened the respect of non-Christians for believers. Of course Paul was not supposing that outsiders could always form a right view of the Christian Church. He had already experienced far worse than lack of respect from non-Christians because of his preaching of the Gospel. Yet he had been morally and practically blameless.

A matter which had cropped up at Thessalonica concerned the Lord's return. Paul had told them about this hope when he was with them and they had gained the impression that this event would take place quite soon. But since Paul had left them some of the believers had died and some debate had arisen about their position when the Lord returned. He now tells them there is no need for them to grieve, for believers who die in the Lord have the same certain hope as those who are still alive when the Lord comes. He describes the event in pictorial language — an archangel's call, a trumpet sound, clouds — very similar to that used in Jewish descriptions of future happenings. The dominant feature is the suddenness of the happening. Paul says nothing about the timing of it. He is sure it will come and is sure he will be present, either as one who has fallen asleep and is raised or as one who remains. It is not possible to reconstruct exactly what Paul's idea of the second coming was, for he writes to people who already have had the benefit of his oral teaching. He describes the suddenness in two ways — as a pregnant woman's travail and as a thief in the night. The latter illustration leads him to remind his readers to be alert and sober, since they are children of light not darkness. It is worth noting that the Jews of Qumran called themselves the children of light, which shows that this imagery was widespread at that time.

Paul puts in a number of brief but telling exhortations, mainly of a social character, such as respect for their Christian leaders, a peaceful attitude to each other, a readiness to help others to cope with their problems, whether it be idleness or discouragement. Revenge is to be avoided. Rejoicing and prayer are seen as God's will for them. There may have been problems over ecstatic experiences, in which case Paul is anxious that no true work of the Spirit should be quenched. There is need for discernment between good and evil, that the former might be developed and the latter avoided. These closing exhortations are valuable because they show the essentially practical character of Paul's thinking regarding the Christian faith at this stage of his mission work. His letters to Thessalonica are in fact among the most practical of his writings.

The closing remarks of this letter are typical, with another prayer for the readers and a request to them for their prayers for him and his companions. There is also a request for the letter to be read to all the brethren, an interesting reminder that Paul saw letter-writing as a method of communication to whole communities. He himself encouraged the public reading of his letters, a practice which must have contributed to their preservation and to the high respect which they later commanded.

70.   *Another Letter to Thessalonica*

(2 Thess. 1:1 – 2:12)

It could not have been long after sending the first letter that Paul wrote a second letter to the Thessalonians. We can only conjecture what happened during the interval. Paul was still at Corinth, but was maintaining contact as far as possible with his churches. Presumably one of his associates took the first letter to Thessalonica. He may have stayed for sufficient time to observe the reaction of the Christians. The main problem arose over the comments in the first letter about the Lord's return. Paul's reference to its suddenness had apparently been misunderstood and some of the Thessalonians had thought the Lord's coming was so imminent that they might as well give up work and wait for it. That this is a fair assumption of what happened is more obvious than the alternative theory that a different view of the Lord's coming is presented in the second letter and that therefore Paul must have altered his mind. Some have even argued on the strength of this that Paul could not have written the second letter. But it is perfectly intelligible if it is recognized that a misunderstanding had arisen which prompted the second letter.

In spite of the misunderstanding, Paul is still thankful that the Thessalonians' faith is growing. He has been boasting about them to other churches. He is impressed because they are still enduring affliction for the sake of their faith. This leads him to reflect on the fact that it is God who will inflict vengeance on those who were afflicting His people. The apostle is taking a rather tough line here. He speaks of eternal destruction for those who do not obey the Gospel. He thinks ahead to the coming of the Lord in glory. This for him is an important event because it means that believers should strive to be worthy of their calling, which forms the burden of his prayer for the Thessalonians. What he is about to say concerning future events has a practical rather than a theoretical purpose.

The coming of the Lord has clearly caused confusion among the Thessalonians. Paul is afraid that some may be unsettled by reports that he holds that the coming is already past. He even mentions the possibility of a letter being sent to them in his name. This would be a daring deceit, but Paul evidently conceives the possibility. There is no evidence, of course, that this had happened. Nevertheless as a safeguard, Paul wrote the concluding part of this letter with his own hand (2 Thess. 3:17), so that they would be able to recognize his authentic signature.

He wants to make the point that there are certain events which must precede the Lord's coming. There will be rebellion, by which he must mean rebellion of a special sort, for rebellions were no uncommon phenomena in those days. The rebellion is linked with a person described as "the man of lawlessness" and "son of perdition." The particular mark of this leader of evil will be his antagonism to the true God and his setting himself up as the object of worship. This amounts to a complete reversal of the truth. There have been many through history who have attempted to usurp the place of God, from the Roman emperors to modern leaders like Mao Tse Tung. The Thessalonians were warned to be alert to the activity of such a person. Nevertheless Paul mentions a "restrainer," and there has been much dispute over what he meant. Some have seen here a reference to the Roman Empire, which at that time was a stabilizing influence in maintaining law and order in the world. Others see the activity of God and yet others the mission work of Paul. Paul's words must have been much clearer to the Thessalonians than they are to us. They had the key, because they had had the advantage of hearing Paul speak to them on this subject (verse 5). We can only conclude that some person of specially evil intent will precede the Lord's coming, and that Paul needed to stress this so that his readers might be prepared. They needed to recognize that the coming could be as a thief, even though certain signs must come first.

As Paul thinks of the "lawless one" he thinks automatically of the "activity of Satan." Pretense and deception are the weapons of his armory. Man's refusal to love the truth is linked with a

God-sent delusion, so that they end up by actually believing what is false. It is a basic conviction of the apostle that those who do not accept God's standards set up opposing standards of their own, in which "error" becomes "truth." Many modern currents of thinking and behavior come perilously near to doing this. Those guilty of such reversal will certainly be condemned, as Paul makes clear.

71. *More Practical Matters*

(2 Thess. 2:17 – 3:18)

Paul turns again to consider his readers, whom he contrasts with those who refuse to love the truth, and he cannot refrain from thanking God for them. They had been chosen by God for salvation. Of course there is a mystery surrounding God's choice, but Paul does not discuss it. He is concerned with accomplished facts. The Thessalonians had believed, and Paul can see no explanation other than God's own activity. He had called them and they had responded. In that contemporary pagan world every convert was a miracle of grace, a person consecrated by the Spirit. Paul had no difficulty in believing in the sovereignty of God and does not hesitate to refer to it in his letters. When he speaks of the glory of the Lord Jesus Christ, he may have been contrasting it with the glory of Greece, which by comparison was infinitely inferior.

At this point in the letter he slips in another prayer. It is a prayer for comfort and steadiness in both word and deed. He is convinced that the best support these Thessalonians can have is the awareness that God loves them. His prayer for them is followed by a request for their prayers for him and his companions. He longs to see the triumph of the Gospel and he wants deliverance from the opposition of evil men. He is convinced that their prayers will count in this spiritual warfare. He knows he can rely on God's faithfulness, and he knows the Thessalonians can do the same. Another prayer follows — that the Lord would direct their hearts — which is a further request for love and steadfastness. As we listen in to Paul's conversation with his converts, we gain some notion of what he meant when he later referred to his "care of all the churches" (see 2 Cor. 11:28).

There were problems of discipline at Thessalonica in spite of Paul's general commendation of them. The main one, which was alluded to in the first letter, but seems now to have become more acute, was idleness. It was presumably connected with wrong views of the Lord's coming, a conviction that it was so near that working was not worthwhile. That some of the Thessalonians had so soon acted like this shows how difficult it was in those early days to explain the true nature of the Christian Gospel. But such literalism was not confined to that age for there have been others in the subsequent history of the Church who have fallen through the same delusion. In dealing with it Paul sets out some clear principles. He first appeals to his own example. His suggestion that the Thessalonians should have imitated the missionaries is not as egotistic as it sounds. In many ways Paul and his companions had to be living examples for new converts, who possessed no manuals of behavior. In the matter of idleness, Paul comes back to what he had already said, not only in his first epistle, but also in person while he was with them. "If anyone will not work, let him not eat." Paul himself acted upon this. He again says that he and the others worked night and day so as not to impose on anyone. He refused to do so, because he wanted to set an example. It must have been disappointing to discover that some had ignored that example. Idlers are most likely to be busybodies. When hands are slack, tongues will wag. Paul is downright practical with these people. Let them work quietly and earn their keep. The apostle never discusses in his letters the problem of labor relationships. He is concerned with spiritual issues. But his dictum about working to eat would not make a bad starting point in establishing good principles of industrial relationships.

The apostle, immersed as he is in the active work of the Gospel, ends on an authoritative note. He expects his readers to obey what he has written. He suggests that anyone who disobeys should be cold-shouldered, not to make him an enemy but to make him ashamed.

He closes with another prayer. "The Lord of peace give you peace." There is nothing that Paul desires more than the effusion of God's peace through the churches. He had begun by mentioning peace (2 Thess. 1:2) and he closes with the same theme.

12

From Corinth to Ephesus

72. *Before Gallio*

(Acts 18:12-17)

Luke is careful to include details of Roman officials, for it was part of his purpose to show the attitude of the State toward the emerging Christian Church. These details are also valuable in providing contacts between the history of the Church and contemporary secular history. Luke's reference to Gallio is especially important, because it helps us to date with fair accuracy the period of Paul's stay in Corinth.

This particular proconsul of the province of Achaia had apparently taken up his duties after the commencement of Paul's work in the city of Corinth. He came from a well-known family, being a brother of the philosopher Seneca, who held an influential position at the imperial court, and an uncle of the poet Lucan. He undertook his duties in Achaia during the reign of Claudius. An inscription at Delphi states when Gallio took office, and the most favored interpretation of the inscription is that the date was A.D. 51, but some prefer the midsummer of the following year.

Paul's Jewish opponents at Corinth decided that it was time to act against him and Gallio's arrival gave them an opportunity. Perhaps they had not acted before because they suspected the previous consul to be unsympathetic toward them. They hoped the new governor would support their charge against Paul, for they were anxious to put a stop to his activities. They were unanimous that Paul was a menace.

The site of the judgment seat or Bema still stands in the ruins of ancient Corinth. It is possible to some extent to capture the atmosphere in which Paul stood, an accused man, before the newly arrived governor. The Jews were probably intending to prove that Paul's preaching was illegal — that Christianity was not in fact a recognized religion in the eyes of the State. As far as religion goes, the Jews were favored by the Romans in being allowed considerable freedom. The Romans were at a loss to understand Judaism, because unlike other subject states, the Jews had no idol-deities to grace the Pantheon. Christianity would, of course, be in the same position, but whereas the Jews could claim religious freedom by law, the Christians could not. The Corinthian Jews hoped to make capital out of this.

The charge that Paul's activity was "contrary to the law" was notably ambiguous. The Jews intended it to be understood of Roman law, but Gallio took it to refer to the Jewish law. Paul was not even given the opportunity to defend himself. There was no need, for Gallio at once made up his mind. The Jews had not brought any charge which was indictable under Roman law. As far as the governor was concerned the Jewish charge was no more than a matter of words, which they should have been able to settle for themselves. In all probability he at once sized up their jealousy. He not only dismissed the case against Paul, but drove his accusers from the judgment area. It was the Jews' first public setback in their opposition to Paul. The official attitude meant that Paul could pursue his work in the province without fear of further opposition from the Jews.

In view of the governor's attitude some of the Corinthians who were standing around seized Sosthenes the synagogue leader and beat him. It may have been intended as a Gentile display to show approval of the snub which the governor had administered to the Jews, whom the Gentiles generally disliked. A Sosthenes is mentioned by Paul in his Corinthian correspondence (1 Cor. 1:1), and if this is the same man, he, like Crispis before him, later withdrew from the synagogue to join the Church. The display of anti-Semiticism in Gallio's presence left the governor unaffected. It is highly likely that he also had no love for the Jews and made no attempt to conceal his dislike.

73. *Journeyings*

(Acts 18:18-23)

After his appearance before Gallio, Paul stayed at Corinth for some time. Luke is vague about the length of time, for his "many days" could indicate a fairly extended period. But this is not important. Paul evidently decided to leave Corinth with the intention of going to Palestine. His farewell is left to our imagination, but there must have been many who regretted the departure of this strong-minded apostle to the Gentiles.

He was accompanied by Priscilla and Aquila. Luke does not mention Timothy, but it seems reasonable to suppose that he also accompanied the apostle. They proceeded to Cenchreae, the eastern port of Corinth, where according to Luke Paul cut his hair, for he was under a vow. This would presumably have been a temporary Nazarite vow which had to last at least thirty days. The cutting of the hair marked the completion of the period of the vow. It may be wondered what he was doing submitting to a Jewish vow, especially when he had argued so strongly over the matter of circumcision that believers were no longer under the law. But he seems to have adopted the principle that as a Jewish Christian he was not opposed to submitting himself to certain Jewish ritual, but as a missionary to the Gentiles he was adverse to imposing Jewish requirements on Gentiles.

After a sea trip from Cenchreae, Paul reached Ephesus, where he left Aquila and Priscilla. Since he himself was to spend considerable time there, it is probable their task was to prepare the way for his return. Paul witnessed in the synagogue and found a readiness on the part of the Jews to hear. Indeed they wanted him to stay, but he was intent on going to Palestine. He assured them he would come back if it was God's will. He was keenly sensitive to the will of God, and would not commit himself, although he must have had some tentative plans in mind.

Ephesus was the most important city in the province of Asia. Its greatest drawback was its harbor, which was constantly silting up. Nevertheless it was a city of great influence, and many cosmopolitan ideas found a fertile soil within its borders. It was to some extent the meeting place between east and west. It was the center of the worship of Artemis, whose temple was its special pride. It was allowed considerable freedom of government under the Romans. The praetorium, the residence of the Roman governor, was located there. Its affairs were in the hands of a Senate and Assembly, and its most influential official was its town clerk. Paul would at once recognize that this city was a strategic center for the planting of the Gospel.

Luke notes rather vaguely that when Paul landed at Caesarea he went up to greet the church, but there has been debate about which church he meant. It is generally agreed that Paul made a brief visit to Jerusalem. Nothing is said of the purpose of the visit. In Luke's mind it was clearly unimportant. Whether Paul saw any of the other apostles is not even mentioned. The historian's interest is to move rapidly on to the third itinerary of the apostle. He compresses journeys amounting to some 1,000 miles into a verse or two.

The visit to Antioch is interesting since it was there that Paul had given a report on the first journey and had been commissioned for the second. The narrative does not describe further reports and commissioning, for Luke has other material to cram into his story. He merely mentions in passing visits to Phrygia and Galatia as if he is anxious to get Paul back to Ephesus as soon as possible. We may reasonably conjecture that on return visits to churches previously established, Paul would have recounted to the brethren something of God's doings in Macedonia and Achaia.

PAUL'S THIRD MISSIONARY JOURNEY.

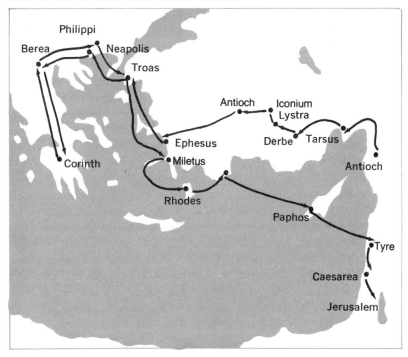

74. *Apollos*

(Acts 18:24-28)

One of the most interesting features of Acts is the occurrence here and there of brief allusions to colorful people. None is more interesting than Apollos. He had come to Ephesus from Alexandria and was apparently there when Priscilla and Aquila arrived. He was clearly a man of considerable ability. As an Alexandrian Jew he may have been fully acquainted with the currently popular teaching of the Hellenistic Jew, Philo. This famous Jewish teacher, who was domiciled in Alexandria, had died only a few years before Apollos arrived at Ephesus. His teaching, which has been preserved in his many books, was aimed to present Judaism in the best possible light for the Greek world. He sought therefore to show by means of allegorizing the Jewish Scriptures that the basic Greek ideas current in his day were to be traced to the Old Testament. His own philosophy was influenced by Plato. Indeed he had a wide acquaintance with Greek authors, showing knowledge of more than sixty of them in his writings. Although nothing certain can be deduced from Luke's bare statement that Apollos came from Alexandria, it is most likely that something of the teaching of this famous Jew would brush off on him.

What had impressed Luke was his eloquence, if this is a right rendering of Luke's phrase, which alternatively could be understood in the sense of a cultured man. He never describes Paul in this way nor any of the other Christian missionaries. Apollos may well have been accomplished in the art of speaking. He may even have received instruction in the rhetorical schools which were at that time prominent in the Greek speaking world, attendance at which would have been expected for a man of culture. But where Apollos would at once be distinguished from the products of the rhetorical schools was in the content of his teaching. As a Jew his mind was bent on the exposition of the Scriptures. One wonders whether in this he followed Philo's allegorical methods, which constantly sought for the underlying meaning as being the true sense. Thus the historical narratives became pegs on which to hang philosophical ideas. Such a method of exposition was in contrast to the literal method favored by the Jewish rabbis, and indeed the method reflected in the New Testament.

Apollos also had some knowledge of Christianity, although Luke does not give the source. He merely says that he was instructed in the way of the Lord. Presumably this was by way of oral teaching and is testimony to the rapidity with which Christian traditions had circulated as far as Alexandria. We are reminded that on the day of Pentecost some were present in Jerusalem from Egypt and there is no reason why some of these Egyptians might not have been converted and have returned home to teach others. This may explain why Apollos was aware only of John's baptism and had received only an inadequate account of Christian teaching.

What Apollos lacked in knowledge he made up for in enthusiasm. When Luke speaks of this he uses the same words as Paul uses in Romans 12:11, which may be rendered "aglow with the Spirit." It is not clear whether Luke means that Apollos was full of zeal or full of the Spirit, probably the former. He was keen to impart his knowledge of Jesus Christ and he did so as accurately as he knew. It must have been refreshing for Priscilla and Aquila to come across this man publicly teaching the Christian message in the synagogue. But they had not been with Paul for nearly two years without developing discernment to detect at once that something was missing. No doubt they invited Apollos into their home as they had invited Paul at Corinth. They gave him fuller instruction regarding the Christian faith. This was the pattern of early Christianity, where Christian homes regularly became centers of teaching. The cultured Apollos was prepared to listen to the expositions of the husband and wife, whom he recognized as more fully informed than himself. It was typical of the international character of Christianity that Italian Jews could instruct an Egyptian Jew in the way of the Lord on the cosmopolitan soil of an Asiatic city like Ephesus.

Luke does not say why Apollos decided to cross over to Achaia rather than stay at Ephesus. It is probable that Priscilla and Aquila had told him of the position at Corinth and had possibly encouraged him to minister in Greece, where his own background of culture would be invaluable. The idea also commended itself to the other Christians at Ephesus, who sent with Apollos a "letter of commendation." He was immediately a tower of strength to the Corinthian believers, especially in public debate with the Jews. His knowledge of the Scriptures stood him in good stead in showing that Jesus was the predicted Messiah. His skill of argument was powerful. He exercised a profound influence on the Corinthian church as is clear from the references to him in one of Paul's letters to that church (cf. 1 Cor. 1:12ff., 3:6, 4:9, 16:12). Although Paul had not yet had personal contact with him, he seems to have regarded him as his successor in the Corinthian church.

75. *Paul Begins Work at Ephesus*

(Acts 19:1-10)

Apollos had already begun his ministry at Corinth when Paul arrived at Ephesus. There were Christians in the city apart from his friends Priscilla and Aquila, as Luke had earlier noted. Luke mentions twelve other believers who knew only of John's baptism. Since Priscilla and Aquila had already instructed Apollos, who was in the same position, they had apparently not come across this group of twelve. Paul at once observes the same lack in them as Priscilla and Aquila had noted in Apollos. There may have been a school of John the Baptist's disciples, who had partially followed the Christian faith and were exerting influence in

The Marble Street of Ephesus.

Ephesus. They may have been converts from Apollos' first preaching. What was clearly lacking was the presence of the Holy Spirit. When Paul inquired about this, he discovered they had not even heard of the Spirit. They must have been poorly informed about the teaching of John, as well as the teaching of Jesus, for John had predicted that Jesus would baptize with the Spirit. Paul had to remind them of this.

Luke naturally condenses the exposition of the Christian faith which Paul gave. In fact he gives only the starting point. It was easy to lead them from John to Jesus, for John himself had been such a signpost. This brief description shows Paul's principle of beginning where he finds his hearers, the same principle which is illustrated by the Areopagus address at Athens.

These men, having heard Paul's exposition of the Christian faith, were again baptized, this time in the name of Jesus. They had presumably confessed their faith in Jesus Christ. Luke does not mention this, for he is more interested in their receiving the gift of the Holy Spirit, which occurred when Paul laid his hands upon them. The Samaritans received the Spirit in the same way when Peter's and John's hands were laid upon them. Yet at Pentecost no such action was needed. Nevertheless, in the present case there are similarities with the Pentecost event, for these Christians spoke with tongues and exercised the gift of prophecy. They greatly strengthened the existing group of Christians at Ephesus and formed a nucleus for Paul's extended ministry in the city.

As usual the apostle went first to the synagogue. Apollos had already preached there, but Luke does not say whether he did so after Priscilla and Aquila's instruction. Although Paul had the opportunity to expound the kingdom of God for three months, he at length ran into opposition. The Jews at Ephesus were at least more tolerant than their compatriots in some of the other places where Paul had worked. At Thessalonica, for instance, hostility had arisen after only three weeks.

By now Paul must have expected such opposition. He speaks in a letter written shortly after his ministry in this city of a veil over the minds of the Jews preventing them from believing. The apostle had learned by now that Jews could not stop at disbelief, but must press on to active opposition. If they considered Paul to be wrong, they regarded it as a duty to oppose him. Luke says the Ephesian Jews spoke evil of "the Way," a popular name for describing the Christian message. Paul had learned by experience that when Jewish opposition developed, his best course was to withdraw from the synagogue. He soon found a new place of meeting, comparable to Justus' house in Corinth, in the hall used by Tyrannus to deliver his public lectures. It was usual in Greek cities for such public lectures to be concluded before mid-morning, which meant that the hall would be available for other use after that. Presumably Paul worked at his trade in the early part of the day and then publicly taught and discussed in the latter part.

This procedure lasted for two years and since Luke says that all Asia heard the Word of the Lord during this period, it is probable that many came from various parts of the province to listen to Paul's expositions. It must have been during this period, for instance, that the churches at Colossae, Laodicea, and Hierapolis, all in the Lycus valley, were established, although Paul himself did not visit them. Men like Epaphras and Philemon, who were known to the apostle, possibly came under his influence in the hall of Tyrannus. Paul's strategy in choosing the main city of a province as his base of operations was a fruitful policy. Since there were seven churches in Asia (excluding Colossae and Hierapolis) when the apocalypse of John was written, it is highly probable that these were founded during the period of Paul's Ephesian ministry.

76.   *The Sons of Sceva*

(Acts 19:11-22)

During his ministry in the hall of Tyrannus, Paul was used by God to perform miracles. Just as people were healed through Peter's shadow falling upon them, so with Paul healing flowed through handkerchiefs and aprons which he had touched. The healing was not only from physical ailments, but also from demon possession. There appears at first sight to be a heightening of the miraculous in this kind of healing which has caused some to question the truth of Luke's account. But once the possibility of miracles is admitted, the means become immaterial. A woman was once healed as a result of merely touching the garment of Jesus. It was the exorcisms of evil spirits in the present case which caused the most stir.

In an age when there was widespread belief in the adverse

influence of spirits on almost all aspects of life, any method of exercising control of evil spirits was eagerly sought after. The Jews as well as the Christians practiced exorcism. In Ephesus there was a family group who claimed power to do this, the seven sons of Sceva, who was in fact a notable Jewish official, for Luke calls him a high priest, which would mean that he belonged to one of the high-priestly families. The term was often loosely used in this way. His sons, who had banded themselves together in a crusade against evil spirits, evidently thought that Paul's technique was better than theirs. They made the fatal mistake of supposing that they could borrow Paul's formula without knowing the secret of life in Christ. Christianity does not consist of incantations, as these men were painfully to discover. On their lips the name of Jesus did not work. They were not in harmony with the Spirit of Jesus. They were using His name as no more than a magic formula. The result was disastrous. The possessed man overpowered the lot of them, tore their garments, wounded them, and caused them to flee from the house. The dramatic effect of seven sorry looking figures fleeing through the streets is not difficult to imagine. It was a powerful demonstration that God would allow no counterfeit to His working. It is no wonder that fear fell on the residents of Ephesus. The extraordinary happenings through the Christian missionaries would be a talking point as news spread through the city. Through it all the name of Jesus was extolled.

The immediate outcome was a remarkable public demonstration by many of the Christians against their former magical practices. The cult of magical spells was widespread at that time, being nourished on the superstitious character of much pagan life. Among the Ephesian Christians there were some who practiced these arts, who had in fact been in the habit of deceiving others. These were in possession of books of incantations which would be used for this purpose. Samples of this kind of book have been preserved. From certain ancient literary sources, it seems that Ephesus was especially noted for these magical books. It is not surprising, therefore, that Christianity made some impact on this kind of cult. What is surprising is that Christians so soon recognized not only the complete incongruity of their former magical textbooks with their Christian faith, but the value of a public witness to their rejection of them. The books themselves were of considerable value and might have been sold, thus giving the Christians some compensation for the loss of their lucrative practices. But they rejected such a course and decided to burn the books in public. As magical books depended for their potency on their secret character, a public burning of them would testify in a powerful way to the worthlessness of the magical spells.

It took considerable moral courage for the one-time deceivers to stand by the bonfire in the presence of many who had been their dupes. It was calculated that the value of the books was in the region of 50,000 drachma, which in comparable modern currency would represent a very considerable sum of money. It is not surprising in view of such powerful testimony that the Word of the Lord was mightily triumphing.

At this point Luke slips in a little note about Paul's plans. He was led by the Spirit to propose a return visit to Macedonia and Achaia and then to proceed to Jerusalem. After that he would go to Rome. As Paul later shared his thoughts with Luke, his companion must have written the words down, for he records them verbatim. Luke was impressed by the steps which led Paul to Rome. Before going on to Macedonia himself, Paul sent on Timothy and Erastus. It seems to have been his practice to use his associates in this way. Timothy has already been used as an emissary of Paul to Macedonia, and Paul has confidence in sending him again on a similar errand. Erastus has not been heard of before and may have been an Ephesian who had joined the circle of Paul's immediate associates.

Old Corinth (at left) and New Corinth (on bay) as seen from Acro-Corinth.

13

Comments for Corinth

77. *A Letter to Corinth*

(1 Cor. 1 and 2)

It was while Paul was at Ephesus that he found it necessary to write to the church at Corinth the letter which is known as 1 Corinthians. It is almost certain in fact that it was not his first letter to that church which he had left about three years before. In 1 Corinthians he refers to having already written a previous letter (1 Cor. 5:9), in which he had urged the Christians not to associate with immoral men. Either Paul had not been sufficiently explicit or else the Corinthians had misconstrued his meaning. They thought he was urging them to have nothing to do with any immoral men, whereas he was thinking of Christians who were indulging in immorality. That a misunderstanding of such a character can arise shows the difficulty of communicating new Christian ideas in a community which has come from a pagan background. This was only one of the many reasons why Paul found it necessary to write again.

While he was ministering with great effect at Ephesus, disturbing reports reached him from Corinth. Among the travelers who were constantly passing through Ephesus were some in the employ of a person called Chloe. Whether she was a Christian is not known, but it is highly probable that she was, since her "people" made an effort to contact Paul at Ephesus. Chloe's people told Paul about the quarreling among the Christians, and probably also about a special case of immorality and a problem arising from lawsuits. All these issues are dealt with in the first part of his letter.

Sometime, either before he commenced the letter or while he was writing it, three men arrived at Ephesus who appear to have been deputed to seek Paul's advice about a number of practical matters. In fact they were probably the bearers of a letter which the Corinthians had sent to Paul and which he answers point by point with a formula which recurs through the letter, i.e., "now concerning" (see 7:1, 25; 8:1; 12:1; 16:1).

With many urgent problems to answer, Paul dictated a letter to his amanuensis, probably one of his associates. In this case it may have been Sosthenes, whom he links with himself in the opening greeting. Before coming to the first issue, Paul included his customary thanksgiving. He recognized that the Corinthians were not lacking in spiritual gifts. They had been greatly enriched in Christ, but the quarreling was a problem which had to be dealt with. The believers were splitting up into cliques under the supposed leadership of Paul, Apollos, and Peter. Some may even have belonged to a fourth party claiming only the authority of Christ, but this is doubtful.

Paul strongly challenges these divisions by asking whether Christ is divided. The idea of a Paul party horrifies him. Reading between the lines, it appears that since the arrival of Apollos at Corinth, some competition had arisen over him. His style was probably more cultured than Paul's, and some of the Corinthians had come to regard him as superior to Paul, while others remained loyal to the apostle. In doing this they went beyond loyalty and were using his name to establish a kind of personality cult. Once hero worship develops it soon spreads, and it is easy to see how Peter's name was brought into it. Neither Paul nor Apollos was an original apostle of Jesus. Peter must, therefore, be superior to both of them and in no time a Peter party had arisen. In some way the Corinthians must have had knowledge of Peter's part in early Christian developments.

Paul is less concerned with personalities than with principles. As he reflects on the Christian ministry, he is convinced its impact does not rest in man's wisdom. Indeed Christian preaching is either a stumbling block (as to Jews) or foolishness (as to Greeks), because it centers on a crucified Christ. Christians in fact go by a totally different kind of wisdom. Indeed Jesus Christ is their wisdom. Most of the believers were not among those whom the world counted wise or great. Paul may be thinking of the Corinthians' love of the pursuit of wisdom and the fact that they may have favored Apollos because of his greater display of culture. But he himself had made up his mind to stress nothing but Christ crucified. Even if his words had lacked the scintillation of rhetoric, his preaching had been with spiritual power, which was much more important. The tension which arose in his mind in preaching the Gospel in an intellectual environment can be sensed in this letter. He has come to recognize that the Christian looks at things from a different viewpoint. The very fact that the Lord of glory was crucified shows the incomprehensible nature of spiritual truth to the advocates of human wisdom.

Paul impresses on the Corinthians a deep doctrine of the Spirit. In fact what he tells them reveals much of his own spiritual life. He would sum up his own position as "taught of the Spirit," which implies some understanding of God's thoughts. Those of the Corinthians who possessed the Spirit would know at once what he was talking about. But those who did not would find his words unintelligible. He is concerned that the Corinthians should know that he and his associates, indeed all spiritual men, have the mind of Christ. Against this high doctrine, the Corinthians' schisms appear petty. Yet Paul has other things to say on this matter.

78. *Paul's Antidote to Schisms*

(1 Cor. 3 and 4)

The contrast between human wisdom and the teaching of the Spirit in the opening part of this letter leads Paul to make another contrast. He thinks of the Corinthians' wrangling as arising from what he calls "the flesh," a term he uses generally of life which is not governed by God but by human passions. He is not using it in the contemporary Greek sense of that which is essentially evil, although it becomes the tool of evil when it is opposed to God. When the Corinthians split into parties under human names, Paul sees this as an evidence of the "flesh."

These Corinthians should know that Paul and Apollos were in the same service of God, although doing different tasks. He uses an agricultural illustration to show that the planter and the irrigator are equal in "God's field." Not satisfied with that illustration, he turns to building and points out the importance of good foundations. In his own work in Corinth the foundation he laid was not himself but Christ. The kind of superstructure to be placed on such a foundation is of utmost importance. Some will stand, others will not. Paul adds a solemn note about the

Judgment Day. It is clear he was taking a serious view of the way things were developing at Corinth. He suggests another line of approach which shows the incongruity of splits. The Corinthians were God's temple, and that is a holy thing. Anyone causing ruin in the Church of Christ would be spoiling God's temple. If the Corinthians had stopped to reflect on Paul's imagery at this point they might have compared themselves with the temple of Apollos with its massive pillars which was situated in their city. To have split it into parts would have ruined the whole. Infinitely more would this be so of the temple of the holy God.

The root problem was a false approach to wisdom. Paul has already spoken of this, but he comes back to it. The thoughts of those who think themselves to be wise are futile. So there is no reason for anyone to boast in Paul, Apollos, or Cephas. Everything is centered in Christ, who is God's. Paul has involved himself in some deep theology over what was essentially a practical matter of unity, but it reminds us that the basis of true Christian unity is doctrinal. Christ is the key.

In his concluding comments on the Corinthians' tendency to split, Paul discusses his own relationship to them. What do they really consider him to be? He tells them what their view ought to be — servants of Christ and stewards of God's mysteries. The main thing about a steward is his trustworthiness. Paul shows that no one can really assess trustworthiness but God. If the Corinthians would only remember this they would not pronounce judgment, they would not in other words attempt to differentiate between Paul, Apollos, and Cephas. It is not their place to condemn or commend. Any commendation must come from God and will be given at the Lord's coming.

The apostle at this point makes a direct personal appeal to the readers. He asks whether anyone sees anything different in them. If Christians are no different from others, their testimony is nil. In any case boasting is utterly inadmissable since all their "understanding" is a gift. It has not come from their own minds. If they molded their lives according to Scripture they would soon see the futility of boasting.

So deeply does he feel about the situation that Paul resorts to a kind of irony. He contrasts their view of themselves, as royal, wise, strong, honored, with the real position of the apostles, which he describes as a "spectacle" to the world, to angels, and to men.

He is borrowing a metaphor from the arena, where great spectacles were regularly organized in which animals and men were subjected to indignities to entertain the masses. It is a striking contrast. The apostles, for the cause of Christ, had become the lowest regarded rank of society, while the Corinthians were trying to make themselves out to be the highest. He even calls his own position "refuse" and "off-scouring." He goes to the rubbish dump for his illustration. He could go no lower. Yet how telling it is when the spiritual meaning is grasped.

In spite of this, Paul was not the man to indulge in self-deprecation. He considers himself to be their "father" in Christ Jesus. He considers his example should be imitated. This was the reason why Timothy was sent to them, so as to recall to their minds his example. This was not egotism, but a basic necessity. The Corinthians must not get out of step with other churches. He will not, of course, leave it all to Timothy. He intends coming himself, but at the moment is tied up with the work in Ephesus. He debates in his mind whether he will need to come with a rod or with love, which shows the mixture of severity and gentleness in his nature. He has said enough at the moment, but when he comes he will judge for himself the effect that these arrogant people have been having.

79.   *Immorality and Lawsuits*

(1 Cor. 5 and 6)

Even against the background of immorality, for which Corinth was infamous, the case of incest which had occurred in the Corinthian church stood out as inexcusable. Even the pagans would not have tolerated a man living with his father's wife. What shocked Paul was the attitude of the Corinthian Christians about it. He calls them arrogant, as if they were tolerant of this sin in spite of their better judgment. Paul has no hesitation in saying that the man should be put out of the church. This first case of discipline being needed over a moral issue is therefore of great importance in that it set the pattern for future disciplinary action. Over such a matter Paul is sure that no place exists for tolerance. The Corinthians should have been deeply grieved.

Paul writes authoritatively. He tells them the conclusion to which he has come and expects them to follow it. What he writes is what he would say if he were present among them. He expresses his view vividly when he says that the man should be delivered to Satan. Some have seen this as a form of excommunication, but Paul probably means that when the man is out of fellowship with the Church he is in fellowship with the world and is therefore associating with those under the influence of the prince of this world. But the apostle regards this as only remedial. His desire is that the man's spirit might be saved.

In order to show the possible harmful effects of the Corinthians' tolerance, Paul uses the metaphor of leaven which affects the whole lump of dough. One case of immorality affects the whole Church. He could not have pressed home the urgent need for discipline in a more vivid way. Thinking of leaven leads him to think of Christ as our Passover Lamb, for the passover feast could only be eaten after all leaven had been purged from the household. He is implying that the Christian celebration of the Passover is impossible while the leaven of sin is present.

There is next a brief reference to the previous letter which the Corinthians have misunderstood. This happens to be relevant to the present matter of immorality, for Paul explains that he meant that Christians should not have fellowship with other Christians who were living immorally. They could not, of course, avoid all contact with immoral persons except by withdrawing altogether from the world, which was no part of the apostle's program.

The matter of lawsuits was a different issue, but similarly reflects the difficulties of an early Christian community adjusting itself to an entirely new way of life compared with their pagan environment. Before Paul and his associates had appeared on the scene, the Corinthians were in the habit of taking their disputes to the pagan judges. When they became Christians it had not occurred to them that was no longer necessary for disputes with fellow Christians. They had not paused to consider the adverse effect on pagans when Christians who claimed to love each other were bringing lawsuits against each other. It was not so much their preference for pagan judges, as their failure to consider an alternative and better course of action. Their newfound faith in Christ had not as yet permeated their human relationships. Paul challenges them. Do they prefer unrighteous people to judge them rather than a brother in Christ? Have they forgotten that they, the Christians, will be judges of the non-Christian world? The apostle makes a common sense suggestion — appoint a Christian umpire in any disputes — that is, if Christians will persist in having lawsuits.

But Paul puts a more spiritual point of view. Why not suffer wrong? The apostle races ahead of his pagan converts. He has already learned to suffer injustice for his faith, but they have not yet done so. In this his moral maturity stands high above the muddling attempt of the Corinthians to modify their living according to altogether revolutionary standards.

Probably the hardest thing for the Corinthians to learn was that Christianity involved a complete rejection of the old standards of morality, or rather the lack of them. The kingdom of God demanded a high moral standard. They had come from a pagan background, but the Christian Church offered no place for their pagan methods of living. When they became Christians they had been cleansed from the past through Jesus Christ. Commitment to Him meant making a clean break. The Corinthians are not the only ones who have found difficulty in recognizing the total challenge of the Christian faith. Wherever the Gospel draws men from adverse backgrounds the same problem arises. But nothing unrighteous from such backgrounds can be tolerated in the kingdom of God.

The apostle comes back to the question of immorality, no doubt a critical one for the Corinthians. But before doing so he enunciated a principle which has become a guiding rule for Christian ethics. "All things are lawful, but all things are not expedient." Many of the other matters to which Paul refers will illustrate his approach. But as far as immorality is concerned he raises this to a spiritual issue by maintaining that the Christian's body belongs to the Lord. In that case any form of prostitution is wholly alien. Immorality in a Christian is a sin against his own body as well as against the Holy Spirit, whose temple he is. Paul's teaching presents a searching challenge to modern sexual permissiveness. Christians who remember that they belong to God, purchased by Him at a price (a reference to redemption), will have no truck with a freedom which dishonors the Spirit.

80.   *Some Comments on Marriage*

(1 Cor. 7)

This is the first of the subjects about which the Corinthians inquired. The precise nature of the inquiry is not known, but again the problem of marriage must be viewed against the loose standards of the pagan world. At the other extreme there were some in the pagan world who admired asceticism. Some of these would have found their way into the Corinthian church. What was to be the official Christian view of marriage? Was it to be regarded as the norm or were Christians to aim for a celebate life? In answering these questions Paul shows clearly that he personally prefers celibacy, but he nowhere suggests that this should be normal practice for Christians.

He first discusses the general principle. He admits that the single state is good, but recognizes that this does not pronounce the married state as not also good. In an immoral environment like Corinth, marriage is to be regarded as the normal state. Faithfulness in marriage is commanded, as well as loyalty to marriage obligations. It is important to recognize that Paul is conceding this because he knows that he cannot command everyone to follow his own example of celibacy. Even the temporary breaking off of marriage relationships must only be by mutual consent. The balanced foresight of the apostle in a matter in which he does not consider himself to be an example for imitation is noteworthy.

Having stated the general principle, he moves on to specific cases. All unmarried people are urged to consider Paul's example, but to marry if they feel they must. Married people are to keep together, as the Lord had commanded. In this case he speaks with great authority since he is not expressing his own opinion. But when he deals with mixed marriages he can give only his own view. This distinction shows the importance attached by early Christians to the sayings of Jesus and the impossibility of words or ideas, even those of the apostles, being attributed to Him. Where a Christian is married to a pagan, all will depend on the attitude of the pagan. If the pagan is willing to continue the marriage, the Christian should concede. But if the pagan is unwilling, the Christian's guiding principle is to choose what makes for "peace," which seems to mean the absence of that frustration which results when partners are unable to live in harmony.

Contentment is a great theme with the apostle, who enunciates a general principle about this. Everyone should be content in the state in which God has called him. He applies this to circumcision or uncircumcision, slavery or freedom. He does not, of course, oppose a slave obtaining freedom if he has the opportunity, but his real point is that Christians of whatever state are on an equal footing. He once again reminds the Corinthians that they were bought with a price.

Another problem concerned virgins. Here again Paul advises that the unmarried state is advantageous, but that the married state is normal. He seems to suggest, however, that some kind of crisis was facing the Corinthians which would make it folly for Christians to enter into new obligations.

Paul is reflecting his own view when he points out that the unmarried are not so committed to "worldly affairs" as the married. He is thinking of the married man's responsibility toward his wife and family. He assures the Corinthians that he wants the best for them. Whatever happens he desires their devotion to the Lord. Undoubtedly he has himself proved the advantage of celibacy in his untiring devotion to the Lord's service.

Having again drawn attention to celibacy, Paul balances this with another example where marriage is preferable to abstinence. His words are somewhat obscure (see verse 36), but he seems to mean that a guardian of a virgin (whether a parent or some other) should not refuse to allow the virgin to marry if this is her desire. But with his strong bias toward celibacy he still feels that he must advise the guardian to maintain the virginity of the girl. There is a certain tension between what Paul considers to be good for himself and what he can see is practical for others.

In concluding his discussion on marriage, he advises widows also to remain unattached, although nothing prevents them from entering into a Christian marriage. In this case, as in most of the others, he stresses that what he is saying is his own judgment. It must be remembered in estimating his approach to marriage that his burning passion was the advancement of the kingdom and that in his own day freedom from marriage ties was undoubtedly a contributory factor in his remarkable missionary work. He was convinced that the Spirit of God had guided him in this but he would have been the first to acknowledge that celibacy was a gift which could not be treated as a norm.

81.   *Food Problems*

(1 Cor. 8)

The Corinthians were bothered about an essentially practical problem affecting food. The meat markets regularly offered for sale meat that had already been offered at a pagan shrine, of which there were many in Corinth. In fact it was impossible to buy any meat with the certainty that it had not been offered in pagan sacrifice. This posed a problem for Christians, who, having turned their backs on idolatry, had tender consciences about eating food which came from an idol shrine. The problem was local to Corinth and its people, but the principle involved in Paul's answer is universal in cases where sensitive consciences are likely to lead to misunderstanding. As usually happens in such cases, some were bothered and others were not, and those who were not tended to despise those who were. The apostle tackles this practical problem in a spiritual manner.

He begins by making a distinction between knowledge and love. Of the two, love is preferable because it is more edifying. Those who were not bothered were the people who claimed to know. They knew that since the idols were "nothings" there was no need to worry about food which had been offered to them. But mere knowledge is never enough. Those who were bothered had not as yet arrived at such an advanced understanding of idols. They still thought them to be "something." The most important thing was for love to be maintained between the two opposing groups.

Paul gives a brief but penetrating exposition of the Christian approach to idols. His view that idols have no real existence was based on a belief in the uniqueness of God. If there is only one God, idols can be dismissed. However many claims there are to alternative gods, Christians, like Jews, believe in the unity of God, in fact in monotheism. Christianity dealt a death blow to polytheism by declaring the multitudinous gods as mere nothings. This leads Paul to make a statement which shows his high view of Christ. It is God from whom all things have come and for whom we exist, but it is also Jesus Christ through whom are all things and through whom we exist. Not only is Christ the agent of creation, but also the source of the new creation of believers. It is not difficult to think of the Corinthians' reactions as they listened to Paul's words being read aloud to them. The weaker brethren with the tender consciences would perhaps have rethought their position. The exalted Christ was so infinitely superior to their former "idols" that it would be folly for anyone to imagine there was anything in them.

Nevertheless Paul shows great sensitivity in acknowledging

that not everyone sees things in this way. The most enlightened minds are those who can make allowances for those who are not so enlightened. Smaller minds would adopt a critical attitude and condemn the unenlightened. But Paul was not guilty of doing that. He recognized that new Christians from pagan backgrounds may still think in terms of "idols" simply because they had always thought that way. In the same way, many converts to Christianity from wholly non-Christian environments have difficulty in discarding their previous non-Christian modes of thinking. There are many counterparts to the Corinthians' situation in modern life. Their "food" problem has become, for instance, the more complex and subtle problems of industrial ethics — for example, is money which has come from questionable sources "clean"? The apostle establishes the principle that the type of food itself is unimportant and will do nothing to commend a person to God. It is the attitude that counts.

The further principle that liberty must never become a stumbling-block to the weak has had deep repercussions. The Christian, in Paul's view, has a social responsibility even in the exercise of newfound liberty. This social awareness acts as a break on many otherwise perfectly legitimate pursuits. In the Corinthians' situation a question of social etiquette could be cited to illustrate the interplay between liberty and restraint. When a Christian received an invitation to a social function at an idol temple, which must have been a frequent occurrence, for the temples were centers of social fellowship in a pagan city like Corinth, what was he to do? Was he to cut himself off from all social fellowship? The people who "knew," the enlightened, said no, for idols are nothing. But supposing an unenlightened Christian is spurred on to follow this example and yet does so with a troubled conscience, has not the enlightened Christian done harm to the unenlightened? At least this is Paul's argument. To harm another Christian is to sin against Christ, who died for that man. Paul is clear as to his own course of action. He would rather abstain than cause offense to a fellow Christian.

The principle is of fundamental importance. But a further question arises. Does this mean that the mature must always bow to the immature, that the weak in fact dictate the actions of the strong? This could never be so in all issues. But love is always more important than rights. In the present case the strong would lose nothing essential in abstaining for the sake of the weak, although their pleasures would no doubt be curtailed. But Paul's principle gives no charter for sensitive consciences to cling to outworn taboos, which long ago should have been discarded. The principle of love affects the weak as much as the strong.

82. *Christian Rewards*

(1 Cor. 9)

Spiritually minded as he is, Paul does not hesitate to speak of money matters. It was a subject which he felt he should mention to the Corinthians. The reason is not quite clear, but we may be grateful to the apostle for giving us the benefit of his mature thinking on this subject, for it is a recurring problem.

First he reminds them of his own position as an apostle. He refers to his experience when he saw the Lord. He regarded the Corinthians as proof of his apostolic office, for they had come to a knowledge of God through his preaching. They were certainly indebted to him. This leads him to discuss his "right." Some apostles were accompanied by wives and were supported by the churches. Paul and Barnabas refused such support, although Paul wants to make it clear that he considers himself entitled to receive support, as any soldier would expect pay, or vineyard worker or shepherd some reward for their work. He is implying that those in the service of God should not expect less than those in other occupations.

He backs up his argument by quoting from the Mosaic law the requirement for oxen, and shows that what goes for oxen must much more hold for men. Everyone engaged in agriculture expects some share of the proceeds. Paul boldly argues that those who have sown spiritual good may expect some material advantage. This principle of his has all too often been ignored by those who have accepted as basic the fact that Christian work must be underpaid compared with similar work elsewhere.

Paul not only supports his argument from Scripture but also from the words of the Lord Himself. He is not arguing for material aid to be given, but only for the recognition that he had the "right" to expect it. It would seem that the Corinthians were being mean in their approach to those who were serving them in the Gospel. Those who serve in temples live by the temples. This was equally true in paganism as in Judaism. Why should the service of Christ be any different? The apostle cites the Lord as advocating that those who proclaim the Gospel should live by it. He was probably thinking of what Jesus had said in His mission charges (see Matt. 10:10, Luke 10:7, 8). It is one of the few cases where he appeals to a saying of Jesus in support of a point of view.

His arguments so far might give the Corinthians the idea that he is appealing for material help, but he hastens to deny this, using the rather strange argument that if they assisted him he would no longer be able to boast that he had supported himself. He could certainly not boast about the Gospel. He had a divine compulsion to preach. This self-confession explains much. It explains why he was prepared to endure constant hardships for the sake of the Gospel. It explains why he was prepared to waive his rights for support. It was sufficient reward to be able to discharge his commission without being a burden to anybody.

The Corinthians might have thought that the apostle was being rather introspective at this point. But we may be glad that he was, for he gives some priceless comments on the approach he adopts in his missionary work; priceless, not only because of their value in assessing the apostle, but also because the apostle's approach provides a basic example for all servants of Christ. It may be summed up in his own words — "I have become all things to all men." The purpose of this policy is "that I might by all means save some."

The outworking of a principle like this was bound to present difficulties, but it shows the great adaptability of the man. Whether he was dealing with slaves, Jews, Gentiles, or weak men, he met them on their own level. It takes a man of great versatility to switch roles like this. For a man who had never been a slave to use the same wavelength as a slave was no mean task, nor for a converted Jew to get alongside Gentiles. But Paul saw the necessity of this principle. Had all Christian preachers grasped the same principle the Christian Church would have developed in a very different form from that which exists today. There are few who can leap over the boundaries of social classes, of national interests, of intellectual differences, even of age ranges. Adaptability is a rare gift which found one of its rarest exponents in the apostle Paul.

There is one other self-revelation which he makes. That is his attitude toward self-discipline. He thinks of the athlete preparing himself for a perishable prize. The illustration, as Paul knew well, would have special point for the Corinthians since the Isthmian Games were regularly held there and every young Corinthian would dream of athletic glory for himself or for his friends. The competitors would allow nothing to stand between them and success. That was the kind of self-discipline which Paul coveted for himself in the cause of the Gospel. He did not relish being like an athlete who had been disqualified because he had not subjected himself to a stringent enough discipline. Throughout all the rigorousness of his Christian service, the apostle was content with the assurance that his reward would be imperishable.

83. *Problems of Worship and Fellowship*

(1 Cor. 10)

For some reason Paul comes back to the subject of idolatry. He wants to dispose of wrong worship before he deals with right worship. There were probably some Corinthians who had not made a clean break with the past. They were clinging to the old idolatry while at the same time professing to worship God through Jesus Christ. It was an understandable mistake on their part. It was easier to compromise than to appear too antagonistic to the old ways. But Paul set about exposing the error of this approach. He begins by giving the Corinthians a history lesson. His Gentile readers in Corinth were probably not well acquainted with Old Testament history, but Paul nevertheless appeals to its testimony.

He reminds them that the history of Israel was supernatural. In fact he allegorizes the history so as to make the rock which features in the wilderness wanderings into a type of Christ. His reason for mentioning the events of the Exodus was to point out that God was displeased with most of them and this gives him an opportunity to warn the Corinthians against idolatry and immorality, both of which were special sins of Israel. The wilderness wanderings contained many examples of God's judgment upon His people. These should make even the best of the Corinthians alert so as not to fall to temptation in a similar way. At this Paul slips in a gem of encouragement. No one can avoid temptations, but God always provides an escape route. It is with this confidence that Paul can encourage the Christians of Corinth, surrounded as they were with pressing temptations.

With regard to the particular temptation to worship idols, Paul appeals to them as reasonable men. They should be able to tell the difference between the Christian communion service and the ritual of an idol shrine. In the former the emphasis is on unity — everyone drinks the same cup and eats the same bread. Everyone therefore belongs to the same body. In Christian communion any idea other than oneness is unthinkable. But in heathen shrines it was very different. Admittedly Christians who participated at such shrines treated the idols as "nothings," but the pagans certainly had a different view. Paul sees the work of demons behind this cult of "nothings." It should have been clear to the Corinthians that the Lord's feast and demons' feasts do not agree. One or the other has to go. Idolatry and all its associations must be exiled as far as Christians are concerned.

This leads Paul to return to the matter of the meat market. He considered further exposition to be desirable, especially in view of his dictum already mentioned (1 Cor. 6:12), that all things are lawful, but not all are helpful. This was a strong conviction with him; otherwise he would not have repeated it. But this postscript brings to light some further valuable advice. The Christian Corinthians were to be persons seeking the good of others rather than their own. This stress on others first, oneself last, so characteristic of the teaching of Jesus, would have made the Christians stick out prominently in Corinth. That principle was certainly not one of the cardinal rules of paganism, neither in its ancient nor in its modern form.

The principle was applicable in the meat market. Paul regarded all the meat as originally from God, whether or not it had any idol associations. There was no need to ask any questions for conscience's sake. But if anyone pointed out that the meat had been offered to idols, the same principle as before would apply — do not eat if another man's conscience would be offended. Christians were always to be alert to the well-being of others.

The apostle's practical advice to the Corinthians should have helped them in other problems. "Do all to the glory of God." What did he mean? If the weaker brethren were offended, that would clearly not be to God's glory. If idols were worshiped, that would not glorify Him. If immorality was indulged in, His name would not be glorified. The glory of God is seen in the saving of souls. Moreover the glory is seen in Christ. Paul calls on the Corinthians to imitate his principle of imitating Christ. It makes a simple but intensely challenging ethic.

84. *Procedure for Public Worship*

(1 Cor. 11)

It is inevitable that groups of Christian people in different environments will have different problems when they come to worship. There were two main problems at Corinth — the position of women and the conduct of the Lord's supper. They belonged to some extent to the local situation, but are still of interest, both for the insight they give into aspects of early Christianity and more especially for the principles which Paul outlines in dealing with them.

The problem of the women concerns a seemingly unimportant detail like headgear. The ancient world would have appreciated the importance more than we do. It was not customary for women to appear in public with heads uncovered. But Christianity had brought liberation to women and there were Corinthian women who were keen to demonstrate their emancipation. They formed a kind of avant garde. But they were jumping ahead too fast. In their enthusiasm for emancipation they were, according to Paul, dishonoring their heads. He compares a veilless woman with a shaven woman, which in those days in Corinth would have been a sign of shame. Yet he thinks that a man praying with covered head equally dishonors his head, which represents a complete turn around for this former Jew, for Jewish men regularly covered their heads for prayer. Paul's argument may not seem valid for western minds, but his principle is that the head-covering represents a subjection to authority. He supports his distinction between men and women with two arguments. One is the order of creation. Man came before woman, which according to Paul's interpretation means that woman was created for man. Nevertheless this is modified to the extent that man has ever since been born of woman. In Paul's time it was conventional for men to wear their hair shorter than women and he brings this as an additional point in favor of women wearing veils. He assures his readers that the advice he is giving reflects the practice of other churches.

Paul's most important consideration in this discussion on women's head covering was to maintain order in public worship. Any action which caused dissension or disorder or misrepresentation should be avoided. The true emancipation of women did not depend on dispensing with an external sign like a veil, but was a matter of the heart. Even if current conventions were to be observed, here was a spiritual equality which was much deeper and more lasting.

Disorders had specially arisen over the Lord's supper. The trouble was not so much the Lord's supper itself as the preceding meal, which was customary in Corinth. This practice may have been more widespread. There is evidence of it later on in Church history under the name of *agape* or love feast. No doubt the idea was acceptable at Corinth, but the working out of it was not. To begin with, its aim was to provide opportunities for fellowship, but the attitude of the different factions excluded this in all but name. There was an absence of the essential quality of love. Many were not concerned whether their Christian brethren had enough to eat. Some were getting drunk through excess of wine. The whole purpose of the love feast had degenerated. The Corinthians had better eat their meal at home and then come together for the Lord's supper. It would avoid stressing the difference between the "haves" and "have-nots." Perhaps Paul was hoping to shame the "haves" into inviting the "have-nots" into their own homes for a meal. But even if this did not commend itself, he is certainly against the humiliation which was happening in public Christian assemblies.

The other problem was the need for a worthy approach to the Lord's supper itself. The Corinthians must have known the details, but Paul sees the need to repeat them. There is some question whether he means to imply that he received the details directly or indirectly from the Lord. Most scholars think that he means that others had passed on to him information which he recognized as coming to him with the Lord's authority, but the possibility of his having received the details by a special revelation cannot be ruled out. What is important is Paul's conviction that the observance of the supper must follow the Lord's own pattern. In the words of institution as he gives them there are differences from the wording in the Synoptic gospels, but the essential meaning is the same. The feast was intended as a memorial and both bread and wine centered in the death of Christ. From Paul's reference to this service it is clear that it formed the central feature of Christian worship at Corinth and there is no reason to suppose that any different procedure was found elsewhere.

What concerns the apostle is more the worshiper's attitude of mind than the form of wording. Self-examination is essential, for without it there is danger of bringing the whole service into disrepute. Paul has a high view of this service. He even considers that a wrong attitude toward it might lead to judgment. Self-examination is preferable to submitting to such judgment. What is essential is order. When the Corinthians listened to his directions being read aloud to them, some of them must have had real qualms of conscience. But the Lord's supper at Corinth could never have been the same again. There must surely have been a greater sense of reverence, even of solemnity, as the words were repeated, "Do this in remembrance of Me."

85. *Spiritual Gifts*

(1 Cor. 12 and 13)

One of the main features of Christianity at Corinth was the importance attached to spiritual gifts. This might at first suggest a spiritually minded church, but problems had arisen. They were failing to maintain the right attitude toward the possession of the gifts. What were intended to be instruments of spiritual effectiveness had become the cause of divisions among them. Paul makes some incisive comments on this state of affairs.

The first thing he wants to make clear is that all Christians possess the Spirit, for no one can say "Jesus is Lord" except by the Spirit. Every one of the Corinthians, coming from a pagan background, had known the transforming power of the Spirit. This must mean that they were all equally indebted to the Spirit.

The problem among them was the claim that some gifts were superior to others, particularly the gift of tongues. The principle that Paul adopts is to stress the unity of the Spirit. With far-sighted wisdom he points to the Spirit's sovereignty in apportioning spiritual gifts as he chooses. If to one is given wisdom and to another the power to work miracles, neither can claim superiority over the other. If the Corinthians were to bear in mind that the Spirit inspires all the gifts, there would be no danger of spiritual pride in the possession of any one gift. Paul sees all the gifts as designed for the common good. As in the earlier part of his letter he is insistent that no Christian can live for himself. He belongs to a group lived in by the same Spirit.

This idea leads Paul to introduce one of his famous metaphors — the body. Being a keen observer of the world around him, he is quick to seize apt illustrations to illuminate his point. Modern medicine has more understanding of the marvelous mechanisms of the human body than the ancients. But Paul speaks with great effect about the obvious harmonies which must exist if the body is to function correctly. By means of some telling rhetorical questions and some imaginary conversations between parts of the body, he shows that each part of the body, feet, hands, eyes, head, and the lesser parts is essential to the others. The fact that he goes into some detail shows how fearful he is that the Corinthians were losing sight of what should have been obvious. The fundamental principle that all the members suffer when one member suffers would avoid all disharmony over spiritual gifts. Each should rejoice in the gifts given to others.

It should have been equally obvious that all cannot perform the same function. God Himself makes the appointments in His Church. Although Paul sets out some of these appointments in a specific order, beginning with apostles, he is doing so to show that all are God's appointments, not to set out a hierarchy.

At this point in his letter the apostle inserts what has been described as an exquisite hymn of love. It is important to note that this is a continuation of the previous discussion and not a digression. It should not be considered apart from its context. It is Paul's "more excellent way," that is, more excellent than any sense of superiority over the possession of spiritual gifts. He shows with unmistakable clarity the uselessness of gifts and achievements when divorced from love. Even giants of spiritual activity can be reduced to mere "nothings" if bereft of love. Paul's statements become disturbingly challenging.

When he proceeds to describe what love is like, his exposition becomes a classic, almost poetic in its conciseness and almost despairing in its demands. The qualities of love may be summed up as kindness, as putting others before oneself, as being tolerant and ready to think the best of others. As the Corinthians listened to these syllables of love they could not fail to apply them to their present situation. Were any arrogant about the gifts they possessed? Paul's poem shows that arrogance does not belong to love. Were any resentful over the gifts they did not possess? Paul shows that resentment and love do not go together. The words he wrote to the Corinthians are of such universal relevance that many, in all subsequent ages, have been saved from the pitfalls of pride and envy through following his more excellent way.

And what would the Corinthians have thought about the apostle's reference to childish things? Was he really suggesting that prophecy, tongues, and knowledge were childish things out of which the mature man grows? He could not have meant that, but he wants them to know the superiority of love over any of these gifts. After all, love will outlast them all. Moreover there will come a time when men will be in the presence of God, and prophecy, tongues, and knowledge will be wholly unnecessary. But not so with love. Love is an essential attribute of God and those who belong to Him share His love. It is no wonder that Paul views love as greater than faith or hope.

We must be profoundly grateful for this hymn of love. It enables us to approach problems which cause differences among Christians with the same approach as God Himself. And one of the most pressing of such problems for the Corinthians was the gift of tongues, with which Paul deals more specifically in the next part of his letter.

86. *The Gift of Tongues*

(1 Cor. 14)

Because this gift was apparently leading to confusion among the Corinthians, Paul singles it out for special treatment. Following his hymn of love, it is significant that he continues his discussion with the double exhortation — "Make love your aim and desire spiritual gifts." He was dispelling the idea that his emphasis on love meant the exclusion of all interest in gifts. When he compares tongues with prophecy, he has no hesitation in preferring the latter on the grounds that it contributes to the building up of the Church. Tongues could only do this when the message was interpreted. Paul is not wanting to make the passing on of information the sole criterion, but is applying his principle of love. Unintelligible utterance is not an apt medium for the communication of love, whatever value it may have for the person who utters it. Love wants to build up others in the faith. It never desires them to be confused.

A vivid illustration springs to Paul's mind, that of out of tune musical instruments blurring the notes. Such instruments can never communicate a musical composition as it should be heard.

In fact, their disharmonies would so grate on the hearers as to put them against the music altogether. Paul unhesitatingly applies his illustration — "so with yourselves." Unknown tongues are as damaging as a bugle whose message is so unintelligible that no one prepares for the battle. In its spiritual conflicts it is essential for the Church's teaching to be clearly understood for men to respond to its challenge.

Paul's point is that within the body of the Church tongues must be accompanied by interpretation, because only then are they intelligible. There is a difference between spirit and mind. What goes on in the spirit is a matter between a man and God, but when he is communicating in public his mind must be active. An appreciation of this distinction would have avoided much misunderstanding over the gift of tongues. Paul admits that he himself possesses the gift, but makes the astonishing statement that five words with intelligence are worth more than 10,000 in a tongue. Those Corinthians who were prizing their gift of tongues would be in no doubt about Paul's comparative estimate of this gift.

There are distinct limitations in the usefulness of tongues. Paul suggests that they may be of some value to unbelievers who hear them, presumably because their unintelligible character would speak to them of God's judgment, as the Israelites of old were overthrown by people of a strange tongue (the Assyrians). Whether the Corinthians got the point is difficult to say, but they could not have failed to appreciate the superiority of prophecy over tongues as a means of communicating to the unbeliever. The apostle is in no doubt that church assemblies should be so conducted that the procedure would convey something to the uninitiated. It is no part of the Christian mission to make the church look like a madhouse.

Paul has a guiding principle for Christian worship. It is simple and to the point — "Let everything be done for building up." This has universal relevance. It is essentially positive. It will make even unbelievers recognize God's presence among the Christians. From what Paul says it would seem that worship at Corinth was a singularly disorderly affair with several people taking part at one time, with the result that no one could hear anything. No wonder Paul compares such procedure with a madhouse. It is fundamental to good order that only one should take part at one time, although Paul is not against two or three participating at once, whether it be tongues or prophecy. But again he stresses the need for an interpreter. There is no doubt in Paul's mind that confusion is wrong for it is alien to the nature of God. The whole message of Christianity is God's communication with man and anything which obscures that message or makes it unintelligible cannot have His support.

Thinking of orderliness Paul mentions another cause of confusion. Women at Corinth were apparently asserting their newfound emancipation in Christ in a manner which was causing problems in the church. To avoid this the apostle counsels silence for them. This embargo he supports by an appeal to the law, presumably Genesis 3:16. The Corinthians were inclined to think they could go their own way, ignoring the practice of other churches, so much so that Paul ironically asks them whether Christianity originated with them. He feels strongly that there should be some uniformity among the churches in this matter.

He feels so strongly that he does not hesitate to command. So sure is he that he is interpreting aright the mind of God that he is confident that this will be acknowledged by all spiritually minded people. It is clear from the sequel in 2 Corinthians that there were some who took a dim view of this. Who does Paul think he is? Why should they take orders from him? Opposition was to build up against him before another letter was written. Was Paul justified in using an authoritative approach? He was surely justified when insisting on decency and order. Only lovers of confusion would deny him that right. He was enunciating a principle which was to become basic in the running of every community whose affairs are dominated by a desire to follow the divine pattern. There is no forbidding of tongues but there is a more earnest entreaty for prophecy.

87. *Thoughts on the Resurrection*

(1 Cor. 15)

In this letter Paul has already touched on a wide variety of practical subjects. It is therefore unexpected to find him suddenly dealing with a doctrinal issue. Whether the Corinthians had consulted him about the subject or whether he had heard of their confusion concerning it cannot be decided for certain. But he is undoubtedly countering objections already made by some Corinthians, especially some who were denying the resurrection altogether.

He first gives some historical evidences about the Gospel which he had preached among them, particularly about the resurrection. The resurrection appearances are considered to be important because of their confirmation of Christ's resurrection as a historical fact. In his list Paul includes the appearance of the risen Christ to him "as to one untimely born." The importance of this rests in the fact that witness of the resurrection was a requirement for the apostolic office and Paul claims to be an apostle, even though he calls himself the least of the apostles. He wants the Corinthians to know that what he had preached was supported by all the apostles.

Those denying the resurrection were clearly going contrary to Paul's preaching. If they were right then Paul was wasting his time preaching. His Gospel of forgiveness through Christ would collapse if resurrection from the dead were impossible. The Corinthians would still be in their sins in a hopeless condition. This shows how central Paul sees the resurrection to be in his Gospel.

It is at this point in his argument that Paul becomes more theological. He talks of Christ's resurrection as the first fruits, a kind of guarantee that other resurrections would follow (that of believers). It is as certain that all "in Christ" (Paul's special word for Christian believers) will live, as that all "in Adam" (those descended from Adam) die. Then Paul makes an astonishing statement about Christ, about His delivering the kingdom to God after vanquishing death. When the time comes for this God will be absolute, for the Son Himself will be subject to Him. This does not mean that Jesus Christ is inferior to the Father in His nature, but only in submission to God in His mission.

Paul leaves his profound statements about Christ as abruptly as he introduced them. He turns his attention to the Christian. Certain experiences of a practical nature assume the reality of resurrection, such as certain baptismal rites (what baptism on behalf of the dead means is not clear) and constant missionary hazards. These would be unintelligible if the dead are not raised. None but a fool would risk hazards for sweet nothings. Paul mentions fighting with beasts at Ephesus, but his meaning has led to divided opinion among scholars. Some take it literally and suppose that Paul was actually arrested and exposed to the arena at Ephesus. There was certainly an arena there and Paul must often have seen it during his ministry. But how did he escape unharmed? Others prefer to take the words metaphorically and see the "beasts" as those who oppose the Gospel. Whichever it is it reflects the fact that Paul's work at Ephesus had not gone unopposed. If he can say "I die daily," opposition must have been quite hot for him in his mission work.

The apostle then turns to another problem — what kind of body do the dead have? He illustrates his answer from nature — from cereals, from animals, from men, and from astronomical bodies. He maintains that the "body" of each is perfectly adapted by God for its purpose. Their glory differs from body to body, but each has its own as God made it.

The resurrection body will be specially adapted for its spiritual function. It will have little connection with the physical body. Indeed Paul vividly contrasts the two. This reminds him again of the contrast between Adam and Christ. Adam lived, but Christ gives life. Adam's origin was dust, whereas Christ came from heaven. Christian believers are between the two, because although descended from Adam they also share the nature of Christ. Those who will inherit the kingdom will be those who were "perishable," but who have now become "imperishable" in Christ. The Corinthians who were denying the resurrection would be in no doubt, having reached this stage in Paul's letter, that their view would make nonsense of his theology. If his lofty arguments are right, the Corinthian objectors were not only tragically wrong, but were missing a most dynamic source of Christian optimism.

The apostle closes this part of his epistle in an unforgetable way. He peers down the future to the end of time. He has no idea how far ahead it is. His concern is to describe the triumphs in store. Transformation, trumpet sound, and thrill of victory all come vividly to mind. Paul sees mortals putting on immortality like people changing their garments. At that moment death is swallowed up and its sting torn from the grave. It all happens through Jesus Christ. It is a magnificent assertion of Christian confidence in the final overthrow of evil. Did the Corinthians see deeper into the soul of Paul on hearing this glorious theme? Did they perhaps understand more clearly why Paul was prepared to "die daily" for the sake of the Gospel? When he encouraged them to stand fast and abound in the Lord's work, they could not deny that Paul was himself the most shining example of his own words.

88. *Future Plans*

(1 Cor. 16)

As the apostle marks off the matters raised by the Corinthians he comes to the last point — the Jerusalem Appeal Fund. It was not the first Christian fund of this sort, for the church at Antioch had already organized its own Famine Relief scheme. There were many Jews at Antioch who had a special concern for their fellow Jewish Christians. Paul's suggestion, however, is for a relief scheme which would demonstrate Gentile concern for the needy Judaean Christians and would be a practical demonstration of Jewish-Gentile solidarity in Christ. It is not surprising that an idea so revolutionary in concept ran into difficulties. The Galatian churches had already been asked to cooperate, and the Corinthians were now to be included. They were apparently not too enthusiastic, if 2 Corinthians 8 is any indication of their initial reaction. They clearly needed some practical advice on the method of collection and Paul suggests regular weekly contributions. He wants the whole scheme to be widely representative and for this reason suggests that the Corinthians should appoint delegates when the time came to convey the contributions to Jerusalem. As 2 Corinthians shows there was to be considerable tardiness in the response to these suggestions.

When Paul wrote this letter, it was probably about Easter time and his present plans were to stay in Ephesus until Pentecost and then proceed to Corinth via Macedonia. By the time he reached Corinth it would be near winter time, when traveling was difficult owing to the closing down of sea traffic, and his thought was to spend the winter in Corinth. It is important to note that in all these plans Paul makes one proviso — if the Lord permits. When he was obliged to alter his plans, some of the Corinthians overlooked the proviso, for they criticized him for being fickle. For the moment he had ample opportunities in Ephesus. There was opposition, but he is not deterred by that. The significant factor was not the presence of adversaries, but the continued existence of an open door.

He adds brief notes about a number of people, all of whom had had some contact with the Corinthian Christians. Timothy was about to pay them another visit, possibly as bearer of the letter. He seems to have been of a rather timid disposition from other references to him in Paul's letters. The Corinthians needed a special request not to despise him. Apollos was a very different character. In spite of entreaties from Paul he resolutely refused to return to Corinth, because he did not believe it to be God's will. There is no knowing his whereabouts at this time. He may possibly have been at Ephesus with Paul. Paul next mentions Stephanus and his household, whom the Corinthians would know well, for Stephenus had come with Fortunatus and Achaicus, presumably bringing the letter referred to by Paul (7:1). This man's household had already established a reputation for devoted service to others. Such men as these were worthy leaders of the Corinthian community.

Aquila and Priscilla were well known at Corinth, for they had been Paul's hosts from the early days of his mission in the city. They were now in Ephesus where a church was meeting in their house. It was worth observing that the Corinthians had not formed an Aquila party as they had done for his illustrious pupil. This husband and wife team sent hearty greetings to the Corinthians. Indeed Paul includes greetings from all the Asian churches.

At the end of this rather long letter, as was his custom, Paul took the quill pen to write his own special greeting. He then added the word Maranatha, a kind of code word meaning, "Our Lord, come!" It was one of the ways in which the early Christians reminded each other of the Lord's return.

14

Back to Europe With More Advice for Corinth

89. Riot at Ephesus
(Acts 19:23-41)

It could not have been long after Paul sent Timothy with his letter to the Corinthians that a nasty situation arose at Ephesus. The Christians were still known as "The Way," a suggestive title for those who followed Jesus, who had used the expression of Himself (cf. John 14:6, Acts 9:2). Opposition arose, as has often happened since, from those whose business interests were being adversely affected by the Gospel. In this case the craftsmen were in protest. Linked with the worship of the goddess Artemis, which dominated the city, was the lucrative trade of providing for worshipers small silver shrines incorporating an image of the goddess. This Ephesian Artemis was the mother-goddess of Asia Minor and the center of a powerful cult. The silversmiths' guild was led it seems by Demetrius, for it was he who organized the protest. His motive was unashamedly selfish. His opposition to Paul and his Gospel was wholly based on the damage the Gospel was doing to his trade and therefore to his wealth. It was the same motive which prompted the antagonism of the owners of the Philippian slave girl, whom the Gospel had delivered from spiritual bondage. It similarly provided the main thrust of the opposition of later slave owners against the abolition of the slave trade, to quote a more modern example.

It is at least a credit to Demetrius that he did not underestimate the power of the Gospel to undermine the powerful cult of Artemis. Had there been less vested interests about the man, he might have marveled at the amazing transformations which the Gospel could bring about. But dwindling profits made him blind to the remarkable character of the phenomenon. The guild of silversmiths in Ephesus had other outlets throughout Asia, but were alarmed because all Asia had been hearing the Gospel. No other power was capable of overthrowing the ingrained idolatry. Yet the bank balances of these men were more important than the people delivered from paganism. They were convinced that the magnificent temple of Artemis would be threatened if this Gospel preaching were allowed to continue.

Riots are usually spontaneous happenings, whose complex causes cannot easily be unraveled. The anger of the silversmiths in the throes of a financial slump is intelligible enough, but why was the whole city thrown into confusion by their predicament? Perhaps their cry "Great is Artemis of the Ephesians" (or perhaps their prayer "O great Artemis") awoke the pride of the Ephesians in their temple, which was of such magnificence that it was numbered among the seven wonders of the world. There was instantaneous confusion as the mob sought for scapegoats. Mob violence has not changed its tactics over the centuries, and what happened at Ephesus has been repeated many times since. Poor Gaius and Aristarchus must have wondered what had hit them. They were Europeans who had apparently joined Paul in Macedonia. The mob bustled them to the theater, a vast building capable of accommodating some 25,000 people. It was a natural meeting ground. In the confusion Paul himself had been missed. Most men would have considered that a piece of good fortune. But not so Paul. His fighting spirit stirred in a scene like this. He wanted to charge into the midst of it all. But his friends would not let him, neither those of his own party nor the Ephesian officials who were particularly concerned with the maintenance of order at public religious gatherings. Having established good relationships with these Asiarchs during his three years' mission at Ephesus, Paul accepted their advice that he should not go to the theater.

It is typical of mob scenes for confusion to reign. Luke pointedly reports that most had no idea what had brought them to the theater. There is a large degree of herd instinct which causes perfectly reasonable people to act completely irrationally when in a crowd. The irrationality of the situation was welcomed by a group of Jews who were as opposed to Paul's preaching as the pagan silversmiths. They had a demagogue at hand who was pushed forward to speak. The Jews, however, had miscalculated the mood of the pagan crowd. Jewish monotheism was as opposed as Paul's Gospel to the idolatry of Artemis and the crowd was at this moment championing Artemis. The intended speech was completely obliterated by the chorus in honor of Artemis. The monotonous cry went on for two hours until the town clerk could stand it no longer.

He was a man of very considerable authority in Ephesus. The Romans had allowed freedom for the continuation of the local system of government, although the town clerk was naturally sensitive that any display of public disorder might cause the Romans to impose their own system of government. This town clerk must have been a man of remarkable presence to have sufficiently quieted the crowd to make himself heard. He appeals to tradition — everyone knows the importance of Artemis and no one need fear her overthrow. If the town clerk really believed this, he had less insight than Demetrius. But he at least sees clearly that no charge of committing sacrilege could be leveled against the Christian missionaries. There was no need for Paul and his companions to make a direct attack on the goddess. It was an indirect approach which had been so effective in undermining her influence. When the truth was proclaimed, error at once diminished.

The town clerk commanded Demetrius to bring his charges before the official assembly, for he knew that the present unofficial uproar would not be tolerated by the Romans. At this the mob, accepting his verdict, went home, while Paul, having said farewell to the Christians at Ephesus, went toward Macedonia.

90. *Another Letter to Corinth*

(2 Cor. 1 and 2)

The normal route from Ephesus to Macedonia passed through Troas, the port of embarkation for the shortest sea route between Asia and Europe. Since writing 1 Corinthians, it seems certain that Paul had had other contacts with the Christians at Corinth. From incidental comments in 2 Corinthians it is probable that he paid them a brief visit which showed up disagreements between himself and them and became a painful experience for him (cf. 2 Cor. 2:1). This visit may have been just after his leaving Ephesus, but was more likely during the period at Ephesus following the writing of 1 Corinthians. It is generally thought

that the letter to which he refers in 2 Corinthians 2:4 is not our
1 Corinthians but another letter written after the painful visit
and sent by Titus.

On his way to Macedonia Paul expected to meet Titus at Troas
so as to hear a report on the Corinthians' situation. But Titus was
not there (2 Cor. 2:13). Nevertheless Paul found an open door
for preaching the Gospel, as he had done at Ephesus. His concern over the Corinthian situation, however, ran deep and he felt
he must proceed to Macedonia on the route that Titus would
take. It was somewhere there that Titus rejoined him (2 Cor.
7:5, 6), much to Paul's relief. It is against this background of
distress and relief that 2 Corinthians must be set. We shall not
expect to find here a calm exposition of doctrine, although doctrine is in fact present. It is rather an expression of many of the
tensions and aspirations of the apostle himself. There is no letter
in which he is more revealing than in this.

He first unburdens himself about his own sufferings. One
particular experience was almost crushing. He calls it an "affliction" which caused him to despair of life. In it he had experienced
the deliverance of God. When a man has put God to the test in
conditions of severe affliction, he has a position of great advantage for encouraging others. Paul regards his sufferings as being
shared by his converts. However distressed he had been about
the Corinthians, he tells them his hope for them is unshaken. He
is clearly wanting to restore good relations with them. He claims
to have behaved among them with holiness and sincerity, although he hastens to add that this was only by God's grace.

He comes next to deal with a charge of fickleness against him.
Titus had told him what some of the Corinthians had said about
his change of plans. He had in mind to visit Corinth both on his
way to Macedonia and on his way back from Macedonia. He had
of course gone directly to Macedonia, but this change of plan
was not arbitrary. Paul reminds the Corinthians that he sought
to follow God's plan, which is always positive. It is God who
had commissioned him and his companions, Silvanus and Timothy. The apostle at this point slips in a choice comment about
the Spirit's seal and guarantee upon them. Even when discussing
practical arrangements he thinks in spiritual terms. This was one
of the profound secrets of this hazardous life.

He was sensitive about the relationship between himself and
the Corinthians. His painful visit and the subsequent letter are

still much in his mind. He remembers the anguish with which he wrote. He remembers his tears. It is not often that he talks like this. The problems at Corinth, particularly the person who caused him most trouble, led to much personal pain. Now he has heard that the majority of the Corinthians have turned against the offender and he fears that they have gone to the other extreme. They must keep showing their love for him. Paul knows that breakdowns in personal relationships become vantage points for satanic activity.

The apostle's mind flicks back to Troas. He vividly records his restlessness at not meeting Titus, but he waits until he has said a great deal more before he tells the Corinthians where he eventually linked again with Titus. His mind becomes deflected again. He possibly remembered a triumphal procession he had seen and this reminded him further of the assured victory of Christ whatever the outward circumstances. Perhaps this kind of thinking meant much to him as he embarked for Macedonia from Troas. He thinks also of the marked difference in the reception of the Gospel — to some a fragrant aroma, to others a deathly stench. In the long run, Paul was kept going by his conviction that God had commissioned him. He was not like a peddler whose desire was to get rid of his stock by whatever method. The minister of the Gospel was fired by an entirely different motive — one of absolute sincerity, a thought which led the apostle into a long digression about the Christian ministry.

91. *The Glory of the Christian Ministry*

(2 Cor. 3)

The glory of a thing is often relative. It depends on one's point of view. Not many observers in that early stage of the Christian mission would have seen much glory in the work of the missionaries. They were a despised group in the eyes of most. The ministry possessed no status. It was rather the object of constant attack. It needed a man of vision to see much glory in it.

Some people at Corinth were concerned about official recognition — letters of recommendation and the like. But Paul looks on the Corinthian Christians as sufficient commendation for him. In spite of his difficulties with them, they were living testimonies to the power of God which had operated through his mission.

The Christians in Corinth were the best advertisement of the glory of the ministry. Whenever the Spirit of God transforms human lives it is a powerful commendation of the Gospel, particularly against a pagan background of moral looseness as at Corinth.

It is important in Paul's mind to show clearly that the ministers of the Gospel, or as he calls them "ministers of the new covenant," are God-powered. This removes any possibility of self-aggrandizement. Of all people Paul had most reason of any of the early Christians to boast, but he knows his own deficiencies and recognizes that the Gentile mission would have been a flop if God's sufficiency had not been available. He had been brought up and trained as a minister of the old covenant, involving a detailed teaching of the law, which he now describes as a "written code." By way of contrast his present ministry is dominated by a much more dynamic motive. The Spirit of God has called him to be a minister of life. Paul remembers only too vividly the deadness of his ministry under the law.

This causes him to reflect further on this contrast. With all its death-producing effects the giving of the ancient law was surrounded with splendor. Perhaps Paul is anticipating some objection that the old order was more splendid than the new, at least outwardly. One of the main problems for the Jews who were attracted to Christianity was the glorious heritage of the old faith compared with the lack of such heritage in the new. In Jewish eyes ministers of the old covenant enjoyed very considerable status. Would not Christians feel that the ministers of the new covenant were a deprived group? Paul gives us the benefit of his own answer to this problem. He argues from the lesser to the greater.

Moses' face was symbolic in the giving of the dead clay tablets of the law. It was the most living and most human part of the whole process. Something of the glory of the God who gave the commandments reflected in his face. The problem was its transience for it soon faded way. Paul argues that since the Christian covenant was lasting, its splendor must exceed the splendor of anything that passes. His purpose is not to lessen the glory of the old, for he held the law to be holy, just, and good (cf. Rom. 7:12). But from experience he had discovered the great superiority of the Gospel.

Thinking of Moses' shining face, Paul sees a parable in it.

Everyone acquainted with the Old Testament would know how Moses was obliged to cover his face because the Israelites could not look upon it. They purposely excluded the glory and found themselves faced with the legal demands of the commandments. Paul switches his thoughts to his own Jewish contemporaries and sees a veil on their hearts. Purists might object that he has transferred the veil from the lawgiver to the recipients and thus radically altered the symbolism of the veil. But what if he has? He has made his point that the glory is still obscured for the Jews in his day as in the days of Moses. He is probably implying that had the veil not been there, they would have recognized that what Moses stood for has been fulfilled in Christ.

Paul had already suffered much from Jews, who in spite of allegiance to the Mosaic law, were nevertheless blind to the glory of the Christian Gospel. The main distinction between him and them was that his veil had been removed. It is intriguing to note how Paul's thought leads from one idea to another as he thinks of what the unveiled Christian can see. He discovers a wonderful freedom presided over by the Spirit. Indeed the Christian's glory was a product of the Spirit. Paul thinks of believers as catching and then reflecting God's glory precisely in the manner that Moses had done. Yet whereas Moses' glory faded, the Christian's becomes more intense in proportion to his nearness to the Lord. There could be no more effective demonstration of the greater splendor of the new covenant. One wonders whether any of the Corinthians, on listening to this letter, looked at each other to see whether any increase in glory could be discerned. Perhaps they remembered on reflection that Paul and his companions had, through the Spirit, shown them something of the splendor of the Christian ministry.

92.   *Earthen Vessels*

(2 Cor. 4)

Having made much of the glory of the Christian ministry, Paul next looks at the real situation. He gives some explanation of the apparent discrepancy between that glory and the hardships and hazards of missionary life.

How does he avoid the temptation to be disheartened? Many happenings at Corinth might have made him discouraged. Moreover he had experienced enough hazards to make any man lose heart, as he mentions later in this letter. What keeps him going is the mercy of God. As a man in the service of God, he had used irreproachable methods. He had relied on clear statements of the truth. The Corinthians would know this. Although they might not agree with him, they could never charge him with using questionable practices.

As he reflects on the impeding veil over men's hearts and ponders the reason for it, he is convinced that it is the work of Satan, whom he describes as the god of this world. Several times in his writings Paul draws attention to Satan's activity. He is deeply aware that men who remain blind to the glory of Jesus Christ must have been blinded by some influence beyond themselves. Only a fool would prefer to sit in a shuttered room when the brilliant sun shines outside. But the fact that all unbelievers are shut out from the light of Christ shows that their minds have been shuttered by a power greater than themselves. Illumination, or the removal of the shutters, must equally be the work of a higher agency. It is the work of God.

This glimpse of the basic spiritual conflict is valuable in assessing the real nature of the Christian ministry. If the missioners were pitting their wits unaided against the forces of darkness they would be sure losers, but the god of this world has a far more devastating Adversary. The preachers were not designing and implementing their own idea — they were proclaiming the Lordship of Christ. Again Paul's supreme conviction about the rightness of his message comes to the fore. He has no fear of clear distinctions. Light and darkness are mutually exclusive. Where light shines blindness disappears. Paul remembers the story of creation. It was God who not only decided but commanded that light should appear. There was no such command regarding darkness. Paul sees the creation as a symbol. It is the same God who created who also commands the spiritual light to shine. In the course of this extended simile, Paul makes two statements which reveal his view of Jesus Christ. He is the likeness of God (verse 4) and He shows in His face the glory of God. Whereas Moses reflected God's likeness, Jesus *was* God's likeness. Such was the exalted theme of Paul's ministry.

Nevertheless he thinks of himself as an earthen vessel, an ordinary clay pot, which after its brief period of usefulness is fit only to be thrown away. If broken pieces of pot (ostraka) were used as writing materials, this would not detract from the force of the illustration which Paul uses. There is no glory about a common earthenware pot. In the same way, if God uses such mundane material in His service, whatever glory there is must be given to Him.

Paul's "earthen vessel" certainly sustained rough treatment — what with afflictions, perplexities, and persecution. He had worked out a kind of spiritual philosophy in coping with these buffetings. None of them could break his spirit. They affected only the body. In a sense they were echoes of the sufferings of Christ. The "earthen pot" could cope with rough handling. The important part was its content — its manifestation of the life of Jesus. It is like a beautiful flower, symbolizing life, set in a pot of earthenware, which apart from the flower would have no claim to distinction. The pot on its own could never symbolize life, no more than Paul himself would ever have made an impact on the pagan world of Corinth. He knew that the Corinthians could testify to the life of Jesus which they had seen in him.

A conviction which meant much to Paul was his assurance that God would one day bring him and the Corinthians into His presence. In a sense Paul was often living in the future. But he never forgot the present. More and more people are yet to experience God's grace. When he thinks of the future, present afflictions appear momentary. The earthen pot may be cracking up, but the spirit grows stronger. The eternal glory is for Paul indescribable. What matters if the pot is chipped or even disintegrates. The unseen is infinitely more important than the seen. Some may dismiss this as pie-in-the-sky philosophy but for the apostle it seemed better to be earthenware now and be possessor of an indestructable glory than something more valuable now with no hope of glory to come. Earthenware has one advantage over gold — it is of little consequence what happens to it. It saves a mass of worry in this life.

93.   *Ambassadors for Christ*

(2 Cor. 5 and 6)

One of the fascinations of Paul's letters is the richness of his metaphors. The earthen pot idea now gives way to the earthly tent metaphor. It is drawn from nomad life, where whole communities are constantly reminded of the temporariness of their dwelling place as pegs are uprooted to prepare for the next journey. It is an apt figure for our present lives. Tents, like pots, are not durable. But the question naturally arises — what happens when the earthly tent collapses? What takes its place? Paul's brief answer is "life." He is sure of this, because the Spirit gives the guarantee of it. It amounts to a strong inner conviction.

Paul pursues the matter still further. He compares life in the present body with life with the Lord. It makes no difference as far as the Christian's motive is concerned. His aim is to please the Lord. Paul thinks ahead to what he calls "the judgment seat of Christ," by which he means the occasion when Christians will account for their actions. It is a solemn thought.

The idea of having to give account for one's actions produces a healthy fear of the Lord. Paul does not hesitate to stress this to his Corinthians readers. He recognizes that God Himself is the only one who knows the whole position. He is still somewhat sensitive to the criticism that he may be commending himself. Some in fact regarded him as mad, but this does not concern him so long as he is mad for God. At this thought he makes another of his brief incursions into theology in this letter. The idea of Christ's love controlling us leads him to think further of what Christ's love has done for us. He died for us to bring about in us a practical result in our lives. The Christian ceases to live for himself because Christ never lived for Himself. Paul had proved the irresistible power which such love unleashes. It was not for his own sake that he had endured hazards galore (see 2 Cor. 11), but for the sake of Christ.

Paul sees Christianity as based on an entirely new concept of living. Believers are new creatures in Christ, in whom the principles which governed their former lives drop away. The Corinthians could remember vividly how this had happened to them. Vice and lust, which were so prominent in pagan Corinth, could not be reformed. They needed to be jettisoned and new controlling factors introduced. Whatever backgrounds the Christian Gospel has since challenged have had to be dealt with in the same way.

The basis of the new life is reconciliation to God. When anyone gets right with God he at once sees where he is wrong with others. Paul understands his own task as one of proclaiming this reconcilation. It is a message of forgiveness and restitution, which is the heart of the Gospel. Those who carry this message are ambassadors, another of Paul's suggestive figures of speech.

An ambassador does not represent himself but his country. He does not express his own opinions. He is told what to say and keeps in constant touch with his government to ensure that he rightly interprets the official viewpoint. It is a noble metaphor for the Christian minister. On his Master's behalf, Paul conveys to the Corinthians the amazing thought that Christ was made sin for us. All who have since pondered these words have wondered at their meaning, but Christians have always recognized that Jesus Christ became so identified with man that He bore man's sin. Anyone who omits this truth from his Gospel is like an ambassador out of touch. Without it, the message of reconciliation makes no sense.

These reflections fired the apostle to make an immediate appeal to his readers. Now is the day of salvation. This has been the burden of his ministry. Paul suddenly decides to give the Corinthians a list of some of the hardships he has suffered to proclaim this Gospel. It is an impressive list of calamities, both natural and spiritual. But he is more concerned about his own attitude while enduring these hardships. It is almost a reproduction of the fruit of the Spirit mentioned in his Galatian letter. It is little use proclaiming reconcilation without showing kindness and love to others. His experiences have been tremendously varied — sometimes he has been well spoken of, at other times not. Many paradoxes are mentioned — sorrowful yet rejoicing, having nothing, but possessing everything. No wonder many have understood little of all this. Yet the Corinthians ought to have understood. Paul's heart is wide, but he fears that theirs are not. Their own emotions were inhibited. If only they would let go, they would give room for the richer experiences of the Gospel!

Some think that the next section of the letter originally belonged to a different context because of the break in the sequence of thought. But digressions are not unknown in Paul's writings. He suddenly advises the Corinthians about their relationships to the world. He views Christians as temples of God and shows the impossibility of their agreement with incongruous things like idols or iniquity. To support his point he quotes some passages from the Old Testament, from Isaiah 52, Hosea 1, and Isaiah 43, which command the separation of the people of God from their environment. No doubt the issue in Corinth was real. The temptation to compromise was constant. Christians were urged to avoid mixed marriages. Real fellowship can exist only between those with a common basis. The problems at Corinth were typical of any situation where light exists in conditions of darkness. The two do not belong together. Paul's principle of separation must, of course, be kept in context. Its positive side has often been forgotten. The key is the Temple idea, for if Christians are God's dwelling-place nothing out of keeping with that is permissible.

94. Titus' Report and the Collection Scheme

(2 Cor. 7:1 – 8:15)

After his long discussion over the ministry, Paul comes back to his personal relations with the Corinthians as a prelude to broaching the subject of his Jerusalem Appeal Fund. He knows it to be a delicate subject. He assures his readers of his great joy over them. They are his pride. Only then does he mention the coming of Titus, presumably because it was this event which turned his previous sorrow into joy. He recalls his distress on coming to Macedonia, but he also recalls God's comfort to him in the news which Titus had brought.

He thinks again of his earlier letter. He had misgivings about it, because it had resulted in strained relationships, but he is glad that the matter was being resolved. The Corinthians themselves had been sorry about the problems they had caused. Paul speaks of their "godly grief," which he contrasts with mere worldly grief because it led to real repentance. He seems to go out of his way to clear the air. He assures them that he recognizes their earnestness and zealousness in carrying out a punishment of the offender. What has impressed him is the enthusiasm with which his instructions had been carried out.

Paul's boasting to Titus about the Corinthians had been fully justified, although there had been distressing moments when he had felt they had let him down. Titus' report must have been quite glowing. He had told Paul about their readiness to respond and their godly sense of fear and trembling. The Corinthians, in spite of all their individual problems, were not without a genuine core of real piety. They had not stood on their dignity, although the conclusion of the letter suggests that there were still some whom the apostle had to rebuke.

Having thus cleared the air for the restoration of confidence between himself and the Corinthians, Paul moves on to the delicate subject of giving. The Corinthians should know about the Macedonians who had magnificently risen to the challenge of his Jerusalem Appeal Fund. Not only had they been passing through persecution (which the Corinthians had been spared as yet), but their material resources were severely limited. Yet in spite of this they gave more than they could afford and begged Paul to accept it. By way of contrast the tardiness of the Corinthians in getting going must surely have shamed them as they listened to the letter being read. With superb tact Paul makes nothing of this. He appeals to their sense of emulation. Since they excelled in other things, why not in this? Was he being sarcastic, or was he being a good psychologist? Surely the latter in view of his careful purpose to commend them!

Then comes another characteristic touch of the apostle. When mentioning an essentially practical matter, he slips in a doctrinal support. The example of Jesus Christ is cited. Though rich, he became poor for the sake of others. This must be a reference to the wealth of His pre-existent state and the poverty of His incarnate life. Paul must have explained this to the Corinthians. He must have told them about the basic facts of the life of Jesus. This is one of those incidental references which show that Paul was not unmindful of the historical Jesus, although he does not make specific reference to the events of His life. The example of Jesus in the present context was powerful. Paul's reasoning depends on the assumption that what was true of Jesus Christ must be a pattern for Christians.

The Corinthians had certainly been slack. They had begun a collection the previous year but had not completed it. They had evidently not acted on Paul's earlier advice (1 Cor. 16). The apostle proposed a kind of social philosophy in his aid scheme. His idea is a simple one. Let those who have abundance at the present time help those who are in need. If ever the Corinthians were in need others would do the same for them. It was a kind of spiritual insurance scheme held together not by legal contracts but by love. It was a policy of "fair shares for all." The apostle sees his fund therefore as a spiritual instrument, a means of expressing Gentile love and concern for the Judaean believers. He thinks of the Old Testament example of the gathering up of manna in the wilderness, where the providence of God worked on the basis of equality for all. Those with strength to gather much were expected to share their surplus with those who gathered little. And Paul sees the same principle as a working idea for the Christian Church.

95. *Liberality*
(2 Cor. 8:16 – 9:15)

After urging his readers to intensify their interest in his collection scheme, Paul mentions that Titus equally shares his zeal for the scheme. He has carried his associates with him — a valuable test for the basic soundness of any scheme. Titus has volunteered to collect the contributions from Corinth, accompanied by a notable man whom Paul nevertheless does not name. The churches have assigned this incognito preacher to accompany Paul. We should like to know his name, but presumably the Corinthians knew, for otherwise the reference would have been an enigma.

There were probably criticisms at Corinth over the whole idea of a relief scheme, for Paul hastens to assure his readers that what he is doing is honorable in God's sight and in man's sight. Moreover there is not only the incognito preacher but also the tested brothers, similarly unnamed, who will accompany Titus. Perhaps these men had worked with Paul at Ephesus. Titus is especially named as Paul's partner and fellow worker. The Corinthians must have been impressed by the delegation from other churches. They could not ignore the fact that they would not only be failing the apostle, but would be out of step with these other churches. They are called upon to give proof to these other churches of their love for the brethren. Regard for reputation is not the highest basis of appeal in Christian issues, but it is not without its place. If other Christian groups zealously support a project it shows up the less zealous and may well stir them into greater action.

Paul, already in Macedonia, has found the Christians there most enthusiastic to give. They had been fired with enthusiasm on hearing from Paul that the Corinthians had promised support. It would be embarrassing both for his readers and for Paul if the Macedonians discovered that the bright example they had followed had completely faded out. Paul wants to avoid such embarrassment by ensuring that the Corinthians' arrangements for the gift are completed before he comes. This reflects how information was disseminated in the early Church. Paul was constantly telling his churches what was happening elsewhere.

It was impossible for any of those early communities to act wholly independently. The collection scheme was seen as a bonding agent to make the various churches recognize their common fellowship.

Paul does not leave the matter there, as he might have done. He wants to give more exposition of the principles of liberality. He draws an illustration from nature. Reaping and sowing are intricately linked. An abundant harvest can never follow a skimpy sowing. The sowing is man's part, the harvest is God's, but man must be liberal with the seeds. Yet what has this to do with giving? Paul wants the Corinthians to know that liberality is more a matter of mind than amount. God gives liberally and loves the cheerful or wholehearted giver. Paul quotes Psalm 112:9 in support. If the Corinthians would think of the liberality of God, they could not fail to develop a liberal mind. The apostle is convinced of the principle that the man who gives is enriched in the giving. He comes back to his agricultural illustration. After all it it God who supplies the seed. Why should man skimp the sowing? It is equally true in the spiritual as in the natural world.

When one considers that the apostle was dealing with Christians who had not long since been pagans, it becomes clear that an entirely new philosophy of possessions and responsibility was necessary. The masterly way in which he works out such a basically Christian approach has left the Christian Church permanently in his debt. An essentially practical matter like having a collection for needy fellow Christians becomes a spiritual expression of thankfulness to God. This raises the whole matter above the begging stage, so often associated with relief appeals. It is not a matter of being stirred by pity, a motive not to be despised, but a case of glorifying God, an infinitely nobler motive. It is characteristic of Paul's whole approach that he ends this section with thanks to God for His inexpressible gift, which was the mainspring for all his fantastic service for God. Such a priceless gift could never be repaid.

96. *Paul Defends Himself*

(2 Cor. 10)

The closing part of this epistle differs from the former part, a difference which has led some to suppose that this last section (chs. 9-13) was part of another letter, perhaps part of the letter which came between our 1 and 2 Corinthians (see 2 Cor. 2:4, 7:8-12). Undoubtedly the tone has changed, for here Paul goes over to the defensive in marked contrast to his expressions of relief and even joy which are features of the first half. Possible explanations of the change of approach are either that Paul has heard further disturbing reports that some at Corinth were still criticizing him, or that he had purposely concentrated on the majority until nearing the end, when he devoted himself to the recalcitrant minority. It should be noted that it is just possible that the minority consisted only of one or two individuals. In any case attacks had been made on the apostle's position and he finds it necessary to defend himself.

The apostle first describes the real nature of his calling, because some are suggesting that he was acting in a worldly manner. This sounds like an accusation from super-spiritual people who were devoting their energies to criticizing others. Of course, if they were right Paul would be inconsistent and insincere. One might think that such charges were not worth answering, but Paul sees a challenge to his whole Christian position and feels an explanation to be necessary.

In the way he tackles such attacks upon his integrity he sets a valuable pattern. He assures his critics that he wants to approach the matter in the spirit of Christ. He remembers His meekness and gentleness. He then echoes what others are saying of himself — i.e., that he acts in a lowly way when present and a bold way when absent. Such a charge really needs firm handling, but Paul has no delight in using severity. His attitude toward his personal detractors is generally conciliatory.

A military metaphor comes to Paul's mind. Like soldiers attacking an entrenched position or laying seige to a fortified city, he and his companions are waging a spiritual battle. As in any battle weapons are important, so in the spiritual warfare appropriate weapons are needed, divine weapons which can remove obstacles. There are many obstacles such as prejudice and corrupt thinking which Paul now regards as prisoners captured in war. Everything, including thought itself, must be brought into subjection to Christ. This shows the breadth of Paul's spiritual psychology. It is because he has disciplined his thinking that he does not hesitate to point out that disobedience must be punished. He does not say how, but he is convinced that any refusal by a Christian to submit to Jesus Christ carries its own consequences. He is obviously hoping that those Corinthians who are still recalcitrant will take stock of his words.

Some of the troublemakers at Corinth appear to have made an issue out of their allegiance to Christ as if this exempted them from paying attention to Paul. The approach is one of spiritual independence. But the apostle reminds them that he too is Christ's (which cancels out any supposed advantage the Corinthians thought they had). Moreover, Paul claims a spiritual authority over them. He is conscious of much harping on this theme, but is nevertheless not ashamed of doing so. It takes great spiritual grace to use authority in Christian concerns without becoming overbearing. Paul could do so only because he was deeply convinced that his authority was not due to his own powers but to his divine calling. He must have received a report of what various Corinthians were saying about him. Rumors travel rapidly. The weight of his letters could not be gainsaid. Even his opponents admitted this. They therefore scorned him because of his bodily presence, which was far less impressive. He was more eloquent as a writer than as a speaker — at least that is what his opponents were saying, and Paul makes no effort to refute them.

He assures them that if he resorts to boasting he will not overdo it. He had no intention of competing with the Corinthian self-commenders — which was a nicely balanced dig at them. On the other hand, he knew they owed much to him. It was through him that they first heard of the Gospel. It was not as though he were boasting about what other men had done. Yet he still wonders whether he might not have some cause for further boasting about the Corinthians as their faith deepened, which was what he most desired.

Paul was always thinking of the lands beyond. It was the constant backdrop to his missionary work. It was not a symptom of restlessness, but a symbol of concern. When a man allows such thoughts to dominate, he will not be greatly concerned with boasting. He has no desire to be commended of men, nor to commend himself. It takes great dedication to the Lord's service to reach such willingness to leave all to the Lord's estimation. This attitude of mind has marked all the truly great servants of God through Christian history. It is only this that enables a man to pursue his mission, come what may.

97. *Legitimate Boasting*

(2 Cor. 11)

Paul decides to mention certain reasons why he feels he can commend himself. He regards this as legitimate because he is so convinced of the commendation of the Lord. He admits that what he is going to say may seem like folly. He is in fact self-conscious about it. Yet he cannot restrain himself, especially because of his rivals at Corinth. He recognizes that some of them were too gullible. They would not detect the difference if another Gospel were preached to them in the name of the apostles. They should have known had they learned properly from Paul, who draws a sharp distinction between rhetoric and knowledge. Many have swayed multitudes through possessing rhetorical skill when their message lacked understanding. The symptoms were already present at Corinth. They preferred the skillful speeches of rival orators to Paul's less eloquent but more profound exposition of the Gospel.

How was he to deal with such a situation? He claims equality with the "superlative" apostles. He considers that if there are degrees of apostleship he comes behind in nothing. In case this seemed presumptuous, he cites the matter of financial support. Some Corinthians may have suggested that Paul must have been inferior if he did not expect support whereas other apostles did. Such an idea makes him indignant. It was not that he was not entitled to support, but he had depended on other churches (especially Macedonia). It was the Corinthians who were at fault. It had probably never occurred to them that responsibility rested on them to provide for the needs of those working among them. Paul boasts about his financial independence to shame them into recognizing the baselessness of their argument.

At the thought of those rival apostles, Paul makes some strong statements. He disclaims all thought of their being on a level with him. They are not true apostles at all, but charlatans. Their claims are wholly pretense, and their supposed office is false. How could men be so base as to deceive like this? To Paul it is no problem. They are merely imitating their master. Satan is so skilled in the art of disguise that he not infrequently appears as an angel of light. The unsuspecting fall for it. It is a more successful ruse than direct hostility.

Now Paul really gets going with his boasting. He ironically

points out that the Corinthians should not mind putting up with the boasting of a fool since they had already fallen for the folly of the false apostles. The passage which follows is a classic for two reasons; for the amazing scope of Paul's hardships in the cause of the Gospel and for the clear way in which he argues his point. To take the latter first, Paul has a masterly command of rhetorical questions. He piles them up, giving his own claims in the process. He admits that in doing so he is talking like a madman. But those Corinthians needed a madman's talk. None of the so-called "superlative" apostles could compare with his claims — he was a Hebrew, a true Israelite and a son of Abraham who had endured an impressing sequence of hardship.

We may be grateful for Paul's mad incursion into self-advertisement. He makes us realize how little we know of his activity from the Book of Acts. We find ourselves listening to the testimony of a giant of a man. The labors, the imprisonments, the beatings, the many near escapes from death, pile up. The fivefold dreadful lashings, the threefold rod beatings, the stoning, the three shipwrecks proclaim the tremendous determination of the man. That Paul's body could stand up to such buffeting is mighty testimony to his indomitable spirit. If this is his kind of boasting, let him continue and let no spiritual dwarfs, who have never suffered a scratch for Christ's sake, dare lift a finger in condemnation. He adds other details — a whole variety of dangers in different environments, not least from false brethren, and the most touching of all — the lack of adequate food and warmth. Yet through all these hazards Paul's mind is more on the churches under his care than on himself. Even his most recalcitrant opponents must surely have been impressed by such a list. We would have liked more details, and could wish that Luke had supplied them. It would have made the Acts a thrilling account of personal endurance in the face of incredible odds. However, that would have glorified the man.

Paul ends his list with a significant detail. He remembers how he felt the day that the Damascan Christians let him down in a basket from the city wall to escape from the evil designs of King Aretas' governor. He had then learned to thank God for his own sense of weakness. What happened afterward was due wholly to God's strength. Escape in a basket was after all no impressive way to commence his service for God.

98. *Visions*

(2 Cor. 12:1-10)

Paul was not in the habit of advertising his inner experiences, but when writing to the Corinthians he felt he must do so. He realized it might not prove profitable, but there are times when inner secrets come vividly to the surface. Paul suddenly reminisces, recapturing the sense of ecstasy he had experienced fourteen years previously. It must have been before his missionary journeys began while he was still in his native Cilicia. The sense of ecstasy was so real that it seemed independent of his body. It was an elevation of the mind. When recording this sensation he speaks of himself in the third person ("I know a man in Christ"), as if he were attempting to take an objective view of his own ecstasy.

Although he feels under an obligation to speak of it, he comes against an immediate difficulty. What he heard were words incommunicable to others. It seems suddenly to have struck him that it was a strange subject for boasting, but he insists that he is making a special plea on behalf of this other "man in Christ." The Corinthians must have been intrigued by this method of arguing, but they no doubt got the point. If Paul had wanted to do so he could have outshone the lot in the breadth of the visions he had experienced. But he prefers to dwell on his own weaknesses.

Whatever visions Paul had had there had been plenty of them. There were enough to make any man overelated. Experiences which lift a man out of the common rut are always dangerous. From his privileged position he surveys the others, still unmoved, with a feeling of superiority. Even the best of men succumb, and Paul was no exception. Ecstatic as the experiences were, they were mixed with others of a less pleasant character. Paul speaks of "a thorn in the flesh," which he also recognized as a "messenger of Satan."

There has been much debate about this thorn in the flesh. We could wish that Paul had been more specific, but his vagueness is not without value. Many have read into his words a symbol of their own buffetings and have derived strength from the same source of encouragement. There may be something to be said for the view that the apostle suffered from some form of ophthalmia (see Gal. 4:13-15). He certainly seems to be referring to some kind of physical defect. Its nature, however, is less important than its spiritual character. That a physical disability can be a "messenger of Satan" in Paul's thinking shows the profoundness of his understanding of spiritual agencies. Modern psychology would of course explain the matter in other terms, but there is a basic element in Paul's description which psychologists often miss. It was not the thorn in the flesh which was most harmful to him. It was the effect it might have had on his mind. His own thoughts had become a battlefield. He had resented the "thorn" and been tempted to question the love and wisdom of God in allowing it to stay. Satan had found a whip to lash up an opposition to God Himself. The great achievement of the apostle was to recognize the device, before his mind became poisoned with doubt regarding the goodness of God.

He tears aside another veil, to give a passing glimpse at the personal problem of unanswered prayer. That even the godly apostle experienced this problem has been an encouragement to many. No one could have prayed more earnestly than he had done on three occasions. He wanted the thorn removed. But God said, "No!" The Corinthians must have known what the thorn was. As they listened to this part of Paul's letter they would gain a new insight into the apostle's mind. They must have been struck by the solution to his problem of unanswered prayer — or rather by the Lord's answer, which although negative was nevertheless a real answer.

Paul does not tell us how the priceless words of encouragement from the Lord came to him. The words were as specific as his own request had been. "My grace is sufficient for you" sounded like a sweet bell across a dark valley of disappointment. The grace was more important than the thorn. A sense of the sufficiency of God is more basic than the sense of one's own insufficiency. For God's strength comes to its fullest maturity in man's weakness. No one ever learned that principle better than Paul. If ever a man became a spiritual Colossus in the midst of infirmities and adversities it was he. With such dynamic resources available it was worth being weak. The apostle's Corinthian critics must have been dumfounded on hearing such a view. All their criticisms would roll off the apostle as water from a duck.

The real secret is contentment. This is not easy when contending with physical infirmities, other people's sneers, hardships, persecutions, and general calamities. That list is enough to make the stoutest heart bend, but the contented man grows stronger as the problems pile up. Paul had reached the point where nothing could overwhelm him, where each new hazard was an opportunity for a display of God's strength.

99. *Plans*

(2 Cor. 12:11 – 13:14)

Paul leaves his reminiscences to defend again his apostleship. He appeals to the signs of an apostle which he had performed among them. This is a fascinating sidelight, for he rarely makes reference to his miraculous powers. It was only the claims of the so-called "superlative" apostles which spurred him to do so now. He gives no details. "Signs, wonders, mighty deeds" were current terms for supernaturally initiated acts. They were presumably mainly healings. They showed Paul to be inferior to none — except, as he adds with a delicate note of sarcasm, that he did not burden them, which implies that the others did.

In the extended conclusion to this letter Paul mentions his intended visit, which in many ways he anticipates with some apprehension. He has no desire to burden them any more than parents want to burden their children. He has no intention of taking advantage of them, any more than Titus did on his last visit to them. Paul had made it a practice to see that he and his associates adopted the same approach.

As the time for another visit drew near, Paul realized that some might charge him with being censorious in this letter. Nevertheless he is convinced that what he has said is necessary. If they heed it they will be edified. But Paul is still fearful. He knows there are some whose lives are no witness to God's grace, who need to repent before Him. He includes another of his familiar lists of sins, mainly of a social kind, as samples of what he fears he may confront when he comes. He is ready to mourn over the immorality of some. This catalogue of vices stands in stark juxtaposition to his own list of hardships. He can be content in the midst of the latter, but never in the midst of the former.

Those Corinthians who had given way to behavior contrary to Christian principles must know that Paul is not the kind of man to deal softly with sin. He has already warned them both by visit and by letter, and he has no intention of watering it down on his next visit. He reminds the Corinthians that the Christ who was crucified is the Christ who speaks through him. But as God's power raised Christ, so God's power dwells in His people. If Paul needs to be tough, it will be by the toughness of Christ.

There are some final appeals. Everyone needs self-examination at times. The Corinthians are no exceptions. They should find out how real their faith was. Paul, with great sensitivity, realizes that he should not speak as if he was immune from that test. Even if he failed, this did not absolve them from doing the right thing. Paul will never be party to the view that if others fail to measure up to God's demands it is no longer worth his bothering. Moral examination of the kind that he has in mind is an individual matter, a matter between each man and God.

No true Christian, and particularly no Christian leader, delights in being censorious. Paul wants to avoid a display of his authority when he visits them at least in a censorious manner. Authority, as he sees it, is for constructive and not destructive purposes. It takes a great man to practice this, for such authority must be wedded to humility, as it was indeed in Jesus Christ.

Paul decides it is time to close. With a few more snappy exhortations he draws to the end. The suggestion that they greet each other with a holy kiss would be an acknowledged symbol of harmony and peace among them. The apostle includes the greetings of other Christians, presumably those in Macedonia, with his own.

The benediction is notable for its Trinitarian form. It has become a favorite benediction in Christian assemblies incorporating as it does the basic Christian ideas of grace, love, and fellowship. The pattern for these is found in God — a thought too profound to be fathomed, but nevertheless of great inspiration to all believers.

So closes what is at once the most turbulent and yet the most revealing of all Paul's letters. It shows the apostle at close quarters grappling with problems and it shows also some of the weaknesses of the Corinthian church. It provides a pattern for solving many of the problems which continue to arise in the modern Church and to that extent is still highly relevant.

15

Great Thoughts for the Imperial City

100. *A Brief Stay in Greece*
(Acts 20:1-6)

It was somewhere in Macedonia that Paul laid down his pen after finishing his correspondence to the church at Corinth. With the situation in Corinth much in his mind, he was moving toward Greece. His Corinthian letters therefore provide a valuable insight into his mental and spiritual state at that time.

All that Luke says about the visit is that Paul spent three months in Greece. He does not even mention Corinth but presumably most if not all of the time was spent there. Those three months were important for a number of reasons. They marked a turning point in Paul's missionary career. He had all but completed his third main itinerary. His mind was now turning away from the east, from those churches which had been brought to birth as a result of his missionary preaching. He was restless so long as there were fresh fields to conquer for the Gospel. His plan was to visit Spain. He mentions this decision in the letter he wrote to the Romans at this time (cf. Rom. 15:24, 28). It would not have been surprising had Paul determined to send one of his associates to Spain. He himself had already encountered innumerable hazards in the cause of Christ. But he did not delegate his pioneer work to others. On the contrary he assigned the work of consolidation to his associates, while he himself undertook the task of spreading the good news. Whether he even went to Spain is difficult to say. There is no positive evidence that he did. Subsequent events may well have caused him to change his mind, yet during that period in Greece he was determined if at all possible to pursue his plan.

The most notable event which took place at this time was the production of another letter from the apostle's pen. It was destined to be different from his previous letters. It would be more theological, concentrating on some of the great doctrines of the Christian faith. It would be somewhat like a treatise although considerably less formal. Its character raises one question which is not easy to answer. Why did Paul write a theological letter like this at this stage in his Gentile mission? And why did he write it to the Romans? The two questions are not unconnected.

It cannot be supposed that the great themes of the Roman letter came to Paul in the act of writing. They had been turning over in his mind during his missionary service. The many profound themes expounded may well have been repeated in his teaching ministry. His reasoning bears the mark of mature convictions. It is not possible to regard this epistle, as some have done, as a summary of Paul's theological position, for there are some important Pauline themes absent from it, such as his views about the Church and about the Lord's return. There must have been a reason why he concentrates on the great theme of righteousness and its implications.

It seems best to suppose that during his brief stay in Greece, word had reached him that the Roman church needed some exposition of this theme. As he anticipates his visit there, following another brief trip to Jerusalem, he wants to prepare the way. It was important that the Romans should know the essence of his Gospel, so as to know what to expect when he arrived among them. His coming to Rome had considerable symbolic significance for the apostle. He looked forward to preaching the Gospel in the imperial city. Moreover, Rome had special significance for Luke for it formed the climax of his story of missionary endeavor.

Another matter which was engaging the attention of the apostle at this time was his collection scheme for the Christians in Judaea. For some time he had been organizing the collection with varying results. The Macedonians had been most generous, the Corinthians more tardy. But Paul had decided that the time had come for the fund to close and for the contributions to be handed to those needy Jewish Christians. It would be a tangible evidence of Jewish-Gentile solidarity in the Gospel.

While he was in Greece his first plan was to sail directly to Syria and then on to Jerusalem, but there were Jewish opponents who had heard of his plans and wanted to stop him. Luke gives no indication either of the reason for their plot or of the method they intended to employ. Having heard of the threat Paul decided against the risk and so proceeded to Macedonia to cross to Asia from there. He appears to have visited Beroea on the way, where Sopater joined his party. He had several others with him from other areas. Secundus and Aristarchus from Thessalonica, the latter having survived his experience at Ephesus with Gaius (Acts 19:29). Gaius was from the Galatian town of Derbe. Timothy was from the neighboring town of Lystra, and Tychicus and Trophimus were both from the province of Asia. All these associates crossed to Troas ahead of Paul, who joined them later, accompanied by Luke (note the "we" in 20:6). It was at Philippi that the doctor rejoined Paul. It appears that for some reason Paul wanted to observe the Feast of Unleavened Bread at Philippi.

101. A Letter to the Christians at Rome

(Rom. 1:1-15)

So far Paul's correspondence has been with churches where he has worked. He has personally known his readers, for he has had much to do with the founding of those churches (at Galatia, Thessalonica and Corinth). He has regarded his readers as his spiritual children. But now he turns to a church where he is not known personally, although it is certain that the Roman Christians had heard of his missionary exploits. Moreover the readers were Christians in a city at the heart of the empire and were consequently more strategically placed than any of those churches established by Paul. Since he was deeply conscious of the importance of strategy in the work of the Gospel, he would contemplate the task of writing to and later of visiting the Christians at Rome with unusual interest. It is fascinating to follow the method he adopts in approaching them.

The first paragraph of his letter is thought by some to be indebted to earlier tradition as if he is repeating or adapting some already agreed statement of Christian belief. Whether this is so or not is impossible to say, but there is no reason to believe that Paul's theological position was at variance with other apostolic preaching. As in all his letters he makes much of his apostleship, which would be doubly important for a church with no personal knowledge of him. It is the "Gospel" which has most emphasis in this opening section. That Gospel concerns God's Son, who is identified as David's descendant. The most important stress, however, falls on the resurrection of Jesus, which was a demonstration of God's power. It demonstrated both the sonship and the lordship of Jesus. Paul packs into few words some of the profoundest aspects of the Christian faith. He is determined that the Romans should be in no doubt about his view of Christ. It was through this exalted Christ that he had received his commission as apostle to the Gentiles. He gently reminds the Romans of this so as to justify his writing to them in this manner.

Following his usual practice he includes a thanksgiving at the beginning of the letter. He has heard much about the Roman church, for their faith is proclaimed in all the world, which must be understood to mean wherever in the world there were Christians they would know of the Christians at Rome. Any reports which reached Paul were a goad to prayer and an impetus to visit Rome. His prayers must have been full of references to churches, for many times he assures Christian communities that he constantly remembers them. He could not think of any group of God's people without praying for them, even when he had never met them. He gives the gist of his prayer for these Romans. He wants to visit them and prays for the opportunity to do so. His comments that this will be so only in accordance with God's will is characteristic. Although at this time he had concluded his work in the eastern regions and was planning to visit Spain, he could not foresee what would happen at Jerusalem, nor that he would spend two years in prison at Caesarea. It must have seemed then that it was not in harmony with God's will for him to reach Rome at all.

In anticipating his visit, Paul's main concern was that it might be spiritually profitable. He looks forward to giving them what he calls a "spiritual gift," by which he apparently means spiritual instruction. In the realm of Christian relationships what men have to share with others can be a priceless benefit, and especially is this so when the giver is an apostle who has been mightly used of the Lord. Nevertheless Paul anticipates that he too will be encouraged by the faith of the Roman Christians. Perhaps he is feeling the need for such encouragement following his disappointments over some of the Corinthian Christians.

Paul was always looking around for harvest fields. He had already found many in Asia Minor, Macedonia, and Achaia. His eyes were on Italy. In spite of the fact that the church in Rome had been established independently of his mission, he still hopes for a spiritual harvest among them. His intention is to preach the Gospel among them. It is worth noting that there is an intimate connection in his mind between the preaching and the "harvest." The one follows from the other. For the apostle the Gospel cannot be ineffective.

In the course of his missionary work Paul has learned to adapt himself to various types of people. As he thinks of visiting Rome, he is reminded that both Greeks and barbarians (the name used by the sophisticated to describe the unsophisticated), both wise and foolish, are to be found there. He considers his commission, however, to embrace them all. He was not called to serve one class to the exclusion of the others. He was implying that the same Gospel is relevant to all.

102. An Assessment of the Gentile World

(Rom. 1:16-32)

Having mentioned the Gospel, Paul sums it up, at the same time giving a concise indication of the main theme of his letter. He sees the Gospel as "God's power for salvation to all believers." This combines God's initiative with man's response. But what did he mean by "salvation"? Again he sums it up in a word — righteousness through faith. It is God's righteousness which becomes linked with man through faith. This is not his own definition. He gets it from Habakkuk 2:4, which has now gained much greater significance through Christ.

But before expounding this theme the apostle needs to show another aspect of God's character — His wrath. This may be considered as the reverse side of His righteousness, His resistance to all ungodliness. Paul is not unmindful of the prevalence of wickedness in the Gentile world and proceeds to give some of the worst aspects of it to show that God's wrath toward them was justified. It is known from other sources that he was not exaggerating the moral decadence of the contemporary world.

Anticipating a possible objection, Paul demonstrates that the Gentile world is without excuse. He bases this on natural revelation, for behind the created order was the powerful person of God. Acknowledgment of this basic fact was, however, ignored. Men refused to ascribe to Him the honor which was due. Paul does not mince his words about people who do not honor the Creator. He calls them senseless fools. They are groping in the dark, groveling before animal images instead of worshiping the true God. The folly of it all is self-evident.

The last part of this first chapter of his letter is the most devastating exposure of man's sinful nature found anywhere in the New Testament. God's giving them over to their own lusts is a sober thought, but Paul is speaking from his observation of the facts. Once man refuses to honor God as He should be honored, he has no standards for his own behavior. He gives way to lust. He sees no wrong in impurity. He has exchanged truth for a lie, a gem for a piece of rubbish. In his mind the creature is more important than the Creator. It is no wonder that Paul says three times that God had "given up" these people. They had willfully chosen not merely an inferior way, but a way which was opposed to all God's revelation of truth.

The details of the kind of life which resulted from this attitude do not make pleasant reading, but Paul does not hesitate to give such details. It is always more effective to specify than to generalize. Undesirable sex relationships were common then as they are now. Homosexuality is specially mentioned. It is noticeable that sexual aberrations are always more flourishing where God's pattern for living is definitely rejected. Those who have wrong relationships with God are most exposed to wrong relationships with others. The increase of moral pollution in any society is generally proportionate to the decline of religious faith.

Sexual indulgence of a wrong kind was not the only moral problem which Paul saw abounding in the Gentile world of his day. He saw evidence of what he calls a base mind. His religious intuition recognized the importance of mental attitudes in social behavior. Conduct follows the dictates of the mind, but if the latter is base, i.e., committed to life on the lowest possible level, the behavior will be equally base. Indeed as Paul lists some of the evils of society he gives pride of place to wrong mental attitudes before coming to the more overt offenses. Wickedness, evil, covetousness, malice, and envy are all in man's mind, although all are manifested in acts which are both alien to God and harmful to others. Murder and strife are the more violent evidences of this "base mind." Some evils are predominantly evils of the tongue like deceit, malignity, gossip, and slander. A base mind has a bias toward hurtful speech. At this point Paul mentions "haters of God," which brings out more specifically the hostile element in the "base" mind toward God.

Man, once having rejected the authority of God, becomes more arrogant and Paul notes three sins of this kind in his list. The concluding instances are more varied. By "inventors of evil," Paul focuses attention on the ingenuity of the "base" mind. In all periods of history evil minds have constantly devised new ways for the exploiting of evil desires. "Disobedience to parents" has an astonishingly modern ring about it, reminding us that our contemporary problems are no new thing. Again when divine authority is rejected human authority declines, and this is frequently most evident in the home. Lack of parental control is not always recognized as an evidence of a base mind.

There is only one thing to be said about such a state of affairs. Men who behave after the manner of this list deserve their fate. Paul notes another characteristic which is true of all rejecters of God. They behave improperly themselves and approve of others who do the same. There is a sort of fraternity among evildoers, as if the approving of others helps to silence the warning voice of conscience in themselves.

As the Roman Christians listened to this letter they would know how realistic Paul was being, for moral evils were as rife in Rome as anywhere else in the Gentile world. The Christians would acknowledge the background out of which they had been delivered by the Gospel.

103. *An Assessment of the Jewish World*

(Rom. 2:1 – 3:20)

Although he does not specifically say so until later, Paul is thinking of a Jewish objector in the next section. He has in mind the self-righteous kind of Jew who would condemn the Gentiles for their vices and yet be guilty of some of them himself, in spite of being a Jew. It would not do to presume on God's patience to His covenant people. That patience is not the kind that tolerates inconsistency, but that gives opportunity for repentance. Paul's typical self-righteous Jew, however, sees no need for repentance. He simply does not recognize that God's wrath is as relevant for him as for the Gentiles. Jew and Gentile are on a precisely equal footing as far as tribulation or glory are concerned. This was a bitter pill for the zealous Jew who was convinced of Jewish superiority over Gentiles. Paul is not exaggerating, for his imagined objector had lived for long within his own breast.

The Jews of Paul's time made much of the law, but their attempt to observe the law gave them no advantage. For the Jews who possessed the law would be judged by the law, while the Gentiles, who had only the law of conscience, would be equally condemned by what law they knew. God knows the secrets of every man and will judge him accordingly.

It was difficult for Jews who made great efforts to conform to the law to admit inconsistency in themselves. Nevertheless in spite of all their boasting the Jews in their history had not been free from giving the Gentiles some cause to reproach them. Paul cites some extreme examples, admittedly, but his point is that men are often blind to those features of the law in which they lamentably fail. The trouble with the Jews was that they placed too much stress on circumcision. A circumcised man became a member of the covenant people, but that did not exempt him from fulfilling the moral demands of the law. Paul establishes the principle that it is better to be uncircumcised and keep the law than circumcised and not keep it. The orthodox Jew would find this hard to accept.

The apostle anticipates an objection. If what he says is right, does this mean that Jews have no advantage over Gentiles? He points out that the Jews, unlike Gentiles, had an inheritance. They were custodians of God's revelation in the past. Even if they failed God, He would never fail them. One of the most dominant features of Paul's theology comes to the fore as he reflects on this. God is not only faithful, but also just. There had been a misunderstanding among some of Paul's hearers when he had expounded this theme, which he thinks is worth mentioning when writing to the Romans. Some had thought that he meant that man's wickedness, because it provided an opportunity for the clearer revelation of God in His dealing with it, was therefore advantageous. This would be an impossible position to maintain. Paul simply says that those who think that he means this are justly condemned.

He has said enough to show that Jews and Gentiles are essentially on the same footing before God. He now quotes a string of Old Testament citations with the aim of demonstrating his point from Scripture. All but one of them come from the Psalms, while the exception comes from Isaiah. The first quotations establish that man's unrighteousness is universal and the rest are samples which stress the nature of man's sin. Paul makes no reference to the context. He regards the words of Scripture as authoritative, regardless of context. This does not mean that he puts an interpretation on the text contrary to its original context, but that he sees a cumulative effect when Scripture is heaped on Scripture. The Jews of Qumran had a similar approach.

Paul gives a parting comment on the Jewish position. The Jews, who acknowledged the authority of Scripture, could not avoid the conclusion that they were included in the "all" who have turned aside. That not even one person can claim to be good eliminates Jewish self-righteousness. Paul can only come to the conclusion that the whole world is answerable before God. Moreover man cannot justify himself. All men who desire to understand the Gospel must accept this conclusion. What Paul proceeds to say to the Romans about God's remedy for man's unrighteousness requires the prior recognition of that unrighteousness.

104. *God Meeting Man's Need*

(Rom. 3:21-4:25)

It may have seemed to his Roman readers that Paul was taking an unduly pessimistic view of human life when he concluded that no single person was righteous. But he was intentionally highlighting man's need. He was not aiming to be gloomy. He could not explain God's redemptive mission without drawing attention to man's complete inability to deal with his own need. God's righteousness becomes meaningful because man has none of his own. That is why Paul says so much about God's righteousness. It is available for all who believe in Christ. It is an act of grace since none can earn it. Its availability is based on God's provision of a means of reconciliation, which in Paul's view is connected with the blood of Christ. The Romans would no doubt have grappled with Paul's meaning here as many have done since. It is deeply theological. It is in fact the core of the Christian faith.

Once anyone accepts such doctrine as this, there is no room for boasting. That redemption has been initiated by God and not by man removes all ground for pride. Moreover it is doubly so because God's provision was at the price of the sacrifice of Christ, which means that justification cannot be by works. Since it is available for both Jews and Gentiles, it cannot depend on works of the law such as circumcision. God does not need man's assistance in providing a perfect means of redemption. Yet Paul is not maintaining that the law can be abolished. It would be a distortion of his position to maintain this. He may be mentioning it because he wonders what the Romans had heard about his views.

As a Jew, he knew very well what some Jewish people might say. They would appeal to the case of Abraham. It was a current topic among the Jews. Paul points out that Abraham's justification was on the basis of his faith and he quotes Genesis 15:6 to this effect. But works expect a reward, not a gift. Paul also cites David's statement in Psalm 32:1, 2, to the effect that a blessing rests on the man to whom the Lord does not reckon his sins, and then he raises the question whether or not this rests on circumcision — an important consideration for Gentiles in the early Church, as the Galatian letter has already shown.

Reverting to Abraham, Paul argues that the patriarch's act of faith was before he was circumcised. Because of this Abraham could be the father of all believers, whether circumcised or uncircumcised. The important thing was not whether men followed Abraham's example of circumcision, but whether they followed his example of faith.

The promise was more important than the law in Paul's view, because it preceded it. If salvation had depended on law, the result would have been an experience of wrath, for law could only point out sin. Moreover, a promise that depended on man's efforts to achieve his own righteousness would lose its essential quality as "promise." Faith consists in accepting what God has said, not fulfilling what God has demanded.

Paul returns to his great theme of grace. It was because God acted entirely on His own initiative that Abraham and his seed inherited the promise. God promised this before his son Isaac was born, when he and his wife Sarah were already both beyond the normal expectation of becoming parents. Even Paul's Gentile readers must have been acquainted with the story of God's faithfulness in the birth of Isaac. Abraham needed a mighty faith to believe a promise which was faced with such odds. But Paul comments that he did not waver. His faith was big enough. He believed that God was able to fulfill His promise. What righteousness Abraham had — and no Jew would dispute that he had it — was based on his faith.

This great theme of justification by faith is not merely bound up with Abraham. It affects all believers. Faith must now, of course, have a different content, but the principle is the same. It is now centered in what God did when He raised Jesus from the dead. The linked historical facts of the death and resurrection of Jesus are vital for Christians. The first deals with their sins; the second witnesses to their justification before God. By the raising of Jesus it was demonstrated that the perfect sacrifice for sins had been accepted. This is the essence of Paul's doctrine of justification.

105. *An Illustration from Adam*

(Rom. 5)

What Paul has just said about justification leads him to reflect on the difference it makes to life. For him it was not merely a theoretical matter, but intensely practical. To begin with it brings peace of mind. What disturbs peace is the nagging feeling that God will hold our sins against us, but in Christ all fear of that is banished. Paul piles up other benefits like grace and hope. But Christians are not exempt from suffering. The missionary who has already passed through many hardships is speaking from experience. He has learned to rejoice because suffering is productive. It sets up a kind of chain reaction. It teaches a man endurance, a quality which gives stability to character. Paul is thinking of Christian character and comes back again to the subject of Christian hope, which is quite different from the "wishful" idea of hope in much modern usage. Christian hope is a solid assurance which never disappoints the person who possesses it. This is because it is dependent on the most dependable factor — God's love for man. Paul thinks of love in terms of a flood which can be poured into empty receptacles. The only limit is the capacity of the containers. This flooding with God's love is through the Spirit. Perhaps Paul had heard of Peter's appeal on the day of Pentecost to Joel's prophecy about the outpouring of the Spirit (Acts 2:18). He uses the same verb.

Then he pauses to reflect on God's love. He points out the unpromising objects to which it was directed. Sinners are not lovable. But what impresses Paul about the Gospel is that God's

love in sending Christ to die for us happened while we were all
sinners. He seems determined that the Romans should be in no
doubt about the nature of God's love. He turns to a more theological kind of argument. Justification involves salvation from
God's wrath, but this is only the negative side of it. If Christ's
death achieves the negative aspect, his life is the basis for the
positive aspect. To escape God's wrath is marvelous for the sin-
ner, but to be reconciled, to have restored relationships as if sin
had never happened, is more marvelous still. Paul's doctrine of
justification implies reconciliation.

It is in this theological frame of mind that Paul turns to Adam
to illustrate his reasoning. It is one of the most important as well
as one of the most difficult passages in his letter. Perhaps he
thought that an appeal to Adam would strike his Gentile readers
more forcibly than his earlier appeal to Abraham. Gentiles at all
acquainted with the Old Testament would know the account of
man's fall in the Garden of Eden and would recognize that
Adam's sin started an avalanche which enveloped all mankind.
There is a reluctance among many to accept Paul's doctrine about
this for it seems to contravene the freedom of man. Yet Paul
was a realist and was approaching the matter from the undoubted
fact that all men had sinned. It was no use contending that only
those since Moses could be charged with sin because until the
law came sin did not exist. That argument would be purely
theoretical. Sin certainly dominated the period from Adam to
Moses. It is no comforting thought that everyone from Adam
onward (except of course Christ) has been affected by Adam's
sin. In spite of the debate which has surrounded the doctrine of
original sin which Paul teaches here, all who ponder the problem
know they have a bias toward sin which their best intentions
cannot overcome.

Paul transfers his reasoning from the widespread effect of
Adam's sin to the widespread effect of the grace of God in Christ.
This is conceived as a free gift, very different from Adam's legacy
to his successors. That gift is remarkable for its capacity for
dealing with trespassers. The gift of righteousness, which no one
can do anything to earn; replaces the legacy of death which
Adam left. Paul is comparing the contribution of both Adam and
Christ to the human race and comes to the conclusion that the
effect of Christ's life was infinitely superior to Adam's. The idea
of a free gift, which was difficult for Jews and was no more

familiar to Gentiles, when it came to the means of getting right with God, is central to the Christian Gospel.

The apostle goes on to make a statement that has caused some confusion. His argument is that as one trespass led to everyone being condemned, so one act of righteousness would lead to everyone gaining life. But elsewhere neither Paul nor the other New Testament writers teach that all would be saved. Paul cannot mean that here. He must mean that Christ's act made it possible for all to have life. This possibility becomes an actuality only for those who exercise faith. He does not mention faith in the immediate context, but his general approach in this letter presupposes it. What he is wanting to do is to contrast the effects of Adam's act with Christ's.

Since Moses' time sin has certainly been more acutely recognized. The more men recognize the nature of sin, the more they can appreciate what grace means. Sin may be king in the region dominated by death, but grace occupies the throne in the realm of eternal life. Roman Christians would appreciate an approach of this kind, for the power of the reigning Caesar would be very much in their minds. The contrast between the best of the Caesars and the grace of God in Christ would at once impress them. The Christian Gospel established a basis of righteousness which Roman justice at its noblest never approached.

106. *Alive to God*

(Rom. 6)

If grace is more apparent when sin is abundant, it is understandable that some might argue that increase in sin is therefore desirable because of its results. Paul at once rejects the thought. He uses the symbolism of baptism to back up his point. Baptism implied a clean break with the past. It symbolized the passing from death to life. It was unthinkable that those walking in newness of life should walk in the same way as they did before. There would be nothing "new" about that. The baptismal ceremony was important to the early Christians, for it stood for a radical change of position on the part of the believer. A deliberate continuation of the life of sin was unthinkable.

Paul's thought turns to the death of Christ and its significance for the believer. Since he holds that the believer is identified with Christ in his death, he argues that he must be similarly identified with Christ in his risen life. This has a twofold implication. The believer must be dead to sin and alive to God. This of course can only happen because he is "in Christ," a favorite and somewhat mystical expression which Paul uses of the believer's relationship to Christ. He proceeds to show the practical outworking of this.

First there is need for a radical change of approach to one's passions. Sin must not be allowed to dominate them. It is important to note that Paul does not consider passion as necessarily wrong, but it is wrong for a Christian to obey passion. A person's bodily functions must become "instruments of righteousness." In the ancient world all Christians would know the radical revolution in thinking and behavior that this would involve. To be alive to God is a highly practical matter. It implies that sin is no longer master.

Paul delights in contrasts. He sees the choice between slavery to sin and slavery to God. He does not hesitate to speak in terms of slavery, but it is a bold metaphor, which he means to be taken seriously. There is no neutral position. In neither position can a man please himself. The Christian has a new standard of teaching, and has no option but to obey it. As he does so, he will become more and more conformed to the standard, which is what Paul means by sanctification. He admits he is using limited language. Slavery is not an attractive metaphor and it might indeed lead to wrong impressions. But the aspect in the metaphor of slavery which Paul wants to stress is the need for obedience.

Continuing his contrast, he compares the rewards of the two positions. Sin's slaves, he concedes, have one advantage. They do not need to bother about righteousness. Once a man is mastered by sin, rightness of conduct ceases to be a consideration. Sin makes no attempt to bind its dupes to any kind of moral code. On the other hand it makes no attempt either to protect its dupes from the consequences of its rule, i.e., from death. Paul is, of course, thinking of spiritual death. In contrast, God's slaves are bound to pursue righteousness. It is part of the terms of service. It cannot be argued about, and is not open to negotiation. Is it then worth pursuing? Paul talks about freedom from sin, which is an infinitely greater benefit than freedom from righteousness. Moreover there is spiritual life in place of spiritual death. God's slaves are on to a good thing.

The topic of rewards recurs in several New Testament books.

Here Paul thinks of it in economic terms when assessing the relative slaveries. Sin's slaves are paid wages. The "wages" are highly undesirable (spiritual death), but they are well earned. Those who receive them deserve all they get. God's slaves, however, earn nothing. Their reward is not the result of their own efforts. What they receive is not wages, but an outright gift. No one in his right mind would prefer wages to a gift. Only those whose pride does not permit them to accept a free offer would prefer to earn their reward. Unfortunately for them and fortunately for all the rest, eternal life cannot be earned. It comes to those who are in Christ Jesus our Lord.

As the Romans listened to Paul's words some must have been caused to think. Was it really as easy as that — just a matter of accepting a free gift? Paul is not through with his arguments yet, for there are struggles as well as triumphs when a man becomes "alive to God."

16

More Doctrine and Ethics for Rome

107. *Inner Conflict*
(Rom. 7)

The apostle is deeply conscious of the need to come to terms with the law. His readers could learn from his own experience, but before he describes this, he discusses the idea of being "dead to the law." The legal position of a married woman is changed when her husband dies. She is free to marry again without committing adultery. Paul applies his illustration in an unexpected way by suggesting that those who have died to law are now free to belong to Christ. He bases this on the assumption that no one can belong to both. Under the regime of law it was inevitable that passions would lead to spiritual death, but the believer has new life in the Spirit. The superiority of the exchange needs no demonstration.

An important consideration is the function of the law for the Christian. Paul rejects at once the idea that the law itself is sinful. There is no doubt that sin has taken advantage of the law, but it has not made the law any less holy. Paul's own unfortunate experience of the law comes to the fore. It made sin revive in him and brought with it death. He is thinking, of course, of the function of law as a means of coming to God. In that respect it had failed.

Paul goes to some length to show that the law was not to be blamed. It was sin that was responsible for the failure. At this the apostle becomes autobiographical. He allows his own tensions to come to the surface, although he admits that his inner struggle baffles him. He cannot properly understand himself. Some of his interpreters have been equally baffled over this passage and have relegated it to his pre-Christian days. They cannot imagine that such a conflict could exist in the mind of a Christian apostle.

But a man whose upbringing has been wholly geared to the fulfilling of the law cannot easily dispose of the tension. Although Paul has been a Christian some twenty years, he cannot put out of his mind the tension caused by the strain between the old and the new.

He is clear about one thing — the law has made the true nature of sin abundantly clear. Paul's awareness of the activity of sin formed a major part of his tension, especially the fact that sin had a hold upon him. He uses picturesque language to describe it (sold under sin). He sees sin as a highly undesirable slave-owner who keeps his dupes in a state of slavery.

The conflict which Paul experienced is vividly described. However much he wanted to do right he found himself doing wrong, in spite of the fact that he hated the wrong which he did. He came to the conclusion, as every man must, that there was an antagonistic principle at work within him which was making him do contrary things. The real problem was that his "flesh," by which he means his lower nature, was a traitor in support of the enemy. It is only because of his awareness of sin that he is aware of the conflict. Whereas these experiences may relate to his pre-conversion state, this is less likely than the view that he is reflecting recurrent conflicts within his Christian experience. Only as a Christian could he fully speak of evil as a thing he did not want to do. The conquering of the sin principle could not be achieved in a day.

It is Paul the Christian who delights in the law of God, but he knows there is a bias within him that pulls the other way. It is a kind of opposing law at variance with his own mind, which precipitates his mind into a state of war. He gives a remarkable psychological analysis of mental and spiritual conflict before psychoanalysis was ever thought of. Obviously such a state of conflict is disturbing. It can only be described as wretchedness. It calls out a prayer for deliverance. The answer is ready to hand, provided by God in Jesus Christ our Lord.

As the Romans read this part of the letter they would gain a more personal insight into the experience of the apostle. They would be able to see him as a man of conflicts like themselves, who was not above the clash between spirit and flesh. As they reflected on his words they in turn would recognize an echo of themselves. They too would know that Christ was the only hope of deliverance from all kinds of spiritual struggle.

108. *Life in the Spirit*

(Rom. 8)

Some experiences are more difficult than others to put into words and this is certainly true of the richness of the new life which Christians find in Christ. One of the classic attempts to do so is found in this letter to the Romans as Paul reaches the climax of his thoughts on righteousness. He aims to show that justification has a practical outworking.

The idea of the Christian life as a walk is not infrequent in the New Testament. Paul here contrasts the walk according to the Spirit with the walk according to the flesh. He is thinking of two quite opposing guides. By flesh he means life which is dominated by passions. He is not intending to imply that the physical side of life is necessarily wrong, except where it shuts out the activity of the Spirit. The believer is a man who is set free from sin and its effects, because Jesus Christ has dealt with sin. Although Jesus lived as a man He never yielded to the flesh as other men had done. Paul says that He condemned sin in the flesh, which is another way of saying that He wholly rejected sin's domination of the flesh. The difference between walking according to Spirit and flesh is reflected most in mental attitudes. The Christian gains a new kind of mind which is characterized by life and peace. This latter quality of serenity is in marked contrast to the hostility of the flesh, a hostility directed against God and His law.

Paul says some great things to the Romans about the Spirit. He talks of the Spirit living in them and of their being in the Spirit. He cannot conceive of a Christian in whom the Spirit does not live. The apostle suggests that as God brought back Jesus from the dead so He will bring new life out of our spiritual deadness. The same Spirit dwells in us as in Jesus Christ. It is an ennobling thought.

The next thing about the Spirit is that He transforms sinners into sons. The Christian has turned his back on slavery to the flesh and to sin. Indeed Paul goes beyond his earlier idea that believers are God's slaves and declares them to be His sons. This is better and more intimate. So intimate indeed that God can be addressed as Father in the most familiar way (Abba). Only the Spirit would dare to suggest this. The Christian knows by the Spirit that he is God's child. Paul goes much further even than that when he suggests that believers are joint-heirs with Christ, which seems to mean that everything that belongs to Christ belongs to us. But this would include suffering as much as glory. Indeed the suffering leads to the glory.

So much suffering has personally confronted Paul that he had to come to terms with it. He sees the whole created order as in the grip of it and thinks of it as groaning for deliverance. By way of contrast, the children of God have liberty, in spirit if not in body. Paul cannot conceive that the physical creation can have any different aspirations from those of the children of God. His mind is reaching out for an application of redemption to the whole creation. This shows the comprehensive character of his view of the redemption which God has provided in Christ. Of course, he admits that this is essentially a matter of hope, but it is a solid hope. The believer has the seal of the Spirit to confirm this. Paul calls the content of the hope "adoption," which echoes what he has just said about the way that believers, having become sons, can address God as Abba.

He wants the Romans to know more of his doctrine of the Spirit, for he proceeds to show how the Spirit intercedes for believers. At the same time he is lost for words to describe it. He mentions "sighs too deep for words" (RSV), but recognizes those sighs to be "according to God's will." It is a great comfort for believers to know that the Spirit's intercession is effective even when noncommunicable.

The Spirit's work is not the only basis for Christian assurance. Another aspect is God's sovereignty, which operates beneficially toward those who love Him. Paul seems at first to be advocating a special providential care over believers, but he does not mean, however, that believers will be protected from hazards that afflict other men, for this would not accord with experience. What Paul evidently means is that whatever the circumstances the believer is convinced that the course of events is for his good. This leads him to introduce more aspects of God's sovereignty in terms of foreknowledge, predestination, and justification. No one has ever exhausted the meaning of the terms and yet Paul assumes that they would be intelligible to his readers. He is, of course, here grappling with profound thoughts, but the general drift of his argument is plain. Looking at things from God's point of view, he sees the assured result of what God is doing as enabling men to share the image of His Son. That is something that man, left to his own devices, could never do.

This part of the letter closes with one of the most confident affirmations in the New Testament. The confidence is based on Paul's knowledge of God. He is on our side. He gave His Son for us. He justifies us. He has provided an intercessor on our behalf. He loves us. It is no wonder in view of such a profound view of God that Paul cannot conceive that anything could come between God and the believer. He makes a list of typical hazards which might do it, some circumstantial, some spiritual. He dismisses them all. All they can do is to make men super-conquerors. When they have done their worst they are wholly incapable of driving a wedge between the believer and God. The Romans must have looked forward to meeting a man with a faith as triumphant as this.

109. *The Problem of Israel and the Justice of God*

(Rom. 9 and 10)

It may be questioned why Paul now turns aside from his discussion of righteousness to deal with the position of Israel. The two subjects are not as separate as some may think. Indeed, unless Israel's problems can be sorted out it might well reflect on God's righteousness, at least for those tempted to think that God has forsaken His chosen people. Paul is clearly convinced that the theme will be of more than academic interest for the Christians at Rome. A proportion of them were Jews in whose minds the problem would figure more prominently than in the minds of the Gentiles.

The people of Israel undoubtedly enjoyed many advantages, but had nevertheless turned against God's provision in Christ. Paul feels acutely the position of his own people. He even makes the point that he would rather himself be cut off from Christ than that Israel should be. A man must feel deeply to make a statement like that, but it draws vivid attention to the problem. It is not God who has failed. The promise to Abraham was continued through Isaac to Jacob. It was all part of the sovereign purposes of God. Even the passing over of Esau is seen as divinely overruled. Paul cites a difficult Scripture in support which shows God's preference for Jacob.

He realizes that God's choice may appear arbitrary to his readers and so proceeds to show that God's mercy is never unjust. The hardening process of God in the case of Pharoah is difficult, but Paul is not intending to exempt Pharoah from full responsibility for his own actions. What he is doing is demonstrating the sovereignty of God. He uses the familiar illustration of a potter at his wheel to show that the clay (representative of man) has no right to question the wisdom of the potter (representative of God). Of course the analogy cannot be pushed, for clay is not the most natural illustration of man, whose personality can hardly be compared with an inanimate lump of dough. Paul's main point, however, is clear — God's real purpose is not wrath, but mercy which extends both to Jews and Gentiles. This universal application is supported by a quotation from Hosea. Those who were not God's people (i.e., Gentiles) were to be called God's sons. As for Israel, Isaiah's statement to the effect that only a remnant was to be saved is cited, together with another statement from the same prophet showing that even the remnant was the result of God's action on Israel's behalf.

By the time that Paul was writing this letter the number of Gentile Christians had far outstripped the number of Jewish Christians. He must often have pondered the reason for this. He had come to the conclusion that the root of the trouble was the stumbling stone, by which he understood Christ. The Jews found a crucified Messiah to be a great obstacle which many could not accept. It was striking evidence of lack of faith on Israel's part.

Although he had come to resolve the matter in his mind, Paul was still deeply disturbed about his own nation. He is aware of their zeal for God, but acknowledges its misguided character. They sought righteousness by their own efforts instead of accepting what God had provided. Man has never been able to achieve his own righteousness. The law of Moses provided the pattern, but gave no power to achieve it. All that is now required is faith and confession. Nothing that man could do would have produced the incarnation (bringing Christ down) or the resurrection (bringing Christ up). God has done it, and all that is now necessary is to confess faith in what God has done and in the lordship of Christ. These simple conditions can of course be fulfilled equally by Jew and Gentile.

As Paul reflects on how men come to believe in God, he recalls yet another passage from Isaiah which extols the preachers of good news. There is no doubt that preaching for him was the major means of bringing men to faith in Christ. We are reminded that his own desire to preach at Rome had been mentioned in the opening part of this letter. He now wants the Romans to know the great importance he attaches to preaching. Nevertheless he admits that not all who hear will receive. He cites yet another passage from Isaiah to this effect.

He is clearly in the frame of mind to quote Scripture, because of its importance for Israel. He cites a Psalm (19:4) to show that all have heard the voice of revelation, and a passage from Deuteronomy which suggested that Israel would be stirred to jealousy by those who in Jewish eyes were a "no-people." Then he again returns to Isaiah (perhaps he had been making a special study of that prophecy at this time), to a passage which shows God's initiative toward those who had made no pretense of seeking Him, as Israel had. Another statement from the same context in Isaiah shows how God had pleaded with His chosen people, who had nevertheless been disobedient to Him.

The whole burden of Paul's problem over Israel is that Israel is thoroughly answerable for their rejection. The Word has been preached and has not been received. No one can blame God for that. Since there were many Jews resident in Rome at that time, this discussion must have been of great practical relevance. It would have helped the Jewish Christians to come to terms with the hardness of their unbelieving Jewish brethren.

110. *God's Solution to Israel's Problem*

(Rom. 11)

Having spoken of the unbelief of Israel, Paul comes to speak of the remnant. It is an important aspect of his theology. He cites the time of Elijah and the considerable number of people who had never indulged in the worship of Baal. He sees a parallel in the contemporary scene. Scattered through most of his Gentile churches were small groups of Jewish Christians in addition to the churches of Judaea. These made up the "remnant chosen by grace."

A remnant which responded implies a majority which rejected, a sad fact which Paul supports from further Scripture passages. He cites yet another statement from Isaiah and also another

from the Psalms. Both of them speak of God's retribution to
Israel because of their unbelief. Isaiah describes their state of
stupor and David the pitfalls confronting them. In reflecting on
this position, Paul sees that all has not been lost, for Gentiles have
come in where the majority of Israel have stayed out. He hopes
this will stir the Jews to jealousy and cause them also to come in.
He ponders on what the result would be if Israel as a whole
believed.

He next addresses himself specifically to Gentile readers and
in doing so magnifies his office as their apostle. Even as he does
so he hopes that some of the Jews might be saved. To illustrate
his point he appeals to dough on the one hand and a tree on the
other. What is true of a part of the dough is true of the whole
lump. What is true of the root holds for the branches. By these
illustrations he seems to be saying that Israel will not be complete until all believe. He has more to say about this later.

It may have been his root illustration which led him to use
his famous wild olive illustration. Although the horticultural
details are somewhat mixed (Paul was evidently no expert on
trees), the train of thought is reasonably clear. Israel is thought
of as an olive tree and the Gentiles as a wild shoot which has
been grafted on to the original stock. Paul warns the Gentiles
not to boast about this, since the branches are dependent upon
the stock. In the long run they are in fact dependent on God's
kindness. They must not forget, however, that there is another
side to His character, i.e., a severity which should lead them to
stand in awe. Moreover, if God can make wild olive branches
productive, He can certainly restore the original tree.

Paul comes back to the basic problem, the hardening of part
of Israel. The word he uses for hardening is drawn from the idea
of a hard crust which makes a thing impervious, and this is how
he sees Israel's position. He visualizes the filling up of the Church
with Gentiles, but also foresees a time when all Israel will be
saved. Much discussion has surrounded this statement. Does it
mean that every single Israelite will be saved? Or, does it mean
that all parts of Israel will be affected rather than just the
remnant? Paul's "alls" are not always comprehensive and it seems
clear that he does not intend this "all" to be. Nothing would,
nevertheless, rejoice his heart more than to see every Israelite
saved by grace, but he recognizes that many will contract out
because of unbelief. Another quotation from Isaiah shows the

promise of a Deliverer for Israel, while yet another is a mixture from Jeremiah about the new covenant and from Isaiah again about the removal of sins.

God has no need to revise His promises. What He has said is unchangeable, because He is unchangeable. Paul notes that there is a discrepancy between the ideal (as seen in the covenant) and the actual (as seen in Jewish opposition to God's Deliverer). It appears at present that Jewish disobedience is making room for mercy to the Gentiles. Yet it is important to grasp, as Paul notes, that God shows mercy to all without distinction. The Jews are certainly not excluded from the mercy of God.

This difficult discussion ends with a magnificent affirmation. Paul searches for words to describe the knowledge of God. He comes to the conclusion that God's judgments are untrackable and His ways inscrutable. If they were not so God would not be God. In face of the many problems which arise when finite minds ponder the infinite, all that can be done is to assert the marvelous wisdom of God. Paul again supports his point with scriptural language, partly from Isaiah and partly from Job to the effect that God is sovereignly independent. How foolish for anyone to think he can understand God's mind or give Him advice! How foolish to imagine that anyone can put God in his debt! Everything originates from Him and exists by His permission and for His benefit. This kind of doxology must have greatly encouraged and perhaps challenged the original readers of the letter, as it must all who seriously ponder its message.

111. *Practical Advice*

(Rom. 12 and 13)

Paul never dwelt exclusively on doctrine. In all his letters he includes practical advice, and this letter is no exception. Indeed, the practical implications of his doctrinal argument are nowhere brought out more clearly than here.

Those who have received the righteousness of which Paul has been speaking have a responsibility to follow it through both physically and mentally. The body needs dedicating to God and the mind needs renewal. This new controlling factor is God's will, which in Paul's view is always perfect, and can be cheerfully embraced.

A constant danger in any community of Christians is pride,

some regarding themselves as more important than others. Paul uses the analogy of the human body to show that each member is equally important. Whatever gift anyone possesses should be exploited to the full in the interests of the whole body. Surely, no reader could fail to grasp the point of this simple but effective illustration.

Such qualities as love, zeal, spiritual glow, joy, and patience are enjoined as essential facets of the Christian character. Even benevolence and hospitality are assumed to be fit themes for general exhortations. Living in harmony with others is essential and must govern one's approach even to one's persecutors. If vengeance belongs to God (and Paul cites the Old Testament to this effect — from Deuteronomy), the idea that a Christian should retaliate when wrongly treated is not only alien to the Gospel, but is also foolishly unnecessary. When Paul talks about giving food and drink to one's enemies, he expresses a sentiment closely akin to a statement of Jesus in the Sermon on the Mount. The Christians' guiding principle is to overcome their opponents' evil with their own good.

The attitude which Christians were to adopt toward the State had not as yet become critical, but some guidance was necessary even at this stage. The Roman Christians were nearer than any to the central government of the powerful Roman empire. They would know at first hand the mood of the governing authorities. So far there had been no clashes between Church and State. Nero had not yet begun his persecution. Roman rule had established a considerable degree of peace throughout the empire. It is against this background of political stability that Paul urges subjection to the ruling authorities on the grounds that these exist for the good of the community. He even calls them "ministers of God." Christians have no need to fear unless they do wrong. Taxation is not to be evaded. Paul does not deal with the problem of what a Christian is to do if demands of the State clash with his conscience. The problem had not as yet arisen, but a time not far distant was to witness a head-on clash between Church and State, involving a matter of conscience.

The apostle switches his mind from subjection to the State to the subject of love. In the Christian approach to other people, particularly to one's neighbor, there is an obligation to love. This is no sloppy sentimentality, but a robust principle, which is unconditional. It does not depend on the subject. It expects the

Christian to show love to his neighbor, whatever the neighbor's character may be like. He may be a rascal, but he still needs love. Moreover, no less a standard is required than the sort of love a person has for himself. Jesus had made the same demand of the rich young man who wanted eternal life and yet when the young man had said that he had fulfilled this, Jesus put him to the test. He really loved his possessions more than he loved his neighbors. To Paul love summed up the law. It was the most positive side of the law. All the other commandments which Paul mentioned were prohibitions (you shall not . . .). But love embraces the lot. No one who really loves will steal or covet, kill or commit adultery. If the Roman Christians had so far received no copy of the gospels, they would have gained from this letter in brief compass an insight into the basic ethical teaching of Jesus.

Perhaps the apostle thought it was too much to expect that all his readers would rise to this height of love, for he immediately appends an exhortation to them to put off the works of darkness. He thinks of a spiritual daybreak which is fast approaching. There comes an hour when it is no longer fitting to remain asleep. It is time for alertness, for preparation for the coming light. The figure of speech is vivid and challenging. Daylight is no time for the works of darkness. New clothing is needed, which Paul picturesquely calls the armor of light. Romans would warm to such imagery. They were used to seeing their victorious armies parading in armor and would readily catch the idea of the spiritual counterpart. The idea of putting on the Lord Jesus Christ as one would put on a garment is striking, even daring. With such a "clothing" gratification of fleshly desires would be utterly incongruous. It was Jesus Himself who had claimed to be Light, and anything savoring of darkness must go from His followers.

112. *The Strong and the Weak*

(Rom. 14:1 – 15:13)

It was bound to happen in the developing Church that differences of opinion would arise over matters of conscience, even over trivial matters. Paul seems to have had specific knowledge of such a case at Rome over what foods were permissible for Christians to eat. This is one of the few practical subjects on which Paul is specific in this letter. The problem was the vegetarian. Those who were not vegetarians were critical of those who were, and that kind of situation at once breeds disharmony. Paul points out the simple yet basic principle that God welcomes even the weak.

An even more far reaching principle is that everything that is done should be done for the Lord's honor, not for one's own. When differences arise over observance of special days, which were a feature of some sections of the early church, so long as each party holds its point of view "in the Lord," criticism of others will vanish. Christians cannot live to themselves even if they want to, for they are committed to live to the Lord. This is implicit in what Christ did for them when he died. Whether in life or in death the Christian belongs to the Lord. This is a conviction which brings a deep sense of contentment and peace.

Paul again discusses the spirit of criticism. He solemnly reminds his readers that everyone will need to answer for his attitude of God's Judgment Seat. He once again cites Isaiah to this effect. Men who live in the awareness of such a future event will not treat lightly their attitude to their brethren in Christ. It is uncomfortable to realize that everything must be accounted for. Nor is this simply Paul's idea. Jesus had said the same kind of thing, even warning that account must be given for idle words on the day of Judgment (Matt. 12:36).

A spirit of criticism can be a real stumbling block. When one calls unclean (Paul probably means ritual uncleanness) what another does not, it is largely a matter of opinion, but if a brother feels strongly about a thing it would be provocative for another to condemn him for it. The matter of meats was a critical one for Christians in the pagan environment. Most meat was offered in idol sacrifices and a moral problem at once arose for certain Christians. Here Paul is not so concerned about the cause of the moral problem as the straining of human relationships which could result. He recommends that Christians should walk in love, which means consideration must be given to anyone else for whom Christ died. This is a comprehensive principle, which means at times that some who see nothing wrong in a practice will refrain from doing it for the sake of the weaker brother. The principle was not intended by Paul to give power to the weaker to dictate to the strong, for he is assuming that an attitude of mutual love exists which would foster mutual understanding.

Paul rarely mentions the kingdom of God, but he does so here to show that spiritual qualities are of much greater importance than material considerations. It is possible to be accepted by God and approved by men, when the prior claims of the kingdom are borne in mind. The approval that Paul is thinking of is, of course, within the Christian community. The peace and strengthening of the community is more important than individual scruples over eating or drinking. In so enunciating a general approach, the apostle set a pattern not only for the Roman Christians, but for all subsequent generations of believers.

The crux of the matter could be summed up as "others versus self." It is no part of the Christian way of life for self-interest to dominate, since Christ certainly did not please Himself. Paul cites Psalm 69:9 as fulfilled in Christ — reproaches rather than self-interest. Such passages were a great encouragement to these early Christians. The readers would have got the point. Harmony among them was expected in Christ, and this became one of the most impressive features of early Christian testimony (cf. Acts 4:32).

Everywhere in Paul's thought Christ Himself is the example. Believers must welcome each other as Christ had welcomed them. His ministry was primarily to Jews (the circumcised), but His purpose was for Gentiles also to hear. Paul again presses home his point from Scripture, citing four passages which all mention the Gentiles (two from Psalms, one from Deuteronomy, and one from Isaiah). If the Jewish-Gentile obstacle could be overcome, no other could stand. Believers, Jews and Gentiles alike, could be filled with joy, peace, and hope. This was not to be accomplished by human effort, but by the power of the Spirit.

113. *Plans and Greetings*

(Rom. 15:14 – 16:27)

In view of what he has just written, it might be supposed that Paul is being somewhat critical of the Romans, but he hastens to correct any such misconception. He considers them to be full of goodness and knowledge, a surprisingly warm commendation. When goodness is partnered by knowledge it is a remarkable combination. Yet to such a group of people Paul considers he must write boldly, precisely because of his calling as an apostle to the Gentiles. He dwells on his experience in this ministry. Looking back on his missionary service, he claims no personal credit, although he clearly has cause to be deeply satisfied. He wants the Romans to know that Christ has been active through him. As we listen to his dialogue with his readers, we recognize how much the widespread response of Gentiles to the Gospel had meant to him. He recalls the "signs and wonders" which have accompanied his preaching. He does not often mention them, but he sees them as evidence of the activity of the Spirit. He thinks of the territory stretching across a good part of the Roman world from Jerusalem to Illyricum on the borders of the Adriatic, where he had preached. It was always his aim to preach only where no one else had worked. Paul was essentially a pioneer. The spread of the Gospel owes much to those who share the same spirit. He cites a passage from Isaiah (52:15) to illustrate this pioneer work.

Turning to his immediate plans, he makes the astonishing statement that he finds no further room for work in the regions just mentioned. This does not mean that the areas have been completely evangelized, for Paul's strategy was to plant churches in important centers and then to expect the developing churches to evangelize the surrounding district. Only by this means was he able to work in so many areas. He was always on the look-out for new fields in which to sow the seed of the Gospel, and conceived the idea of going to Spain. Whether he ever went there is uncertain, but as he looks forward to his visit to Rome he definitely intends going on from there to Spain. He may well have had to change his plans. He is about to depart for Jerusalem with his collection fund, contributed by Christians in both Macedonia and Achaia, which was designed to alleviate the distress of the Jewish churches of Judaea and was also seen as a token of Gentile-Jewish concern. In a world in which Jews were not a particularly loved race of people, this gesture on the part of Gentile churches was impressive.

There are some apprehensions in Paul's mind as he thinks of his visit to Judaea. He wants the Romans to pray for him. He knows he has enemies at Jerusalem — he calls them "unbelievers," but we can guess what is in his mind. He is also somewhat uncertain what the Jewish believers will think of his collection scheme. Even Jewish Christians still shared the characteristic pride in their nation, and to accept help from Gentiles was none too easy. Nevertheless Paul expects to discharge his task in Jerusalem and then to proceed to Rome to gain refreshment through his fellowship with them.

Because a benediction is included at this point and because the rest of the letter is mostly made up of greetings, many scholars treat the whole of chapter 16 as originally belonging to a different letter. The theory cannot be proved, and it is by no means impossible to regard the greetings as part of the letter to Rome. It has been thought that a difficulty arises over so many people being known by name to Paul in a church he had never visited. At any other place than Rome the difficulty would be more acute, but because Rome was the hub of the empire and all roads led to Rome, it is not surprising that many who had known Paul elsewhere had since traveled to Rome. They would provide useful contacts when the apostle visited the capital.

In the list which he gives, many of the names are no more than names to us. We would like to know more about the people. Illuminating comments are attached to some of them: the deaconess, Phoebe, who was known for her helpfulness and was coming to Rome; Aquila and Priscilla, who were last heard of in Ephesus and who had exposed themselves to danger for Paul's sake and were evidently patriots of Rome (they had a house church, as Aristobulus and Narcissus also probably did); the first Christian convert in Asia (Epaenetus' chief claim to fame); one man, Rufus, who is known as "eminent in the Lord," whose mother had evidently been kind to Paul; two men, Andronicus and Junias, who are described as "fellow-prisoners," a description which conjures up some unrecorded event in which Paul and his kinsmen fell foul of the authorities. Some are described simply as "beloved," others as "in the Lord." It is an intriguing list which characteristically ends with a greeting from all the churches.

An unexpected warning about false teachers who deceive is inserted before the letter ends. One wonders why nothing has been said about it before. It seems improbable that the deceivers have yet affected the Roman Christians and all that is needed therefore is to urge them to be on their guard. Their enemy Satan will then deserve no better fate than to be crushed underfoot.

A few more greetings from Paul's associates are added, including such people as Timothy, his scribe, Tertius, and Erastus, presumably the city treasurer of Corinth, a reminder that there were at least a few people of influence in the Christian church. A magnificent doxology brings the letter to a close. It fits the majestic character of the whole letter. Its theme is the mystery, once hidden, but now revealed. This is the core of the Gospel which Paul has preached already and will preach at Rome.

EPHESUS AREA.

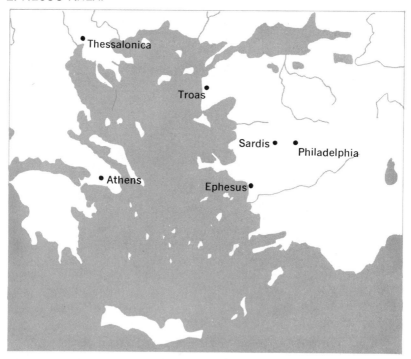

17

Journey to Jail

114. *From Troas to Miletus*
(Acts 20:7-16)

Paul encountered many adventures on his journeys which Luke does not record. Special focus therefore falls on those which he particularly related. Few happenings were more dramatic or unexpected than the restoration of Eutychus. Some of the details are left to the imagination, but it is not difficult to reconstruct them. While still at Troas Paul had gathered together some of the believers for the breaking of bread and the exposition of the Word. It was a Sunday, and by this time it seems to have been the usual practice for believers to assemble together in this way. Presumably on this occasion they had not been able to meet until the evening when the day's work was done. Paul was intending to leave Troas the next day en route for Miletus.

Although the apostle had already been in Troas for a whole week, this final evening evidently meant much to him. He had much to say. The flickering wick lamps in the third story room where they were meeting helped to dispel some of the darkness as Paul's sermon continued until midnight. It is not surprising that the atmosphere became drowsy through lack of oxygen. Even the incomparable privilege of listening to an exposition by the apostle to the Gentiles was not enough to keep all the audience alert. Whether Eutychus was bored with the sermon or whether he fell asleep through sheer mental exhaustion is of no importance. Paul's midnight sermon came to an abrupt close. The young man who must have been near a window fell to the ground. Other members of the audience were clearly not sufficiently alert to notice the danger that threatened Eutychus. It was too late. He lay dead on the ground.

Luke says nothing about Paul's immediate reactions. It may be conjectured that he rushed down the stairs to the scene of the tragedy. Luke says that he bent over the boy and embraced him. That was enough. He was convinced that the boy would revive. Luke telescopes the details. He includes nothing about any prayer that Paul ·presumably offered before the restoration, nor any details of the method he followed. Indeed Luke's account concentrates on Paul's remark that life was still in him and at once describes the continuation of the service. Even so stupendous a miracle as this is almost crowded out by the greater importance of Paul's spiritual ministry. The young man was taken home, much to the comfort of his associates.

When the apostle returned to the upper room, the congregation had still not dispersed. The sermon was not resumed. They went straight into an observance of the Lord's Supper. Even after that the congregation did not move away, for Paul was still conversing. It is futile to conjecture the subject of conversation, but a man with so rich an experience of missionary service as Paul could never have been lost for topics of conversation. The people of Troas stayed to listen till daybreak. Some years were to elapse before Paul visited Troas again, on an occasion when he left behind his cloak and parchments (cf. 2 Tim. 4:13) with a man named Carpus. It was near the end of his life.

Luke resumes his narrative. He remembers that he and others of Paul's party had embarked on a ship for Assos, some miles further south from Troas. But Paul himself for some reason preferred to go over land. He met the ship at Assos, a place built on a rocky headland some 700 feet high. It was at that time a formidable fortress situated in Mysia in the province of Asia.

The sea voyage from there to Miletus passed uneventfully. Luke jots down a list of places visited. The chief interest in these details lies in the evidence they give of his meticulous concern for details. He probably kept a daily diary. He notes for instance that it took three days on the way from the Mitylene on the island of Lesbos to Miletus, with a call at Samos en route.

Miletus was further south than Ephesus, where the ship was not calling. Paul's urgency to get to Jerusalem in time for the feast of Pentecost is noted as the reason for his not stopping at Ephesus. Nevertheless he feels he cannot rush past without meeting the Ephesian elders. He decides to send for them to meet him at Miletus. The boat was evidently stopping at Miletus for a while. No previous mention has been made of elders at Ephesus, but presumably some time during his three years' ministry there Paul had appointed them. They came to him at once. There must have been a close understanding between them and the apostle for them to travel the 28 miles to see him. The strong bond of Christian affection between them is in fact seen in the touching farewell following Paul's speech to them.

115. *Advice to Church Elders*

(Acts 20:17-38)

Luke does not say whether the hastily arranged "retreat" of Ephesian elders was held in the open air or in some nearby room. He is concerned only with the words which flowed from Paul's lips on that occasion. It was an address which gives many insights into Paul's character.

Paul's first remarks appeal to both past and future, as a prelude to his dealing with the present. There is a value in appealing to the testimony of the past, as distinct from living in the past. Some are so anxious to avoid the latter that they never do the former. Paul reminds the Ephesians of what they already knew. His ministry among them was marked by humility and even by tears and trials, but it was centered in the Lord, not in them nor in himself. He recalls his method, which consisted of public meetings and private conversations. He had approached both Jews and Greeks with the Gospel. Both alike were exhorted to repentance and faith. It is a valuable exercise to remind oneself and others of what the Lord has already done, for this increases confidence for the future.

As Paul looks ahead his comments contain much advice which is timeless in its application. He disclaims being a free agent, but maintains that he is "bound in the Spirit," by which he means that the Spirit has constrained him to go to Jerusalem. Nevertheless, he is clearly apprehensive (cf. Rom. 15:31). He is not afraid to say that he has no idea what will happen to him in Jerusalem. He expects nothing but imprisonment and afflictions, a conviction which, borne of the Spirit, has been increasing in each city as he moves on toward Jerusalem. By now he has become more than ever convinced that his enemies will not let such an opportunity slip. It is the nature of the Gospel to arouse opposition, and Paul has come to terms with this. His concern is more for the faithful completion of his ministry than for his own safety. The Ephesians would know this was a characteristic of the apostle's approach to his missions, which were based on disregard for his own comfort or security. He was consumed with a passion to proclaim the grace of God. He could have had no greater aim.

At this point Paul takes stock of the present. He stands as it were at the end of an era in his life. Turning his back on his mission activity in Asia Minor, Macedonia, and Achaia, he now looks toward Spain. This is therefore in the nature of a farewell. Paul affirms that he has discharged his responsibility to the Ephesians. He puts it strongly. He claims to be innocent of their blood, the same kind of expression as used by Pilate at the trial of Jesus. Moreover, he claims to have set before them the "whole counsel of God." It was a great claim, but undoubtedly justified in his case. He set the pattern for all subsequent servants of God, whose commission does not permit them to choose for themselves the content of their message.

Having looked to the past, the future, and the present, Paul now turns to a final exhortation. The Ephesian leaders were to take stock of themselves and of the church, which is an exercise which bears constant repetition. Particularly is this so for elders who recognize themselves as being appointed by the Spirit. Their task is illustrated through the imagery of sheep and shepherds. It involves responsibility for the shepherds, who cannot afford to neglect self-examination. Especially is this so for the leaders of God's flock, which is of priceless value. It was purchased by nothing less than the Lord's own blood.

Eastern shepherds needed constant care to guard the flock against enemies. Wolves were a special threat and Paul transfers the figure to violent enemies of the Church whom he foresaw would arise. Moreover, undermining would come from within in the form of perverse speech. When those purporting to belong to the flock use their influence to lead astray, it is one of the most devastating of all attacks on the Christian Church.

Another valuable exhortation called on them to remember Paul's constancy among them. His was no fleeting example. The Ephesians had for three years heard his earnest admonitions. With typical wholeheartedness he adds "day and night," meaning to indicate presumably that there was no time of day or night during which he refrained from admonishing them if it were necessary. He reminds them of his tears on their behalf. Tears are always eloquent. The Ephesian leaders responded in the same way when the time came for Paul's departure. He now commends them to God for building up and for enjoying all that God has prepared for them. There is no thought of them being able to stand on their own feet, for Christians have a more secure basis than that.

In a parting comment Paul indulges in personal reminiscence. He denies covetousness. But why? Had some charged him with working among them for what he could get out of it? This is unlikely. It is more probable that he wished to forestall such a suggestion. His mission work had indeed demanded great self-sacrifice. His gnarled hands could bear testimony, for the rough canvas had taken its toll, but had enabled him to be self-supporting. Moreover, he had been able to dispense charity rather than rely on it. Paul quotes a statement of Jesus — "It is more blessed to give than to receive" — which is the clearest example of a saying of Jesus not recorded in the Gospels. It must have been orally preserved as an epigrammatic saying. It is fitting that Paul's final words to the elders should be the words of Jesus.

The farewell is particularly moving. The whole company — the elders and the members of Paul's party — knelt and prayed as Paul led them. There was not a dry eye as, with warm Christian affection, they embraced the apostle, gave him the customary farewell kiss, and escorted him to the ship. With saddened hearts they returned to Ephesus to tell the church there about Paul's message.

116. *At Tyre and Caesarea*

(Acts 21:1-14)

Luke was in Paul's party as more sea voyages were undertaken. They passed many places of considerable interest, but the historian has no inclination to enlarge on these. He may, of course, have been disinterested, but more likely the pressures of space and purpose forbade any descriptive comment. They visited the mountainous island of Cos, famous as the seat of the medical school founded by Hippocrates. The following day they came to Rhodes, site of the famous Colossus, and from there sailed on to Patara, a harbor in Lycia which was much used for transshipment to Phoenicia. It was not difficult for Paul and his party to transfer to another ship en route for Tyre. On the journey there the ship skirted the island of Cyprus, but did not stop. The sight of it must have revived memories in Paul's mind of his first missionary visit in company with Barnabas, a native of the island.

While the ship was unloading cargo at Tyre, Paul and his party had time to visit the Christians there. Luke gives no details about them. It will be remembered that some of the people of Tyre had heard Jesus teach (Mark 3:8, Luke 6:17) and since then must have become His disciples. Tyre itself had had a notable history, but was past its prime. It had been besieged by Alexander the Great nearly four centuries before Paul's time, but had recovered under the rule of the Seleucid kings. It was a strategic place for the planting of a Christian church. The apostle to the Gentiles seized the fleeting opportunity to have fellowship with the Christians there and to encourage them.

They were men of the Spirit. They felt convinced that they should dissuade Paul from going to Jerusalem. He did not heed their advice, for he was equally convinced by the same Spirit that he should proceed with his plan. It is not uncommon for God's people to suggest what other people's leading should be, only to find that the others do not share the same convictions. In the long run Paul had to decide for himself what the Spirit wanted him to do, which was to finish his journey. The Christians of Tyre accepted this decision with grace, for they all, including wives and children, accompanied him from the city to the harbor. It was another impressive farewell scene as all the Christians kneeling on the beach prayed together. Onlookers must have been puzzled, but some may have been deeply impressed by the concern which these Christians were showing for each other.

Paul and his company continued their journey to Ptolemais, a port about eight miles north of Carmel on the Phoenician coast, across the bay from the modern Haifa. In Paul's day it was a Roman colony because some of Claudius' veterans had been settled there. The apostle may have been there before. On the present occasion, he had only one day to spare, but succeeded in locating the brethren in order to spend that day with them.

From there it was not far to Caesarea, which they reached the next day. Their host was well known as one of the earliest to be appointed to non-apostolic office. But Philip had long since forsaken administration for the work of an evangelist. Moreover his example was such that his four daughters all devoted themselves to prophetic ministry. His was certainly an unusual household. It must have been of special interest to Luke, whose appetite for collecting information of a historical kind was already whetted. It was almost certainly from Philip that he gleaned some of his information about the earliest stages of Christian history.

But Luke's main interest during that visit to Philip's was in the arrival of Agabus. He was a notable Jerusalem prophet, who had already made a startling announcement at Antioch regarding the coming famine and had inspired the church there to send relief to the Judaean Christians. On that occasion his prophetic gift was exercised by the Spirit. Once again he prophesies by the Spirit, this time in a dramatic way by binding his hands and feet with Paul's girdle. This symbolic action, reminiscent of the Hebrew prophets, was predictive of Paul's destiny at Jerusalem. The Jews would bind him and hand him to the Gentiles.

It is not surprising that such a prophecy had a disturbing effect. All in Paul's party were alarmed, in spite of Agabus' claim to speak as the mouthpiece of the Spirit. Their immediate reaction was to try at all costs to prevent such a disaster. Yet they were not only being unduly protective toward Paul, they were setting themselves against the prediction of the Spirit. Nevertheless the tension they showed was intensely natural. Where strong human attachments appear to conflict with spiritual convictions, it is difficult for the latter to supplant the former, but in Paul's case it did. His one desire was to fulfill his mission in the name of Jesus. If that meant captivity or even death in Jerusalem, it could not deflect him. Yet he was thoroughly human and the tears and attempted persuasions of his closest friends were disturbing. He urged them to stop, at which they had no option but to pray that God's will should be done.

The incident raised a problem which constantly recurs. Was Paul foolhardy in following his convictions? Would not a more cautious approach have been wiser? Was he pigheaded to resist the advice of his friends? The more calculating might be tempted to answer in the affirmative, but pioneers of the stamp of Paul are not the kind of characters to put personal safety before devotion to their calling. Maybe Luke, as he recorded the incident, remembered his own futile attempts to persuade the apostle to change his plans.

117.   *Arrival at Jerusalem*

(Acts 21:15-26)

From earliest days the Christians sought to serve each other. Paul's brief stay at Caesarea had sufficiently commended him to the Christians there for some to accompany him and his party to Jerusalem. Moreover the Caesareans appear to have made the arrangements for accommodation for the travelers at Jerusalem. There was a man of Cyprus who was able and willing to offer them hospitality. The host, Mnason, had been a disciple of Jesus since early times. This offered Luke another good opportunity to collect information about the ministry of Jesus.

Evidently James and the Jerusalem elders were aware of Paul's coming, for the day after his arrival a reports meeting was arranged. It is not clear whether any of the apostles were present, for Luke does not mention them. Paul had an appreciative audience, in spite of the fact that some of the Jerusalem Christians had been party to the attempt to impose circumcision on Gentiles as a condition of the Gospel. The meeting must have taken some time, for Luke says that Paul related one by one what God had done among the Gentiles. The historian probably had his notebook to hand, if he had not previously recorded the main features of the events which Paul reported.

The Jerusalem Christians were thrilled by what they heard. They glorified God for what was happening among the Gentiles. That these Jews rejoiced so generously over God's activity among the Gentiles showed they had come a long way toward a true Christian understanding. But there were many Jewish Christians who had other views of Paul's activity. A report was circulating that he was urging Jewish Christians to forsake Moses. The Jerusalem elders did not support such an interpretation for they had come to an understanding with Paul. It is nevertheless significant how easily well-meaning Christians could believe and circulate a false report, which their own leaders had effectively denied by extending to Paul and Barnabas the right hand of fellowship. Two false deductions were being made — one that Paul was legislating for Jews and the other that he was advocating the forsaking of Moses. It is clear that even at this early stage in Christian history damage was being done through irresponsible reports.

The problem of how to deal with such misrepresentation is an ever present one. The Jerusalem elders proposed a compromise. If Paul specifically did something to show the Jewish Christians that he was not opposed to the Mosaic law, it would do much to lessen the criticism leveled against him. Having placed himself under a Jewish vow, Paul was asked to associate himself with four others who were also under a vow. If he identified himself with them by paying their expenses most of the sting would be removed from the Jewish accusations. The elders wanted it to be seen that Paul ordered his life according to the Mosaic law.

Some have seen a problem in the readiness with which Paul agreed to the elders' proposal. Since he had been so adamant over the circumcision of Gentiles, was it not inconsistent for him to continue the ritual observance of the Jewish law? There was, however, a difference between imposing new restrictions on Gentiles and continuing established practices among Jews. Paul was proud of his Jewish heritage. He did not hesitate to adhere to standard Jewish practice in the matter of a vow. The Christian Gospel was independent of the Jewish tradition, but Paul saw no harm in observing the latter. Although on this occasion he was anxious to avoid giving offense, the plan did not succeed as the sequel shows.

Something of the problem facing early Jewish Christians is seen in the dilemma of these Jerusalem elders. They themselves had made wide concessions over the admission of Gentiles. They told Paul of the letter they had sent. But why did they draw attention to this at all? If Acts 15 is to be relied on, Paul knew all about it. Yet the elders are not so much informing him, as reminding him. Their proposal about the vow must be seen against this background, for they were on Paul's side.

118.   *The Arrest of Paul*

(Acts 21:27-40)

The plan of the Jerusalem Christians appeared to be succeeding without incident. The period of purification for the vow which Paul had undertaken covered a week and was almost over. His regular visits to the Temple had not been noticed until he was recognized by some Asiatic Jews. If these were men who had dogged the work of the apostle in Asia and whose repeated attempts to thwart the progress of the Gospel had failed, their strong reaction on recognizing Paul can be easily appreciated.

In Jerusalem there would be many ready to support any move against a man who had had an undermining effect on the synagogues of the Dispersion, particularly among the proselytes. The Asians soon roused many of the Jerusalem Jews to mob violence. As usual the seizing of Paul was not based on rational judgment. They regarded him as a religious revolutionary. He was definitely regarded as anti-establishment (which in their mind consisted of the people, the law, and the Temple). Officialdom never likes anti-men, but neither do gullible crowds which have been convinced that the anti-men are against their best interests. Such times offer no opportunity for a reasoned examination of the evidence to discover whether the rumors are correct.

There were three steps in the logic of these Asians, which led to a wrong conclusion. First, they had seen Paul with a Gentile, Trophimus, in the city; secondly, they had seen Paul with other men in the Temple; and thirdly, they concluded that Paul had taken a Gentile into the Temple. The fact that it was necessary to prove that Trophimus was one of these men was disregarded. The idea of a Gentile in the Temple was enough to stir the blood of all loyal Jews. It was a perfect situation for a riot. Luke picturesquely says that the whole city was roused and dragged Paul from the Temple. It was a riot with a strong religious motive, the worst kind for acts of inhumanity. Paul sustained blows and beatings until the army intervened and formally arrested him.

It is typical of mob violence that no clear picture can be obtained of the cause of the trouble. The Roman official's attempt to obtain a reasonable explanation from the crowd was doomed at the outset. No consistent picture emerged. Some said one thing, some said another. What they agreed on was a common opposition to Paul. Much religious persecution in the subsequent history of Christianity followed the same pattern.

Mob violence brings out the worst in men. So incensed was the crowd that soldiers had to carry Paul up the barrack steps. The cry, "Away with him," is reminiscent of the clamor of the crowds for the crucifixion of Jesus. It is a solemn reminder that the disciple can expect no better treatment than his Master. But Paul was a veteran in this kind of situation. He had often suffered indignities for Christ's sake. On this occasion he was once again remarkably cool-headed. Always alert to seize opportunities, he addressed the Roman tribune while in the process of being manhandled into the barracks. The official, amazed that Paul spoke in Greek, must have been muddle-headed about the whole affair. He had supposed that Paul was a noted Egyptian revolutionary, who had headed up a considerable revolt only recently. It does not seem to have occurred to him that a character who had marshaled four thousand supporters would not have appeared without escort in the Temple at Jerusalem. No doubt this was another case of unconfirmed rumor, but the official was taking no chances. It was Paul's command of Greek which made him wonder.

There is a dignity about the apostle's reply. He made it clear that he was no Egyptian, but a Jew, which must have made the tribune puzzled. Why then had his soldiers had to rescue Paul from the Jews? The apostle also stated his city of origin, Tarsus in Cilicia, which he proudly described as no mean city. He had some cause to describe it in this way. It was one of the four university cities of the ancient world and was renowned for this reason. The Roman tribune must have known this. In view of his own mistake in assuming the wrong identity of Paul, he appears to have been more disposed toward him. In spite of the fact that Paul had been the center of a near riot, the official gave him permission to speak, perhaps already convinced that there was no hope that he would make himself heard. He must have been astonished when, by no more than a movement of his hands, he hushed the rabble. Paul must have had some spiritual dignity which shone through his tortured body so as to compel even those who had just shouted "away with him" to want to listen. It was only after the hush had begun that they noted that he spoke in Hebrew, which at once gave him further rapport with the hostile Jews.

119. *Paul Addresses a Crowd*

(Acts 22:1-21)

Faced with a mob whose resort to violence he had done nothing to provoke, Paul decided to make a defense of his position. Most men would have seized the opportunity to escape into the security of the barracks, but Paul was made of sterner stuff. Even in adverse conditions he could not forget his mission. It is instructive to note what line he took when the clamor had sufficiently given way to quiet for him to make himself heard.

He decided on personal testimony. In a tense situation, this was likely to be most effective. An evangelistic sermon was out of the question. His testimony on this occasion provides some fascinating insights into his character.

The first part of this testimony gives his pre-Christian history. The Jerusalem audience would have been impressed by several salient points — that Paul was a Jew, that he was educated in Jerusalem under no less a teacher than Gamaliel, that he had a zeal for the law, and that he persecuted those who belonged to "The Way." There must have been many in that crowd who remembered the zealous Pharisee who had sought out Christians in their own homes to persecute them. Although he mentioned the matter it was never a subject of pride when he recalled the ruthlessness with which he pursued his goal, persecuting women as well as men. He gave in his own testimony a confirmation of what Luke had earlier recorded of his pre-Christian days. He remembered those official letters from the high priest and council. He recalled his specific intentions to arrest the Damascus Christians and transfer them for trial to Jerusalem. It was still vivid in his mind.

The next paragraph recounts Paul's remarkable encounter with Jesus Christ on the Damascus road. The details are the same as in Luke's earlier account, but they take on a new flavor when related in the first person. The journey, the light, the prostration, the conversation with the heavenly Jesus now come with the force of personal testimony. Nevertheless the account is not embellished. Paul mentions one detail omitted from the earlier account, that is his own question, "What shall I do, Lord?" and the Lord's answer directing him to go to Damascus, where instructions would be given. On the other hand Paul makes no reference to his blindness lasting three days. He gives no information about his thoughts during this period. He was concerned only to bring to his audience the essential facts.

His encounter with Ananias made a deep impression upon him. He may have had this man on his list of prospective victims for persecution. He knew that he was well spoken of by the Damascus Jews. It would be important for his Jewish audience to know that the human agent used in his conversion to Christianity was a man of irreproachable character in the eyes of the Jews. The words that Ananias addressed to Paul are much abbreviated in Paul's own account, concentrating on his restored sight. Moreover, the terms of his commission, which in the earlier account are given to Ananias, are in Paul's account recalled as Ananias imparted them. Again Paul concentrates on those details particularly relevant to his present purpose. His appointment in the Christian mission was made by "the God of our fathers," a typically Jewish expression with which none of his Jewish audience could find fault. Moreover, the idea of knowing God's will was equally important, since this was the ostensible aim of all pious Jews. The mention of the "Just One" would appeal to the Jewish sense of God's righteousness. The call to witness to all men was stated generally at this stage. Paul did not refer to Gentiles until he had reached the climax of his testimony. His mention of baptism and the washing away of sins would also cause no perplexity among Jews. There appears to have been some emphasis on this in the Qumran community and the idea was probably also familiar to many outside that community.

In his earlier account of Paul's conversion, Luke says nothing about his trance at Jerusalem, but he relates it here because of the importance of its location (i.e., the Temple). It is not without irony that the very place where God had communicated with Paul in a special way was the same place where the Jews had seized him. Moreover, in the trance he was told to get out of Jerusalem, yet his present predicament was caused by his determination to visit Jerusalem, in spite of the pressure of others against the idea. The reaction of his audience to the statement that Jerusalem would not accept the testimony about Jesus Christ is left to imagination, but the return to violence was not far distant.

Paul sets out his own change of position, referring again to his persecution of the early Christians and his partial responsibility for the martyrdom of Stephen. The crisis came when he referred to his commission to go to the Gentiles. His typically Jewish audience could not conceive that God would ever send a man to Gentiles, who in Jewish minds had no hope of salvation, in preference to work in Jerusalem. This shows the narrow limits of their idea of God and of His plan for mankind.

120. *The Binding of a Roman Citizen*

(Acts 22:22-30)

It was the mention of Gentiles which broke the hush and again unleashed the fury of the Jewish crowd against Paul. This abrupt change is indicative of the animosity which existed in the first century world between Jews and Gentiles. Moreover, the Jews were prepared to stage an immediate demonstration against Paul. It takes little to vocalize deep animosity. Intensity of feeling in crowds is demonstrated by loudness of clamor. "Away with such a fellow from the earth" would hardly seem a justifiable demand because Paul had mentioned the Gentiles or referred to his conversion experiences, nevertheless, seen against the background of religious and racial discrimination, it becomes intelligible, especially in view of the many parallels which history could furnish. When the Jewish mob took upon itself to decide who was fit to live, it was usurping the prerogative of God. The waving garments and dust-filled atmosphere added to the confusion. Such methods do not contribute to clarity of understanding, but no incited crowds are noted for logic.

The Roman official felt he must intervene by ordering his men to take Paul into the barracks. He had probably completely misunderstood the aim of Paul's speech. It is unlikely that he had understood the Aramaic. He seems to have assumed that Paul's words were revolutionary in character. He orders examination by scourging, a barbarous method of making men confess,

Roman milestones in Arnon Valley, Moab.

used for slaves and aliens. As soon as Paul realized what was to happen, when a centurion proceeded to bind him, he announced his Roman citizenship. Such citizenship protected a man from scourging and in fact required a proper trial before punishment. With all its much vaunted sense of justice the Roman State reserved for its more privileged citizens the advantages of a fair hearing without torture. The Roman tribune in Jerusalem does not show up too well in his handling of Paul's case, for he appears to have acted more on impulse than on information. He may well have given up the attempt to reason with turbulent Jews and had automatically classed Paul among them.

It was a serious offense for a Roman official to subject a Roman citizen to indignity without a trial and it is no wonder that the centurion at once reported the matter to the tribune. Something similar had happened at Philippi, although on that occasion Paul had already been beaten. The senior official at once dealt with the matter himself. He had purchased the privilege of Roman citizenship and prized it highly. No one appreciated its value more than a man who had paid dearly to obtain it and this would make him all the more conscious of having abused a fellow Roman citizen, especially when he discovered that Paul was a citizen by birth. Evidently his parents possessed the privilege. The intention to examine Paul by scourging was at once dropped. Those responsible withdrew and left Paul alone with the tribune. Luke reports that the Roman official was afraid. Paul must have observed this in his demeanor and told Luke about it later. It is extraordinary what effect an appeal to Roman citizenship could have and makes one wonder why Paul did not make more use of it. It may well have been the blind hatred of the Jews against him which caused him to do so on this occasion.

The tribune lost no time in summoning the Jewish Sanhedrin in order that a proper examination could be carried out. The Sanhedrin held considerable powers under the Roman system and would be regarded as the constitutional body to which most matters affecting the Jews would be referred. Since it was this body which had condemned Jesus to death, there was little possibility of Paul's case receiving sympathetic consideration. The sequel shows the continuance of hostility against this most energetic apostle of the crucified Messiah.

18

Defense Before Agrippa

121. *Dissension Over the Resurrection*

(Acts 23:1-11)

If Paul had ever been, as some think, a member of the Sanhedrin in his pre-conversion days, it would have been a challenging experience for him to face some of his former colleagues in
defending his actions. He was at once made aware that his
presence was not welcomed. The high priest Ananias ordered
him to be struck on the face after his first few words. There was
clearly an official policy to deny a fair hearing to the Christian
missionary. The fact that Paul appealed to his own clear conscience before God was of no consequence to the high priest. The
implication was that anyone who dared to claim such a thing
when, as they thought, he had apostatized, deserved only to be
silenced immediately.

The manifest injustice of the high priest's action roused Paul
to strong protest. Fearlessly he described the Jewish leader as a
"whitewashed wall," a striking metaphor which focused attention
on the man's hypocrisy. While claiming to be competent to pass
judgment according to the law, he was in fact acting contrary
to the provisions of the law in denying to the defendant a fair
hearing. There were not wanting those ready to defend the high
priest, since his office was surrounded by a certain sanctity
through his being regarded as God's representative. Indeed, this
was recognized by Paul, who cited Exodus 22:28 in support. He
claimed, however, to have been unaware that he was addressing
the high priest.

Presumably when he became aware that the high priest was presiding at the Council, he at once knew that Sadducees were present, for these were the ruling party. As a former Pharisee, Paul would be well aware of the strong disagreement that existed between these two Jewish parties on the subject of the resurrection and he at once seized the opportunity to stir up contention in the Council. Paul was proud of his Pharisaic upbringing. In his pre-Christian days he would have believed in the resurrection in contrast to the Sadducees who denied it. His letters bear eloquent testimony to the central place which belief in the resurrection held in his Christian theology. It was easier for a Pharisee than for a Sadducee to grasp the significance of Christ's resurrection. As soon as Paul claimed that it was on the grounds of his resurrection hope that he was before them, the Council was at once divided into two factions. A body of men who could not restrain themselves from contending with each other, however strong their differences, was hardly fitted to make impartial judgments. It is not surprising that an uproar developed which made any further examination of Paul's case impossible.

When some of the Pharisees supported Paul's innocence the reaction of the opposing party became so violent that the Roman official, who had called the Council to secure a fair examination, feared for Paul's safety and ordered him to be removed from the Council chamber. Evidently the Sadducees were so incensed against the apostle that they were even threatening to use violence against him in the Council. It is strange that matters of theological conviction, which should be a strengthening influence, sometimes become the cause of violent dissension. Judaism is not alone in showing instances of this, for the Christian Church has many times been torn into factions of considerable violence through theological causes.

It is significant that Paul at once received spiritual encouragement from a far more consistent source, for the Lord Himself spoke to him in a vision that same night. In one sense it was encouraging, yet in another sense it was challenging. The tension was by no means over yet. It was in fact to be repeated in Rome as it has been in Jerusalem. At least, a similar opportunity would be given for Paul to bear the name of Christ before governors and leaders.

122. Sworn to Kill

(Acts 23:12-35)

The hearing in the Council had shown the triumph of violence over voice. When justice is stifled by such a method, further violence may be expected. There were not wanting many Jews who were the more determined to stalk their prey. An action group numbering more than forty made an astonishing and somewhat macabre oath to abstain from food and drink until they had murdered Paul. To make such an oath, they must have burned with intense hatred against the apostle, a hatred which must have been the accumulation of many years, in some cases probably going back to their reactions at the time of Paul's conversion.

The action party, with its considerable numerical support, announced its plans to the chief priests and elders. Paul was once more to be called before the Council, an ambush was to await his transference from his place of confinement, and the murder was to be committed before Paul ever reached the Council chamber. The high priest did not object to the ethics of the plan. On the contrary he seems to have accepted the scheme as a tidy solution to what might otherwise prove a troublesome case. Jewish casuistry at that time would find little difficulty in justifying a mob execution of this kind in the interests of religious truth. It would be a similar principle to that which prompted Caiaphas to demand the death of Jesus. It is in situations of this kind that the real character of any religious system is most clearly seen. Contemporary Jewish leadership could not rise above the level of exerting its authority by violent means. It is to be noticed that this group of violent men were not only would-be murderers, but were also prepared to urge the high priest to practice deceit.

The security arrangements for this conspiracy went awry, for news of the plan leaked out and was picked up by a nephew of Paul. By what means the nephew managed to gain access to the barracks to tell his uncle, we do not know. As soon as Paul heard of the ambush he at once informed one of the officers that his nephew had important information to give the commanding officer. For obvious reasons the details were not noised abroad. In fact the commander consulted the young man in private and learned from him the nature of the plot. In view of the size of the ambush an ugly scene might well have developed. Swift military action could, however, forestall the threat to Paul's life and maintain public order. The commander lost no time in implementing his plan. Paul's nephew had done a good piece of detective work and in so doing had helped to save his uncle's life. He needed, however, to keep his interview with the commander strictly secret.

The military solution to the problem of the threat on Paul's life was to remove him at once to Caesarea. So urgent did the commander consider the matter to be that he ordered a company of 270 armed men to escort Paul on the journey commencing at 3 A.M. Such a movement of troops could not have been done with complete secrecy, but no doubt no one supposed that it was anything more than a maneuver or one of the familiar emergency calls upon the armed force in those troublesome times. Claudius Lysias, the commander, was taking no chances.

The governor of the province at that time was Felix, to whom Lysias was ultimately responsible. An official letter was sent explaining the circumstances, in which Claudius stated his opinion that Paul deserved neither death nor imprisonment. This is another example in which a Roman official was favorable toward a Christian preacher in face of the determined opposition of the Jews.

Having reached Antipatris, about 26 miles south of Caesarea, the company of 200 foot soldiers returned to Jerusalem, leaving the 70 horsemen to complete the journey with Paul. Both the letter and the prisoner were presented to the governor, who agreed to a hearing as soon as Paul's accusers arrived. He was to be kept in custody until then.

Luke does not report what happened to the men who had entered into their rash vow. They must either have ignored their ill-conceived oath or else have died of starvation. It is not likely that they chose the latter alternative. The chief priest and his advisers must also have been in a dilemma because of the command to provide witnesses before the governor. The whole incident supplies another testimony to the overruling hand of God in the affairs of His servants. Paul's time had not yet come. No plots of men could prevent the fulfillment of God's plan for him.

123.   *Paul Before Felix*

(Acts 24)

Because of the governor's command, the high priest Ananias was obliged to provide witnesses to accuse Paul. He decided to go himself, no doubt assuming that his presence, as official representative of the Jewish people, would impress the governor with the seriousness of the accusation. Nevertheless, he must have had some qualms about the strength of his case against Paul, since he was not only accompanied by some of the elders, but also by a professional spokesman.

Tertullus, the orator, stated the case against Paul. Luke gives a summary of his speech, which began with customary flattery of the governor, especially for public services which are attributed to him. This commendation was intended to dispose Felix to listen favorably to the charge. Tertullus had obviously been given a defamatory picture of the apostle. He describes him as a pestilent fellow, an agitator among Jews, and a ringleader of the Nazarenes (his description of the Christians). The only real charge was one of profaning the Temple, but even here no supporting evidence was cited. It would certainly appear that Tertullus had a poor case to present. He even suggests that Felix should examine Paul himself. The rather shaky charge was, not unexpectedly, vigorously supported by the Jews.

Paul's defense before Felix is notable for its reasoned character. He gives a factual account of the events in Jerusalem that led to his arrest. He affirms that his purpose in the Temple was worship and not turmoil. Moreover at no time had he stirred up trouble anywhere in the city. What he is glad to admit is his allegiance to "The Way," although he is at pains to show that he is in full agreement with his accusers in his reverence for the law and the prophets. As so often in his clashes with the Jews, he appeals to his belief in a resurrection, in which he knows he will have the support of the Pharisees. He must have assumed that among his accusers were members of the Pharasaic party. He would not forget that some of that party had been favorable to him when he was charged before the Jewish Council.

It is obvious that Paul's collection scheme had great significance in his mind. He regarded it as evidence of his patriotic concern for Jews in need. Since this was his purpose in coming to Jerusalem, how could he be charged with causing tumult? As

Paul proceeded, Tertullus' case was made to look increasingly thin. Where were the Asiatic Jews who had caused all the trouble? Why had they not been called as witnesses? The apostle persists relentlessly — what charge was proved by the Jewish Council, except his belief in the resurrection? This was a sore point with the Sadducees, among whom was Ananias the high priest.

On this occasion Paul made his points so well that his defense is a good example of the promise that Jesus gave of the assistance of the Spirit when His disciples had to answer for their faith before kings and governors. In the present case the governor appears to have been better informed about the Christian movement than the Jewish accusers. He was clearly not impressed by the manner in which the charge was presented. Luke comments that he had a fairly accurate knowledge of The Way, which presumably meant that he recognized that it was not as politically disturbing as the accusers were implying. The governor decided to await the arrival of Lysias who had sent Paul to him.

Among the various imperial officials mentioned in Acts, Felix is one of the most intriguing. He shows himself on the one hand more enlightened than some and on the other hand more spurred by baser motives. He shows his friendliness to Paul in his stipulation that his captivity should be liberally interpreted so that he might have access to his friends. But he shows his lack of a sense of justice in that he kept the apostle in this state for two full years. He could not have been waiting for Lysias' arrival all that time. Luke comments that he was hoping for a bribe in order to give Paul his liberty. By some means the governor must have thrown out hints to the apostle, who had informed his friends about them. It is important to note that neither Paul nor his friends considered it to be a justifiable procedure to buy his liberty to enhance the resources of a Roman governor. Certainly the governor himself did not come out of this incident with unscathed honor.

One thing can be said in favor of Felix. He was prepared to listen to Paul's exposition of the Gospel and was prepared for his wife also to hear. The apostle did not hesitate to speak in terms of future judgment. Felix did not respond, but procrastinated until he become hardened. If he seriously thought that Paul would be prepared to bribe him, he had understood very little of the spiritual content of the Gospel. It is not surprising that at the conclusion of his term of office, Felix was more concerned about pacifying the Jews than with releasing Paul. The matter of justice was secondary to political expediency. Felix certainly did not exemplify the Roman renown for just dealing.

124. *Appeal to Caesar*

(Acts 25:1-12)

During the decade culminating in the seize of Jerusalem, the Jewish nation had a succession of Roman governors, who seemed incapable of understanding the people under their control. The Jews were notorious for their independence and indeed for their hostility toward the occupying power. Festus, as much as Felix, was conscious of tension in dealing with this turbulent people. They were both anxious to avoid any unnecessary confrontation. Where possible they would show the Jews a favor. In such an atmosphere of political intrigue it was not to be wondered at that Paul became a mere pawn, whose case was regarded more as an occasion for political bargaining than for social justice.

Festus lost no time in making contact with the Jewish leaders in Jerusalem. He left his official residence in Caesarea only three days after taking possession, so strong was his desire to establish favorable relations with the Jews. The Jewish leaders saw an opportunity to take action against Paul. Their murderous intentions had been thwarted ever since the apostle had been kept in custody in Caesarea. But they reasoned that a new governor would be more disposed to accept their charges and send Paul to Jerusalem. In spite of the failure of the earlier plot, the Jews still intended to take the matter into their own hands and to arrange for the murder of the apostle. All that it needed was an ambush when once the apostle was en route for Jerusalem. Luke must have received information about these intrigues after the event. For some reason the governor declined to allow Paul to be moved. He may have been told by Felix of the Jewish leaders' particular antagonism to the apostle. He ordered the accusers to attend a hearing at Caesarea. In all this the hand of God may be seen as Paul is preserved from the murderous intentions of the Jewish antagonists.

The historian clearly has access to detailed information about the movements of Festus during the first days of his official residence in Palestine. He notes the time spent by the governor in Jerusalem, presumably to emphasize that it was no more than a fortnight after his taking office that Paul was brought before him. The Jewish accusers were not lacking in serious charges, but were bereft of evidence to support them. It is significant that after pursuing their prey for so long, they could put up no better case against him. It is not surprising that they had decided on the ambush execution idea. They were clearly conscious of the weakness of their accusations in law.

Paul's defense was categorical. He denied having committed any offense. Moreover, when the governor asked whether Paul wished to be tried at Jerusalem, he expressed his confidence in the effectiveness of the existing court at Caesarea. Then, for some reason, he appealed to Caesar. As a Roman citizen he was entitled to do this, but the question arises why he decided to do so. The answer lies in the nature of the charges brought against him and his assessment of the effect of the governor's conciliatory policy toward the Jews. It would appear that the Jewish accusers had not been content to restrict their charges to agitation among the Jews as they had done before Felix. They had introduced a charge of offense against Caesar, which Paul specifically denies. But an offense against Caesar was serious enough to be referred to the arbitration of the emperor himself and would at once take the initiative out of the hands of the Jews. Moreover, Paul was evidently apprehensive about Festus' approach to the Jews. The Roman governor might well have considered it expedient to hand over an insignificant prisoner to appease his subjects. Nevertheless it must not be imagined that the apostle was concerned only for his own safety. He may have seen his present circumstances as an opportunity to gain the emperor's recognition that the whole Christian movement was not subversive to the State. Festus, no doubt with some relief, acceded to his request to lodge an appeal before Caesar.

The Roman Emperor at this time was Nero, who later became infamous for his manner of persecuting the Christians. It was still, however, during the first five years of his reign when he was under the restraining influence of his advisers Seneca and Burrus. This period became known as the quinquennium of Nero, in which Roman rule throughout the Empire was renowned for its justice.

125.   *Festus and Agrippa Discuss Paul's Case*
(Acts 25:13-27)

Although Festus had agreed that Paul should be allowed to appeal to Caesar, he was in a dilemma for want of an adequate charge to refer to the imperial court. He must have had the case much on his mind, since it became a topic of conversation when he was visited by King Agrippa and his sister Bernice. The king was paying a courtesy visit to the new governor. This Agrippa was the son of Herod Agrippa I and was granted jurisdiction over a region in the northeast of Palestine. His sister, who lived with him, had formerly been married to the king of Chalcis (her uncle). When her husband died she married again, but did not get on well with him and returned to live with Agrippa. Her second husband was the king of Cilicia. Later, after the siege of Jerusalem, she accompanied Agrippa to Rome, where she had an affair with the Roman Titus.

It is illuminating to consider Festus' report of his recent dealings with the Jewish elders. He first mentioned the Roman procedure of refusing to hand over a prisoner for sentence until he had had a fair trial. Festus is keen to inform Agrippa how speedily he had arranged for Paul to have a hearing in his presence and to have an opportunity to defend himself against his accusers. No doubt he wished to impress the king with his efficiency and fair-mindedness. In his report of the charges, he made no mention to Agrippa of any suggested sedition against Caesar. He mentions that the real cause of the hatred between Paul and the Jews was religious. He uses a word which means either "religion" or "superstition." It makes little difference which interpretation is preferred. As far as Festus was concerned he was no doubt intending his comments to be complimentary to the Jews. The real problem was the resurrection of Jesus, which had been the main contention between Paul and the Sadducees and to a lesser extent between him and the Pharisees.

When the governor told Agrippa of Paul's appeal to Caesar, the Jewish king expressed a wish to hear him, no doubt mainly out of curiosity. He may have heard of the work of the apostle. He was well aware of the Jewish background against which Paul's position had to be assessed and therefore had a definite advantage over Festus. The latter agreed to arrange a hearing, for he was obviously glad to have some assistance in framing a charge against Paul.

The occasion was marked with considerable pomp and ceremony. Since an assembly had been arranged, it was evidently desired that both the prisoner and the witnesses should be impressed with the official character of the hearing. Festus no doubt hoped that Agrippa, with his greater understanding of Jewish affairs, would be able to detect some reasonable charge to be reported to the emperor. The case was opened by a brief and somewhat formal statement by Festus to Agrippa. The governor wished the audience, which consisted of all the notable people in Caesarea, to know of his dilemma. He admitted to the whole company that he could not reasonably send Paul to Rome without more definite charges than he had yet been able to formulate. It was a strange dilemma for a governor who had so recently taken office. As far as Luke is concerned the chief interest in this assembly for him is the opportunity which it gave Paul to make his defense before Agrippa.

Although the historian has already twice related the story of Paul's conversion, he considers it worthwhile to include it again in Paul's defense. There is no doubt that he highly esteemed the significance of that momentous event. What interests him most in the present scene is the effect that the recording of the experience had on both Agrippa and Festus.

126. *Paul's Defense Before Agrippa*

(Acts 26:1-23)

The apostle, having gained experience in defending himself before official judges, shows no sign of being intimidated by them. His opening words to Agrippa reflect his skill in adapting his words to suit the occasion. He recognizes Agrippa as a man whose expertise in Jewish affairs should make him amenable to hearing Paul's defense. The apostle expresses the wish that he would be patient.

The first part of his defense appeals to his Pharisaic origins. It was important for Agrippa to know how thoroughly Jewish, even orthodox, those origins were, since the accusations were based on the assumption that Paul was aiming to undermine Jewish customs. The second point is that his position is supported by God's promise in the past. He was probably thinking mainly of God's covenant with the patriarchs. These ancient promises which were precious to every pious Israelite could be fulfilled, in Paul's opinion, only through a resurrected Messiah. He does not, however, at this stage mention the Messiah, only the resurrection and even that only indirectly in the form of a question. Agrippa and his audience knew that the resurrection was the major cause of the clash between the prisoner and his accusers. He challenged, "Why should it be thought incredible?" Those who maintained that it was would be limiting the power of God.

In order to emphasize the remarkable change that had come over him, Paul gives a concise description of his pre-conversion experiences. It was marked by determined opposition to all connected with Jesus of Nazareth. The intensity of his hostility and the thoroughness of his persecuting zeal was an important step in the development of his defense as it had been in his defense before the crowds in Jerusalem (Acts 22). He had no natural liking for the new Way. His raging fury was sufficient testimony to that. The extent of his persecutions reaching to foreign cities was evidence that he would stop at nothing in his antagonism to Jesus of Nazareth. Agrippa must have been impressed by the dedication with which the Jewish prisoner had attacked the very movement which he now represented and which his Jewish accusers hated.

The account of his conversion which follows is similar to that which Luke has recorded twice previously (Acts 9 and 22). The journey to Damascus, the brilliant light, the challenging heavenly voice, the conversation, and the directions are all present. This is the only account where Luke records the words, "It hurts you to kick against the goads," reflecting the imagery of an ox kicking its heels against a sharp point which has been so held as to spur it on. Paul would only recognize after the event the nature of the goads — those many influences which were leading him to change his position, but which till then he had never acknowledged. In his own account he omits the incident in which Ananias conveys his commission from the risen Christ, but he gives in some detail the terms of the commission. He informs Agrippa of his appointment as a witness to the risen Christ, of his task to illuminate the Gentiles. His task was in fact to turn men from Satan's power to God's and to proclaim forgiveness. By the time he stood before Agrippa he had proved effectively how powerfully the preaching of the Gospel had achieved these aims.

The conclusion of the defense concentrates on a personal affirmation. In a direct address to the king, Paul claims that his obedience to the heavenly vision had led him to preach at Damascus, Jerusalem, Judaea, and among the Gentiles the need for repentance. His accusers were therefore opposing what was in fact a divinely authenticated message. The arrest and plot by the Jews to kill him must be judged against this fact. Moreover, Paul claimed to have done nothing contrary to Moses and the prophets. It was essential in early Christian apologetics to show that a suffering Messiah was foreseen in the Scriptures, for this was a major Jewish stumbling block. Linked with the idea of a suffering Messiah was the indispensable Christian truth of the resurrection. There was no more for Paul to say, once he had established that his mission was divinely appointed and scripturally based.

127. *Decisions of Innocence*

(Acts 26:24-32)

When Luke had recorded Paul's defense, he noted the different reactions of the two main hearers, Festus and Agrippa. His comments provide in cameo form interesting character studies.

The Roman had clearly appreciated very little of Paul's speech. He had as yet had insufficient time in Palestine to learn much of the Jewish situation and without such knowledge he would find it difficult to grasp the religious problems involved. His conclusion was that Paul was mad, a not uncommon conclusion among those who find others unintelligible. He did not, however, write off Paul as an ignoramus for he recognized his great learning. Festus belonged to that group of matter-of-fact people who find spiritual issues incomprehensible and who assume that those who do not must be somewhat mentally unbalanced. Paul's answer to the charge of madness was courteous but firm. He denied madness and then at once turned his attention to Agrippa because of his greater acquaintance with Jewish affairs. It looks rather as if Paul was bypassing Festus, because of his failure to understand. He was shrewd enough to know that Agrippa was more likely to grasp the significance of the case.

Paul gives Agrippa the credit for knowing the facts, for he claims that all that had happened to him had not been done in a corner. Whether this was a true assessment or whether Paul was merely being courteous is not clear. It must, however, have taken Agrippa completely by surprise when he received a direct challenge from the prisoner — "King Agrippa, do you believe the prophets?" Without waiting for an answer Paul asserts, "I know that you believe." Agrippa's response was cautious. He hedged the question addressed to him and suggested that Paul was aiming to make him embrace Christianity. Whether the king was seriously affected or not is unknown, but his remark gave Paul the opportunity to express the wish that all his hearers might follow his example, except of course for the chains. Whether a man is free or captive, he has still to make personal decisions about his basic religious faith. Agrippa said no more to the prisoner.

The governor and the king and his sister withdrew to discuss their impressions. Neither Festus nor Agrippa could find any fault in Paul. His sincere explanation of the events which had led up to the present imprisonment had evidently convinced them that the charges brought by the Jews were false. Agrippa, indeed, is inclined to the opinion that Paul should be released, but recognizes that his appeal to Caesar cancels this out. Since the Jews had consistently failed to obtain a positive verdict condemning Paul, Festus must have known how precarious it was for him to send the prisoner to Rome without more adequate grounds. No doubt, realizing how great a stumbling block Paul was to the Jews, he deemed it wisest to transport him out of the area, and the appeal to Caesar supplied an admirable pretext for him to do this. This was not the only occasion when governors have been nonplussed by the claims of Christianity. History has repeated itself many times.

19

A Stormy Passage to Rome

128. A Storm at Sea

(Acts 27:1-20)

Luke does not say how long it took for arrangements to be made for Paul's shipment to Rome. He takes up the story at the time of embarkation, when he himself apparently joined the same ship. Paul and some other prisoners were under the charge of a centurion named Julius. In addition to Luke there was at least one other of Paul's associates on the boat, for Aristarchus, the man who was involved in the riot at Ephesus, was a passenger on the boat which was homeward bound for the port of Adramyttium on the coast of Mysia in Asia Minor. Passengers bound for Rome would need to change ships at one of the ports of call along the coast. When the boat docked at Sidon, the centurion allowed Paul to visit his friends there. This city was known for its Greek learning. Many of its inhabitants had heard the teaching of Jesus (cf. Mark 3:8, Luke 6:17, 10:13, 14). It was probably some of these whom Paul visited, for there is no mention in Acts of any mission which he conducted there.

Leaving Sidon the boat sailed round the north side of the island of Cyprus, which may have revived Paul's memories of his first missionary journey. Similarly as the boat passed Cilicia, Paul would have been close to his place of origin. There were no stops, however, until Myra in the province of Lycia, where the passengers for Rome transferred to an Alexandrian ship bound for Italy. There was frequent traffic on this route, which was plied by the grain ships from Alexandria delivering their indispensable cargo to the center of the Roman Empire.

Sailing conditions were none too favorable. It must be remembered that in those times there was one period of the year when sea travel was considered too dangerous, two periods of the year when it was hazardous but usable, and one period only when conditions were favorable. It was evidently toward the end of autumn when Paul was being shipped to Italy, i.e., toward the end of a risky period and approaching the dangerous. This needs to be borne in mind in order to understand Luke's account of the voyage. He notes the difficult progress that was made after leaving Myra and comments that it was necessary for the ship to steer south of Cyprus because of contrary winds. He gives many precise details regarding location, but it is the human part of his story which is most fascinating.

Arriving at the Cyprian harbor of Fair Havens, Paul ventures to express his opinion to the centurion that it was hazardous to proceed with the journey. It was not surprising that the Roman officer preferred to be guided by the captain rather than by Paul. A seafaring man would be expected to size up an adverse situation at sea, but hardly so a landlubber like Paul. Nevertheless the approach of winter should have been sufficient warning to anyone that the voyage was highly dangerous. The problem for the captain was that the harbor at Fair Havens would not give sufficient protection for his ship, and he wanted, with the support of the majority, to reach Phoenix, a more adequate harbor on the island. There is no certainty about the location of this, but it was probably on the western side. It was no great distance, but the journey was nevertheless dangerous.

The captain was not to know that a northeasterly tempest would rapidly blow up as they set sail from Fair Havens with a gentle southerly wind. Until the tempest struck, the centurion and the captain no doubt considered that Paul's counsel had decisively been shown to be wrong. But when the wind whipped the sea into a fury the position was different. Luke notes how they had to let the boat ride before the wind and then notes the steps the crew took to strengthen the boat, mainly by undergirding, in which ropes were passed under the boat to give added support. When the storm continued unabated, the cargo was first jettisoned and then the tackle.

Amid all this activity Luke says nothing about the reactions of the crew, the passengers, and the prisoners, except the brief statement that hope had been abandoned. No doubt by this time, or indeed long before this, the captain wished he had taken Paul's advice. The darkness of the storm was matched by the desperate state of the minds of those aboard — except for the mind of the apostle. Luke's portrait of the composure of the apostle is set against this background. It was not, of course, the first time that Paul had faced hazards at sea. In 2 Corinthians 11:25, 26, he mentions several perils at sea, including three shipwrecks. He had learned from experience how to face danger with equanimity.

129. *Shipwreck*

(Acts 27:21-44)

When everyone else in the boat had given up hope, Paul could refrain no longer from issuing a gentle rebuke for the foolishness of setting sail from Crete against his advice. It would have been cold comfort if this was the sole content of his comment, for it would then have savored of vindictiveness. The apostle was not that kind of man. He rebuked only to add weight to his encouragement. He announced that in a vision he had been assured that the whole company would be saved. It tied in with Paul's conviction that in the plan of God he was to appear before Caesar. Indeed this was reaffirmed in the vision. On the strength of the vision he encouraged all in the boat. Had it not been for the uncanny accuracy of his former advice, they might have been ill disposed toward this visionary prisoner. In any case Luke records nothing of the reactions of the passengers or crew. Since they had been some days without food, they probably still considered the chances of survival to be remote.

The only hope was to reach land but the position of this was not easy to predict from a boat drifting in open water. But after soundings had been made they realized that land was near. It was a tense moment which Luke must have vividly remembered, for it was midnight when the discovery was made and not until daylight could they discover what type of coastline they had struck. Anchors were dropped for fear that the boat would be dashed on the rocks.

A dramatic incident occurred at this stage involving the sailors and the apostle. Some of the former tried to escape to land in a boat, forsaking their responsibilities toward the others in the ship, but Paul's quick protest led the soldiers to forestall the plan. Luke brings out clearly that Paul appears to be more in command of the situation than either the captain or the centurion. It is significant that even those who should have been in control were now more ready to heed the advice of this non-seafaring missionary prisoner.

Paul's next directive was that everyone should eat food. Again it is extraordinary that such a suggestion had to come from the prisoner rather than from the captain. Paul's presence of mind sprang from his deep conviction that all would be saved. Luke notes that Paul ate in the presence of the others (who numbered 276), who then followed his example. After doing this the ship was further lightened by the jettisoning of the wheat in its hold.

It was now daylight and a beach was seen to be nearby, which offered the possibility of running the ship ashore. But before reaching the shore the ship struck a shoal and began to disintegrate. At that moment the soldiers were about the kill the prisoners, since they would have been responsible had any escaped, but the centurion took charge and prevented them. Luke wastes no words on the scramble to shore of the 276 people. It must have been an epic operation, some swimming, some clinging to pieces of wood. One wonders what the reaction of the rest of the company was when, as a result of the roll call, it was realized that Paul's prediction had been precisely fulfilled. Not a single man had been lost.

It may be asked why Luke decided to devote so much of his limited space to such a detailed description of a storm and shipwreck which contributed little to his main purpose of narrating the spread of the Gospel from Jerusalem to Rome. His reason must have been his desire to show the character of Paul in the midst of highly dangerous circumstances. No doubt he could have illustrated this many times over in view of 2 Corinthians 11, but chose this shipwreck incident because he himself was a witness of the extraordinary coolness, authority, and foresight of the apostle, which stood out against the background of general despair. The secret was in Paul's firm belief in the overruling hand of God. It is a secret which is open to all men of faith, and we may be grateful to Luke for providing so outstanding an example of the triumph of faith in adverse circumstances.

130. *Hospitality in Malta*

(Acts 28:1-10)

It was fortuitous that the shipwrecked people after their ordeal found themselves on a friendly island. For the great number of people, who were dripping wet, the fire which the natives of the island had quickly kindled was a most welcome sight. One can imagine something of the thoughts of the captain of the vessel as he reflected on the sorry sight of his smashed-up boat and thought of his foolishness in not heeding Paul's warning at Crete. Now it was too late.

Whether other members of the shipwrecked party gathered sticks for the fire, Luke does not say, but Paul is not slow to give practical assistance. His doing so led to another dramatic incident which is related by Luke. A viper sprang from his bunch of sticks and fastened on his hand. The Maltese, who knew the deadly character of the creature, took it as an omen that he should die. Recognizing him to be a prisoner, they at once concluded he must have done something worthy of death — he must be a murderer. It was the kind of snap judgment which men are inclined to make without sufficient supporting evidence. They had in fact been altogether too hasty, for Paul was able to shake off the viper into the fire. Popular reaction was again hasty and on the basis of this unexpected deliverance concluded that Paul must be a god. So sudden an extreme about-face may reflect something of the superstitious approach of the natives who were clearly disposed to attribute circumstances to some ulterior cause. Nevertheless this kind of hasty judgment is not uncommon in the more sophisticated environment of modern society. Once again the apostle is seen to be under a divine protection, in keeping with his assurance that he must stand before Caesar.

The next incident was no doubt of special interest to Luke since it involved a healing. Moreover it concerned a relative of the ruler of the island whose estate was nearby. Publius the ruler acted with great generosity in housing the shipwrecked people for three days. It was during this period that Paul learned of the illness of Publius' father, who had dysentery. By some means he managed to pay him a visit. The centurion must have become particularly lenient with his prisoner, who took the opportunity of praying with the ill man and effecting a cure. News of the healing of a man of such status soon spread through the island and others with illnesses came to Paul and were cured. Luke's narrative here is compressed. We would like to know whether Paul preached the Gospel as he healed. It would certainly be out of keeping with all we know of him if he had not done so. The people of Malta would not soon forget the visit of this shipwrecked prisoner, whose prayers had been mighty to heal. They would not easily forget the name of Jesus. Moreover, as the soldiers continued to observe their unusual charge, they too must have wondered what kind of man had been entrusted to them. Whatever the accusations against him which had led to his being taken to Rome, his army guard must have learned much of his noble character as they accompanied him. The experience on the island of Malta, which lasted for three months, must have presented many opportunities for the apostle. These are left unrecorded, but can be imagined. When at length sailing conditions permitted the party to move, the Maltese again showed their hospitality by loading more gifts on to Paul and his associates. Indeed the New Testament contains no record of warmer hospitality than that shown by these people.

131. *In Rome at Last*

(Acts 28:11-31)

Throughout the enforced delay in Malta, an Alexandrian ship had been docked waiting for the end of the winter period. Its Twin Brothers figurehead must have caught Luke's eye, for he specially notes this feature of the ship which conveyed them to Rome. A brief halt was made at Syracuse in Sicily and the ship then headed for Rhegium, a port on the Italian mainland on the strait of Messina, which separates Italy from Sicily. This strait was particularly hazardous because of the whirlpool of Charybdis and the rock known as Scylla, both north of this port of Rhegium. The harbor was, therefore, invaluable for ships to take refuge until a favorable south wind enabled them to negotiate the treacherous passage. Luke notes that such favorable conditions arose only the day after their arrival at Rhegium. Their next port of call, Puteoli, was reached two days later, and from there Paul and his party proceeded overland to Rome.

Luke notes that at this place there were brethren who gave them hospitality for a week. Nothing is known of the origin of this group of believers. What is significant is their knowledge of Paul's arrival and their readiness to assist. News of his movements had evidently preceded him, as a result of which Christian fellowship was shown in a practical way. Again the military guard must have wondered when they saw the strong bonds of fellowship between the Puteoli Christians and a Christian prisoner whom they had presumably never met before.

The demonstration of Christian fellowship was further seen some miles before the party reached Rome, as some of the Roman Christians had traveled south as far as the Appii Forum, a town some 27 miles south of Rome on the Appian Way. Others met him at the nearby Three Taverns, another staging post on the same route. It speaks much for the warm concern of these Roman Christians that they made the effort to come. It is understandable that Paul was greatly encouraged by their action. They had no doubt heard much about the apostle and had read his letter to the Roman church. But to met him face to face was, an occasion of special rejoicing. To be escorted to Rome by such warm brethren in the Lord did much to ease the apostle's mind as he entered the capital city. By this time the centurion had clearly become deeply impressed with Paul. He must have been mystified as strangers communicated with him as if they were close acquaintances. He was sufficiently convinced that Paul could be trusted without a full guard. He seems to have granted him considerable liberty in his access to others.

In spite of his status as a prisoner, the apostle still adhered to his missionary principle of seeking out the Jews, and this he does even at Rome. He called for the local Jewish leaders to visit him so that he could explain to them his present circumstances. He is at pains to show that he had done nothing against the Jewish nation, although it was the Jews who had delivered him to the Romans. He explains also why he had appealed to Caesar. It is in some ways strange that the Jews in Rome knew nothing of the charge against Paul. Perhaps their Jewish compatriots had been thwarted by the appeal to Rome and preferred not to advertise their frustration to their Roman brethren. The latter were quite ready to give Paul a hearing, especially as they had heard much about the Christian sect and had observed the opposition it had everywhere aroused. In all probability this was a polite way of showing their own inclination to oppose it.

When the hearing was arranged, a considerable audience of Jews assembled to hear Paul's exposition of the Christian faith.

He devoted the whole day to expounding the kingdom and laid special stress on the fulfillment of Moses and the prophets, which would be of vital importance to his Jewish hearers. The response was mixed, some believed and some did not. The apostle would not have been surprised, for this was his common experience when witnessing among Jews, who were generally more unbelieving than believing. His parting words to them were a quotation from Isaiah 6:9-10, which points to the hardness of men's hearts in hearing the message of God. Then he challenged them with the statement that Gentiles would listen to the message of salvation.

According to Luke, Paul continued to enjoy a considerable amount of freedom in receiving visitors at his own apartment. He was placed under house arrest, an arrangement which continued for at least two years. The note on which Luke chooses to end is the unrestricted preaching of the Gospel by the imprisoned apostle in the imperial city. What happened after that he does not tell his readers. It is reasonable to suppose that the book was published while Paul was still under house arrest, in which case the inconclusive ending is understandable. From the evidence in the Acts it is highly probable that Paul was released. This may have happened through the default of witnesses within a reasonable time or through a favorable verdict due to inadequate support of the charges. What we know of Paul's movements subsequent to this Roman captivity is culled mainly from the pastoral epistles (1 and 2 Timothy and Titus). What we know of Paul's own thoughts during this period comes from a study of the captivity epistles (Philippians, Colossians, Philemon, and Ephesians) which will next be examined. It should be noted that some scholars date these letters much earlier, on the assumption that they were produced during a supposed Ephesian imprisonment. The traditional view is that they were written from Rome and this view has been adhered to in the following description of them.

20

A Glimpse at Two Churches

132. A Letter to a Warm Community
(Phil. 1)

It was some time since Paul had been last at Philippi, but his memories of the Philippian Christians were still vivid. They had been kept alive by constant prayer. He had also received reports about them, especially from one of their number, Epaphroditus. Indeed, the main reason why he decided to write to them was because Epaphroditus was returning to Philippi and could act as the bearer of such a letter. Moreover, although he is still a prisoner in Rome, Paul is optimistic that he will soon be released and in that case intends to pay them another visit as soon as possible. Before that time he proposes to send Timothy to them. The letter has therefore a very practical setting.

Among the letters of Paul which have been preserved, this is notable because of the warmth of his thanksgiving to God for all the news he has heard about the Christians at Philippi. He thinks of his relationship to them in terms of a spiritual "partnership." He may possibly have in mind the contribution which these Christians have made toward his material support, but his thoughts are mainly on the common bond between them in Jesus Christ. He even boldly declares that he loves them with the same kind of affection which Jesus Christ shows. Nevertheless, in spite of his warm regard for his readers, he is not yet satisfied. He wants them to show much more love yet. He goes in for a wholehearted approach to everything. He wants to see evidence of yet greater spiritual productivity among them.

It is understandable that Paul was at this time reflecting on his present circumstances as a prisoner for the sake of the Gospel. He had pondered what part this seeming misfortune had in the plan of God. He had set his heart on preaching at Rome in the same way as he had done throughout the eastern provinces. His freedom to preach at Rome had been severely restricted. His audiences were confined to those who had found their way to his guarded apartment. In spite of his own restrictions, he rejoices that others have found great liberty to preach Christ, inspired perhaps by his example. Some in fact were doing this from wrong motives, supposing to goad the apostle to envy, but he shows his nobility of spirit in exulting in the preaching of Christ from whatever cause. He had learned that Christ was more important than the preacher. In fact the imperial body-guard, part of which was responsible for the security of prisoners, had learned that Paul was captive for Christ's sake. His chains were speaking louder than his freedom could ever have done to those whose military calling made them difficult to approach with the message of the Gospel.

The apostle's mind was naturally dwelling much on the future. He wondered how his imprisonment was going to turn out. Whatever his outward circumstances, he was an optimist in the best sense of the word. His optimism was not based on wishful thinking, but on a solid Christian assurance. He was buoyed up by the Philippians' prayers. He was strengthened by the Spirit of Christ. He had come to the conclusion that the issue of life or death was less important than the honoring of Jesus Christ. He was like a man stretching out his neck so as not to be ashamed. He made no room for apathy in his spiritual approach.

When he discusses the dilemma of the future, Paul shows the delicate balance which marks him out as a man of maturity. His assurance regarding the future would be unshaken by the decision of any court considering his case. If death were the outcome, the spiritual benefit would be an ushering into the presence of Christ, which Paul at once concedes would be a highly desirable gain. Nowhere in his epistles does he more vividly announce his complete confidence in the triumph of Christ over death. His statement is in direct contrast to the continual fear of death in the world at that time (cf. Heb. 2:15). A man who could face the last enemy with such confidence had learned a secret which men of all generations need to know.

Paul writes as if he is in a real dilemma, as if he is faced with the need to decide whether he would choose death or life. He could not have expected his readers to take the dilemma literally. The choice was with God. Nevertheless he admits that there would be some benefit to the Philippians if he were spared. If he were able to pay them another visit, he sees this as a cause to make them boast in Jesus Christ.

As so often in his letters, Paul gives practical advice. He first recommends unity. This is a strong conviction of his. "Striving side by side for the faith of the Gospel" may be seen as a kind of trademark of a true community of believers. Any military commander knows that a united front is essential if opposition is to be overcome. Paul uses an illustration of a pack of horses stampeding before the advance of the enemy to show what must be avoided in the Christian conflict. Unity is linked in Paul's mind with dauntlessness. There is no promise that the Christians will escape unscathed. They must be prepared to suffer for Christ's sake. The apostle points to his own example in the service of Christ, but no one had a greater right to do this than he.

133. *A Humble Mind and a Workable Salvation*

(Phil. 2)

If unity is to have any real meaning in any Christian community, selfishness and conceit must be banished. These are the real enemies, but they are the most difficult to be rid of. Humility is not a virtue which comes naturally to many. It was a despised quality in the ancient world. The Romans encouraged pride, and it must not be forgotten that Paul is in process of writing to a Roman colony. Certainly if self-interest is to be banished and humility enjoined, a powerful incentive would be needed for those who were proud of their Roman privileges. Such an incentive was ready at hand – the example of Jesus Christ.

The manner in which Paul proceeds to describe the self-effacing character of the mind of Christ is both profound and poetical. He may be adapting some Christian hymn or he may be composing a hymnlike passage. Whichever it is, it should be realized that the purpose of appealing to Christ's example of humility was essentially practical. In doing so Paul introduces some of the most profound statements about Christ found anywhere in his epistles. Since the apostle is thinking mainly about the mind of Christ, it is not surprising that his statements have been much debated as to their essential meaning. He was, after all, attempting to express the infinite in finite terms, and some limiting of his clarity is not therefore surprising. What must have struck the Philippians most forcefully when the epistle was read was the immense submission of Christ to become obedient as He did.

In order to appreciate the extent to which Christ humbled Himself, it is essential to consider what He was before the humbling began. Paul talks about "the form of God" which Christ had, by which he meant His divine nature. He also shows that equality with God was something that Christ possessed as a right. Such a high view of what Christ was is the background against which to see His humiliation. Paul talks of Christ emptying Himself, by which he means that He laid His glory aside. Instead He assumed a servant's status and became obedient to death. That is a remarkable thought, for only One who had power over death could become obedient to it. All other men are mortal and have no choice. In no more emphatic way could Paul bring out the voluntary character of Christ's death.

The extreme humiliation of Christ was not in death itself, but in the ignominy of death by crucifixion. In Roman eyes crucifixion was a symbol of utmost degradation. Yet since becoming a Christian Paul had gloried in that cross. It was in fact the path to glory, for it led to remarkable exaltation. There is no mention here of the resurrection but it is implied in Christ's exaltation about all others. No knee would fail to bow in acknowledgment of the Lordship of Christ. Paul does not say that all would come to believe. But some kind of homage to Jesus Christ was unavoidable. This was a status that He did not have to snatch, as Satan suggested He should at the temptation. Every Christian acknowledges without compulsion the Lordship of Christ. This passage in the letter must have warmed the Philippians' hearts as it has the hearts of countless millions since. In contrast to the growing contemporary pagan practice of addressing Caesar as Lord, the Philippians would recognize the superiority of their allegiance to Jesus Christ.

Although the apostle makes profound statements on Christian doctrine, he has an essentially practical approach to salvation. He tells the Philippians to "work it out," by which he means that they are to examine how it affects every aspect of life. This is no mean task, which should be accompanied by godly fear. But Paul knows very well that no amount of human effort could achieve this, without God's enabling. No one can "work out" until God has first "worked in."

Salvation should work in any environment. Paul calls the Philippians' background "a crooked and perverse generation." Against such a background he makes some astounding demands. They were to be morally blameless. They were to be brilliant lights against pagan darkness, or rather they were to reflect the "word of life." Moreover, their behavior affected him, for he did not want to be ashamed of them on the final reckoning day. On reading this, the Philippians would recognize how much they and he were bound up together. He was like a poured out offering ready to be sacrificed. With such an example the Philippians could not ignore his earnest entreaties.

Paul's references to his fellow workers are always illuminating and in this letter he mentions two of them. Timothy is well known and is mentioned several times in Acts. Paul speaks warmly of him here. He is unequaled in his concern for others. This single-minded companion is to be sent to the Philippian church and will report on Paul's welfare before his visit to them.

Epaphroditus belonged to Philippi. He was now returning home. He had been a great help to Paul, who describes him in glowing terms as a brother, fellow worker, fellow soldier, and minister. Moreover, he had endured some "hazard" in his service to Paul as the Philippians' representative. Whether this hazard was some severe illness or other threat to his life is not certain. He was a credit to the Philippian church. He had apparently visited Paul in the first place as the bearer of some gifts which had been sent (see 4:8), but had stayed on to minister.

134. *Warnings*

(Phil. 3)

It looks as if Paul had intended finishing the letter soon after mentioning Timothy and Epaphroditus, but he suddenly issues some sharp warnings. The explanation might be that he realizes there are troublemakers in the vicinity and fears lest the Philippians will fall prey to them. On this issue, he does not mince his words. He seems to have in mind Jewish groups who are persuading people to be circumcised as a necessary part of their Christian profession. So strongly does the apostle feel that he does not hesitate to advertise his own Jewish pedigree. Not only was he of Hebrew origin, but also a zealous Pharisee. It is not often that Paul includes self-advertisement in his letters, but when he does, it is illuminating, for he proceeds to give what amounts to a spiritual profit and loss account.

Paul had many assets of a national and religious kind. But these go into the loss side of the account. He had reason to boast in his heritage as a reputable Pharisee, but he dubs all this as refuse. Nevertheless he is convinced that he has made an indisputable profit, for on the credit side he places the surpassing worth of knowing Christ. He had not come by this through any efforts of his own. He had not earned it, as the orthodox Jew believed he could earn righteousness by fulfilling the demands of the law. He had received it by faith.

Not only had he come to know Jesus Christ, but he had also discovered the possibility of a new power. It was the same power as that seen at the resurrection of Christ, a power that could shatter the power of death. It may involve suffering with Christ, but what was this compared with the power? It is no wonder that Paul's previous "assets" now seemed so utterly worthless. His account had become lopsided on the credit side. Nevertheless he is a realist and could never delude himself into thinking that he had yet arrived. On the contrary, when he compares what he ought to be with what he is, he finds a strong motive for pressing on. It has both a negative and a positive side. To press on means to look constantly ahead and to refuse to look back. It reminds us of the plowman in Jesus' illustration, who could only plow a straight furrow if he kept his eye ahead. Those who look back are not fit for the kingdom. Paul calls it "the uplook call of God in Christ Jesus," which acts as a kind of spiritual magnetism drawing men to their spiritual goal. As the Philippians listened to these words, they would see new spiritual horizons spread out before them.

It is not surprising that a man with such spiritual assets should base his exhortations to the Philippians on his own experience. When addressing the mature minded, he does not hesitate to tell them to imitate him. They would understand. They would not suppose that it was a sign of arrogance on his part. It must be remembered that converts from pagan environments would value the example of any whose life had been molded to a new pattern, and their regard for the apostle would make acceptable such an invitation to imitate him.

Paul is aware of other enemies of the Gospel who were distinct from the Jewish opponents alluded to earlier. He now thinks of perfectionists who are so deluded in their folly that only God could illuminate them. These are not merely enemies of Christians, but of the cross of Christ. This can only mean they were adopting a position diametrically opposed to the Gospel. They may have called themselves Christians, but if so their life was totally opposed to their profession. So highly significant has the cross become to the apostle that he can think of nothing worse than those who become enemies of it. He is moved to tears at the thought of how foolish they are.

His mind goes to the Christian's advantages. He is writing to people who were proud to belong to a Roman colony. Nevertheless he uses the word "colony" in a different sense. He thinks of Christians as belonging to a colony of heaven. Citizens of this heavenly colony have not yet reached their full privileges. A wonderful transformation awaits them. Their present physical limitations will disappear and be replaced by a body of the same form as the glorified Christ. Paul is thinking of the return of the Savior, a theme on which he delights to dwell, for it provides him with great inspiration. Although there may be enemies who now despise Jesus Christ, Paul is convinced that Christ's power is so extensive that all creation is to be subjected to him.

135. *Spiritual Qualities and Fragrant Gifts*
(Phil. 4)

In the closing part of his letter to the Philippians, the apostle makes several choice comments on Christian qualities which are relevant for all time. He wants his readers to stand firm in the Lord, but is concerned about a specific threat to their unity. Two members of the Philippian church were at variance with each other. They were two women, Euodia and Syntyche, and so important did the apostle consider this unfortunate disagreement that he exhorts a third member, whom he calls "true yoke-fellow," to act as go-between. He evidently knew these people well and probably understood the cause of the trouble. These women were active members of the Christian Church and had worked side by side with the apostle. Quarreling can mar the usefulness of even the noblest workers, and those who can act as peacemakers are blessed indeed.

A note of joyfulness has already been sounded in this epistle, but it bursts into its greatest expression as Paul nears his conclusion. He even exhorts his readers always to be joyful. On the surface this seems impossible, but presumably Paul had found it practical in the midst of a wide variety of hazards, including his present predicament as a prisoner. If ever a man could demonstrate that true joy was independent of circumstances it was the apostle. Perhaps some at Philippi would remember the night of the earthquake when Paul and Silas sang praises to God in spite of their tortured backs. The Christian jailer would ensure that others heard of that remarkable rejoicing.

Another needed quality is forbearance, which in any community is necessary if peace is to be maintained. But the most urgent need for the Philippians was to bear in mind the coming of the Lord. The saying, "The Lord is at hand," which Paul injects into his letter was probably used by early Christians as a method of greeting (cf. 1 Cor. 16:22 and Rev. 22:20). It was a salutary reminder and undoubtedly exerted a powerful effect on Christian behavior.

Anxiety states, which are increasingly prevalent in our modern world, were not unknown in Paul's day. His answer was to be found in a true attitude of prayer which he claims should lead to the banishment of all anxiety. Some will find it hard to believe that an anxiety-free existence is possible, but Paul is convinced that a positive approach to prayer which is all-inclusive and based on thankfulness to God will result in a state of peace. Thankfulness is important because it saves prayer from becoming self-centered and makes it God-centered. Paul paradoxically thinks of peace in terms of a military metaphor. It becomes like a sentry on duty to guard our hearts against the ravages of worry.

There is no doubt that a mind so garrisoned with peace will be capable of much previously beyond reach, and Paul points to some of the qualities which should flourish in true Christian thought — things true, honorable, pure, lovely, gracious, excellent. This at once shows the high plane on which the Christian mind moves, for these qualities are to become the norm. In the midst of a pagan environment, in which impurity and immorality invaded thought as well as deed, the Philippians were to set their minds on a loftier plane. Paul is confident that he has shown the way to this himself and does not hesitate to urge them to follow.

The letter ends with a passage about Paul's Christian contentment which is deeply self-revealing. His remarks are bound up with the gifts which the Philippians have sent to him. They had presumably had no opportunity to contribute to his support for some time, either because of their own poverty or more likely because of their contributions to Paul's collection scheme for the poverty-stricken Christians in Judaea. He wants to assure them that the lack of material support has in no way affected his peace of mind. He has learned the secret of true Christian contentment. It is not automatic, for the Christian has the choice between "abased" or "abounding." Paul had learned to choose the latter even when circumstances were against him. His positive approach is most vividly seen in his astonishing claim that he could do all things through Christ. A man with such confidence could be resilient in any situation.

The apostle finally turns his thought to the Philippians' gifts and in so doing so uses the language of commerce. Their former gifts had accrued interest. This is more important than the gifts themselves. He even talks in the language of receipts for payment. But this kind of language is not to his liking so much as religious language. He prefers to think of the gifts as an act of worship, like incense which wafts its fragrance to God. It is a striking metaphor, which would let the Philippians know how deeply valued their gifts had been. Perhaps Paul fears that they have stinted themselves and so assures them of the abundance of God's supply for their needs. He speaks from his own experience, which is the reason why he includes a doxology at this point.

In his conclusion, he includes an intriguing greeting from those of Caesar's household. These were probably members of the civil service, who were at that time mainly slaves. The Christian Gospel had found converts in the heart of the imperial service.

136. *A Letter About Christ*
(Col. 1)

Not all the churches in the province of Asia were founded by Paul. One of the places which he had never visited was the town of Colossae, in the Lycus Valley, about 100 miles inland from Ephesus. It was not the sort of place that he would have considered strategically important, for it was off the main trade route. But a church had sprung up there, apparently due to the witness of one of Paul's converts, Epaphras, who had somehow found his way to Rome and had made contact with the apostle.

The report that Epaphras brought spurred the apostle to write a letter to this community of Christians, whom he had never met face to face. There were problems in the church through certain people who were teaching false doctrine. The errors seem mainly to have arisen from wrong views about Christ, and this is the reason that Paul sets out some great doctrine in this letter.

What he has heard about the believers at Colossae rejoiced his heart. He speaks of their faith, love, and hope, three cardinal Christian graces which he links elsewhere (1 Thess. 1:3, 5:8, 1 Cor. 13:13). It is a thrilling thing when Christian communities arise from pagan environments. Paul's thrill can be appreciated, especially since he knows that the Gospel is bearing fruit among them. Indeed, the church was very much alive. Paul clearly has great respect for Epaphras, whom he thinks of as his own representative among them.

Paul's prayers are always an inspiration. In this letter he lets us hear how he prays for those he has never met. He desires spiritual understanding for them. Perhaps he felt, from what Epaphras had told him, that they were somewhat undiscerning. He is not thinking of ordinary knowledge or wisdom, but an insight into God's will, which is essentially practical, issuing in good works. Paul is not interested in theorizing without action. He is nevertheless not unmindful of the difficulties in doing God's will and consequently prays for adequate power for the Colossian Christians, no less than God's own glorious power. What might have seemed impossible becomes eminently attainable with such resources. He recognizes that these Christians are living in the midst of pagan darkness, but have been transferred to the kingdom of light. It is a striking picture of transformation which has been brought about by redemption. Redeemed people do not continue living as if nothing had happened. They belong to a new realm. It is worth noting that Paul did not initiate this imagery. The people of Qumran called themselves the Sons of Light and other men the children of darkness. Jesus also spoke of light: indeed He claimed to be the Light of the world.

This statement about redemption leads Paul immediately into several profound statements about Jesus Christ. Some take these statements to be part of a Christian hymn, which Paul has included in his letter. If this is so, the hymn fully endorses Paul's own conception of Christ. The Colossians on reading it would catch a glimpse of a majestic view of Him. They would see Him as Lord of creation. They would hear Paul describe Him somewhat enigmatically as "the image of the invisible." He may have been thinking about Adam being in the image of God and have been reflecting on the superiority of God's likeness as seen in Christ. It is a tremendous statement which at once shows Jesus Christ as more than a perfect man. The supporting statement that He is "first-born of all creation" does not mean that He is no more than a creature, but that He is prior to all creation. Nowhere in his letters does Paul paint a more exalted view of Jesus Christ. Not only for the Colossians, but for all time the truth of His Lordship over creation is reassuring, especially in our modern age devoted to the conquest of space.

Another important statement is that Christ is Head of the Church. This vividly illustrates the essential unity of the Church. Moreover, the astonishing implication is that Christ is in some ways dependent on the community of His people. The head cannot function without the body. Nevertheless the head is pre-eminent. All that can be known of the fullness of God dwells in Him. Paul's statements stagger the mind. No one has yet plumbed the depths of them.

One of the recurring themes in Paul's letters is reconciliation. He is never tired of pointing out this priceless benefit of what Christ has done on the cross. The Colossians would not need a worked-out doctrine of the Atonement to appreciate the meaning of reconciliation. They used to be hostile to God, but now that was changed. Their new aim was to be holy and blameless, a high ideal, to be sure, but the transforming work was to be Christ's not theirs.

The thought of such a powerful Gospel makes Paul proud to be a minister of it and leads him to comment on his task. It certainly involves suffering, which he conceives as a continuation of the sufferings of Christ. The purpose of his ministry is perfectly clear — to make the Word of God fully known. The Colossians had never had the advantage of hearing Paul's exposition of the Gospel, but the reading of this letter must have whetted their appetite to do so. There could be few to equal this expositor of the mystery of God. He had a rich theme, as applicable to Gentiles as to Jews. The Gospel, as Paul saw it, included both negative and positive aspects: it was a warning as well as an instruction. Those who heeded it were in his judgment the only spiritually mature people. It was worth the expenditure of much effort, but the energy required for such a task was not his own, but Christ's.

137. *Warnings Against Deluding Doctrines*
(Col. 2)

As Paul writes to the church at Colossae, he thinks also of the neighboring church at Laodicea on the other side of the valley. He had visited neither, but considered both as within his province as apostle to the Gentiles. He has certain specific desires on their behalf. He wants to see them united together in love. Love is the best kind of cement in any community, especially in Christian communities. But love needs linking with knowledge to ensure a sane approach. Otherwise it might deteriorate into sentimentality. Knowledge, however, is of a special kind, defined as the "treasures of wisdom" which are hidden in Christ. This means that Christians have many new treasures to discover. These priceless experiences contrast vividly with the delusions which some were trying to pass on to the Colossians as true wisdom. In the face of such delusions what the readers needed was stability. Paul thinks of them in terms of an army ready to face the enemy, and rejoices that reports have come to him that they are presenting a solid front. He then changes the metaphor and desires that they make sure of their foundations. Their firm footing was in fact to be Christ. As so often when he writes, Paul stresses the need for a continuous relationship with Jesus Christ.

Although he had the false teachers in mind when writing so sublimely about Christ, he now comes to more specific details about them. It was a local problem, but Paul's method of dealing with them has given his words continual relevance. The Christian faith has always been threatened by speculative philosophy which makes a strong appeal to intellectual pride. To Paul such philosophy deserved no better fate than to be linked with "empty deceit." In no higher category can he place "tradition" or the "elementary spirits." The former seems to refer to Jewish tradition, which enjoyed equal status with the law. The latter describes those spiritual agencies which were believed to control the material world. But Paul considers these to be feeble compared with Christ, in whom all the fullness of Godhead dwells. This is certainly a high view of Christ. The Colossians may have heard some of the deluders talking about the "fullness," a term used by later Gnostics for the absolute and unapproachable being. In Christ the unapproachable has become eminently approachable.

He who is our life is also head of all dominion and authority. As the Colossians listened to these words, yet further vistas of the majesty of Christ opened up before them.

At this point Paul switches to circumcision and baptism. In all probability some were urging the Colossians to submit to Jewish circumcision, but Paul reminds them of a new kind of circumcision, which involves the putting away of the old nature. In place of a merely formal rite like circumcision, Paul speaks of Christians as "buried with Him in baptism," "raised with Him," and "made alive together with Him." In other words, the answer to all deluding doctrines is Christ. The most important feature of a Christian's experience of Christ was forgiveness through the cross. Of course, the Colossian believers knew all this, but it must have warmed their hearts to be reminded of it. It was good to remember that no more demands could be made upon them. It was as if all their offenses had been recorded on a notice board and nailed to the cross. Then there was another switch in Paul's imagery. He thinks of the spiritual agencies, which were believed to be antagonistic to man, as a bunch of captives led in shame in the triumphant procession of Christ. He draws his illustration from a Roman victor's public procession in which he exhibited all his prisoners of war. Reliance on such defeated agencies would make any philosophy look foolish in the extreme.

One of the delusions being advocated among the Colossians was a narrow interpretation of ritual, which denied to Christians any liberty in the matter. It was not simply a question of observing certain festivals and scruples over food. It was a question of how far these were essential to Christian faith. They were an important part of Judaism, but Christian faith had to break loose from its Jewish moorings. Paul sees these things as no more than shadows and therefore no more important. It is weighty when a former Jew can say this. Whether the worship of angels was also being introduced by Jews is not clear, but whatever the source Paul saw this practice as detracting from Christ. Since He is pre-eminent, there is no need for other go-betweens in approaching God. In any case this angel-worship was having a disastrous moral affect — its worshipers were puffed up with sensuality. Perhaps the worshipers were conceited because they considered their angel-worship to be of a superior kind to that of the rank and file of Colossian believers.

The true Christian approach is very different. All believers are members of the same body with Christ as head. The relationship between them is extremely close. Being an organism, growth is expected, but no member can grow at the expense of another. Paul is thinking of the growth of the whole.

Once again he speaks of the "elementary spirits," but reminds the Colossians that in Christ they have died to them, which means that these no longer have any power over them. All the taboos which the deluded doctrinaires were wanting to impose are regulations which the Christian must reject. Although they may appear to be wise measures for the disciplining of the body, they are in fact dismal failures when it comes to checking self-indulgence. They are essentially of human origin in contrast to the glorious life in Christ which Paul next discusses.

138. Life on a Higher Plane
(Col. 3:1 – 4:1)

When compared with the program for living favored by the teachers of human wisdom, the Christian has a much superior scheme. He shares in Christ's risen life, which gives him the incentive to aim for the highest aspirations. Christ's life is centered at the right hand of God. It is a noble target. It means a new mental incentive as well as spiritual. The direction of the mind to higher things must result in nobler actions. Those interests which are tied to materialistic considerations are dead as far as the Christian is concerned. His whole destiny is bound up with Christ's, which opens up a vista of glory. Not only is his present life derived from God ("it is hidden with Christ in God"), but his future hope is centered in the appearance of Christ. With the present and the future so securely based in Christ, the poor substitute offered to the Colossians by the deluded doctrinaires looks even more shabby.

What Paul has just said gives the basic principles, but he does not leave it there. He goes into practical details. He would know something of the background of these Colossians from what he had heard from Epaphras. There are certain features of the old life which need to be stripped off. Paul mentions evils like immorality, impurity, passion, evil desire, and covetousness. These were all rife in any pagan city in Paul's time. A modern list would not look very different. It encompasses sins of the body as well as sins of the mind. None of them is allowable as part of a Christian's new life in Christ. The new nature involves different standards — a banishment of falsehood, a development of godly knowledge, a disappearance of racial, religious, and social distinctions. Paul never got beyond the wonder of the broken down barrier between Gentiles and Jews. If this had been the only barrier demolished it would have been a major feat. The antagonism between these groups was formidable. Yet when the equally formidable contempt for slaves is added, the unparalleled power of the Gospel shines through. No other agency in the ancient world could hope to unite these socially antagonistic groups. There could be no question about distinctions of this kind among Christians, who were all hid in Christ.

In addition to his list of things to be stripped off, Paul specifies some of the qualities which must be put on. They are attitudes of mind like compassion, kindness, humility, gentleness, patience, and forbearance, none of which come naturally. Because of this Christians should stand out by their possession of them. In an environment in which many of these qualities would be regarded as a sign of weakness, it was necessary for Christians to make a determined effort to "put them on." When others cause offense, Christians must forgive because the Lord has forgiven. Similarly they must exhibit love and peace, two qualities which more than others help to cement the members of the community into a single body.

Paul includes suggestions for fostering this community spirit. He thinks of the whole Christian teaching (which he calls "the word of Christ") as a constant companion, dwelling among the Colossian Christians. This is more than just a nodding acquaintance with the Gospel. It implies a consistent and intelligent understanding of the Gospel. Indeed, there must be provision in the community for instruction and admonition of one another. This comment gives a fleeting insight into Paul's thought about how a Christian community should be run. In addition to instruction there was to be the opportunity for communal singing. Paul recognized the value of singing in encouraging a sense of community. What he meant by hymns and spiritual songs is not certain, but it is probable that from earliest time the Christian religious genius found expression in the creation of lyrics, which gathered up the essential characteristics of faith. It is notable that every period since Paul's day which has been marked by religious revival has witnessed the birth of new hymns to express faith. The apostle's insight is further seen in his emphasis on thanksgiving, for again strong religious faith is inseparable from a thankful spirit. He gives some basic guidance for everyday Christian action when he urges that everything should be done in the name of the Lord Jesus.

Another insight which Paul shares is the dramatic transformation which Christianity makes on home life. Wives and husbands, children and fathers are all brought under a new obligation. Wives are to see to it that their relation to their husbands is "in the Lord." If this is done, the question of subjection to their husbands is easily solved since both are in subjection to the Lord. Love is to be the dominating feature of the husband's view of his wife. Similarly obedience of children to parents is related to the Lord, which means that parents should not provoke children.

The relation of slaves to master was an important problem in Paul's day. Many slaves belonged to the Christian Church, and no doubt Colossae numbered not a few among its members. Slavery was so prevalent that some practical advice on attitudes was essential. Naturally slaves who had non-Christian masters were in a more difficult position than those who belonged to Christians. Paul's advice to any slave was to act as if serving the Lord. The problems of putting this advice into effect if the master was unscrupulous can easily be imagined, but Paul does not allow for modifications of his principle on this score. If the slave is wrongfully treated, this can be left with the Lord. Christian masters have a responsibility to give fair treatment to their slaves, since they themselves are bondslaves of a heavenly Master. Christ transforms all human relationships.

139. *Christian Counsel and Christian Greetings*

(Col. 4:2-18)

As he draws near to the end of his letter to Colossae, Paul reminds the Christians to watch for certain things. First, they are to develop a consistent prayerfulness. Paul himself is the best example of this, especially "with thanksgiving." The Colossians must have detected this as they listened to the letter. The apostle was to a notable degree "a thankful Christian." He makes one special request for prayer — that he and Timothy might have an open door to preach the Word. This figure of speech is interesting in view of the apostle's present imprisonment. The closed door of the prisoner did not quench his enthusiasm for wider horizons. His confident expectations could be supported by their prayers. The fact that they had never met him was no bar to their praying for him. This wonderful solidarity between the Gentile churches and the Gentiles' apostle was responsible in no small measure for the remarkable spread of the Gospel. God had already opened many doors and there was no logical reason why a further door might not open for the enchained apostle.

The second advice was for wise behavior. It was not so obvious that Paul had no need to include it. In writing to Christians in a pagan environment, he knew what temptations would face them. He knew what wisdom was needed in social relations with those who were outside the Christian community. Opportunities must be seized for commending the Gospel.

Speech was another essential point to watch. Conversation is the most important medium for communicating the Gospel. Christians must watch the way they speak. There was to be a graciousness about their words that other people would note. Words, like salt, could be purifying and curative. The advice has never become obsolete. Whenever the Christian Gospel has been taken seriously, it has had a powerful effect on the type of language men use.

His counseling concluded, Paul next mentions people. He refers to several, and imagination can fill in some of the details that he omits. First there is Tychicus, who like Timothy was a member of his group of assistants. He was one of those who accompanied Paul from Macedonia to Jerusalem at the conclusion of the third missionary journey. He seems to have been specially commissioned by Paul for various tasks (cf. Eph. 6:21, Titus 3:12, 2 Tim. 4:12). Paul calls him "faithful" and "beloved," both words that he never lightly used. He seems to have had some magnetic quality which drew to him devoted associates. After he joined the apostle, Tychicus evidently did a considerable amount of traveling, acting like Timothy and Titus as Paul's representative. His present task was to take the letter and give a personal report. Paul can trust Tychicus to give the sort of report that will hearten and not depress them. He will be accompanied by one of their own members, Onesimus, of whom we know from Paul's letter to Philemon that he was a runaway slave who had been converted.

Other people whom Paul mentions send greetings to the Colossians. Whether they had ever had personal dealings with them is not known, but clearly they must have known them by repute. Aristarchus is another who accompanied Paul on his last journey to Jerusalem and who was with him on the sea crossing to Italy. He must have shared the shipwreck off Malta. He is now sharing Paul's imprisonment. He was from Thessalonica (Acts 27:2). Then there was Mark, the cousin of Barnabas, who had accompanied Paul on part of his first journey, but had been the subject of sharp contention at the beginning of the second journey. Now he is again with Paul. Time has healed the breach, and Mark had so far deepened in Christian understanding that he was soon to write a Gospel (if he had not already done so). Paul wants the Colossians to receive him well if he visits them. Jesus Justus is not mentioned elsewhere. Perhaps he had contacts in Colossae. The three just mentioned were Jews but there were three Gentiles who also send greetings.

Epaphras has been named earlier in the epistle. He is staying with Paul to minister to him. The apostle is deeply impressed by his constant concern for the Colossians and for the neighboring churches of Laodicea and Hierapolis. Luke was another of those described as "beloved," a physician who later turned his hand, not only to the writing of a Gospel but also to a narrative of the beginnings of Christian history. Demas is the third Gentile, who later deserted the cause through love of the world. At the moment he is still loyal.

A brief reference to the Laodicean church is informative. One particular household is singled out, that of Nympha. But what is most fascinating is Paul's request that this letter should be exchanged with one from them. It seems probable that he wrote to Laodicea at the same time a letter which has now been lost. The practice of exchanging letters suggests that Paul himself encouraged this process. It throws light on the distribution of the letters.

The strange note about Archippus needs comment. Evidently this man needed encouragement from the Church. He had probably taken over as leader from Epaphras.

As Paul takes the pen from his scribe to add his own greeting, the creaking of the chains leads him to urge the Colossians to remember them. As the last tones of the public reading of the letter died down, the gathered Christians would know for certain that here was a man whose spirit was not chained.

21

A Personal Note and a General Letter

140. A Personal Plea
(Philemon)

Of all Paul's correspondence there is no letter which reveals so much of the apostle as his brief letter to Philemon. The few words he writes are eloquent with exquisite tact and understanding. The letter concerns the runaway slave mentioned at the end of the Colossian letter. This reference enables us to reconstruct the historical situation. Onesimus was a slave of Philemon, a Colossian Christian, who evidently had a group of Christians meeting in his home. Onesimus had absconded with some of his master's possessions and escaped to Rome, where by some means he had come in contact with Paul. Through the ministry of the apostle, Onesimus became a Christian, and at once the problem of his social circumstances became acute. Contemporary practice was severe in its penalty against runaway slaves and Onesimus' reluctance to return to his master may readily be imagined. He would not at once recognize the difference that the Christian Gospel could make to master-slave relationships. Nevertheless Paul would not have been slow to point out to Onesimus that he could expect Philemon to have a forgiving approach. Yet how could Onesimus be sure? The apostle decides to write a letter of pleading, and Christians have ever since been grateful that he did, for the letter has become a classic of Christian advocacy. It appears from Colossians 4:9 that Onesimus returned to Colossae in company with Tychicus, who delivered Paul's letter to the church there.

It was a delicate subject to broach. In addressing Philemon, Paul not only includes his associate Timothy in the greeting, but also Apphia and Archippus in the address. Apphia was probably Philemon's wife, while Archippus, as Colossians 4:17 suggests, was the leader of the church. The problem of Onesimus' reinstatement was a problem for the whole community, not just for Philemon alone. In this case Onesimus was fortunate. His master was a Christian of considerable stature. He is warmly commended by Paul for his love and faith, which have found expression in practical ways. The "saints" have been refreshed by him, which suggests some material as well as spiritual assistance. A man with such open-heartedness was not likely to have a niggardly attitude toward his recalcitrant, but now repentant slave. He had already brought great joy to Paul, which encourages him to begin his pleading.

After dismissing from his mind the idea of commanding Philemon, Paul decides to begin by pleading his own circumstances. He was an ambassador in bonds for Christ's sake, which shows the limits to which he has been prepared to go in his service for Christ. Philemon could not fail to be impressed by sacrificial service.

What would he have thought when Paul next describes Onesimus as his "son"? If Philemon has any esteem for Paul, could he deal harshly with his "son" even though that "son" happened to be Philemon's own slave? Presumably Paul means that he has led the slave to Christ. That very fact should have rejoiced Philemon's heart. Who can doubt that it did? In a kind of aside, Paul makes a word-play on Onesimus' name, which means "profitable." As a Christian he can now live up to his name.

Then the apostle makes an astonishing statement. In sending Onesimus, he was sending part of himself. He had clearly become attached to this converted slave, who had evidently been most useful to him in view of his own limitations as a prisoner. Philemon must have wondered at the transformation which had taken place in his slave.

Paul's next suggestion is daring. Perhaps Onesimus' defection was overruled, since he is now returning as a Christian brother rather than a slave. In no more eloquent way could Paul express the powerful effect of the Christian message on the social problem of slavery. When master and slave are both brothers in the Lord, a different relationship is unavoidable. The Christian message undermined the system of slavery from within.

There was, of course, the problem of repayment of what Onesi-

mus had taken from his master. Paul's strategy is again irresistible. He offers to pay it himself. The idea must have seemed
ludicrous to Philemon — how could an imprisoned man pay the
debt? But the apostle adds a comment for Philemon's guidance —
to the effect that Philemon owes him his own existence as a
Christian — a far greater debt than that incurred by Onesimus.
Indeed, Paul writes a kind of IOU in his own handwriting, but it
cannot be imagined that Philemon followed it up. He would
refresh Paul's spirit by writing it off — although the apostle deli-
cately only implies this. He is confident that Philemon will do
more than he has asked. Some have interpreted this as a hint
that Philemon should send Onesimus back to Paul to continue
his profitable ministry. In view of Philemon's character, it is at
least not impossible that this was in the apostle's mind.

In closing the letter, Paul asks Philemon to prepare his guest-
room so that he can visit him on his release from prison. It is
impossible to say whether Paul ever paid the visit, but he was
optimistic of a speedy release. If he ever did occupy that room
the host would no doubt have shared with him the reactions he
had on receiving this letter. There were greetings from Epaphras,
Mark, Aristarchus, and Luke, all mentioned in the Colossian
letter and all presumably known to Philemon.

141. *A Letter of Christian Reflection*

(Eph. 1)

About the same time as Paul wrote his letters to the Colossians
and to Philemon, he wrote another which was sent to the Ephesians. It may have been sent to other churches in Asia as well,
like a circular sent to a group of churches based on Ephesus, as
some have suggested. In either case, it shows Paul in a more
reflective mood than in his Colossian letter. Moreover, it does not
deal with a specific problem. It develops some of the positive
aspects of the Colossian letter without mentioning the false
teaching which led Paul to present them.

It is fitting that the apostle begins with a doxology which sets
the tone for the whole letter. It is not the easiest passage in the
epistle, since it introduces many sublime themes. These will be
appreciated most if they are regarded as subjects for meditation
rather than as definitions of doctrine. So profound are the

thoughts that even the language becomes unwieldy through the weight of them. There are three main themes in the doxology — sovereignty, redemption, and inheritance.

God's sovereign choice has always been difficult to grasp, but Paul does not hesitate to speak of it. The One who blesses with spiritual blessings is the One who chose. Even before the creation God's purpose was to have a "holy" people, whose main characteristics are purity and love. There is no problem about this, for such a purpose is wholly in harmony with Paul's conception of God. The new family that God had planned would make men glorify Him. It would be a supreme exhibition of "grace" (God's free favor). But the problem arises over Paul's idea of God's choice. We are inclined to ask, "Why some and not others?" Yet Paul is not dealing with the problem of God's choice, but only with the conviction that Christians are chosen, which is another way of saying that God took the initiative with them. Since the gift was bestowed only through the "Beloved" (i.e., Jesus Christ), non-Christians will have no awareness of not being chosen. The divine choice will be meaningless to them.

The second theme is that of redemption or deliverance. The word was used of the freeing of slaves on the payment of a ransom. Paul thinks of the blood of Christ as the means of release. Christians have received remission of sins. They are no longer slaves to sin. The metaphor vividly brings out the sense of relief. Whenever Paul thinks of God's grace, he tends to use superlatives, as if words were not weighty enough to convey his wonder. Here he speaks of its lavishness. The result of this is that God has uncovered His mystery — His purpose in Christ. Paul talks of the "fullness of time" when everything will be united. It is a staggering view of the extent of the redemptive activity of God. The "plan" makes man at one with his environment, because all creation was to be "in Christ."

The theme of inheritance is tied closely with that of sovereignty. Paul is still thinking of God's plan. He sees everything through God's will, which is the all-important consideration. Paul classes himself among those who first hoped in Christ, and then he links in his readers who have heard "the word of truth." There is no difference. His readers, whom he calls "saints" in the opening of this letter, were sealed with the Holy Spirit. He uses a metaphor drawn from the sealing of a document as a sign of its authentic nature. The Spirit is the believer's mark of authentication, a badge of ownership. He is also a "guarantee" of what God will give us as an inheritance. The present possession of the Spirit was a foretaste of what was to follow.

After this extended doxology, the apostle comes to his usual prayer for his readers, and even this is fuller than usual. He knows of his readers' faith and love, which causes him to give thanks to God. His special prayer for them is for illumination — always a relevant prayer for all Christians, for none have too much of it. Even the wisest can still do with more wisdom of a spiritual kind. Paul links it with the word "revelation," the kind of wisdom which comes from another source than man himself. It is capable of leading to a fuller knowledge of God. The knowledge consists of knowing more about the Christian hope, the wealth of inheritance, and the greatness of God's power. Paul again piles up superlatives. Those first readers, like all sincere readers since, had much profound food for thought as they sought to follow the apostle's moving words.

To Paul the Christian faith was dynamic. It released the same kind of power as seen in the resurrection of Jesus. No greater spiritual energy has ever been known. Moreover, the exalted Christ is so far superior to all other agencies in all ages that His power is unchallenged. Further, this astonishingly superior Christ is head of His people, the Church, His body. Paul grasps at the truth that the body shows the fullness of the head. It is a bold idea, as if in some sense Christ is incomplete without the Church in whom His fullness dwells, an idea already expressed in the Colossian letter. Paul's words border on the mystical, but even those who do not understand the meaning cannot fail to sense the awe with which he contemplates the riches of the Gospel.

142. *God's Workmanship*

(Eph. 2)

One of the greatest sources of inspiration for the Christian is to reflect on the wonders that God has done. Paul gives a number of fruitful suggestions. First, think about God's raw material, the men and women in the clutches of the "prince of the power of the air" (i.e., Satan). The pagan world, then as now, was dominated by passion and selfish desires. It thoroughly deserved the divine wrath. It was from such a background that God was taking people with the express intention of working on them to transform them into new creatures. The mercy of God comes most vividly into focus against the reality of His wrath, as light shines against the background of a dark cloud.

Paul sums up the Christian's new position as "alive with Christ," again in contrast with the former state of "deadness" through trespasses. It is well to remember that such a transformation could never have taken place apart from God's mercy and love. Paul reminds his readers that he is talking about personal experience. There is nothing abstract about this. God loved us, that is Paul and his readers. This is not speculative but experiential. Paul knows and all believers know that this is a matter of grace — he and they had done nothing to merit it.

God's mercy shows itself in revitalization, resurrection, and reward; in the first by providing a new way of life (the Christ-life); in the second by providing a share in Christ's resurrection; and in the third by enabling believers to sit with Christ in heavenly places. Of course, words are a poor medium to express the wonder of new life in Christ. It needs to be experienced, and none are more conscious of it than those who have come to Christ direct from paganism. When this effective result of God's grace is contrasted with the former state, it shines like a jewel in a rubbish dump. Paul insists that the transformation is God's work not man's. He is the master craftsman who fashions men "in Christ Jesus" to show "good works." God's creations are contrasted with the devil's dupes. His people are governed by an entirely different standard of action. They walk along a different pathway.

One important aspect of all this is the relationship between Jews and Gentiles. God's workmanship could not be confined to the Jews. It was a matter of experience that God's grace had been extended to Gentiles, which must mean that the breach between Jew and Gentile had been closed. The Jewish view of the status of the Gentile was pessimistic in the extreme. They were aliens and were actually thought of as "no-people," a measure of the gap which separated the Jew and Gentile in Paul's day. There seemed no hope of reconciliation — until Christ came. Now the "far off" have been brought near. The blood of Christ had bridged the gap.

Paul thinks of the transformation in terms of the collapse of partition. He was thinking of the Temple, with its strict rule that Gentiles were not allowed beyond the outer court. The middle wall of partition was a constant reminder to them that they were an inferior species. No wonder hostility existed. Yet the impossible happened when in Christ the partition was demolished. The rift between the Jew and Gentile ran deep because it was a mixture of religious exclusivism and racialism. The cross is seen as a powerful force in that it was capable of making a unity out of the rival factions. The peace between these contemporary divisions is a foretaste of the remarkable unity which the Gospel was to effect among many different groupings, racial, religious, social, and economic. No other power on earth possesses such unifying potential. It is easier to fan hostility than to preach peace. When Jew and Gentile come to God through the same way of access with no distinction between them, it is evidence of the activity of the Spirit of God. No other explanation is credible. When the Spirit dwells in a Jew and a Gentile, how can there remain hostility between them?

The apostle sees a new temple, not made with stones but with people. He talks of the household of God. All partitions are swept away. All members of the household belong together as fellow citizens. Paul thinks of the foundation of this new temple. Instead of saying that the foundation is Christ, he makes the surprising statement that the "household" is built on the apostles and prophets. He was probably thinking of the testimony of the apostles and prophets to Christ, which played so large a part in the growth of the Christian Church. He is in no doubt that the real key or cornerstone is Christ Himself. This spiritual building is such that it serves as a dwelling place of the Holy Spirit. It is important in modern discussions on unity to note the stress that Paul laid on the activity of the Spirit. There is no doubt that where the Spirit dwells there is a deep unity which is capable of expressing itself irrespective of external organization. The apostle again and again shows how practical problems can be solved only by spiritual methods.

143. *Ministering a Mystery*

(Eph. 3)

There is no more effective way of commending profound truth than by personal testimony. Having said so much about the Christian faith in this letter, Paul now comes to his own commission as a minister of the Gospel. He uncovers for his readers some of the aspects of this commission. To begin with it is independent of his circumstances. He is in prison, but he is conscious that his lack of liberty is for Christ's sake. Then it is described as a stewardship of grace, not accomplished in his own strength. Thirdly it involves a mystery which God had made known to him. He has a noble idea of what the ministry is all about. To be the bearer of God's secret is a high calling which has deeply impressed the apostle. The readers of this letter will already have had an opportunity to discern his understanding of the mystery. Although he is thrilled with the privilege of making it known, he is deeply conscious that his own understanding is due entirely to the Spirit. What has also impressed him is the long period during which the mystery was still closed, and therefore the great privilege of now being God's agent for making it known. The mystery involved the inclusion of Gentiles on an equal footing with Jews, in a partnership: "fellow-heirs, members of the same body, and partakers of the promise." Paul never lost the wonder of the corporate fellowship which can be enjoyed by all men.

He next comes to what prompted him to become a minister and his answer may be summed up in a twin statement — God's grace and God's power. Paul is not however saying anything new, for he has said it before. It meant so much to him that it bears constant repetition. It was not a theory, but an experience. The more he ponders God's grace, the more convinced he is of his own unworthiness, which accounts for his description of himself as "the least of all saints." In some men such words would amount to mock humility, but set over against the indescribable privilege of dispensing the riches of Christ and making known "the plan of the mystery," it reflects a deep appreciation of what God's grace can do for a man. To unlock the divine mystery to a puzzled world was an unparalleled privilege.

Paul moves on to comment on the function of the Church. It is to be an exhibition of God's wisdom. Since every individual member is a miracle of grace, such a function is not surprising. But what is surprising is the nature of the spectators of this exhibition. Paul identifies them as spiritual agencies in heavenly places. One would have expected him to suggest the non-Christian world. Yet so convinced is he of the marvel of salvation that he sees even the spiritual world marveling at it. This was not an accidental afterthought, but part of God's eternal purpose. The Church as He planned it cannot be other than a spectacle to the unseen spiritual world.

The apostle has already included in this letter a moving prayer for his readers, but he cannot refrain from including another. He thinks first of all of his confidence in approaching God. This is important, for there is no point in praying unless there is a firm assurance that the prayer will be heard. Paul talks of boldness and confidence He knows he has access to God even though at present he suffers imprisonment. He is personally not worried about his bonds and urges the readers not to be perturbed.

In his second prayer, Paul senses the greatness of the God to whom he comes. His bowed knee testifies to that. Yet he comes to God as Father, the most intimate name for God. Since all human fatherhood is derived from God, fatherhood is seen to be an essential characteristic of God. He did not suddenly become Father. He is Father because he has a fatherly nature. A similar beginning to prayer is found in the Lord's Prayer (Our Father).

Before specifying his requests, Paul dwells on God's resources. They are certainly not inconsiderable. Paul tries to describe them as "the riches of His glory," by which he must mean His resplendence. If such a God will listen to man's petitions, none need fear His ability to respond. There are four parts to Paul's prayer for his readers, the kind of fourfold petition that is relevant for Christians in any age — first for inward strength, then for the indwelling Christ, thirdly for comprehension, and fourthly for fullness. A man strengthened by the Spirit is powerful, and Paul assumes that this should be the pattern for all believers. It is almost the same prayer, although expressed in another way, when Paul desires that Christ should dwell within them. Of course He lives in every Christian, but Paul yearns for Him to have complete mastery. The third prayer is the most astonishing — nothing short of comprehending the incomprehensible. Since the Christian is rooted in love, he ought to make some effort to understand that divine love. Paul visualizes a man intent on exploring it who finds there are no limits in any direction — breadth, length, height, or depth. Such a man is attempting to know the unknowable, but it is an attempt that he must make. This is a major burden of Paul's prayer. The last petition is more astonishing — to be filled with God's fullness. There is no greater request. It is tantamount to being perfectly like Christ. This may seem idealistic and unattainable, but Paul knows the value of praying prayers commensurate with the God to whom he comes.

It is no wonder he closes this part of his letter with a doxology, in which he affirms his belief that God can do more than we ask (even after his stupendous requests) and ascribes all glory to Him. His magnificent view of God makes insignificant the paltry view that many have of him when they pray.

144. *Living in a New Way*
(Eph. 4:1 – 5:2)

If what has preceded seems profound and theological, what follows is essentially practical. It is an exposition of how the power of the Gospel can affect the life. Paul begins by entreating his readers with a serious exhortation. A high calling demands a worthy life. There is no escape from this. But what is a worthy life? Paul gives a specific answer. It involves such qualities as humility, meekness, and patience, none of which comes naturally. Indeed they are not qualities which find much admiration in the world. Neverthless they are basic to Christian unity, which is the main burden of Paul's thought at this point in the epistle. Meek men are more likely to show tolerance than proud men, and Christian tolerance is essential to Christian unity.

Paul is quite clear about the kind of unity he desires — "the unity of the Spirit in the bond of peace." The Spirit dwelling in one believer cannot be at variance with the Spirit dwelling in another believer. They are bound together with an inseparable bond. Paul speaks of a sevenfold unity. One body, Spirit, hope, Lord, faith, baptism, God — these are a unity which all believers share in common. Moreover all have received the same gift of grace. When this comprehensive statement of the spiritual nature of unity is set against the long history of disagreements and splits among believers, it may be wondered whether Paul was not speaking purely idealistically. Yet there is no doubt that he considered it to be a realizable aim. It is important, however, to note that he points out that each believer shares the same grace, which is conferred, not in accordance with the achievements of each person, but wholly in accordance with Christ's own measurements. Unity has often been impeded by failure to appreciate this. No one is superior to any other in this matter of grace.

In reflecting on the subject of gifts, Paul thinks of Christ, as the ascended Lord, distributing His bounties to men. He pictures a victorious king who could lead "captivity" itself captive and dispense the spoils of His triumph. But the gifts are offices which carry responsibility. Paul mentions apostles, prophets, evangelists, and teachers as gifts, which at first seems surprising. It is, however, a penetrating thought, for it means no holder of any of these offices ranks higher than another. They owe everything to God. It is impressive to note that the purpose of all the gifts is the same, for equipping Christians, for ministering to others, for building up the Church. They are meaningless except in terms of service to others. The final aim is the maturity of God's people, the perfect example of which is Christ Himself.

Maturity is manliness (in a Christian sense) as opposed to childishness. The latter is seen when men are tossed about in an unstable way, like leaves blown by gusts of winds. In his Colossian letter Paul has warned against false teaching, and here he warns against cunning and craftiness. Shallow Christians have always been ready dupes for unscrupulous people who have misled them by false doctrine. Paul shows prophetic insight in his strong warning against them. The mature Christian presents a striking contrast. He can be candid in a loving way. His aim is to grow up into Christ, that is to become progressively more like Christ. A whole group of such mature Christians is like a body working in a perfectly balanced way, in perfect harmony in all its parts. When each member is in full obedience to the head (i.e., Christ), each will be dominated by love.

Then Paul comes to more specific aspects of the new life. What does it involve? As so often elsewhere, he contrasts the past with the present. It is always a worthwhile exercise. The apostle's description of the background out of which his readers have come is vivid. Futility of mind, darkness of understanding, alienation of spirit, and hardness of heart are all of a piece. They lead to callousness and immorality. The apostle was not exaggerating his description of the current Gentile world. Christians had a revolutionary attitude toward their former background. When they "learned Christ," as Paul expresses it, they turned toward altogether different principles. This learning process had a negative as well as a positive side. There was a stripping off and a putting on. The old nature, with its ruinous effects, must be discarded and the new garment of righteousness and holiness put on. The transformation is radical, involving the adopting of no less a pattern than God Himself. Some may say "impossible," but Paul does not so much as hint at this, although he could not have been unmindful of the difficulty of his advice.

A striking feature of Paul's letters is their practical character. The new nature is not left in abstract terms. Paul gives some examples of what is involved. Indeed most of the remainder of the letter sets out practical advice. The stripping process is illustrated by the banishment of falsehood, anger, theft, and other evils. In the midst of all these there is the injunction not to grieve the Spirit, a reminder that these evils are completely alien to the Spirit's character. The positive side of the transformation is represented by such qualities as kindness, tenderness, and forgiveness, all of which are seen in their purest form in God Himself. In fact, Paul draws special attention to God's forgiveness, which serves as a powerful motive for Christians to forgive each other. He then goes on to urge his readers to be "imitators of God," which amounts to thinking God's thoughts after him. No one could have a higher aim. It involves loving as Christ loved, which remains a constant "fragrance" for the believer. Love and sacrifice are never far apart and their odor rises like incense to God.

145. In the World, at Worship, and at Home

(Eph. 5:3-33)

Paul has already had much to say about the pagan background of his readers, but he comes back to the theme with special mention of the sins of immorality, impurity of mind, and greed. These were so prevalent in the non-Christian world, as they are still, that they permeate common conversation. The apostle makes the stringent demand that such evils should not be mentioned by Christians. Conversation reveals character and Christians are expected to have pure lips. When lips are inclined to utter impurity, Paul's remedy is that they at once turn to praise. Members of the kingdom of God are not the kind of people to give way to immoral action or sinful motives.

It was a true impulse of the apostle to recognize the power of words. In modern times with mass media multiplying the bombardment of words, his comments are even more relevant. Empty words, i.e., words devoid of truth, are plentiful, but Paul warns against them. They are the objects of God's wrath. The best procedure is to take evasive action and avoid associating with those whose words are empty. The apostle is, of course, thinking of close association and not mere casual acquaintance, for the latter is unavoidable. He sees the world about him as plunged in darkness with men groping around. He sees Christians as people with a light shining on their path, leading to the kind of life which is pleasing to God. Then comes a command for action — exposing the unfruitful works of darkness. Some kind of protest against a dark environment is unavoidable. The more those deeds, which men would rather hide, are dragged into the light the more shameful they are seen to be until they become intolerable. Most evils are more hidden than seen. Paul pictures, in what may be an early Christian hymn, Christ calling men out of the dark sepulchers of sin into the marvelous light. In the world the Christian finds no fellowship, but only challenge.

Among fellow believers the position is different. First of all there is a sense of obligation over the use of time. Time is too precious to be frittered away foolishly. It must be used wisely, and the best guide Paul can give for this is God's will. It is a searching test for it means that Christians must always be inquiring whether their activity at any time is the best use of that time in God's sight. While this does not exclude relaxation, it certainly excludes excess of wine and all that flows from it. This is never honoring to God. On the positive side Christians who are filled with the Spirit will want to find expression for their fellowship and Paul mentions the psalms, hymns, and spiritual songs which he had already referred to in his letter to Colossae. He was clearly impressed with the importance of singing, not just in a formal way, but spiritually minded singing ("to the Lord") with all the heart. Some sections of the Christian Church have been scared of religious heartiness, but Paul would have none of this. Singing springs from thankfulness, and there is no time when Christians have no grounds for gratitude. Such singing delights the heart of God. As we think of Paul the prisoner writing in such vein we remember that he set a magnificent example on his first visit to Philippi. He was not theorizing, but speaking from experience.

The real test of Christian faith is in the home, and in the next passage in this letter Paul focuses on domestic relationships. He begins with a general spiritual principle which places all his other remarks in perspective. "Be subject to one another out of reverence for Christ" is so mutual that it excludes all possibility of one party lording it over another. The apostle next comments on the attitude of wives. In urging a submissive approach, he is not recommending a slavish obedience, but a spiritual understanding. He makes a surprising comparison between the husband and Christ. It makes sense only when it is recognized that the same bond must exist between husband and wife as between Christ and the Church. That bond is a love which makes service a delight. No wonder Paul imposes on husbands the highest possible standard of love toward wives, the same kind of love which Christ has for His people — wholly sacrificial; a love which gives rather than commands. It is significant that this thought leads Paul to a doctrinal statement in the middle of his practical advice. This is another evidence that for him doctrine and practice are always closely linked. The love of Christ in preparing the Church for Himself in a pure and holy form is seen as a pattern for Christian husbands. It is a high ideal, for it means, as Paul points out, that there is a much deeper spiritual union between Christian husbands and wives than would be true for non-Christians. In a sense the human analogy, because it is so intelligible, illuminates the relation between Christ and His Church. When home life becomes a reflection of the life of God, human relationships are at once placed on a higher plane.

146. Children, Slaves, and Enemies

(Eph. 6)

Continuing his comments on Christian homelife, Paul turns his attention to children. In view of his high idea of the relationship between husbands and wives, his exhortation to children to obey parents is not surprising. He bases it on the first commandment. He does not question the need for discipline in the home. He sees it as part of the divine ordinance for man. His words may not appeal in modern times when children all too often reject the authority of their parents, but the fault may lie with the parents who have failed to match up to Paul's pattern for their domestic life. Even in Paul's day this recognition of parental authority would present a challenge. It also presented a responsibility for fathers, whose position of authority must never be regarded as giving license for provocation. Indeed Christian parents have great responsibility for seeing that their children are instructed in the way of the Lord. Had Paul been able to look down the centuries he would have seen innumerable blessings which followed from his advice. The Christian Church is deeply indebted to the profound influence of Christian homes.

It may have been because the case of Onesimus was still in his mind that the apostle adds a fairly extensive note about slaves and their masters. It was a matter of some relevance in those days since many slaves were numbered among the Christians. The advice is essentially practical — a plea to slaves to show obedience and singlemindedness, as if they were serving Christ rather than their human masters. It is not difficult to imagine, however, that slaves would frequently experience frustration, particularly with non-Christian masters, many of whom were tyrannical. Paul gives them the assurance that reward rests with the Lord. Similarly Christian masters are reminded that they, as well as their slaves, have a heavenly Master who makes no distinctions on the grounds of social status. Even if Paul could do nothing about the evil system, his sound advice did much to mitigate the position of Christian slaves who had Christian masters.

In concluding this fascinating letter, Paul thinks of the spiritual conflict in which all Christians were engaged. He thinks of a military man's armor and weapons and uses the imagery for spiritual purposes. He is in no doubt about the opposition — spiritual enemies of determined character, led by the devil himself. These superhuman agencies of darkness, who exercise such power in the world, are directed by a master strategist. "The wiles of the devil" is more than a picturesque phrase. It is a serious appraisal of the skill of the enemy. It may not be fashionable in the twentieth century to speak of invisible forces of evil, but Paul was convinced that the Christian Church was engaged in spiritual warfare. He was nearer the truth than much modern opinion. The devil's cleverest device is to persuade men of his nonexistence.

In view of the opposition, the Christian warrior needs both defensive and offensive weapons of a spiritual kind and Paul makes some penetrating suggestions. The defensive equipment is truth, righteousness, peace, and salvation. Paul thinks of the enemy shooting arrows with fiery tips which are incapable of penetrating the Christian's defenses. It is those who are uninstructed in the basic truths of the Gospel who succumb in the spiritual conflict. But defensive action is not enough. "The

sword of the Spirit" is provided for attack. This is Paul's picturesque description of the Word of God, which carries with it
the authority of God's revelation. Spiritual opposition can be
shattered in no other way. Of course the whole operation must
be supported by prayer, a fitting reminder that spiritual resources
come from God.

In his concluding sentences Paul appeals to his readers to pray
especially that he might have boldness in proclaiming the Gospel.
This may seem a strange prayer for an imprisoned man, but his
spirit is not imprisoned. He may be in bonds, but he is still an
ambassador. No one can take from him the high privilege of
representing his Master. He wants to seize every opportunity to
speak for Him, limited though those opportunities might be.

In almost the same words as he used at the end of his letter to
Colossae, he commends Tychicus to the readers. He is clearly
the bearer of the letter and may also have been the scribe who
wrote it. Paul dispenses with any personal greetings. If the
letter was designed as a circular, this would be intelligible. He
sends his greeting of peace, love, faith, and grace to all his Christian readers. So ends a letter in which the apostle plunges into
profound doctrine, but links it with down-to-earth practical
advice. It has been called, not without some justification, "the
crown in Paulinism."

22

Letters to Two Friends

147. *Paul Writes to Timothy*
(1 Tim. 1 and 2)

It seems certain that Paul must have been released from his Roman imprisonment, because when he writes to Timothy he is no longer a prisoner, but has been traveling once more in the eastern countries. He has recently been to Ephesus, where he left Timothy to continue as his representative. No information has been preserved about the course of the trial or the manner of Paul's release. It may either have been because the charge was dismissed or because no adequate witnesses presented themselves in support. It is also difficult to be sure what Paul's movements were immediately following his release. He seems to have abandoned his earlier plan of going to Spain and decided to return to Asia. Indeed, he must have revised his plans before writing his notes to the Philippians or to Philemon, in both of which he anticipates a visit in the near future.

After leaving Timothy at Ephesus, Paul proceeded to Macedonia, from where he writes this first letter to his associate. It must be supposed that much of what he writes he had already communicated to Timothy orally. The letter is, therefore, to a large extent a written confirmation of what Timothy already knew.

He had been left with several tasks at Ephesus, one of which was to deal with teachers of false doctrine. This doctrine appears to have been a mixture of myths and speculations. The one thing which stands out is its unprofitable character — it leads to empty discussions and unintelligible assertions. The history of Christianity has many times thrown up comparable movements which have been marked by views based on a lack of understanding of the Gospel. In the case of the teachers at work at Ephesus, their attempt to pass as teachers of the law leads Paul to comment on the function of the law. He reckons it to be good for the law-abiding, but not so for the law-breakers. He lists some examples of evils which it condemns, a list which contains both attitudes and actions. It is a grim list, but he wants to highlight the effects of wrong teaching. We need not suppose that the Ephesian false teachers were all guilty of the sins which Paul mentions, but he is concerned about anything which is contrary to the Gospel which he preaches. He regards this as a sacred trust from God.

The apostle's mind moves on to personal reminiscences of God's dealing with him. He recognizes that his call to service was an appointment by Christ. He is thinking back to the heavenly vision on the Damascus road. He could never forget it. Nor could he forget his former life or his persecuting zeal. The one factor which stands out was God's mercy to him. In all his letters he brings in at some point the grace of God. It may legitimately be regarded as his theme song. Moreover as he contemplates God's dealing with him, he sees himself as an example to others. If God's grace can do so much for him, others would see the possibilities for themselves and would believe. At this thought Paul inserts a doxology — quite characteristic of him when he has been dwelling on some great theme. But this doxology is distinctive because of the title "King of ages" which he never uses elsewhere. It is nevertheless an expressive title emphasizing the sovereignty of God.

Then he addresses himself personally to Timothy. He calls him his son because he was instrumental in his conversion. He reminds him of certain prophetic indications of his calling, by which he probably means some insight given to him by others. Whatever the occasion, Timothy knows his calling to a spiritual conflict, and should take courage from the evidence that he is so commissioned. Two features are important in this warfare — faith and conscience. For the Christian a good conscience follows when he is reconciled to God and knows forgiveness of sins. Where this fundamental Christian position is rejected, shipwreck follows. Paul knows of two people in this category — Hymenaeus and Alexander. Presumably Timothy also knew them. Paul does not say where they were, but this unimportant. He sees the danger and classes them as blasphemers. His remedy is strange, for it consists of delivering the men to Satan. We may compare 1 Corinthians 5:5, where Paul delivered another man to Satan for a remedial purpose. It is his figurative way of saying that the men are in Satan's realm. There is, however, a way for the men to return. We would like to know the nature of their error, but in all probability it was doctrinal (cf. 2 Tim. 2:17, 18).

Paul next gives general advice to Timothy, first on the subject of public prayer and then on the status of women. Prayers are to be for all men, including the rulers. It is a comprehensive suggestion which shows that Paul's mind worked on a broad horizon. He had no place for restricted prayer because he had a high view of God. When a man dwells on God's salvation, on His provision of a mediator, and on the self-giving of the mediator as a ransom for all, how could he pray small prayers? Moreover, he solemnly reminds Timothy of his appointment as preacher, apostle, and teacher of the Gentiles. Did Timothy need such a reminder? Perhaps not. But Paul felt the need to draw attention to his own commission.

The second advice was about the adornment of women. No doubt Paul had observed that some Christian women were adorning themselves in an extravagant way, and for this reason he enjoins modesty. There is no need to suppose that he is suggesting that Christian women should have no thought for their appearance. His real point is that a woman's pious life is more an adornment than ornaments. His injunction about women keeping silent has been misunderstood. Against the contemporary practice of women's chatter in synagogue services it becomes intelligible. When Paul refers to Adam's superiority over Eve because Eve fell first, his words create problems. Women have redeemed their position through childbearing. Yet they still need Christian graces.

148. The Church: Its Officers and Its Detractors
(1 Tim. 3 and 4)

In his other letters Paul has little to say about Church officials. Here, when writing to his close associate, he gives advice on the choice of such officials. The reason for the difference is clear. The apostle recognizes that because the time remaining for his active service is short, the need for his successors to be properly briefed on Church order has become urgent. In all probability Timothy was fully aware of Paul's principles, but needed them in writing to support his own handling of Church organization.

At first sight the qualifications for bishops appear remarkably elementary. Was it really necessary for Paul to tell Timothy that a drunkard should not be appointed? Against the pagan background of Ephesus, a reminder was needed lest it should be thought that moral behavior was less important than ability to organize. Not only so, a candidate for the office of bishop must not be a new convert, must have some ability to teach, and must manage his own household well. It is evident that the bishop was not an autocratic official, but an elder of the Church with special responsibilities. There could therefore be more than one bishop. It was essential for the smooth running of the Church that the right men should be appointed. Moreover, the office-holders were the public representatives of God's people in the eyes of the world and must therefore be beyond reproach.

Similar, though not so comprehensive, suggestions are made about the appointment of deacons. The main feature is that they must be "proved" men, upright in behavior and loyal to the truth. Again the requirement that deacons should rule their households well shows the importance that Paul attached to this and the close relationship which he saw between domestic and ecclesiastical authority. The women to which Paul refers in the course of discussing deacon's qualifications were evidently the deacon's wives, whose behavior must be in keeping with their husband's office.

At this point in the letter Paul becomes more personal. He hopes soon to come to Timothy. He anticipates a possible delay and gives his fear of this as a reason for writing. He wants to strengthen Timothy's hand for his task. He thinks of the whole Church in terms of a fortress for the truth. If the Church is a bulwark, so must its leaders be — a strong reason for Paul's concern over Timothy. He then quotes what appears to be a Christian hymn which exalts Jesus Christ. It shows the kind of hymns which emerged at an early stage in the development of the Church. Rhythmic statements of doctrine are easier to recall than prose.

After the hymn comes a warning for the future. There were some who would follow wrong doctrines, so seriously wrong in fact that Paul calls them "doctrines of demons." He is sufficiently sure of this to claim a direct revelation of the Spirit in support. Not only is there to be a wrong doctrine, but a wrong practice — a devotion to spirits which lead astray. It is clear that the apostle is predicting an intensification of Satan's activity which would make men insensitive to truth and devoted to religious taboos such as celibacy and asceticism. Paul rejects such taboos because they are against God's creation. Instead he enjoins devotion to the Word of God and to prayer, by which anything which God created could be sanctified.

The apostle gives no indication when these serious deviations will occur, but he sees the need to give Timothy some specific instructions for his immediate task. He is to warn the "brethren" and to instruct them in good doctrine. There is always a negative and positive side to the ministry of the Gospel. Clearly the minister needs some practical guidelines for his approach, and Paul gives Timothy some hints. Avoid empty myths and develop godliness, which is a man's most valuable exercise. It is valuable both for now and for the future. Even if the present brings toil and effort, hope is set on God, which brings a wonderful stability and optimism.

There are other activities to which Timothy was to devote himself. He is to show authority in teaching and to set an example in living. Some were probably contemptuous of Timothy's "youth," which could indicate any age up to forty. He needed this boost from Paul. He was to read the Scripture in public — which was the only way that most of the Christians in his charge would ever come to know it. Private copies of the Scriptures were expensive. Paul makes another reference to the "prophetic gift" (cf. 1:18), i.e., the spiritual equipment received at Timothy's call. He reminds him what happened at the laying on of hands. In Acts this action is frequently associated with a special imparting of the Spirit, and there is no reason to exclude this here. The ministry requires a considerable degree of devotion. Moreover some visible evidence of progress must be expected. The minister is under the public gaze. He must do a frequent stocktaking to discover where he stands. As Timothy read these pointed exhortations addressed to him, did he flinch at the challenge? Perhaps he knew himself well enough to know how necessary such challenges were. Paul's words show how forthright he could be when dealing with his closest associates.

149. *Discipline Among Christians*

(1 Tim. 5 and 6)

Paul is convinced that Christians should do things in an orderly manner and with this in mind has no reserve in recommending a disciplinary approach within the community. A family approach is necessary.

The first group about whom he speaks to Timothy are the widows. Because no welfare state existed, the plight of widows was a real concern to the Christian Church. There was no problem for those who had relatives, for these had a responsibility to provide for them, but solitary widows must, in Paul's view, be the responsibility of the Church. He has severe words for Christians who refuse to face up to their family responsibilities. Such people he judges to be worse than unbelievers. In no clearer way could Paul have stressed the greater responsibility of Christians.

When dealing with the solitary widows, Paul makes a distinction between older and younger widows. The latter, he feels, should not be placed on the register of official "church" widows. His opinion of what would happen if they were enrolled is not flattering to them, but he is no doubt arguing on the basis of general observation. It seems to him that marriage is the answer. He does not discuss the position of younger widows who receive no offers of marriage. The older widows without other support must be the responsibility of the Church, although even these were expected to be people who bore a good testimony in the community. What Paul is most concerned about is the image or the Church in the eyes of those outside. All too often the opponents of Christianity have had just cause to revile the Church because its approach to social problems has been sadly below the standards set by the apostle in this letter.

There is special advice regarding elders. As already mentioned the bishops were almost certainly elders with special duties. Paul is concerned that elders should be well treated. He cites a passage from Deuteronomy 25:4, which he had earlier quoted in his first Corinthian letter (1 Cor. 9:9), and he also echoes some words of Jesus (cf. Luke 10:7), to the effect that God's servants should be provided for. Those elders who are sincere servants of God should not therefore be rebuked, but those who make a habit of sin should be publicly censured before the church. Paul recognizes the difficulty of maintaining impartiality when discrimination is necessary, but he reminds Timothy that his judgment must be arrived at in God's presence. He is probably thinking that God Himself is the perfect example of impartiality.

At this point, Paul gives some miscellaneous advice which is revealing for Timothy's character. He is not to lay hands on people hastily, which suggests he is given to somewhat impetuous judgments. He is, moreover, not to become involved in other men's sins, which suggests he may not have been as discerning as Paul desired. He apparently had some stomach trouble which the apostle appears to have diagnosed as due to infected water and suggests the drinking of wine instead, because it was believed that wine had medicinal properties. Evidently Timothy's health was delicate, and this together with his timid temperament explains why Paul writes to him as he does.

A brief note on the position of slaves is added to give Timothy guidance, although he must have known Paul's views on such matters. Paul makes no attempt to challenge the existing order and is most concerned lest the work of God should come into disrepute. He takes the view that Christian slaves should be exemplary in the respect they show their masters, whether their masters are Christians or not.

Although he has already spoken of the false teachers, the apostle returns to the theme before closing the letter. He again rejects any teaching which is not in keeping with the teaching of Jesus, by which he probably means teaching about Jesus, i.e., the accepted body of teaching. It is clear that the false teaching was leading to various forms of ungodliness. One of the most disturbing features was the inclination to greed. The false teachers were using their doctrine as a means to material gain.

Because of this emphasis on gain the apostle urges the superior claim of contentment and then comments on the share of riches. He makes his well-known statement that the love of money is the root of all evils, which has often been misinterpreted to mean that money itself is the root of all evils. Paul has a penetrating understanding of human motives. Materialism in its broadest sense is undoubtedly the cause of a mass of other social evils. Many have found themselves deflected from the Christian faith for the same reason. Paul includes special injunctions for rich men, which would go far to mitigate the adverse effects of wealth. They are to banish arrogance, a frequent partner of wealth. They are to pin their hopes on God rather than riches, which would remove the temptation to regard wealth as all-powerful. More positively, wealth is to be used in generous actions. There is an echo in Paul's words of the advice of Jesus to His followers to lay up treasure in heaven.

The apostle gives more practical advice to Timothy of a personal nature. He is to have a high target — nothing less than righteousness and all that implies. Moreover, he is reminded that he is in a conflict and must wage a spiritual warfare as in the presence of God. Paul then gives his associate a solemn charge to keep the commandments until Christ's appearing. Did he fear that Timothy might fail to do so? Perhaps all that he intends is to remind Timothy of the solemn responsibilities laid up him. No serious minded Christian is above the need for such a charge. As Paul thinks of the second coming he includes a majestic description of God which brings out His uniqueness of power and essence.

As a parting piece of advice he again warns Timothy to avoid empty talk and what he calls "contradictions." He can only describe this in terms of an archer who never manages to hit the target, which in his view is "the faith."

150. *Rules for the People of God*
(*Titus 1:1 – 2:10*)

About the same time as Paul wrote his first letter to Timothy he also wrote to Titus. He is still free to move around and appears to be at Nicopolis at the time of the writing of this letter. This place was probably on the west coast, on the Adriatic sea. Paul had decided to spend the winter there. He is no longer able to contemplate extensive journeys in winter as he previously had done. Age has caught up with him, but he is still intensely active in the service of the Lord. He has a variety of issues on which to advise Titus, some of which are on similar topics to the ones touched on in the letter to Timothy.

For some reason the apostle's introductory greeting to Titus is fairly full and somewhat theological. It uses such ideas as faith, election, knowledge, truth, godliness, eternal life, promise, and preaching. Much is condensed into small compass, but Titus was well acquainted with Pauline exposition of theological truth.

As with Timothy, so with Titus, the apostle warns about the false teaching. Titus has been left in Crete, and from the apostle's remarks it is clear that he has a tough assignment. To begin with he had the responsibility of appointing elders in every town, which involved him in problems of selection. He was instructed about the qualities needed and many of these are identical with Timothy's list. An interesting difference is the omission of the note about not appointing new converts. Perhaps it was impracticable at Crete, where the church was not as long-standing as that at Ephesus. It was especially necessary in Crete for bishops to be men capable of refuting false teaching. These false teachers were again (as at Ephesus) more concerned with financial gain than with truth. Paul is emphatic that they must be silenced, a task which was not going to be easy. The Cretans had an unenviable reputation. Paul cites a Cretan poet as proof of this. If one of themselves had so poor an estimate of his compatriots as to call them all liars, they must have been liars par excellence. But linked with lying was bestial behavior, a combination highly reprehensible. Moreover, the false teachers in the island had got mixed up with Jewish myths. The main feature about them was their corrupt minds, recalling the warning of Jesus that the things which defile are the things which come out from a man. It is all the more dangerous when corruption hides beneath the cloak of religion and a profession to know God is belied by the person's behavior. Titus is not alone in having to cope with such hypocrisy. Many times in the history of the Church a similar state of things has recurred. Paul's advice is definite and uncompromising. Rebuke them sharply. Soft words were not made for those whose deeds are dishonoring to God.

There is more positive teaching, however, for Titus. His instruction is to be "sound." The word has been misunderstood, but it is vividly to the point. It has been mixed up with dull orthodoxy, but Paul's idea is linked with healthy teaching, free from all moral disease. It is doctrine which is eminently sane. Of course, there must have been a clear understanding of its content. It cannot be imagined that the apostolic Church spoke with multifarious voices. The early Church would have had a clearer notion of what "sound doctrine" meant than many of its modern interpreters. Paul, at least, was not afraid to lay a charge on Titus to proclaim it.

As so often in his epistles, Paul gives specific advice for different groups within the community. Older men are to be serious, sensible, and sound, not merely in doctrine but in faith, love, and steadfastness. No better advice could be given to those who wish to grow old gracefully. Older women are also to be reverent, to be good teachers of younger women, and generally to set a good example. Both younger men and younger women must watch their behavior so as not to cause any discredit to the

Christian community. The advice to young men would be rejected by many in contemporary society as too authoritarian, but self-control is needed as much now as then. Paul's advice to Titus is that he should show integrity and "gravity," by which he means seriousness of purpose. Christian youth in all ages has never attained its noblest expression unless impelled by a dominating quest for truth. Titus had the task of setting a noble example. The slaves needed a special word. Their job was to be faithful, by which means they would adorn Christian doctrine. It must have brought a new nobility to the drab existence of the slaves that their example might enhance the doctrine. This was not just making a virtue out of a necessity, but laying a solid basis for social relationships. Slavery has gone, but modern industrial relationships in many economic systems imply a virtual subservience, if not to a man at least to a State, which imposes as many problems for the Christian as ancient slavery. Christians in trade unions, for instance, might watch that they adorn the doctrine. Paul's advice to Titus has a universal ring about it.

151. A Theology for Living

(Titus 2:11 – 3:15)

In the first section of this letter Paul has just mentioned doctrine, which he now proceeds to develop. For him doctrine is summarized in the idea of grace, the unmerited favor of God, which he here thinks of as a kind of instructor for living. It warns against ungodliness and encourages a godly way of life. Grace and godliness are never far apart.

This leads Paul to think of the Christian's hope of the return of Christ. It is surprising how often he mentions this hope in relation to Christian behavior. It is clearly intended to have a sobering effect. Those awaiting the appearing of Jesus Christ could not fail to watch the kind of lives they live. One thing leads to another and reference to the Savior leads Paul to dwell on His redemption. The people of God have become what they are only because He has released them from sin. The self-giving of Christ on behalf of His people is the core of Paul's Gospel. It was never far removed from his thoughts. When describing the redeemed people, he uses a word which really means "a peculiar treasure." He thinks of the Christian community as a special possession of Jesus Christ. It is no wonder that they are expected to be zealous for good works. When a man knows he is not his own but Christ's, his motives will be governed by what most pleases his Master. These positive aspects of Christian faith are to be the subject of Titus' public proclamation. Moreover he is not to hesitate to adopt an authoritative approach. Paul assumes Titus' right to do this and even encourages it.

Then follows some practical advice. Christians must generally accept the authority of the State so as to show a good example. Paul probably feared that the Cretan Christians would find themselves caught up in some political agitation. Instead they are urged to gentleness and courtesy, qualities which do not make the strongest appeal to activists who feel Christianity should be strong-minded in society. Nevertheless the Christian Gospel has at its center the most perfect example of gentleness and courtesy.

When the apostle thinks of the superiority of Christianity over paganism, he again makes doctrinal statements which are rich in theological meaning. The marvel of the Gospel is best seen against the background of paganism with its foolishness, its bondage to passions, and its antisocial manifestations. Salvation in the Christian sense is not merely *to* a life of holiness, but also *from* a life of sin. Again and again Paul strikes the note of man's inability to save himself. Titus, of course, knew it already, but he must be reminded again. It was all a matter of mercy, another familiar Pauline theme.

Paul uses two other important words — regeneration and renewal. They both speak of transformation, of the endowment of Christians with new powers, which in their pre-Christian state they did not possess. This transformation is effected by the Holy Spirit, given to every believer through Jesus Christ. This again is a special Pauline theme. He could not conceive of a believer who did not possess the Holy Spirit (cf. Rom. 8:9). There is no need to suppose that when he proceeds to speak of justification, he is using the term in a different sense from that in his earlier letters because he makes no mention of faith. Justification by grace is in essense identical with justification by faith, for faith is needed to grasp the very nature of grace. Again Paul thinks of the Christian's inheritance, which he has mentioned in many of his letters.

The apostle closes this letter with general admonitions. Again he urges Titus to encourage Christians to apply themselves to good works, not as a means of salvation but as a result of faith. As in his letter to Timothy, he urges Titus to avoid unprofitable controversies and advises fairly tough discipline for the man who is factious. There is no virtue in being too soft with those likely to disrupt the community.

The apostle's final words concern the movements of some of his associates. Artemas is not mentioned elsewhere and nothing is known of him, but Tychicus was the bearer of his letters to the Colossians and Ephesians and was clearly one of his most trusted associates. The lawyer Zenas is nowhere else mentioned, but Apollos is well known from the Acts and the Corinthians correspondence. A parting exhortation follows, urging good works toward the needy, as if Paul cannot leave the theme. Then with the customary greeting the letter ends. What became of Titus after he received this letter is not known, but he is remembered, not only as its recipient, but as a man who was entrusted with some of the more difficult of Paul's assignments (Corinth, Crete).

152. A Farewell Letter to Timothy

(2 Tim. 1 and 2)

This was the last letter which Paul wrote. He is once again a prisoner and does not anticipate regaining his freedom. It forms a noble farewell from a missionary statesman to his young lieutenant. It consists mainly of personal advice, but also includes directions of an organizational kind.

After a customary opening greeting Paul goes into reminiscence. He is reminded of Timothy's faith and of his upbringing. His references to the influence of Timothy's mother and grandmother, who instructed him in the Scriptures, are significant as showing the powerful effect of a godly home. The reminder of this was intended to be an encouragement to Timothy, who was urged to kindle afresh the "gift of God" received at his ordination. This need not imply a lack of enthusiasm on Timothy's part, but is an exhortation to keep the fire at full flame. Moreover, timidity is to be banished. This may well have been the younger man's besetting sin.

A man like Paul, who writes as a prisoner for Christ's sake, has a right to exhort others not to be ashamed. He was never tired of dwelling on his calling and recognizing that that calling had involved suffering. In his other letters he mentions some of the hardships he had endured. Here he gives something of his attitude to suffering. It is governed by his deep awareness of the greatness of the Gospel. It is with a discernible sense of pride that Paul mentions his appointment as preacher, apostle, and teacher. The suffering was an unavoidable accompaniment of the office. When he thinks of it Paul makes one of his great personal assertions — "I know whom I have believed." Faith for him had within it a strong element of personal experience. Two specific injunctions are addressed to Timothy after this — follow the pattern and guard the truth. The veteran apostle is concerned that all that he had stood for should not be lost when he has gone. But he recognizes that the Holy Spirit is the best guarantee of this.

Men of God sometimes have disappointments, as they see those who promised well fall away. Paul mentions the Asiatics. It amounted to a personal landslide. Two are singled out — Phygellus and Hermogenes, of whom nothing else is known. Timothy must have known them. How different was Onesiphorus, who seems to have been a man of warm hospitality who sought out Paul when he came to Rome. The apostle speaks of the help he had been both at Rome and Ephesus. Perhaps he regarded Onesiphorus as a compensation for all the defectors in Asia.

After this Paul again turns to direct encouragement and exhortation. Timothy's task is to pass on the instruction received from the apostle, who sees a kind of chain reaction as other faithful men pass on the message. It is significant that the sole requirement for bearers of the tradition is faithfulness. Timothy is also urged to persistence as a soldier, or an athlete, or a farmer. None of these would get anywhere without single-mindedness. It may be that Paul recognized that Timothy was apt to fail in not sufficiently applying himself.

As he writes Paul thinks of his chains and tells Timothy to think about the Gospel which has led to his present sufferings. This is no mere creed about Jesus' resurrection or His Davidic descent, although it includes that. Paul speaks from an experience of salvation which makes his suffering abundantly worthwhile. Nothing can put chains on the Word of God. All he is concerned about is that men may come to salvation. To back up his point he cites a hymn which contains many ideas he has himself expressed elsewhere, as for instance the idea of dying with Christ. So close are believers to Christ that what happens to

Him happens to them. It would be against the nature of Christ to be faithless to His people. It would amount to a denial of Himself.

At this Paul thinks of the false teachers and gives Timothy further advice on how to deal with them. He gives both negative and positive advice. Timothy is twice told to "avoid." There are some forms of error which deserve no better treatment. They can be summed up as "godless chatter," and the Christian Church has had to suffer them in all ages. Paul uses the metaphor of a gangrene, which leads to disastrous consequences, to describe these errors. A case in point is the error of Hymenaeus (cf. 1 Tim. 1:20) and Philetus, who held wrong views about the resurrection. So central is this doctrine that error about it jeopardizes a man's faith. How necessary to make sure of one's foundations! Other positive advice is that Timothy should be a good workman with truth — the very antithesis of the false teachers.

In considering Timothy's task, Paul's mind goes to the distinction between honorable and dishonorable service, which he illustrates from the different kind of vessels used in a great house. The analogy must not be pressed, but the meaning is clear. Some advice of a more personal nature follows. Again, Timothy must avoid controversies. At the same time he must have a right target, which involves the development of Christian qualities and the growth of Christian attitudes. Where love and peace dwell in the heart, kindliness will show in relationships with others, even with opponents. The Christian teacher's aim is not to crush but to love. The devil's dupes cannot be delivered by using the devil's methods. He knows nothing of the incomparable power of love.

153. Trials and Triumphs

(2 Tim. 3 and 4)

Paul cannot help looking to the future, for all men must at times muse on things to come. He paints a picture of moral decadence, which he sees as characteristic of the last days. His picture is gloomy, but has many times found a partial fulfillment in successive ages when men's religion has become powerless. Some of the worst aspects of moral decline are noted by Paul. It is no wonder he again urges Timothy to avoid such people. He numbers among them those who captivate weak women, who are a constant prey to unscrupulous men. When he cites the case of

Jannes and Jambres, who opposed Moses, he is appealing to some tradition which is not preserved in the Old Testament. Yet their opposition to God's servant made them representative of all who oppose truth. Paul's words are still relevant. The men of any age in which error is passing for truth would do well to heed his warning.

The apostle lapses into a reminiscent mood, but with a didactic purpose. He has set an example for Timothy to follow, which will involve his teaching, behavior, and faith. He cites examples of what he had himself endured on his first missionary journey at Antioch, Iconium, and Lystra. Timothy was not then associated with the missionary enterprise, but since his home was at Lystra, he must have had vivid recollections of Paul's sufferings at that time. Indeed, his initial impression of the apostle was conditioned by his observance of how he endured hardship. Paul now reminds Timothy of how he overcame the difficulties, or rather how the Lord delivered. The younger man is also reminded that evil would not diminish, with the implication that further persecutions must be expected. Later on Timothy himself was to know the hardships of imprisonment (cf. Heb. 13:23).

The brief further reminder to Timothy of his godly upbringing throws valuable light on Paul's approach to Scripture. Acknowledging its importance as a contributory factor in Timothy's development, he then proceeds to comment on its inspiration. He does not give any doctrine of inspiration, but he supplies some insights on which an adequate doctrine can be built. It may be supposed that he is either giving Timothy information which he did not possess, or more probably is making a statement about inspiration to formulate what has always been implicit in his ministry. It cannot be supposed that Timothy was wholly unaware of his doctrine of Scripture. Nevertheless in these final instructions to his closest associate, he sees the need for some definitive statement. There can be no doubt that his words mean that the text of Scripture in its entirety was inspired and was therefore profitable. This is borne out by his authoritative method of citing its testimony throughout his letters. Moreover, he would share this view with all pious Jews. It was essential that Timothy, as he contemplates the continuation of the mission, should have no lesser view of Scripture. This is a major part of the equipment of the man of God.

The farewell letter is nearing completion, but Paul cannot

refrain from addressing another serious injunction to Timothy, so serious in fact that he links it to the judgment activity of Jesus Christ. The main burden is preaching, teaching, and evangelizing. The work must not be restricted to favorable circumstances, nor marred by lack of toughness or of patience. The man of God must not be deflected by people's whims, or by those who prefer myths to truth. Paul predicted the rise of such and a survey of Church history shows how right he was. Timothy's target is plain — to fulfill the ministry whatever it involves. It is the long succession of Timothy's successors who have acted on that advice that has thwarted the determined attempts of evil men to stamp out the message of the Gospel.

As Paul thinks of the immediate future he thinks in terms of an offering about to be sacrificed. It is a figure of speech he has used before (Phil. 3:17), but now the action is imminent. Nevertheless he does not dwell on this metaphor. An athletic illustration springs to his mind and he sees himself just about to cross the tape. It has been a contest in which he has pressed on to the end. There is a note of triumph here. The athlete's mind is on the victor's laurel, which in this case is awarded not simply to the first past the post, but to all who faithfully finish the course. Paul picturesquely calls it the "crown of righteousness."

Only matters of a personal nature remain — the movements of his associates, the desertion of Demas, the request for his cloak and his books and parchments, the opposition of Alexander. In few words Paul gives glimpses into many personal experiences. Most poignant of all is his sense of loneliness at his trial — except for the presence of the Lord. The old warrior is near his end, but he approaches it with supreme confidence. He knows that the Lord will deliver and save him — which leads to a typical doxology.

A few greetings and a request for a visit from Timothy close the last letter the apostle wrote. What happened after that is not recorded in the New Testament. A tradition exists that Paul was beheaded at Rome, the end of a fruitful missionary life, but only the beginning of centuries of profound influence on the life and teaching of the Christian Church.

23

A Word of Consolation

154. *Son of God and Son of Man*
(Heb. 1 and 2)

No one knows who wrote this epistle, although numerous suggestions have been made. Many of the ancients were convinced that Paul was the writer, but there are so many difficulties that few scholars now maintain such a view. It is generally supposed that the writer was closely associated with the apostles and wrote this letter to a group of Christians who met in a house, possibly at Rome. It is not even possible to be sure where the writer was when he wrote. His reason for writing, however, will become clearer as the letter itself is examined. He calls it a "word of consolation." It has no opening greetings and none of the usual marks of an epistle. It was possibly a transcript of a sermon preached to a congregation and is therefore more of a written homily than a letter.

The first part of the epistle centers on the superiority of Christ. There is a kind of introductory paragraph which shows Christ to be the final revelation of God. There had been other revelations, like those through the prophets. The writer is convinced that God had spoken through them. Indeed the whole epistle appeals to the Old Testament on the assumption that all of it speaks with the voice of God. Yet when God spoke through Christ the revelation was not only infinitely superior, but final. No fuller revelation could be made. The statements about Christ are certainly worth considering. He is Son; He is heir of all things; He is Creator; He is the bursting out of God's glory; He is the stamp of God's character; He is the purifier of sins; and He is at the right hand of God (i.e., in the position of authority). In this brief compass the writer has condensed much profound theology.

He leaves his readers in no doubt at all about his exalted view of Christ. Whatever else he says about Him must be squared with this.

It will seem strange to Western minds that after so exalted an introduction, the writer states the superiority of Christ to angels and then proceeds to support this affirmation with a chain of Old Testament texts. What was he getting at? It must be supposed that some people among the readers known to the writer were paying too much reverence to angels. We know that Jews had high respect for them. There is evidence for this from several sources. Whereas the title Son of God is nowhere given to an individual in the Old Testament, the superiority of Christ is seen in His right to the title, as compared with the angels.

All the quotations are from the Psalms, which suggests that the writer had made a special study of these, especially since he links together so many passages to illustrate his point. Some think that he used a quotation book with passages listed under themes. Such a book would have been valuable, but no evidence is available that this kind of manual existed at this time. The writer is obviously a man with a remarkable knowledge of the Old Testament text. Moreover, he cites Scripture in such a way that its authority is undeniable. What he shows by his quotations may be summed up in the following way.

The first (v. 3) shows the eternal character of Christ's Sonship, linked with His incarnation, which resulted in a new status; the second (v. 5) shows the promise to David more perfectly fulfilled in Christ than in Solomon; the third (v. 6) shows the superiority of the first-born (i.e., Christ) to the angels; the fourth and fifth (vv. 7-9) show His superiority in that Christ occupies the throne of God, whereas the angels are but servants; the sixth (vv. 10-12) shows Christ as Creator, as the unchanging One; and the seventh (v. 13) shows His superiority by His present and future triumph over His enemies. It is an impressive introduction to the next section, which shows His humanity.

Before coming to grips with the problem of the incarnation, the writer gives a warning. It is the first of several which are interspersed at various points throughout this letter. The first warning furnishes a clue to the purpose of the whole letter. Some were tending to drift away and needed to be exhorted not to neglect the salvation which the writer is about to expound. He sees it as of first importance because the salvation is the same as that proclaimed by the Lord. It is an authenticated message, confirmed by signs and wonders and spiritual gifts.

Now for the problem! If Jesus was superior to angels, how could He be lower, as He must have been, at the incarnation? Jewish Christians might well have been bothered about this, since they had brought into Christianity a high view of angels. The answer is to be found in much greater exaltation of Jesus. None of the angels were crowned with glory and honor, because none of them suffered and died. It is a strange kind of crown which can only be gained by self-sacrificial death, but that is God's way of doing things. Indeed the writer considers that this fits in perfectly with the nature of things, since for Christ suffering was the means to the perfect fulfillment of God's purpose for Him.

All this would sound self-centered, if Christ's action were inward looking. But it is not. It is geared to bringing men (sons) into the same glory. In fact, the identification of Jesus with men is extensive. He shares our nature and we share His glory. He destroys the devil's power and we find release from death. It is no longer a taskmaster, for fear has fled. Not only so, but because Jesus took our nature He has power to sympathize, and this idea leads to the central idea of this epistle. Christ is our high priest. Jews would understand. Their high priest was their representative before God. A representative must understand the people he represents, and Christ can do this because He has passed through the same temptations as His people. Although there was no answering sin in His mind as there is in ours, He knows the intensity of spiritual conflict.

Although the letter begins on a high theological level, the author at various stages throughout his arguments presses home the practical implication of his words.

155. *Superior to Moses and Joshua*

(Heb. 3:1 – 4:13)

The Jews were naturally inclined to compare everyone with Moses. So great was the esteem in which the law-giver was held that any Christian, desiring to win Jews or strengthen weak Jewish Christians, must be able to demonstrate the superiority of Christ to Moses. This epistle proceeds to do this. The main subject for comparison is the faithfulness of both. In the glory which each gained, the glory of Christ outshone the glory of Moses. There was a fundamental difference between them, the difference between a servant and a son. The contrast could not be more vividly described, for a son has rights which a servant does not possess. The writer uses the illustration of a builder who must always be superior to the house which he has built. Such imagery has limitations since people are being compared with an inanimate object like a house but the builder is likened to God. Whereas Moses served in the household of Israel, Christ rules as Son over the Church, the new Israel. Nevertheless, the new Israel consists only of those who continue in faith. The theme of faith is a dominant one which recurs throughout this letter.

Faith has its opposite number in unbelief, on which the writer comments, illustrating his views by reference to the history of the Israelites. He first quotes Psalm 95:7-11, which was an exhortation to the readers to obey the commands of God on the strength of the Israelites' wilderness experiences. They were not to harden their hearts, and the present writer feels that his readers need a similar exhortation. The theme of rest, which is introduced at the end of the quotation, inspired the writer to develop the idea in a kind of Christian application of lessons learned from the past. But before doing so, he fastens on the first word of the quotation, i.e., "today," and sees it as a challenge to an urgent situation. There is no room in Christian experience for procrastination, which leads to hardening. Faith in Christ is an ever-present experience, a holding on to the end. The writer is clearly fearful that some of his readers are in danger of being as rebellious as the Israelites had been under the leadership of Moses. All those people had failed to possess the inheritance which God had provided for them, which the writer summarizes under the word "rest." Because of their rebelliousness the leadership of Moses was seen to have failed in its objective. It is implied, but not explicitly stated, that Christ is a more successful leader than Moses.

The message is applied directly to the Hebrews. They have the promise of "rest." They also need a warning. "Let us fear lest any of you be judged to have failed to reach it." In spite of Israel's failure there is still a "rest" to be enjoyed by faith, a "rest" as old as creation itself. This idea leads the writer to link up the "rest" with God's sabbath, His resting at the end of the acts of creation. The comparison between the sabbath and the rest of God was a well-known rabbinical idea, which would no doubt have been appreciated by the Jewish Christian readers.

It is at this point in the argument that Joshua is introduced. The tragedy of the Israelites was not simply the failure to inherit an earthly Canaan. The writer wants to make clear that God had provided a spiritual type of "rest" which was superior to Canaan. If Joshua's conquest had been all that God had intended, there would have been no more to say. There is a danger, however, that these Jewish Christians had not enough vision to see the much greater spiritual provision which God had made for them. They may have been hankering after a restitution of an earthly Canaan instead of enjoying their spiritual blessings in Christ. Joshua, in spite of his heroic conquests, was no more than an earthly commander. But Jesus, superior in every way, leads His people to a spiritual and therefore an eternally enduring reward. Maybe the writer sees some significance in the fact that the name Joshua in Greek is the same name as Jesus. There is no doubt in his mind which is the greater "Savior."

This section ends with another exhortation linked with a significant assertion. The divine Word, which represents the powerful activity of God, is described as a sword, a vivid metaphor which highlights both its penetrating and its discerning power. It is well to remember the impossibility of concealing anything from God. There is no place for delusion. The writer probably has in mind the ease with which man can convince himself of his spiritual well-being, when God's estimate of him is in strong contrast.

156.　*The Priesthood of Christ*

(Heb. 4:14 – 5:10)

Some hint of the priesthood of Christ has already been given in the letter (cf. 2:17), but now the writer concentrates on this important theme. Nowhere else in the New Testament is this idea expounded with such detail. It was of special interest to Jewish Christians, who would be familiar with the high priest theme, to know how it fitted into their newfound Christian faith. It also has much value for Gentiles in enabling them to understand the spiritual interpretation of the Old Testament cultus.

The first proposition is that Jesus as high priest acts in a heavenly sphere, which at once raises His office above those who performed the Jewish ritual. Moreover, our high priest is Son of God, undreamed of in the long history of Jewish high priests. Another fact which is of great practical importance is the ability of our high priest to sympathize with His people. The uniqueness of Christianity lies in this fact that man's representative is sufficiently identified to be able to understand, and sufficiently dissimilar to be without sin. Temptation without sinning is alien to man's normal way of thinking, but Christians have a perfect example of it in Jesus Christ. With such a high priest it is no wonder that Christians are exhorted to approach confidently the throne of grace, an immensely suggestive name for the throne of God.

Having briefly commented on Jesus Christ as high priest, the writer proceeds to compare Him with Aaron's priesthood. This would be a matter of great significance for Jewish believers. High priests cannot appoint themselves, and in this Jesus was no exception. He was called by God to this office. But a contrast exists between Aaron and Jesus. The former had to offer sacrifice for his own sins, whereas Jesus had no sin of His own. At this point in the discussion the writer introduces two quotations from the Psalms. The first, from Psalm 2, stresses the divine origin of the Son, and the second, from Psalm 110, establishes His priesthood as that of Melchizedek. Much more will later be said about Melchizedek, but for the moment the intention is simply to introduce a new priestly order distinct from Aaron's.

It is not often in the New Testament epistles that details are given about the historical life of Jesus. The writer makes some penetrating statements which directly link the earthly experience of Jesus with His priestly office. He is clearly fully familiar with the agonizing prayer of Jesus in Gethsemane. The mention of tears draws attention to the stress through which the earthly Jesus passed, which the writer sees as a valuable qualification for the office of high priest. When faced with death Jesus had not shrunk from it, but had learned the way of obedience. One may hear the echo of the strong affirmation of Jesus — "nevertheless not my will, but thine." That this theme of the obedience of Jesus captured the imagination of the early Christians is seen from its appearance in the Christian hymn in Philippians 2:8. It is difficult to understand how Jesus Christ, without sin, could be made perfect, but this is what the writer says. Clearly Jesus

Christ was never less than perfect. But the writer seems to use the word "perfect" in relation to God's plan of salvation. In this sense Jesus Christ became "perfect" when His perfect obedience to death provided the basis for man to come to God. This marked out His priesthood from others and led to the idea of a new order, which the writer links with Melchizedek. His reasoning at times seems involved, but his choice of Melchizedek as an alternative priestly order was prompted by the quotation in the psalm. After a diversion in which a stern warning is issued to the readers, the Melchizedek theme is further developed in Hebrews 7. It is clear that the writer considers it to be valid to apply Old Testament statements in a new way.

157. *An Exhortation and an Exposition*
(Heb. 5:11 – 7:28)

It has by this time occurred to the writer that his theme may appear rather tortuous to some. Indeed he speaks of his readers as "dull of hearing." He knows them well enough to make this judgment. These people have evidently been Christians for some time. They are, moreover, people of some ability since the writer considers that they should be using their time in teaching others. It is this statement which has led most scholars to conclude that the readers were a small part of a larger church, perhaps a house group of more intellectually minded people who were forming a separate community instead of contributing to the enrichment of the whole. The writer is rather scathing about the attitude of his readers — he thinks of them as having a milk diet like children instead of a diet of meat like strong men. Some interesting expressions are used to describe what they need. Their target should be "the word of righteousness," which is distinguished from "the first principles of God's word." Every Christian is expected to progress in understanding and thus to mature. It is only mature Christians whose faculties are fully discerning.

In the next part of the letter, the writer warns about those who not only do not mature, but who are even contemplating leaving their faith in Christ altogether. Any who do this are placing themselves outside the sphere in which repentance operates. It amounts to recrucifying Christ, a vivid and challenging figure to describe the serious consequences of apostasy. The writer is supposing the condition of those who, having experienced the benefits of Christianity — the heavenly gift, the Holy Spirit, the goodness of God's Word, and the powers of the new age — deliberately reject and hold in contempt the Son of God. This condition suggests a hardened attitude toward Christianity. The writer implies that there is no more hope for those who adopt such an approach than there is for land whose only produce is thorns and thistles, destined for burning.

The proposition has been stated in a hypothetical form, for the writer immediately proceeds to assure himself that his readers are not guilty of such contempt. Indeed, their work and love on behalf of other Christians shows that something other than "thorns and thistles" are being produced. Nevertheless there is room for improvement. Their faith is sluggish — not having yet reached the exhilarating state of "full assurance of hope." As is clear from the latter part of the epistle, the writer attaches considerable importance to the value of imitation in matters of faith. The "sluggish" can be goaded into greater effort by observing the example of others who have "arrived." It is a major aim of this epistle to encourage Christians to press on in faith to take full possession of their inheritance.

The thought of inheriting the promises leads to some comments about Abraham. The patriarch stood out like a giant in matters of faith. He almost personified the kind of faith which implicitly acted on the promises of God. He took God at His Word without any oaths to back it up. That God had said it was enough. This implies a strong belief in the changelessness of God, which the writer shared with the patriarch. Since God's nature as well as His Word is changeless, there is no possibility that what He said at one time will not hold for all time. This for Christians is a strong basis for hope and is strengthened still more by the fact that Jesus acts on their behalf in the presence of God. The writer puts the whole matter metaphorically. He visualizes hope in the shape of an anchor finding its hold in the inner shrine, i.e., the holy of holies. Although the metaphors are mixed, the ideas are clear. The holy of holies was symbolic of approach to God and no surer anchorage could be found than faith in a high priest who has already made access possible.

At this the writer goes back to the Melchizedek theme and compares his order with Aaron's. Melchizedek is a shadowy figure, a priest-king to whom Abraham offered tithes. The Old Testament says nothing about either his origin or his end, and the writer deduces from this that his priesthood was therefore continuous. The idea may, at first, seem strange, but no doubt what is in mind is the contrast with Aaron's priestly order, whose origin and dimensions are recorded in detail. Because of his kingly nature, Melchizedek was moreover more fitted to be a type of the Son of God.

The argument is pushed still further. It was important in Aaron's order for genealogy to be established. Only genuine descendants of Levi were eligible candidates for the priesthood. Had this applied to the order of priesthood to which Jesus belonged, it would have raised a difficulty since He was of the tribe of Judah and not Levi. But the order of Melchizedek is superior because antecedent to Levi, who was not yet born. Moreover, Levi's ancestor Abraham acknowledged the superiority of Melchizedek by offering tithes.

The writer again quotes Psalm 110:4 as his authority for maintaining not only that Christ's appointment to the order of Melchizedek was a divine appointment, but that it was continuous. In spite of the sanctity attaching to the Aaronic order, the writer has no hesitation in describing its "weakness and uselessness" and in pronouncing approach to God through Christ as "a better hope."

This superiority theme is developed still further. The new covenant is better than the old. The old priesthood was constantly needing renewal because of the death of its representatives. But the priesthood of Christ is permanent. His intercession for His people is constantly effective. It does not depend, as Aaron's did, on daily sacrifices. His one sacrifice, infinitely superior because He was both offerer and offered, never needs repetition. As the writer meditates on the Christian believer's high priest, he can only find one word to describe Him — perfect.

158. *The New Covenant*

(Heb. 8:1 – 10:18)

Having given an exposition of his Melchizedek theme, the writer then gives a summary of his positive ideas of the new high priestly order. The earthly order of priests is regarded as a pattern for the superior priesthood of Christ. This idea of pattern is important throughout this letter, always linked as it is with the thought that the new, the fulfillment of the pattern, is infinitely superior to the pattern itself. The relationship is like that between a shadow and its substance. The new covenant, with its perfect ministry, puts the old covenant in the shade and shows up its imperfections. The author thinks of what Jeremiah had said about a new covenant (Jer. 31:31-34) and quotes a considerable passage from his prophecy. He sees Jeremiah's predictions of a covenant which rests upon an inner acceptance of God's laws as fulfilled in Christ. "I will be their God and they shall be my people" has been effectively achieved in the Christian Church. It will be remembered that Jesus Himself claimed to institute a new covenant through His blood at the Last Supper. No longer need people be in bondage to the old, for the new covenant has made the old obsolete. Such an idea would have burst like a bombshell on the contemporary Jewish world which held the old covenant in such reverence.

Having established his point about the new covenant, the writer nevertheless comments on the regulations for worship under the old. He describes the main features, making his focal point the inner shrine, the holy of holies. It is noticeable that he is not describing the Temple, but the tabernacle. He is going back to beginnings, which are as important for the worship as for the priesthood. What he is concerned about is the basic inadequacy of old regulations to provide a permanent basis for approach to God. Then he conceives of the holy of holies as a spiritual sanctuary into which Christ the perfect high priest entered with the perfect offering, i.e., Himself. This offering could do what all the Levitical offerings could not do, that is purify the conscience. What the author is doing is finding a spiritual meaning in the old order to explain the greater effectiveness of the Christian way.

He has not yet finished with his interpretation, for his thought now switches to the idea of a mediator, i.e., someone who acts between the two parties in an agreement. But before identifying the mediator as Christ Himself, his mind dwells on the alternative meaning of the word for covenant. It is also used for a will which a man makes to dispose of his estate, and from this the writer argues that, as a will only becomes effective when the testator dies, so the death of Christ is necessary for the new covenant to become effective. He illustrates from the fact that Moses had to sprinkle animals' blood when the old covenant was ratified (Exod. 24). Indeed everything was ritually cleansed with blood under the old order. What the old demonstrated in fact was that "without shedding of blood there is no forgiveness of sins." This is a principle basic to Christianity. The vital difference between the old order and the new lies in the effectiveness of the sacrifice. The Christian Gospel is based on an offering so effective that the writer can declare it to be "once for all." Its glory rests in its finality. There is no need for a repetition. The only return will be the second coming of Christ, which is not, however, for the purpose of redemption.

It is natural that this kind of discussion would have had a special relevance for Hebrew Christians, who would be able to see the old ritual of Judaism in a new light. If at first sight it may seem less relevant to Gentiles, it must be remembered that the Old Testament cultus within the accepted Scriptures of the Christian Church would have seemed more of an enigma. It was undoubtedly because of the light that this letter shed on the Christian interpretation of the Old Testament, which, among other reasons, led the Gentiles to admit it as part of their New Testament.

As the writer reflects on the fact that through the centuries interminable offerings had been made, he finds a vivid testimony to the utter ineffectiveness of the system. The strong contrast between this and the finality of Christ's offering so impressed the writer that he several times repeated the same idea. Animal's blood could not remove sin. It could only remind the worshipers of the existence of their sin. The sacrifice of Christ is of a wholly different kind because it involved a voluntary obedience on the part of the offered. The key is found quoted in Psalm 40:6-8, especially, "Lo, I have come to do thy will, O God." It is no wonder the writer repeated this part of the quotation to draw special attention to it. In the same way he reiterates the onceness of Christ's offering. Then comes the repetition of a theme which came at the beginning of the epistle — Christ seated at the right hand of God, after purging our sins (Heb. 1:3). This is clearly one of the major purposes of the author, to show the completeness of Christ's work. All His enemies were to be subdued. His work was to be a triumph.

With this thought the writer repeats his new covenant theme, quoting again from Jeremiah 31 and ending with the statement "I will remember their sins no more." He sees the fulfillment of this only in the finality of the offering of Christ, which is undoubtedly the most important message which the Christian Church has to proclaim.

159. *Exhortations, Warnings, and Encouragements*
(Heb. 10:19 – 11:39)

The doctrinal argument has demonstrated that Christians have a high priest who is effectually able to lead them to God. All the barriers are swept away. It is as if the curtain, which kept people out of the holy of holies, has been removed — nothing remains to prevent them from coming to God. As the writer now thinks what effect this should have on Christians, he moves into the more practical part of his letter.

He notes first of all that believers should have confidence. There is no question about it. He speaks of "full assurance of faith" and of a conscience which is fully cleansed. There can be no assurance without the removal of guilt, but since this has been achieved in Christ there is no longer any obstacle. In the world of the twentieth century no less than in the first century, this message has a constant relevance. The author's threefold exhortation is not outdated. "Let us draw near" is a constant call to fellowship with God. "Let us hold fast" is a constant reminder to stand on the foundations of our faith. "Let us consider" is a constant need if Christian living is to be based on an intelligent pattern. An important aspect of the last of these is its corporate aspect. No Christian can live to himself. Because he is a member of a fellowship, opportunities for mutual encouragement must not be allowed to slip. It seems likely that some of those being addressed were not sufficiently joining in the fellowship of the whole Church. Isolationism in Christian worship and Christian living is always inadequate, because it gives no opportunity for mutual "stirring up." The lone Christian is not entering into the full effects of the Gospel.

Rather unexpectedly a warning is suddenly introduced. It is a warning to Christians against deliberate sinning, which seems to mean a hardening attitude of sin. The writer can see no prospect for anyone with such an attitude except judgment. He does not mince his words when speaking on this theme. He introduces the idea of a fury of fire. Some modern scholars would reject such language as inappropriate to our day, but the writer of this letter did not share this feeling in his own time. He claims that such people have spurned the Son of God, profaned the covenant blood, and outraged the Spirit. In some quarters anyone in our contemporary society who used such language would be despised as a heresy hunter. The judgment theme is not popular, but was nevertheless integral to the early Christian idea of God.

Of course, the Christians addressed in this letter were not in this class. They had produced strong evidence of their Christian faith. They had suffered for their faith and been exposed to public abuse. Some had had belongings stolen and had taken it in a truly Christian manner. They had learned that property was not as important as spiritual possessions. It requires considerable maturity of faith to adopt a position like that. In our contemporary materialistic age, Christians are not infrequently guilty of placing more value on material possessions than on spiritual realities. In view of their past experiences, the readers are warned not to throw away their inheritance. Perseverance is needed on their part (and Old Testament statements are included which inculcate this), but the writer is convinced that neither he nor his readers, are among those who shrink back.

Mention of men of faith leads him to give a brief survey of some of the great names in the past to demonstrate the important part played by faith. Before doing so he gives his own definition of faith as assurance and conviction about things which have not yet come about. It is strongly dependent on the validity of God's promises. It was because the men of old took God at His word that they triumphed. From the period before the flood the writer cites Abel and Enoch as the most notable examples. Noah is a conspicuous example of a man who heeded God's warning when it seemed ridiculous to those who lacked his vision of faith.

It is natural for much to be said about Abraham. His faith made a deep impression on Paul (see Romans and Galatians). It is also appealed to James in his letter. Abraham was revered by Jews as the father figure. His faith is noteworthy on several grounds. His calling to a land far from his land of birth, his trust in God's promise about Isaac, and his willingness to offer up Isaac to God are the most notable events in the patriarch's life and are all evidences of faith. Jacob and Joseph get briefer mention, but Moses, because of his key place in Israel's history, is given more space. Once again the faith element is stressed, both in his former life in Egypt and in his leadership of the Israelites out of Egypt. At the end of his list, the writer briefly mentions the Jericho incident, some of the judges, David, Samuel, and the prophets. He would clearly have liked to extend his list in more detail. He contents himself with mentioning some of the circumstances over which faith has triumphed. It is an impressive list, involving many kinds of torture, as well as positive achievements in the realm of conquest. No wonder it is said at the end that the world was not worthy of such men of faith. The writer had sufficiently demonstrated his point. Faith does not depend on sight.

But the most astonishing statement is that which concludes this portrait gallery of faith. God has provided something even better for us Christians. The faith of the men of old was limited, because of the limit of the revelation which they possessed. Their sort of faith needed for its perfection the kind of faith which Christians have in Christ, no longer just steadfast endurance, but also personal commitment to Christ. It should follow that men of Christian faith can achieve even more than the heroic men of the past, who counted no sacrifice too great for the spiritual cause to which they were committed.

160. *Sufferings*
(Heb. 12)

In a rather mixed metaphor, the writer visualizes those men of faith in Israel's history as spectators in a sports arena in which the Christians are the participants. Athletic games were well known in those days, especially in Greece. Participants would subject themselves to considerable self-discipline with the hope of achieving victory in the games in the same way as modern Olympic contestants. All encumbrances would be jettisoned. Moreover the mind would consciously be fixed on some famous pattern. This writer sees sin as the encumbrance and Jesus Himself as the pattern. Christians could have no more demanding pattern of self-sacrifice or of endurance. The shame of the cross is, however, linked with the glory of the throne. The writer will not let his readers forget that Christ is seated on the right hand of God. It is against this background that his discussion of suffering must be approached.

The exhortation "Consider Him" (i.e., Christ) in His sufferings is characteristic of this epistle. The writer focuses throughout on Christ. Since He endured the hostility of death on a cross, these Hebrew Christians should not be disheartened, for they had not had to endure violent death among their number. Moreover they should regard as a means of discipline whatever suffering they have endured. Proverbs 3:11, 12 is quoted in support of this view. Discipline is no sign of God's anger, but of His love. The family analogy is used. No father can afford to neglect the disciplining of his children. The writer would give no support to the modern cult that children must discipline themselves. He sees distinct value in parental authority. Maybe his argument in this part of his letter would be wholly lots on those who have given up the struggle to exercise discipline over their own children. He belongs to the school of thought that maintains that true discipline brings respect rather than resentment. There is room for a reaffirmation of this approach in our modern age, in which all forms of parental authority are at a discount. Discipline, according to this writer, bears such fruit as righteousness in those who submit to it. Many who reject it do so solely on the basis of the pain which it brings.

Having established this point, the writer proceeds to give exhortations to his readers which may be summed up as follows. 1) Pull yourselves together (expressed in the picturesque words echoed from Isaiah 35:3 and Proverbs 4:26 [LXX]); 2) Live amicably with everyone if possible; 3) Avoid bitterness (another Old Testament echo from Deuteronomy 29:18 [LXX]); 4) Avoid immorality and irreligion (illustrated from Esau's example, Genesis 25:29-34). All these exhortations are practical as well as being timeless.

It is not clear why the writer at this point introduced his impressive passage on the theme of the awesomeness of God. It may be that mention of Esau and of his rejection led him to contemplate the serious consequences of underestimating the majesty of God. The Christian does not approach God as Moses did. The law was given in an atmosphere of holy isolation, with impressive evidences of the majesty of God. Even Moses was afraid. But this kind of awesomeness is different from the sense of reverence which Christians know. The writer visualizes a spiritual concourse of worshipers in what he calls the heavenly Jerusalem, surrounded by angels. A later writer visualizes a similar heavenly scene (cf. Rev. 4 and 5). Christ is here seen as the mediator, which makes sense since this letter has had so much to say about His work on man's behalf. But this mediator uses

His own blood to ratify His new covenant in a much more effective way than Moses ever could.

The thought returns to exhortation. The earthly scene is compared with the heavenly. When warnings were ignored in the history of the past disaster followed. This is seen as a spiritual pattern. "Him who warned on earth" (v. 25) is probably God speaking through Moses, while "Him who warns from heaven" is God speaking through Christ. Anyone who rejected the former would certainly reject the latter. It is a solemn thought.

Then the imagery of an earthquake is used as a means by which God speaks. It is so regarded in the Old Testament (e.g., Isa. 2:19, 21). A quotation came to the writer's mind from Haggai 2:6 in which the prophet thinks of God's activity (a shaking of heaven and earth) in fulfilling His promise to restore the temple. When the Greek translators worked on this passage they gave it a significance which could belong to a future stage in human history and not simply to the period covered by Haggai. The writer of this letter sees it as pointing to the transitory character of the world. This is important to him because it contrasts with the stability of the spiritual order of Christ. He sees the Christian way as an impregnable rock which will withstand the most violent earthquakes. It is like a kingdom which is above the movements of revolution. Nothing can shake it.

Such contemplation on the nature of the kingdom did not lead the writer into complacency, as well it might have done. On the contrary he feels that the only appropriate response is reverence and awe. Although his whole purpose has been to show the approach to God through Christ, he never loses sight of the majesty of God. His close acquaintance with the Old Testament reminds him of a statement in Deuteronomy 4:24 that God is a consuming fire, which does not mean that he sees Him only as a God of judgment, but that he sees the quality of mercy against this background. It is no credit to the Christian Gospel when the just demands of God are dismissed or forgotten.

161. *Responsibilities*
(Heb. 13)

The close of this letter is marked by a variety of exhortations and at the same time contains many echoes from themes which appear earlier. The writer, like Paul, is convinced that Christianity must have a practical outworking.

Brotherly love was necessary. The Christian faith was never intended to exist in isolation. Concern for others was an essential part of the faith. Not only is this true in a Christian's attitude toward other believers, but also in general social concern. Hospitality and care for those in prison or suffering through bodily persecution are singled out as notable examples. Thinking of hospitality, the writer echoes the Old Testament occasion when Abraham entertained angels unaware of their identity. Marriage is to be honorable and the approach to wealth free from avarice. Contentment is to be regarded as the best antidote to the love of money and such contentment comes to the Christian when he recognizes his true relationship to his Lord. If God is always present and utterly dependable, what possible reason has anyone to fear? The writer quotes two passages, one from Deuteronomy 31:6 and the other from Psalm 118:6 to support this line of reasoning.

The next advice concerns the relation of Christians to their leaders. The writer does not define these by their office, but by their teaching and preaching ministry and by their quality of life. They were evidently worthy men. It is not clear whether these leaders were still alive, but since the readers are exhorted to remember them it is highly probable that they were now dead. At this point the changelessness of Jesus Christ is mentioned, perhaps by way of contrast to the leaders who have passed away. It is an anchorage for Christian faith to know that whatever the age or circumstances, Christ is always the same. Indeed it is this conviction which makes relevant not only what this epistle says about Him but the whole message of the New Testament.

It is not easy to see why the writer turns rather abruptly from the changelessness of Christ to a warning about strange doctrine, unless it be the vivid contrast between the diversity of the latter and the constancy of the former. There will always be room for warnings of this kind, for strange ideas exert a fascination over certain kinds of mind. In this case it was bound up with food taboos and recalls similar warnings found in Paul's epistles (e.g., Rom. 14:2f; Col. 2:8, 16-23; 1 Tim. 4:3). The Christian faith does not, however, depend on ritual rules about what may or may not be eaten. It depends on grace, God's free gift, which is a very different matter.

Thinking of food leads the writer to mention the Christians' altar, which is different from the Levitical priestly system, where

the altar provided sustenance for the priests. The priests, representative of those who belonged to Judaism, have no part in the
Christian's spiritual worship. In other words no Jewish Christian
could ever continue to receive benefit by relying on the Jewish
ritual. A clean break must be made. The writer has in mind the
distinct possibility that there would be some Jews, who having
tasted Christianity, would try to retain a share in both. The same
idea is continued under a different imagery — that of the Day of
Atonement. The special sin offerings on that day had to be
consumed outside the camp according to the Levitical regulations. The priests were not allowed any part of these offerings
as they were the other sacrifices. The writer sees a spiritual
picture here. Jesus was crucified "outside" Jerusalem, but His
offering was unlike the burnt offering of the Day of Atonement,
since all believers can share in the benefits of it. This imagery
gives the writer the idea to exhort his readers to go outside the
camp (of Judaism) and identify themselves with Christ, which
brings the real point of the letter to its climax. Jewish Christians
must expect to bear something of Christ's reproach, but it is
impossible to remain in the camp of Judaism and share the full
benefits of the Gospel.

The spiritual nature of the ideas comes out in the contrast
between Jerusalem (the center of Judaism) and the coming city
which is eternal (the future hope of the Christian Church [cf.
12:22]). In the old cultus occasional peace offerings were specially associated with thanksgiving and involved offering the
fruits of the earth. The writer again interprets this in a spiritual
way, reminding his readers that they can come continually, not
with earthly fruits but with "fruits of the lips," by showing true
Christian fellowship with others in need. The superiority of
this approach over the repetition of ritual requires no further
elaboration.

The letter closes with more direct advice and request. The
leaders must be obeyed. No details are given about them. The
essential requirement is to acknowledge their leadership joyfully.
Maybe the readers had been acting independently or had been
critical of their leaders. Another pressing need is for them to
pray for the writer, a request reminiscent of many of Paul's
letters. He hopes to visit them soon.

Just before his final words, the writer slips in a magnificent
benediction, a rich prayer for his readers which has brought its

encouragement to many outside the original circle. The descriptions — God of peace, Jesus, the great shepherd, the eternal covenant — are vivid. The petition — for full equipment to do God's will — is remarkably comprehensive. It is a noble close to a great letter.

One or two personal notes are added and then the pen is laid down. Timothy has been in prison, but is now released. There is no way of knowing the circumstances. There are some Italian Christians with the writer and they send greetings. These may have been travelers in the provinces or residents in Italy sending greetings to their fellow believers in Rome. These closing notes stamp the whole as a true letter.

PROVINCES IN ASIA MINOR.

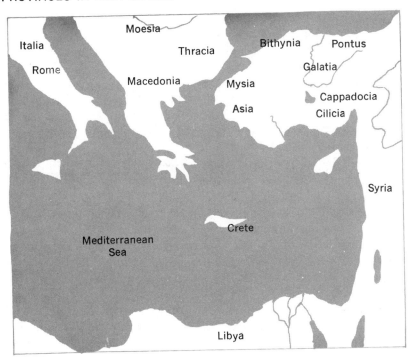

24

Peter Takes to Writing

162. *Peter Writes About Christian Salvation*
(1 Pet. 1:1 – 2:10)

Many years have elapsed since we last heard of Peter at the assembly in Jerusalem which discussed the circumcision issue. Nothing is known of his movements since then, nor is it certain where he was when he decided to write a letter to the Christians in a number of provinces, in what later came to be known as Asia Minor. Two of the provinces, Galatia and Asia, had been the scene of Paul's ministry, but the others had not. It may seem surprising that Peter, who was apostle to the circumcision, should write to areas where Paul had labored. But it need not be supposed that territorial boundaries were enforced. In any case Paul may by this time have died. Although the churches were predominantly Gentile, as the letter shows, they would no doubt have appreciated a letter from the chief apostle to the Jews. Many of the allusions which Peter makes shows that he assumes a fair knowledge of the Old Testament, especially the exodus of Israelites from Egypt. His opening greeting shows marked echoes from the ratification of the old covenant (cf. verse 2 with Exod. 24).

Peter reminds his readers that they have a marvelous and secure inheritance promised to them. Security belongs to the present as well as the future, even though the Christians were facing persecution. Peter at once gives his own recipe for facing trial, by drawing attention to its refining effect. There is no doubt that those who are called to endure any form of hardship for Christ's sake find faith strengthened as a result. The real key to Christian salvation is one's relationship to Christ. Christians are those who love Christ even though they have not seen Him. Peter is conscious that not all have the privilege of having known Jesus in the flesh as he had, but it makes no difference to the reality of their love for Him.

The early Christians soon learned to recognize the continuity between Christian salvation and what the men of old had foretold. Peter's speeches in Acts show many Old Testament allusions. Here he points out, probably as a result of considerable meditation about the matter, that the Spirit had directed the prophets to predict the sufferings of Christ and the same Spirit had made the facts known to the readers. Believers had come to have more insight into salvation even than angels. The apostle has keen insight into the tremendous privileges of Christian salvation.

Nevertheless, privilege always brings responsibilities. Peter's mind turns to the manner of life appropriate to believers. Mental discipline and moral reformation are indispensable, but the pattern which Peter suggests is surprising. Indeed it sounds impossible — nothing less than the holiness of God Himself. This kind of pattern was not entirely new, for it occurs in the Old Testament (Lev. 11:44, 45), but applies even more directly in the Christian era. Holiness is not just a pious idea, but an active principle of life affecting every action and attitude.

Peter's mind still works in Old Testament imagery as he compares Christians to the Israelites who wandered in the wilderness. Both have experienced deliverance through redemption, but with a vital difference. Whereas the Israelites were redeemed by animal sacrifices, Christians are redeemed by Christ's own blood. The idea is taken from a slave being ransomed by money, but Peter sees the Christian's freedom as based on an infinitely more precious purchase price. The thought of Christ as a spotless lamb reminds us of the first announcement by John the Baptist to the earliest disciples (John 1:29). Peter would not have forgotten that, but would have come to understand the deeper significance of it. He adds a note that this redemptive act was predestined. The passion of Jesus was not accidental. Peter had mentioned this in the first sermon he had preached (Acts 2:23). The conviction had not faltered. It was God who had presided over the salvation of His people.

Again Peter pauses to apply his doctrine. Christians are called on to love one another. He would vividly remember Jesus' command on the night before He died (John 15:17). He can do no more than repeat it, for no doubt the course of the years had confirmed it to be the only way. He recalls another of the messages of Jesus — about the new birth — and shows that this is now a reality. This means the rejection of all that belongs to the old life (malice, envy, and the like) and the building up of oneself on pure spiritual sustenance. Peter's mind dwells on milk as illustrative of good nutritive value, by which he presumably means the sustenance derived from the Word of the Lord.

The idea of Christians as a kind of new Israel again comes to his mind and here he uses a variety of metaphors to express his meaning. He thinks of Christ as the rejected stone, and of Christians as forming a community (a kind of building), illustrating the oneness of all believers in Christ. His thought is that Christ is the cornerstone into which all believers fit. From the notion of a building Peter's mind next turns to the Church as a spiritual temple, which then leads him to think of believers as priests, offering spiritual sacrifices. Three Old Testament passages are quoted in support (Isa. 28:16, Ps. 118:22 and Isa. 8:14, 15). The first two show the stone as an anchor stone, while the third portrays the stone as a stumbling block. There is no place for neutrality in Peter's thinking. Men are either believers or disobeyers. It will be remembered that he had himself heard Jesus use the same quotation from Psalm 118:22 (cf. Matt. 20:42). He has come to see the significance of it. He could also recall that the religious leaders on that occasion had determined to reject Him.

163. *About Christian Relationship*

(1 Pet. 2:11 – 3:12)

All the New Testament writers are concerned about practical Christian issues. Peter turns especially to such matters in the next part of his letter. First of all he is concerned for the Christian's relation to the world around him. His advice is succinct. "Maintain good conduct" among people in general. Of course, there is sometimes room for difference of opinion in the application of such a general principle, but Peter clearly assumed that a Christian's behavior in society should be recognizable as "good." It is important to note how alert the early Christians were to the need for impeccable behavior, so that even those who were hostile could not fail to acknowledge the evidence of God's power in the life of believers. Yet however much the non-Christian world takes stock of the example of Christians, the latter will always be regarded as aliens. As soon as they turn their backs on their passions, they are at once out of place in a society dominated by such passions.

So far Peter has considered non-Christian society in general, but now he comes to the important problem of the Christian's attitude toward the State. Again he proposes a general principle that those in authority should be respected, from the emperor downwards. Christianity was never intended to antagonize the State. Peter does not discuss the problem of what Christians should do when the State is corrupt or where it puts itself in direct opposition to Christian principles. So far this had apparently not happened. The importance of Christian behavior is again stressed, as believers are urged to live a life which befits the servants of God.

From the State, Peter turns to domestic matters. Slavery in those days was too deeply ingrained for the Christian Church to expect to dislodge it speedily. Some guidance was, therefore, necessary for slaves who had become believers. Paul had already given advice and Peter's suggestion is on the same lines. A slave would be expected to submit to his master, whether the master was good or bad. A Christian slave could not expect preferential treatment. If he was ill-treated unjustly he would have a supreme example to follow, for Christ was the most just person ever to die unjustly. But Peter realizes that such suffering was foretold in Isaiah 53, whose language he echoes. It was vital for the Christian slave to remember that Christ Himself is his example. Although this did not overturn a system which was degrading to human dignity, it did provide the slave with a way of looking at his lot, which made it more tolerable. Peter points out, moreover, that Christ was more than an example, since He bore our sins. He was doing something on behalf of all who would believe, whether they were slaves or freemen. Everyone was like a straying sheep, but the Shepherd cares for His own. No doubt Peter remembered Jesus calling Himself the Good Shepherd, and now he realized what it all meant.

From slaves, Peter turns to wives and thinks specially of those with unbelieving husbands. Recognizing the principle that action is more effective than words, Peter reminds such wives of the possibility that their Christian submissiveness may win their husbands. Such an approach may seem outdated in an age in which women's liberation movements clamor for equality, yet the principle that restrained behavior is more effective in personal relationships is ageless. Peter's approach to adornment is essentially spiritual. In those days hair styles and fashions were often ostentatious, which he regards as unbecoming for Christian women, who could exert more influence through spiritual qualities. There has never been a time when a gentle and quiet spirit has not been a choice quality. Peter thinks back to the case of Sarah, who acknowledged submission to Abraham, although in this case it was not the husband who was unbelieving. Nevertheless, he sees Sarah as typical of what Christian women should be. There is for him a kind of continuity about pious womanhood.

Husbands are treated with less detail, but are nevertheless strongly exhorted. Their main responsibility is to treat their wives with consideration. This was by no means widespread in the contemporary world. Women were not honored but despised for being the weaker sex. In only a few areas of the ancient world was a more enlightened approach encouraged, as for instance in Macedonia. The Christian Gospel revolutionized family relationships by insisting that both husbands and wives were on an equal spiritual footing. They were joint heirs. When they prayed together their prayers were equally valid. True Christian faith is the most revolutionary leveler, overturning established conventions from within.

This section on relationships now turns to the broader issue of Christian unity. Peter saw clearly the need for this. Unity does not come from organization, but from love, tenderness, and humility. Retaliation is a great wrecker of unity. Peter advises the substitution of blessing for vengeance. In spite of the difficulty in putting it into practice, there is no doubt that this advice is in full agreement with the spirit of the Master. Psalm 34 also provides support and Peter cites a fair portion of this to back up his advice. He sees it as authoritative. Evil is strongly contrasted with right. The burden of the psalm is that the evil can and should be left to God, whose face is against evil.

164. *Reflections on Suffering and Discipline*
(1 Pet. 3:13 – 5:14)

Suffering has always been a problem, but a special problem arises when people suffer for Christ's sake. Peter offers some encouragements for Christians being persecuted because they are Christians. He seems to have in mind cases of prosecution in court. The sufferer is assured that the experience will bring blessing. Reverence for Christ will oust the fear of man. Moreover in any defense before men, the deportment of Christians was to be in gentleness and respect, even when they were treated wrongfully. Most important of all was to keep a clear conscience. In this early phase of the Christian Church believers were having to forge out principles of action in difficult circumstances. Peter's advice to his own time has been a tower of strength to many succeeding generations of believers.

As he reflects on the believer's true approach to suffering, he could not fail to recall the example of Christ. He remembered that Jesus Christ had suffered wrongfully, the just for the unjust. This is another example in which moral advice leads to an illustration which contains a profound doctrinal truth. Those confronted with wrongful punishment or persecution for Christ's sake can find no greater source of encouragement than the thought that He also suffered without cause — except that He died for sins. At this point in Peter's argument he introduces a strange reference to Jesus Christ preaching to spirits in prison, which he links with the patience of God in the period before the flood. His readers may have understood more clearly than we are now able to do, but Peter does not stop to explain more fully. He follows his reference to the flood by an allusion to baptism. Again the connection is not clear, but baptism is further linked with the cleansing of the conscience. His thought comes back to Jesus Christ, whom he thinks of in His exalted state at the right hand of God.

Peter sees the need to make a distinction between suffering in the flesh and indulging in the flesh. Christ Himself endured the former, but never experienced the latter. His is the kind of pattern that these Christians are to follow. Peter knows well their former background. They were used to indulging in the flesh in common with current Gentile practice. Evils like licentiousness, drunkenness, immoral behavior were accepted conventions. The Christians could no longer accept such standards, which made them objects of abuse in the eyes of their former associates. Their experience has been repeated in every age since. Yet there is a firm conviction that those who indulge in passions will later be called to give account for their actions. This conviction is borne out by all the New Testament writers, for the idea of judgment is inseparable from the Gospel.

The thought of judgment is not only a solemn reminder to non-Christians, but also a serious challenge to Christians. Certain principles of behavior are set out such as soberness, love, hospitality, liberality, authoritative speech, and service. All become important as means by which God can be glorified in a Christian's life. What is most prominent in Peter's list is the emphasis on doing things for other people rather than for oneself.

The theme of suffering is again introduced, this time with special focus on a particular experience, which is called "a fiery trial." Some have connected this with the fear that Nero's persecution, with its public burning of Christians, would spread to the provinces. Although there is no evidence that the provinces were affected, it is easy to see why Peter warns these Christians about the possibility. His advice is threefold — be prepared; remember that a share in Christ's sufferings brings with it a share in His glory; and remember the contrast between suffering as a criminal and suffering for Christ's sake. Whatever happens Christians must glorify God. Once again judgment is stressed, but this time referring to Christians. A quotation from Proverbs 11:31 [LXX] adds a solemn note to this. If Christians are only just saved, what fate awaits the unbeliever? Peter does not dwell on this. He prefers to leave all to a faithful Creator, confident that what He does will be right. The all-important factor for Christians is to live according to God's will, even if this involves suffering.

From the subject of suffering Peter turns to discipline, both corporate and personal. He points out that the job of elders is to tend the flock. He no doubt remembers the time by Galilee when Jesus commissioned him to do the same. He is most concerned about attitudes. Those who exercise authority are greatly tempted to domineer, but such an approach is inappropriate in Christian circles. The leader is set up as an example. His reward for being so is assured, but is a spiritual and not a material reality. Peter adds a special word to young men to show humility towards their elders. His advice here is reinforced by another quotation from Proverbs 13:34.

On the believer's personal life Peter has some pointed remarks. Anxiety must be banished by remembering God's care. Peter no doubt recalled the similar thought of Jesus from the Sermon on the Mount. If the heavenly Father cares for sparrows, will He not much more care for you? Moreover Christians must watch for and resist their enemy the devil. Did Peter here remember the comment of Jesus that Satan had desired him, but that Jesus had prayed for him? His concluding statement is another assurance for the suffering Christian that he will share the eternal glory of Christ.

Evidently throughout this letter Silvanus has been doing the writing — hence Peter's mention of him at the end. Mark is also with the apostle and sends greetings. They are both with the church in "Babylon," most probably a cryptic name for Rome.

165. *True Knowledge*

(2 Peter 1)

Peter is writing another letter presumably to the same people to whom he wrote the first (cf. 2 Pet. 3:1). Although many scholars do not accept this letter as genuine, there are still those who can see no conclusive reason for rejecting it. There is nothing in it which Peter himself could not have written. He may have used a different scribe from the one used for the other letter. He does not mention Silvanus at the end.

Every Christian has to live in a corrupt world. Yet each one has access to a divine power which is absolutely adequate to sustain him in a life of godliness. True knowledge, in Peter's view, can be summed up as knowledge of God. He has no place for speculative ideas. He sees the promises of God as of great value in enabling Christians to escape the corruption of their environment. They are people who share God's nature and therefore God's triumph over evil. Such an assurance cannot come through man's efforts, but Peter goes on nevertheless to speak of the Christian's responsibility.

Virtues do not sprout without effort. In a sense their growth is progressive. The development of one makes easier the culture of another. Peter's sequence is worth pondering. He starts with faith and ends with love. All the intervening virtues are personal qualities. A person who possessed them all would be well set up for a fruitful life. Yet Peter does not present any of them as optional. Anyone lacking them is described as blind and short-sighted. This is all the more reason for pressing on zealously.

The same assurance of eternal reward is given here as in the first letter.

Peter now becomes reminiscent. He has reminded his readers of truths which are not new to them. He is almost apologetic at having mentioned them. Yet he is fully convinced that it is necessary. So long as he lives he considers it to be appropriate to remind them. He fears they have short memories. Such fears are not unreasonable, for ever since then the stirring up of the minds of believers has been an essential part of the Christian ministry.

In some way or other, Peter knows that his time is short. He does not say how he knows, but such premonition does at times seize men's minds as the end approaches. He recollects what Jesus had told him by Galilee, when he predicted that others would gird him. He may often have wondered what it meant. Tradition has it that he was crucified upside down, but he could have had no inkling of this possibility when he wrote this letter. When he promises his readers that they will be able to recall what he has told them after his death, he probably means through the contents of the present letter. He sees it, therefore, as a kind of final testimony to them.

What suddenly made him think of the transfiguration and his own part in this incident is not clear, but an interesting suggestion is that it arises from an association of ideas, for he has just used the same word for his own departure (exodus) as Luke says was the topic of conversation between the transfigured Jesus and Moses and Elijah (Luke 9:31). Peter remembers vividly the majesty of that scene. He was convinced that it was no clever myth. He remembers the heavenly voice with its witness to the beloved Son. He tells his readers "we were with Him." It was a hallowed occasion. When he now recalls it, he describes the mount itself as holy. Its sacred association with that never-to-be-forgotten event had made it so. The hearing of that authoritative voice had made him more confident of the voice of the prophecy. Once having seen the majestic nature of Jesus, the testimony to the coming Messiah by Hebrew prophets took on new meaning.

This gives Peter a cue for pressing home an important point. The prophetic Word is like a brilliant light shining in a drab dark place and leading to Christ. He wants his readers to ponder this. How foolish to continue living in night when dawn has arrived! Peter no doubt recalled hearing Jesus claim to be the Light of the world and remembered Him urging His disciples to walk in that light.

The prophetic Word needs explanation. Interpretation has proceeded on many different principles, but Peter allows only one — the interpretation given by the Holy Spirit, who moved men to write. Christians were not to regard the Scriptures as human productions, but Spirit-prompted. He gives a hint here of a spiritual understanding of the origin of Scripture. His unsophisticated mind saw no need to expand further the method of the inspiration. He devoted no space to the problem of a divine source which used human agents. He is content to accept that whatever has been produced through the Spirit's agency must command the believer's most careful attention. Nothing inbreathed by God can be ignored. It carries with it an inescapable authority. This Word is as relevant to succeeding generations of Christians as it was to those to whom Peter was writing.

166. *False Knowledge*

(2 Peter 2 and Jude)

The linking of the next section in this letter with the epistle of Jude is because they both deal with similar themes and use many similar phrases. The exact relation between the two is not certain. Some think that Peter knew and used Jude's letter; others that Jude used Peter's letter; and still others that both used a common source. The main difference between them is that Jude is rather more harsh on the false teachers than Peter, while Peter's descriptions are more extensive than Jude's.

Both Peter and Jude stress the secretive and therefore insidious character of the false teachers and both mention their ungodliness and denial of the Master. In very similar ways they illustrate from past history God's judgment on the ungodly. Both mention God's judgment on the fallen angels, while Jude precedes his statement with a comment about the destruction of the unbelieving Israelites who were delivered from Egypt. Both then focus on the fate of Sodom and Gomorrah, while Peter alone mentions Lot, his revulsion at the unrighteousness of the people around, and God's keeping power in such adverse circumstances. Both writers note that God's judgment on these wicked cities was intended as an example.

Against this background of the certainty of judgment, both

Peter and Jude proceed to describe the nature of the men who were deviating from the truth. The first characteristic is what both describe as "reviling the glorious ones," which seems to denote an utter disregard for all authority, whether heavenly or earthly. Peter mentions angels, who refrain from pronouncing the judgment, whereas Jude refers to a specific instance of this in the archangel Michael's contending with the devil over Moses' body. Since this is not recorded in the Old Testament, Jude must have been thinking of a traditional story. The story may in fact have been taken from a Jewish work known as *The Assumption of Moses*. The false teachers are shown to do what angels dare not do, such was their irrational behavior. Both Peter and Jude in fact describe them as animals, a strong indication of their surrender of themselves to their passions. The condemnation contained in these letters has relevance wherever men exalt immorality and greed as a way of life.

Peter does not mince his words. He calls these people "blots and blemishes" and gives details of their immorality and greed. Jude omits these details, but agrees with Peter that these people are followers of Balaam. Since we meet with Balaam again in the Book of Revelation in connection with false teaching, this Old Testament character was clearly regarded as symbolic of wrongdoing. Again Peter goes into greater detail by mentioning the dumb ass which rebuked him, while Jude includes a passing allusion to Cain and to Korah, both men who disobeyed God.

Both writers use some vivid imagery as they describe the false teachers. Jude speaks of blots at love feasts because of immodest carousals. Peter thinks of the uselessness of waterless wells, and both conjure up pictures of clouds pushed by winds, which never disperse their refreshing rain. Jude includes other imagery to describe these men — fruitless trees which are due for uprooting at the end of the season, or wild waves which create much foam, which is all display, or moving stars which have no stability and vanish into the darkness. Here his descriptions are more vivid; all his images speak of futility. He then includes a statement about God's judgment on the ungodly which he appears to have taken from the Book of Enoch, a Jewish work which was probably produced in the second century before Christ. He recognizes the truth of what this Jewish author had attributed to Enoch, and then gives his own very unflattering description of the ungodly people he is writing about (see Jude 16).

Peter points out one characteristic which Jude does not stress. The false teachers are not only open in speaking about their ungodly behavior, but open in their enticements of others. What they promise turns out to be a delusion. Peter is specially concerned about those who have already known something of the power of Jesus Christ to save, who are inclined to be deceived by these loud-mouthed teachers. He issues a serious warning that it would have been better for such never to have known the Christian way. Is he perhaps thinking of Jesus' parable of the unclean spirit, in which the last state was worse than the first? He quotes a proverb about animals who wallow, and again implies that those who follow these ungodly men are no better than beasts who act unintelligently.

Jude's conclusion to his letter is worth noting. He quotes a statement of the apostles to the effect that scoffers will arise at the end of the age. If Jude has adapted 2 Peter, this is intelligible as a reference to Peter. In any case the prediction is fully in line with predictions made by Jesus Himself about the end of time (cf. Matt. 24). Jude notes that such men are without the Spirit, an important method of distinguishing them. It is only Christians who can pray in the Spirit, and these have a sure defense against false teaching.

The sequence of exhortations which Jude gives is comprehensive — build yourselves up, pray, keep in God's love, wait for Christ's mercy, convince doubters, save others, show mercy on others, hate what defiles. Jude is a master of succinct expression. In a few words he sets a pattern which it takes a lifetime to follow.

His brief letter ends with a magnificent doxology, which stresses the keeping power of God, His saving activity, and His majesty. There could be no more striking contrast to the miserable concepts of the false teachers.

167. *Challenge*

(2 Peter 3)

In drawing his second letter to an end, Peter issues a reminder. Memory constantly needs a jog. Some effort is needed to recall even what the prophets have said and what Jesus Himself had commanded. This is the positive side of the Christian's combat with false teaching. The best antidote to error is always a positive approach to truth. There has never been a period in Christian history when conscious effort to recall the apostolic teaching has not paid dividends.

Peter proceeds to give an explanation of what he means by the prediction that scoffers would come. These are people following their own passions as described in the previous section. But one characteristic not so far mentioned is a misrepresentation of the second coming of Christ. The scoffers were denying the coming on the assumption that nothing had happened. In the way that scoffers do, they were exaggerating, suggesting that the world was carrying on as it had been since the creation. But they had forgotten that creation itself was God's work. What was to happen to that creation was in fact in God's hands.

Peter had earlier in the letter mentioned the flood and he makes another allusion to it here. It had clearly impressed him as an awesome example of God's judgment. He cannot free himself from this sense of judgment on ungodliness and foresees another time in the future when God will act in catastrophic judgment, involving the destruction of the existing creation by fire. The language is probably borrowed from apocalyptic imagery, but the reality of God's condemnation shines through unmistakably Peter's answer to the problem of the delay in the second coming is that God is merciful and forbearing. Delay is therefore an act of mercy. But delay is also a relative term. What seems an age to men might not be to God. His method of calculation is different. A thousand years is no more than a day. The scoffers were, therefore, badly miscalculating in calling a few years a "delay."

Peter uses the same imagery as that used by Jesus to explain the fact that no one knows the timing of the coming, any more than a man can predict the precise hour when a burglar will strike. If the timing is unknown, Peter is in no doubt about the certainty of the final destruction of the earth. He sees the material world as essentially transient.

These profound thoughts about judgment lead him to think of the effect this should have on Christian people. His comments show clearly that the practical effect of Christian teaching about coming events is of more point than any speculation about the nature and timing of the events themselves. His rhetorical question "What sort of persons ought you to be?" is as relevant now as it was then, in spite of the fact that the "delay" now extends over more than nineteen centuries. While they wait, Christians are to develop holiness and godliness. The possibility of the imminent coming of Christ and the thought of judgment on ungodliness cannot fail to exercise a salutary effect on Christian living. The Christian approach to the future is profoundly optimistic, for what is destroyed will be renewed and the new will be governed by righteousness. Men have dreamed of a Utopia on this present earth but Peter's point is that the present environment needs to be replaced by one in which righteousness is the norm.

If the future vista is dominated by righteousness, there is no reason why the present should not be for Christians. What is needed is not the passive acceptance of a different standing, but a zeal for purity. Peter is here acting in character. He advocates wholeheartedness in Christian behavior.

Conscious of the fact that the false teachers are apt to twist the Scriptures, he appeals to Paul's letters, although admitting his difficulty in understanding some parts of them. Christians in all ages have echoed the same sentiments. But the theme of God's forbearance is clear for all to see.

Anyone who possesses such guides to truth as Paul's letters and other Scriptures should be able to resist the guiles of these false teachers. It is a question of being firmly based. Peter's closing exhortation is for spiritual growth in grace and knowledge. Again his approach is positive. He does more than decry error, for he encourages Christians to develop. His approach should serve as a pattern for those confronting modern errors.

25

Brief Letters from John

168. *John Writes About Fellowship*

(1 John 1 and 2)

There is little information about what happened to the Apostle John after the last mention of him in Acts. There is a strong tradition that he went to Ephesus and exercised a wide ministry among the churches of Asia. If this tradition is correct it is reasonable to suppose that this happened after Paul's ministry in that area. It was probably at Ephesus that John wrote his gospel, followed by the three letters which appear under his name. It is from these brief letters that some indications may be obtained of his characteristics. His favorite term for describing his readers is "little children," which suggests that he himself is now a man of advanced years. It introduces a flavor of intimacy, which permeates the whole letter. The apostle does not produce a treatise. He keeps repeating himself, but the warm reality of his themes carries his readers along with him.

The general theme of the letter may be described as fellowship, not only with God and with Jesus Christ, but also with fellow Christians. This he makes clear in his opening remarks, which incidentally lack all marks of a normal letter opening. He neither introduces himself nor his readers, but plunges straight into his credentials for writing — nothing less than the claim to be an eyewitness of the "life," which can be no other than the life of Christ. Clearly a letter of exhortation from one who had been in personal touch with Jesus would carry considerable weight. John had heard Jesus talk about eternal life and about fellowship and he wants to share his experience with his readers.

One feature of the teaching of Jesus which John cannot forget

378

is that fellowship with God demands purity. He remembered how Jesus spoke of Himself as Light and pictures the world as being in darkness. The idea of any darkness existing in God is unthinkable. But this raises an acute problem over man's fellowship with Him, for man also must dwell in the light. The necessity for some remedy for lapses into darkness is all too evident, but John sees the answer in the cleansing blood of Christ. All that is needed is confession of sin. It is not improbable that he knows of some among his readers who were perfectionists, claiming to have reached that state when they believed themselves to be beyond sin. But John recognized the serious consequences of such a view — it amounts to self-deception. He is not, however, taking a fatalistic view. He realizes that the believer should aim to be without sin, but he is realist enough to recognize that the provision of an Advocate to plead for us, who has made an effective atonement for sins, is essential. The thought of Christ as an Advocate is reminiscent of what John records in his gospel of the Holy Spirit as an Advocate. He sees the true need of man for someone other than himself to act on his behalf.

Fellowship has its practical aspects and John pays some attention to these. One is obedience to God's commands. The Christian must "do" as well as 'know." John does not hesitate to call a man a liar whose actions do not match his profession. A new road lies before the believers in which God's ways become the norm. Anyone who loves God will want to fulfill His Word. He will want to walk as God walks — a vivid metaphor which describes the high example which a Christian has.

When writing about commandments, John is not only thinking of the old law, but of the entirely revolutionary command of Jesus, which he calls "new." He remembers hearing Jesus speak a command to love (cf. John 15:12). It was new in the sense of the quality of love demanded. It contrasted with hate, as light contrasted with darkness. Those who have come into the broad daylight have quite different standards from those who grope in the darkness. No doubt John is thinking of similar words of Jesus, which he records in his gospel (John 8:12).

He sees fellowship as applicable to and making demands on all age groups. He links children, young men, and fathers in a sequence of exhortations, the main gist of which is the power to overcome the evil one. One secret is to "know." Those who know the Father need have no fear of what the enemy can do. Another secret is the abiding of God's Word in the mind. Young men, who feel naturally strong, are reminded, that the abiding Word is the key to their victory. A general piece of advice is to reject wordliness. John uses the word "world" of society dominated by sin and passion. He is not, therefore, suggesting that Christians must withdraw from the world, but that the world must never dominate their affections. It is the "will of God" which must do that.

As John looks ahead at the environment in which Christians must live, he is aware of approaching threats. He speaks of the coming antichrist, who is the embodiment of all that is opposed to Christ. Not surprisingly many had already arisen who possessed this characteristic, and John saw this as evidence that the last hour had come. He wants his readers to be prepared. Some of these "antichrists" had actually been in the Christian community, but had withdrawn. He defines the antichrist as one who denies the Father and the Son. True believers are like anointed men, set apart; they are not uninformed; they have the promise of eternal life. There is no need for such Christians to seek knowledge from any source other than God, or the "anointing," as John expresses it. He repeats the one requirement as "abiding" in Him (i.e., in Christ).

169. *The Family of God*

(1 John 3:1 – 4:6)

The idea of Christians as constituting God's family is found in many other parts of the New Testament, but John makes much of it. His favorite name for God is Father and he calls Christians "children of God." There is no analogy more intelligible to man. When anyone belongs to a family he is affected by all that happens to the other members. If the Father is snubbed by the world, it is not surprising that the world snubs the "children." Certain kinds of social ostracism have often affected Christians, but this is insignificant compared with the privilege of being God's children. Such privilege carries with it the prospect of becoming like Christ at His appearing. This is a spiritual hope which has a direct effect on the life. It incalcates purity. In our present age, in which materialistic values are set more highly than moral purity, this may appear poor consolation, but John has no doubt which is the more permanent and profound.

The apostle returns to the subject of sin and this time gives its definition as lawlessness. But Christians have an answer to this, because Christ came for the purpose of removing sin. Those who sin, in the sense of habitually sinning, are wholly out of touch with Him. In fact they are the devil's men. But John sees the achievement of Christ as victory over the devil. This broadens the idea of His work as not only removing the guilt of sin, but also the power of sin. God's children are recognizable by their desire to do right, which the devil's children have no wish to do.

Previously John has stressed the command to love one another and he now proceeds to illustrate what happens when hate displaces love. The case of Cain furnishes an admirable example. Hate led to murder and both sprang from an evil heart. John does not labor the point, for the moral is obvious. This early instance of lack of all love in Cain for Abel is symbolic of the tragic result whenever men turn to hating each other. Indeed John sees hate and murder as identified. Where love exists, as it should exist among brothers in Christ, it is indisputable evidence that they no longer belong to the kingdom of death, which knows nothing of the true meaning of love. Suddenly the apostle senses that he has been discussing love too much in the abstract, and gives some specific examples. The supreme example is the self-giving love of Christ. Believers could have no nobler pattern. But another example shows its outworking in social concern — like a wealthy man who ought to show compassion for a fellow believer in need. Love must be translated into deeds. Jesus had said the same thing.

Repeatedly in his letter John brings out the importance of knowing. The path to assurance lies through knowledge and experience. Even when we find ourselves overwhelmed by self-condemnation, we can find reassurance in the fact that God knows better than we do. Moreover, John contends that we can maintain a confident attitude by doing what pleases God. When we do this, there will be no room for self-condemnation. There will be, on the contrary, much room for effective prayer, for whatever we ask when our minds are set on pleasing God will be answered. There would be fewer problems over unanswered prayer if Christians first examined whether their requests were within the context of God's will. Thinking of the necessity for keeping His commandments, John points out that the special "commandment" consists of "believe" and "love." This is a development from what he had already said about love being a commandment. This is paradoxical, for neither faith nor love can be commanded as a duty. The characteristic of this kind of commandment is spontaneity, mixed with authority. We respond to the leadings of the Spirit and in doing so recognize the authoritative nature of God's Word. We come to see that "believing" and "loving" are not the result of our good intentions, but our response to His commands. Once again the state of abiding in Christ summarizes the Christian experience.

Having mentioned the leading of the Spirit, John recognizes the danger that some may be misled. He advises his readers to "test the spirits." There is one unfailing guideline — the Spirit of God always prompts confession in the coming of Jesus Christ into human life as a real man. John probably has in mind some who were claiming to teach by the Spirit of God that the incarnation was not real, but only appeared to be. It is known that a group referred to as Docetists advanced such a view, and it is not impossible that John has in mind the forerunners of this movement. Nevertheless he states principles rather than attacks specific heresies. He sums up all such movements as "the spirit of antichrist." He classifies all false concepts of Christ as opposed to Him, and then proceeds to mention again the contrast between the people of God and the world. Another contrast is between truth and error. For John there is no place for compromise. Everything is either black or white.

170.   *Love and Faith*

(1 John 4:7 – 5:21)

The spiral character of John's thought is seen by the constant repetition of the theme of love. In returning to it here he makes some profound statements about it. He finds its basis in the nature of God, for he maintains that God is love. Such a view of God was unparalleled. There are many glimpses of the love of God in the Old Testament, but nothing which approaches this simple identification of God with love. The most outstanding evidence of that love is God's sending of His Son. John is echoing here a statement included in his gospel (see John 3:16). He elaborates on it. The initiative was with God, who not only sent His Son but gave Him a special mission — the propitiation of sin, a thought which John has mentioned earlier (1 John 2:2). Such love as this is profound. It comes as a shock to realize that it serves as a pattern for Christians. If God's love for us is the standard for our love for each other, it is no wonder that the exhortation to love one another needs constant repetition. No one can afford to be complacent, because no one has yet reached the ideal. Yet John does not hesitate to suggest that God's love can be perfected in us. He has the highest possible standard for Christian behavior.

This process is forwarded by the gift of the Spirit and by the testimony that God sent His Son to be our Saviour. These are the basic facts which enable men to abide in God — John's way of describing the absolute dependence of the Christian on God. Love comes as a result. This love promotes confidence even when contemplating the day of judgment. It cannot co-exist with fear, for fear results from guilt and certainty of punishment. Fear was a powerful factor in first-century life. To discover an effective way of banishing it was like balm to a wound. The ancient world knew only gods which increased the fear, but the Gospel proclaimed a God of love which made fear of Him incongruous. Once again John is concerned to translate his high notions of Christian love for God into practical terms — if a man loves God he cannot hate his brother. It is an infallible test. When hate begins to well up in any Christian, he should at once meditate on Christian love and the hate will dry up, for love and hate are implacable enemies.

John now turns more particularly to the theme of faith, although he still echoes his theme of love. In speaking of a victorious faith, he first reminds his readers of its basis — faith in Jesus as the Christ, or Messiah, which includes not merely the name, but the mission of Jesus. No one can call himself a child of God except on this basis. But a child should love and obey his parents, and this serves as a pattern for us in our approach to God. John takes it for granted that victory over the world is assured to those who have faith and love. However powerful the adverse forces in the world are, they are not comparable to the power of the Christian life. Such conviction is impregnable.

Because faith must have an object which is unchallengeable, witness is important. Can it stand up to investigation? John mentions a threefold witness — the Spirit, water, and blood. He may be thinking of the Mosaic requirement that testimony is valid only if supported by two or three witnesses. He undoubt-edly remembered that Jesus had spoken of the Spirit of truth, for he records such statements in his gospel. But what do the water and blood signify? Since these are directly related to the coming of Jesus Christ, they must relate to His baptism and death, to the beginning and ending of His public life. In both occasions, John sees the testimony of God; in the former to God's seal on the mission of Jesus and in the latter to God's seal on His sacrificial work. Because of this threefold witness to what God has pro-vided, the gift of eternal life offered to men is assured. This life is in the Son — that means it cannot be obtained in any way other than faith in the Son.

It is not until he is nearing the end of his letter that John states his purpose. This is also a feature of his gospel. There is in fact some similarity between the two statements of purpose (cf. 1 John 5:13 and John 20:30, 31). The difference is that the gospel was written that men may come to believe, whereas this letter was written that those who have believed may "know" that they have eternal life. It is John's intention to lead his read-ers into a firm and intelligent conviction. Another result of our knowing is the conviction that God answers prayer. John includes in his gospel some sayings of Jesus about prayer and he now writes in a way which suggests that he has proved it for himself. He suggests that prayer should be directed on behalf of those not hardened in sin (this hardened state he calls "mortal" sin). He is convinced that Christians do not make a habit of sinning, because God keeps them. It is impossible in these circumstances for the enemy to overcome them. Perhaps John remembers how Jesus told Peter that he had prayed for him when Satan desired him.

There are two other facets of the Christian's knowledge with which John closes his letter. We know we belong to God and we know the purpose of the coming of Jesus Christ. Both these assertions have already been made, but John wants to emphasize them again and again. Then, out of the blue, he warns his readers against idols. He has just reflected on the fact that the whole world is in the power of the evil one and sees it concentrated in the pagan worship around him. Those who have taken to heart his profound sayings about the Christian view of God would have no temptation to return to their former idolatry, but the word of warning must be given.

171. *Two Personal Notes*

(2 and 3 John)

In both these brief letters the writer introduces himself as "the elder," but both of them have been attributed to John from early times. It seems reasonable to suppose, therefore, that they were written by John and that he preferred the title "elder" when writing them. They differ from all other New Testament letters except Philemon and the Pastorals in being addressed to individuals.

The letter known as 2 John is addressed to "the elect lady and her children." It seems most natural to suppose that she was a Christian lady well known to John. This is better than to suppose that the lady was a church and her children were church members, as some have suggested. The key word in this letter is "truth," which occurs three times in the greeting as well as later in the letter. The lady concerned is well loved by Christians generally because of her loyalty to the truth.

On some occasion John has met the lady's children and is delighted to find that they too were followers of the truth (clearly a name for the true Gospel). He mentions this and then refers to the "new" commandment in precisely the same terms as he had done in 1 John. He cannot refrain from urging Christians to love one another, although he concedes that this commandment has ceased to be "new" for the lady or for himself.

What appears to be the real point of the letter is a warning about deceivers and these are clearly the same people who are alluded to in 1 John as those who are denying the true human nature of Jesus. He tells the lady what he told the readers of the other letter that such people are antichrists. He is obviously concerned lest the lady should be taken unawares and reminds her of the position of anyone who does not abide in the doctrine of Christ. He gives her practical advice. She is advised to decline hospitality to anyone who does not adhere to this true doctrine. Moreover she is not even to greet such a person, so as not to be identified with him.

An intimate note closes the letter. John confesses that his preference is not for pen and ink, but for a personal visit which he hopes to arrange soon. He passes on greetings from the lady's sister's children, whom he has presumably recently met.

The other brief letter is addressed to a Christian named Gaius, who was apparently a leading member of a church known to the apostle. John has received encouraging reports of Gaius' stand for the truth, which has greatly rejoiced his heart. He regards Gaius as one of his "children," as he did the readers of his first letter. He advises him to offer hospitality to other Christians, even to strangers. The value of hospitality in the spreading of the Gospel cannot be exaggerated. Unless Christians received into their homes those who were traveling around in the interests of the Gospel, they would be obliged to use hostels, which were anything but conducive for Christian people. While the same circumstances do not now exist, it is still true that Christian hospitality can do much to further the cause of Christ. True Christian hosts became identified as fellow workers with those they were entertaining for Christ's sake.

John's main reason for writing is the attitude of Diotrephes, who seems to have assumed a position of authority and to have used it in an overbearing manner. Although John has written to him, his letter has been ignored. He may have seized office in the church to which Gaius belonged or to a neighboring church. In either case John feels that Gaius should know that Diotrephes is not only antagonistic to him personally, but has declined to receive other Christians whom John has sent. He had even gone further in excluding from the church any who wanted to receive them. This is separation of the wrong kind. Diotrephes may have been sincere, but was certainly misguided. He was also intensely arrogant.

John wastes no more words on him. He gives a further exhortation to Gaius to imitate good and then mentions Demetrius as being well spoken of. No other information exists about Demetrius, but it is probable that he was among the itinerant preachers who had been sent out by John.

The same comment about preferring personal conversation to pen and ink, which John had made to the lady, he now makes to Gaius. Greetings are sent from "the friends," evidently the circle of Christians associated with the writer. The same general description is also used for those with Gaius. Perhaps John remembered at this point what Jesus said in the Upper Room — "I have called you friends" (John 15:15).

26

A Glimpse Into the Future

172. John Writes to Some Asian Churches
(Rev. 1:1 – 2:11)

The Book of Revelation is in a class of its own within the New Testament. It consists of two main sections — letters to seven churches and a series of visions. The two parts belong together, which means that the visions were as much a part of John's message to the churches as the letters. This must be borne in mind in our approach to the visions. These have seemed so obscure to many that they have ignored them, and so intriguing to others that they have taken them too literally. It is best to suppose that these visions were intended to be understood in their original historical context, even if they have further relevance for the future.

In his opening remarks John makes clear that what he is about to write is a divine revelation. He does not intend his book to be taken as his own reverie. Indeed he at once sets the tone with some authoritative and impressive statements about Jesus Christ and about Christians' relation to God through Him. He places the whole message in the context of the churches of Asia. He first gives a general greeting from God, described by the cryptic phrase "who is and who was and who is to come"; from the Holy Spirit, under the figure of the seven spirits (seven being a symbol of perfection); and from Jesus Christ in His threefold office as Witness, Victor over death, and Ruler of all.

At once the basis of man's approach to God is stressed — freed from sins by Christ's blood and made priests to God. A general statement about the return of Christ is made to provide the scene for the general visions to follow.

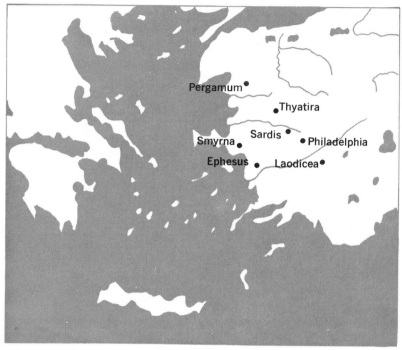

SEVEN CHURCHES OF REVELATION.

John describes the occasion for the visions as a day when he was exiled on the island of Patmos, off the coast in the region of Ephesus. He notes the day — the Lord's Day — as if he attached special importance to this. He is convinced that on that day he was prompted by the Spirit in a specific way. The book was to be directed to a group of named churches, presumably those with which he had been associated. It is clear from the letters that he knows much about each of the churches.

He then sees a vision of lampstands which concentrates on the person in the midst (said to be like the son of man). This is clearly a pictorial way of describing Jesus Christ in the midst of His people. It is not a heavenly scene, but a present reality. The description of Jesus Christ, however, is impressive for its dignity, its awesomeness, and its brilliance. One wonders what John might have made of an attempt to describe the Transfiguration. There is a clear warning in the vision, in the flashing eyes, the thunderous voice, and the sword projecting from the mouth. It presents an impression of a Christ who is a judge among His people. It is no wonder that John fell awestruck on his face in homage.

Although here and there in this book are the softer sides of revelation, in salvation and mercy, its prevailing picture of Jesus Christ is as the righteous Victor. John's homage is typical of what he expects of all his readers in face of the splendor of visions. But he hears the reassuring words of Jesus and is reminded of the victory which He has gained over man's last enemy, death, and its accomplice, Hades. Only the Victor Himself can allay the fears of His people as they face death. Many who first read this book were fearful about the future, but John sees it as a word of encouragement and of challenge.

The seven churches to which John writes his messages are placed in an intentional order, following a circular route begining from Ephesus to the most northerly at Pergamum and then proceeding to the most southerly at Laodicea.

The first two letters will be included in this section and the rest in the next. Of all of these churches only the first and the last is mentioned elsewhere in the New Testament, the first being one of the scenes of Paul's labors and the last being indirectly referred to in Paul's letter to Colossae. There is a strong tradition that the Apostle John spent his last days in Ephesus. It is reasonable, therefore, to suppose that he used Ephesus as a base to extend his influence toward the other Asiatic churches.

The message to the church at Ephesus has on the whole an encouraging theme. The Ephesian Christians have been consistent in their profession and service and are specially commended for resisting false teachers. They possessed sufficient spiritual discernment to differentiate between true and false apostles. They had moreover persevered in their faith in face of opposition. All this speaks highly for them. Yet Jesus Christ, through His servant John, reveals one basic weakness. They have cooled off in their love and are strongly exhorted to repent and get back to their former position. This criticism is perennially relevant, for few churches can sustain the first enthusiasm of love. Nevertheless, this is what Jesus Christ desires for His people. It seems that the Ephesians were more concerned with truth than with love, for they had rejected, even hated, the works of a group of false teachers known as Nicolaitans. It is sadly possible to be strong in hate and yet weak in love; to excel in the negative and yet fail in the positive.

The church at Smyrna receives a message of encouragement to face future sufferings which are predicted as imminent. The

Christians were apparently subjected to special attack from Jewish sources. John sees the real power behind their antagonism as the work of the devil. He does not hesitate to call the Jewish synagogue a synagogue of Satan. It is strong condemnation, but he is deeply aware of the spiritual conflict involved, as is clear from the entire book. These Smyrna Christians are facing a severe testing. Some may even face death, and are exhorted to be faithful.

We note that in both letters the Spirit concludes with a special message to the conquerors. John knows that he writes under the direction and inspiration of the Spirit.

173. Messages of Warning and Encouragement
(Rev. 2:12 – 3:22)

Whereas at Smyrna John locates Satan's synagogue, at Pergamum he locates Satan's throne. Another church was, therefore, set in an environment of spiritual antagonism. John notes a commendation to this church for remaining true to Christ in face of an opposition which did not stop at killing one of their number, Antipas. Yet the Christians at Pergamum were not as discerning as those at Smyrna, for some of them had been misled by false teaching, which is called after Balaam's name, and had fallen for the teaching of the Nicolaitans. There is no knowing what these false teachings were, but they were undoubtedly deviations from the truth. A serious warning is delivered to the people at Pergamum to repent. Otherwise judgment is certain. A special encouragement is given to those who overcome. They will receive a white stone with a new name on it which only the recipient will know. This may be an allusion to the Urim and Thummin, which Jewish high priests wore and which bore a name they were not allowed to disclose. This would tie up with the hidden manna which was stored in the ark of the covenant, which was placed in the holy of holies where the high priest alone was allowed to enter once a year. Perhaps the false teachers were offering an alternative method of approaching God. In that case, the Christians are being reminded that each one of them has as much right as the Jewish high priest to come to God.

More toleration of false teaching was found at Thyatira, reminding us of the prevalence of devious philosophies and sects throughout Asia. John calls it here the deep things of Satan. This sect was associated with the name of Jezebel, who was presumably not so much a person as a movement, which showed the characteristics of Ahab's apostate wife. The teaching which was deluding some at Thyatira was mainly a devotion to immorality and to the eating of food implicated in idolatry (a clear echo of the trouble at Pergamum). The major problem is clearly the former. In view of the widespread immorality in the contemporary pagan world it is not surprising that some insidious inroads were made into the Christian Church. When this is linked with false teaching, as in this case, the warning is severe. Nevertheless not all at Thyatira had been affected. Indeed the Church as a whole is commended for its faith, love, and endurance. Unlike Ephesus its latter works were better than the first. There had been definite progress. The main need is for persistence, as the exhortation "hold on" shows. In this church the overcomers are promised power in phrases strongly reminiscent of the Old Testament Psalms, but which point to the believers' share in the ultimate victory of Christ, the Morning Star (cf. Rev. 22:16).

The church at Sardis comes in for strong rebuke. It was situated in a city which had seen more glorious days and the same comment could be made of its own history. But its real state was now one of deadness. Most of the Sardis Christians were soiled by their immoral environment, and these are called on to repent. Their moral deficiencies have had a soporific effect on them. They need to shake themselves awake. Those who have remained unsoiled are described as "few" and "worthy." These are promised white garments, symbols of purity. Moreover they are further assured that their names will never be blotted out — which offers these faithful Christians an unshakable confidence.

The Christians at Philadelphia have been loyal to the truth, but lack power in their Christian witness. Their weakness has prevented them from seizing the opportunities confronting them. John records the promise of Jesus to make their opponents recognize His love to His people and His promise to keep His people in the hour of trial. The whole world is going to be implicated. It is tremendous encouragement to know that Jesus Christ is Himself the Guardian of His people. Another hope is His coming, a hope which is echoed in many parts of the New Testament. For this church the reward for overcoming is to be a pillar in the spiritual temple. The figure of a pillar speaks of solidarity and strength. Moreover an inscription on the pillar testifies to the name of God. This is witnessed to by the name of the new Jerusalem, which would need none of the props of the old city, and by the new name of Jesus Christ (perhaps His name as Lord).

The concluding letter is not at all commendatory. The trouble with the Laodiceans was sheer mediocrity. They were steering a comfortable middle course which was achieving nothing. The city was famous for its wealth, its merchandise, and its medical school. The Christians belonged to an affluent society, whose attitude was dominated by materialism. They were completely misguided about their true condition. The scale of values they prized was wholly reversed by Jesus Christ. They are advised to seek true riches and true raiment and to anoint the eyes with eyesalve (Laodicea was well known for its eye ointment). The reaction of the risen Lord in rejecting the materialistic lukewarmness of these Christians may at first seem surprising, but the letter shows them to be virtually keeping Jesus Christ outside the door of their experience. They were missing the deep, rich fellowship with Christ which a whole-hearted faith enjoys. A wonderful promise is given to the conquerors in this church — to sit with Christ on His throne, which is another way of saying "to reign with Him." In no more striking way could the believer's identity with Christ be portrayed.

No wonder at the close of each of these letters John adds the exhortation to hear what the Spirit says to the churches. Each one conveys a message which is timeless.

174. *A Vision of Heaven*

(*Rev. 4 and 5*)

As the visions of events showing the drama of the spiritual conflict between Christ and the devil were about to be described, John relates a remarkable vision of heaven. It is as if the events affecting earth and its people must be viewed from the point of view of the enthroned Christ. This is the key to the whole picture.

An open door and a trumpet-like voice inviting John to see the revelation are an impressive introduction, which at once convinced him that he was under the inspiration of the Spirit. The description of the throne is reminiscent of Ezekiel and speaks of the majesty of the scene. The accompanying twenty-four seats, occupied by elders in white, draws attention to the purity which belongs to this exalted position. They may well represent angelic beings. Any attempt to describe in words the awesomeness of the Throne was bound to be inadequate. John makes use of imagery drawn from a serious thunderstorm as being the nearest analogy. Similarly the "seven" Spirits which he sees are symbolic of the perfection of the Holy Spirit. The four living creatures distinct from the elders appear to represent the submission of all creation (man, animal, cattle, and bird) to Him who occupies the throne. By means of "wings" and "eyes," the velocity and vigilance of these representatives of the natural world is portrayed.

At this point John notes the worship of the creatures in heaven. Although previously seated, the elders remove their crowns and offer homage to the One on the throne, who is described as eternal. An anthem of praise is then addressed to Him, extolling His worthiness. The main theme is His creative activity and purpose, which is a fitting theme in a scene which shows the submission of the creation to the Creator. Glory, honor, and power are all attributes of God which are His by right, but His creatures must acknowledge them as they do in this vision. This heavenly exercise of worship may serve as a pattern for the worshiping Church on earth, calling for great reverence and adoration for God.

The revelations which are about to unfold are inscribed on a seven-sealed scroll, which has writing on both surfaces. It was the general practice to write only on the inside, but in this case there was too much in the contents to do this. The scroll was held in the hand of the one on the throne, which shows clearly where the initiative lies. No one answered to the challenge of an angel for one to open the book, which caused great grief to John, who had already been assured that the book of the future would be revealed to him. The touching episode of one of the elders comforting the weeping seer introduces a human concern into an otherwise overawing scene. The elder was able to announce that Jesus Christ was worthy to open the book, under the figure of the Lion of Judah and the Root of David (cf. Gen. 49:4 and Isa. 11:1, 10 respectively). These were both titles associated with the Jewish Messiah, but here the idea goes beyond the Jewish hope of a deliverer. The victory which entitles Jesus Christ to open the book cannot be other than His redeeming act, because He is also identified as the Lamb, which appeared to have been killed. The conjunction of Lion with Lamb in these descriptions

is remarkable, bringing out the link between judgment and mercy
in His character. The seven horns and eyes represent the perfection of Christ's power and knowledge. The explanation that these
are the Seven Spirits shows unmistakably the close connection
between the Spirit's and Christ's work. It is worth noting that the
emphasis falls on the Spirit's activity throughout the world. This
marvelous scene in heaven is not divorced from the happenings
on earth. Indeed this is the message of the whole book — that all
things are known by Him who has won the victory over sin and
death.

It is not until the Lamb has taken the book that the twenty-
four elders worship Him with music and incense (which symbolizes the prayers of Christians, after a typically Jewish method).
It is the anthem they sang which shows most clearly that the
dominating factor in Christ's worthiness to open the book was
His passion — conceived as a ransoming of men for God. The
inauguration by Him of a new kind of kingdom, comprising
priests before God, is a comprehensive picture of what redemption means to the people of God. They may now act as their own
priests and make their own way to God.

This song of the elders set all the created world singing the
praises of Christ. The first chorus by heavenly beings echoes
similar sentiments. It is worth noting that glory, honor, and
power, which in the earlier part of the vision are ascribed to God
are now ascribed to the Lamb. Other attributes of the Lamb
included in the song are wealth, wisdom, and blessing. Words
are poor instruments to describe Him! Another chorus echoing
the other two sung by all creatures in heaven and earth, and
links adoration to God with adoration to Christ. The act of worship closes with the living creatures' amen and the elders' further
adoration. The whole scene is full of a wonderful consciousness
of the glory and majesty of Jesus Christ, which sets the stage
for the next revelations made known when the seals are opened.

175. *The Seals*

(Rev. 6 and 7)

The book which the Lamb proceeds to open was sealed with
seven seals, each one of which conceals some coming revelation.
The first four, when broken, reveal a succession of riders, who
represent the various woes which belong to the last days.

The emergence of each horse and rider is dramatically announced by one of the living creatures, i.e., by one of God's highest agents. The four variously colored horses may be derived from Zechariah 6:1-8, where the riders are seen as ministers of God's will. Here the first rider is seen as a victorious warrior, a personification of coming judgment, whereas the other three represent specific woes — war, famine, and death. These woes are inescapable in times of judgment and typify the worst aspects of human suffering.

The opening of the fifth seal revealed martyrs under the altar. If their position at first seems surprising, it must be remembered that this was regarded as a place of honor and security. What strikes John most forcibly is their plaintive cry for vengeance. This kind of prayer may seem at first to fall short of the approach of Stephen with his prayer for forgiveness for his enemies. It is more in the spirit of the Old Testament. And yet it is not out of keeping with the aim of this book. The problem of the righteous suffering has always needed explanation. All righteous people long for justice. The martyr's plea is a longing that God will show His real nature — holy and true. In answer, each was given a white robe, symbol of his true standing in Christ. Patience is needed for a little longer until the full number of martyrs is completed. They are reminded in this way that they are not the only ones. There were many others to follow. The full number is not yet complete. Christians are still being martyred for their faith.

When the sixth seal was opened, a tremendous earthquake occurred, accompanied by catastrophic disturbances among the heavenly bodies. The composite picture which the writer describes is one of stark upheaval. In vivid poetic language he pictures the rolling up of the sky and sees mighty mountains being jolted out of place. It is as if he describes his personal impression of some gigantic earthquake, in which it seemed as if everything was collapsing around him. The hiding of all classes of people in clefts of the tottering rocks and their terror, expressed in the desire for the rocks to put them out of their misery, vividly portray the attitude of mind of those who fear the Day of the Lord. There was much more to happen before that day arrived, but men whose consciences were stabbed alert in the cataclysm mistook the cosmic chaos for the inauguration of the day of wrath. These catastrophes were, however, mild compared with what was to come.

At this point there is an interlude before the opening of the seventh seal, during which John sees a vision of four angels restraining the four winds from blowing, because had they been released they would have been harmful. The idea of angelic agenices behind the elements would not have been unfamiiar to Jewish minds. It is a fitting reminder that the spiritual world is more powerful than the natural world. In John's vision a fifth angel introduces a note of mercy. It is a welcome relief amid the clashings of judgment. The angel has a seal to seal the number of the elect by imprinting on their foreheads. The seal in ancient times was used both as an evidence of ownership (or authentication) and as an assurance of security. Possibly both meanings are present here, with the emphasis falling more on the second. With catastropic happenings around them, God's people may rejoice that their future is God's responsibility — a remarkable contrast to the cringing of the non-Christian world, following the earthquake of judgment. There is no need to take the 144,000 literally any more than the other imagery. But who are these people who are called the sons of Israel? Are they Jews, Jewish Christians, or the New Israel (i.e., all Christians)? Since the same number occurs in Revelation 14:1, where it can only be understood of the whole Church, it seems mots reasonable to understand it in the same sense here. It will be remembered that James in the opening of his letter addresses the twelve tribes of the dispersion, but clearly has Christians in mind. As to the number twelve, this occurs frequently in this book and undoubtedly has a symbolic meaning. Especially is this true of the vision of the New Jerusalem, with its twelve gates, twelve angels, twelve tribal names, twelve foundation stones, twelve apostolic names. The city is symbolically described as a cube with sides of twelve thousand furlongs. There were twelve jewels in the foundations and twelve pearls in the gates. Who can doubt that in this apocalypse the number twelve stood for completion.

Next John sees the multitude of the redeemed, in white robes, triumphantly praising God. This time the crowd was too vast to be numbered. The scene is one of magnificent worship as all the heavenly creatures, angels, elders, and living creatures included, join in a doxology to God.

At this point there is a dialogue between John and one of the elders. The seer has become part of the vision. He is asked to identify those in the white robes. It is essential for the interpretation of the whole series of visions that he should know the answer. But because he is not sure, he leaves the elder to explain. The key to the identity lies in their having been redeemed — hence the white robes of purity. They are in the blessed position of continual worship of God and of exemption from the trials of human life (famine, scorching sun, sorrow). The view of the Lamb as Shepherd leading His sheep by springs of water and tenderly wiping away all tears is touching, for it savors of the Gospel.

176. *Six Trumpets of Doom*

(Rev. 8 and 9)

It is the opening of the seventh seal that leads into the sequence of seven trumpets. Before this further revelation there was a period of silence, the purpose of which was to allow the prayers of the saints to be heard.

Before the trumpets sound, John notes that the trumpeters were angels, drawing attention once again to the divine nature of the revelations to be made, for they are the servants of God. An eighth angel had the special task of holding the censer containing incense. The idea seems to be that the prayers of God's people are aided by the incense which ascends. This is not, however, to think of angels as performing the work of a mediator, for the New Testament reserves such a function for Christ alone. The abrupt action of the eighth angel in hurling fire from the altar to the earth vividly demonstrates the beginning of judgment (cf. Ezek. 10:2). What John is about to see relates to the end of the age.

When the trumpets sound, the form of the first four judgments bear some resemblance to the plagues which afflicted the Egyptians at the time of the Exodus. John would clearly understand the significance of what he saw—the violent storm which scorched, the sea of blood, the bitter waters, and the darkened heavens were all calamitous abnormalities of nature which spoke unmistakably of the judgments of God. Yet in each case only a third of the world of nature was affected. It might be expected that men would at once heed the warning and repent, but they refused to do so.

No doubt John's own feelings were reflected in the cry of the eagle expressing woe for the inhabitants of earth, because there were still three more trumpets to sound. The first four disasters were severe enough, but there were still others to follow. The fifth trumpet releases a plague of demons in the form of locusts. The poet can describe them only in familiar imagery. They come swarming out of the bottomless pit, a vivid metaphor which describes the abode of evil. Their density is so great they are like a cloud which blots out the light of the sun. They possess considerable powers of torture, but not of destruction. Moreover they had power to harm only those who were not sealed by God. Even so their powers of torture were of limited duration. However terrible the judgments of God, John continually draws attention to the fact that evil forces do not have the final say. Certain details of these evil agenices are worth observing. Their cavalry-like formations, their crowns, their human-type faces, their long hairy antennae like women's hair, their strong lionlike teeth, their ironlike scales, their deafening wings, their scorpionlike tails, all build up a picture of considerable horror and ugliness. Having abandoned his role as an angel of light, their king is seen as Apollyon (which means "destruction"). When this embodiment of evil sheds his deceptive disguise, he shows his terrible nature, as becomes increasingly clear in the following visions.

The sixth trumpet further focuses on destruction. John sees four angels in the vision, whose sole task was destruction. As the Israelites hoped to keep their worst enemies at bay on the other side of the Euphrates, so John understands that these agencies of destruction are to be released from beyond a spiritual Euphrates. The vision was one of a cavalrylike charge of very considerable proportions. Many would die in the onslaught, but the enemy's terrible power was again restrained, for not more than a third of the people were killed. It is difficult to imagine horses with lionlike heads, poisonous burning breath, and serpentlike tails. The impression created by such an incongruous description is startling. The sixth woe is terrible to contemplate.

John's sad commentary that those unaffected by the plagues did not repent is highly typical of men in general. Their foolishness in actually worshiping demons in various forms (mainly idolatry) and their immoral practices show men at their blindest. For John, as he continues to look at these visions, the idea of judgment is inescapable.

177. *The Seventh Trumpet*
(Rev. 10-12)

Following the sounding of the sixth trumpet, a considerable interlude occurs before the seventh is heard. But the interlude sets the scene for the drama unfolded by the last trumpet. It emphasizes the nearness of the end, John's authority for prophesying the special protection given to God's people and the effectiveness of true witness during the period in which antichrist is dominant.

The first of these facts is conveyed by the vision of an angel with a book. John describes the angel in impressive imagery — with blazing face and legs of fire and a massive voice like a lion's. Thunders rolled when he spoke. Obviously greatly impressed, John was about to write when he was commanded not to do so by a heavenly voice. Strangely enough no hint is given of the reason for this prohibition. It was evidently a special personal message which was intended to add an air of mystery to the revelation about to be made known. The mighty angel with legs astride announces with an authoritative voice that no further delay will occur before the end. This is clearly intended to show the climactic character of the seventh trumpet, and the fact that the many prophecies of the end were about to be fulfilled.

A direct word from the heavenly voice to John gives a commission to prophesy. Like Ezekiel centuries before, he is commanded to eat a book, a symbolic way of saying that what he must prophesy does not come from himself. The mixed taste of the book shows that John's announcements would contain both encouragement and judgment. In harmony with such a commission, he is given a measuring rod. He does not provide his own yardstick in his assessment of the Temple and its worshipers. The Court of the Gentiles, however, was not included. The vision shows God's people surrounded by hostile elements which would overrun the Holy City (Jerusalem). The whole scene typifies the history of the Christian Church in a society dominated by hostile forces. Jerusalem has now become the representative of oppression, as Sodom and Egypt had before them (cf. v. 11:8). Nevertheless there is a limit to the oppression, expressed in terms of three and one half years (which finds an echo in Revelation 12:6, 14). It is by no means certain that this period should be understood in any literal sense. It undoubtedly sets a limit on the tramping down of God's city.

During this period when the antichrist's influence is dominant, God does not leave Himself without a witness. Indeed, two special witnesses, clothed in sackcloth, symbolize the testimony of all God's people. In describing them John uses language from the prophecy of Zechariah, who saw in his vision two olive trees supplying continual oil to the candlestick. Here, however, two lampstands are seen to bear light during that dark period. They are formidably powerful, which shows that God does not intend their preaching to be hindered. Their powers in fact recall those exercised by both Moses and Elijah.

At the close of the period, the "Beast" from the Pit will be allowed to kill them. He is the personification of all that is opposed to God. The leaving of the two corpses unburied in the streets speaks of the scorn and ignominy to which the Church is subjected. John sees this happening in the very place where Jesus was crucified. The witnesses were continuing the sufferings of their Lord. The enemies of the Church would gloat over their downfall, but again for only a severely restricted period (as the symbolic three and one half days shows). Then God gives renewed life to His people through His Spirit, as the Spirit had brought quickening to Israel (cf. Ezek. 37). This so astonished the oppressors that they were terrified — especially when they saw the resuscitated witnesses caught up to heaven. As the earth trembled beneath them and a sizable part of the city collapsed, killing a very great number of people, the survivors at last showed some kind of acknowledgment of God. But all this was only the prelude to the seventh trumpet.

Although this trumpet is supposed to pronounce the third woe (the fifth and sixth also pronounced woes), the details are not given until later. Instead the coming of God's kingdom is announced, which leads to another description of a majestic scene in heaven during which the twenty-four elders offer homage and give praise to God. Another thunderstorm description is given as the temple was thrown open to reveal the ark of the covenant, the symbol of God's promises to man.

At this point a vision appears in the sky showing the birth of a child, which is clearly intended to represent the Messiah. The symbolic character of the event is seen from the fact that no resemblance is discernable to the historic incarnation of Jesus.

What the vision is intended to teach is the hostility of the Dragon to the Messiah, but his intentions are thwarted by the ascension of the Messiah to heaven. The woman, representing the people of God, is protected during the period of the antichrist's reign.

The removal of the Messiah marks the outbreak of war in heaven. The Dragon, who represents Satan, attempts to retrieve his loss, but is overcome and hurled to earth. As John watches the scene he is aware of a loud announcement in heaven to the effect that the Dragon had been conquered by the blood of the Lamb. This is important, for he can no longer accuse the people of God. All he can do is to vent his fury against the Church on earth. He appears as a sea monster who pursues the woman even into the wilderness by belching water after her, but she is preserved. This is a powerful picture of the security of God's people in the face of the severest antagonism.

178. *The Beasts and the Martyrs*

(Rev. 13 and 14)

In the previous section John has been introduced to the major enemy of the Christian Church, i.e., Satan himself. In this he sees the second and third enemies under the name of beasts. The first is described in terms which are calculated to bring out the worst features of brutishness, the sudden spring of the leopard, the slow, powerful progress of the bear, and the conquering roar of the lion. Its horns and heads intensifying its terrifying appearance, further stressed by the incongruity of its browns. The overall impression is of great authority, and the beast itself would seem to represent the power of world governments under the domination of the Dragon, the prince of the world. The beast had one special peculiarity — one of its heads which had been mortally wounded revived again. It seems best to interpret the mortal wound as the deathblow to Satan resulting from Christ's work, and the revival of the head as the intensification of Satan's power over those outside the community of believers. Certainly the beast's fury is unleashed against the Christian Church, pursued with great blasphemy. The remarkable thing is that men worshiped the Dragon because of the superiority of this atrocious beast. This illustrates the hypnotic effect of sheer power. Clearly in face of such opposition God's people need strong faith and endurance, but they have the certainty of His protection.

The second beast is more deceptive, with its lamblike horns and dragonlike voice. It proceeds out of the earth in contrast to the first beast, which comes from the sea. It represents the religious agency through whom the Dragon exerts his influence. It has power to work signs through which men are deceived. Its greatest achievement is to cause men to make a statue of the first beast and then to lead them to offer homage to it. John's readers would not find it difficult to see in his description some allusion to emperor worship, which the Romans developed to provide a religious unifying factor among its variegated peoples. A more modern example is in Communist China, where the people are expected to treat the State as an object of reverence. The mark of the beast shows that its bearers are loyal to the Beast. The curious number 666 must have been intelligible to John and to his readers, but baffles the modern mind. It may have been merely symbolic, since 6 is a number of imperfection. But John gives a broad hint that it stands for a man's name. It presumably appears in this cryptic cipher for security reasons.

The opposition of these two beasts — the world and a false spirit of religion — is so intense that the thought of it might well depress. At this point, however, John sees another of those scenes of encouragement, which intersperse the whole book. It is a vision which gives the true spiritual counterpart to the activities of the forces of evil. It pictures another group of people who do not bear the beast's mark on their foreheads, but the name of the lamb and of God. Moreover true worship is offered by the redeemed, which makes the homage to the beast's statue look paltry. Again, as so often before, the accompaniments of a natural storm form the background to the worship. A new song of praise accompanied by harpists is sung before the throne. This echoes the earlier scene of worship in heaven. Although the precise number of the redeemed is said to be 144,000, this was symbolical of the whole people of God. It is therefore in a spiritual sense that their chastity must be understood. Such purity of mind is in marked contrast to the habits of the world. Moreover falsehood and reproach are banished from them. Their main concern is to follow the Lamb. Sandwiched between passages which speak of the activity of the beast, this vision is a relevant reminder that God can keep His people pure in the midst of the most adverse conditions. John was not writing merely for his own times, but for all times.

Nevertheless, the vision of encouragement was but an interlude. John sees an angel with the everlasting Gospel. The angel announces the coming of the hour of judgment, which shows that the Gospel is not the good news of grace, but the message that God will vindicate His people. The angel does not call on men to repent, but to offer homage, thus acknowledging the supremacy of the Creator.

A second angel announces the doom of Babylon, which would in all probability have been understood by John and his readers as the Roman State. It contained in prophetic form an assurance of the final overthrow of the persecutor of God's people. Yet another angel loudly proclaims judgment on those who bear the beast's mark. In contrast to Rome, which had made nations drink the wine of passion, her dupes will drink the wine of God's wrath. Judgment is described in terms of torture because this is the most vivid way to express just retribution. But the symbolical character of this book must not be lost sight of. The main message is that when judgment begins there will be no more room for mercy — a solemn warning.

God's people will naturally be in a threatened position at such a time and are thus urged to steadfastness. They need not fear death. They are on the contrary happy to die. This is vouched for by a heavenly voice.

John next sees a vision of the messianic king who is linked with these announcements of judgment, for almost immediately a fourth angel announces the time of harvest, a well-known scriptural figure for judgment. At once the messianic king thrusts in the sickle. Yet another angel, described as the controller of the altar fire in the temple, harvests grapes of wrath. The reason for this description is not clear, but the idea of a winepress of wrath is an echo from Joel 3:13. Judgment is a terrible thing. John sees coming from the winepress, not grape juice, but blood. His measurements suggest an incredibly vast area, which heightens the awful effect.

179. *The Bowls*
(Rev. 15 and 16)

In the last section visions of the end have been given, but in this more scenes of judgment are described, which shows that John's visions are not arranged in chronological order. The idea seems to be that a sequence of different series of woes will build up an impression of the nature and certainty of divine judgment. The trumpets had disclosed various plagues, and there is a remarkable similarity with the bowls seen in this next vision, only these are more comprehensive.

First John sees seven angels. The background to their pouring out the bowls of wrath is a chorus from those who had conquered the beast. The scenery is again symbolic. The sea of glass reminds us of the similar scenic detail in the earlier vision of worship in heaven. Here it is merged with some reminiscence of the Red Sea, when the Israelites stood beside it to sing the song of Moses. A vital difference is that the redeemed sing the song of the Lamb. In both cases the name of God is extolled. What John hears is a rhapsody on the wonderful doings of God, of His truth and holiness. It provides an oasis of praise in the midst of judgment, but is nevertheless necessary to show the justness of the judgment.

The seven angels are seen to come from the heavenly tent of witness (another Old Testament allusion). Their dress suggests that they are appearing in the role of priests. It is one of the living creatures who gives them the golden bowls of wrath, which underlines the essential authority of the judgments. As John watches, he notes the smoke which, as so often in Scripture, accompanies divine revelations of special majesty. It was a smoke of glory which masked Mount Sinai at the giving of the law. It was appropriate that a similar symbol should be seen at the execution of judgment.

The authoritative command for the pouring out of the bowls comes from the midst of the temple, again stressing the divine character of the wrath. As one angel after another pours out his bowl, it is noticeable that the judgments are described in terms of intensity. The sores which afflicted the men were particularly foul, and no one seems to escape them. The sea not only turned to blood, but to dead men's blood, killing all the sea creatures. All the rivers and waters became blood, which brings out comments from the angel of the water and from the altar to the effect that God's judgments are just. Here John uses poetic licence in personifying both the water and the altar. Moreover, the sun in its entirety is affected, becoming so intense that men are burned. At this point John notes that in spite of the severity of the judgments, the men concerned showed no evidence of repentance. Their rebelliousness against God had gone too far.

This hardness of heart comes out again when the fifth bowl was emptied, which brought darkness, only aggravating the suffering from ulcers which was introduced at the first bowl and was evidently still continuing. This shows clearly the cumulative nature of the judgments.

When the next bowl was poured out, a rather different effect is produced. The drying up of the Euphrates no doubt reminded John of the drying up of the Red Sea for the salvation of the people of Israel. Here however the effect is different since judgment is still in mind. This must affect our understanding of the "Kings of the East," who now have no barrier to overcome in order to advance. In John's day the chief menace from the east were the Parthian armies, but there is undoubtedly a further allusion to a future event in which the Kings of the earth would meet in final conflict at Armageddon. This was a symbolic place which would become a kind of magnet to attract all the kings to gather, aided by the deceptive activities of demons sent to act on behalf of the Dragon and his agents. Their froglike characteristics are intended to illustrate their repulsive nature. In the midst of this revelation, John hears words which must have reminded him of some words of Jesus — "I come as a thief." The solemnity of the judgments makes a warning necessary for God's people.

With the seventh bowl comes the announcement of the end. It is made in a loud manner, for it is decisive. Both the heaven and the earth become convulsed, with violent storm and devastating earthquake. John sees the tottering of men's citadels as a result. The furious wrath of God is irresistible. The judgment blows are vividly described by him as massive hailstones of considerable weight, which crushed those on whom they fell. The whole series of visions in the bowls sequence shows the infinitely greater power of God over man's mightiest efforts to defy Him. John is showing the Almighty having the last word, and none can challenge His power.

180. *Babylon*

(Rev. 17 and 18)

Although in the last section the end was announced, there are further revelations, developing in detail various aspects which have already been mentioned. The focus falls now on Babylon, her opposition to the Church of God, and her ultimate fall.

First of all, John is shown by an angel "the great harlot" who has been responsible for the debauchery of the kings of the earth. The kings clearly represent the temporal power. But who is the harlot? She is introduced later as Babylon, as the mother of harlots. She appears to be the quintessence of all that is base. Many see her as the temporal power of the Roman empire, since seven hills are mentioned in 17:9. Others see a reference to papal Rome, but this would not have occurred to John's readers and cannot have been the original intention. It is perhaps best to see the harlot as purely symbolic of all those manifestations of evil which are a counterfeit of the true Church of Jesus Christ.

The garb and appearance of the woman is gorgeous. Outwardly she glitters, but inwardly she supports filthiness and immorality. She stands for the spirit of the world in all its outward attractiveness, but in fact is a sham compared with the Christian Church, which is also represented as a woman, but a woman, who is chaste and pure (cf. 19:7, 8). It is noticeable that John sees on her forehead a name of mystery, since "mystery" in the ancient world had strong religious associations. This glittering spirit of the world is a tool of the Beast — she rides upon it — and is seen as a major agency in Satan's opposition to the people of God, whose blood has been shed.

Noting John's amazement, the angel explains. The renewal of the Beast's existence is only temporary. This renewed energy amazes the world outside the Church. The seven heads are perplexing since they are described as both hills and kings. Many see both as evidence that imperial Rome is meant. But when the seven kings become ten kings it complicates the picture. The major idea seems to be temporal power and authority. The harlot is borne along by such temporal power. John could not fail to see a manifestation of this in imperial Rome. Yet the real climax comes when the ten kings rebel against the harlot. This shows the principle that evil has within it the power of its own self-destruction. Many times in history temporal power turned against the spirit of false devotion and debauchery which gave it birth. It is simply that God at times uses the devil's own agents to execute His judgments. Some see the great city, with which the woman is identified, as the counterfeit of that other "great city" of which John writes, i.e., the heavenly Jerusalem.

As the vision continues, John is conscious, no doubt by way of contrast to the harlot, of the resplendence of the angel who next speaks to him. Even the earth reflects the brilliance. John is aware that the announcement is backed with considerable authority, as if some great victory had been gained. Indeed Babylon had fallen. It had become desolate as a wilderness, where it was believed that demons dwelt. Again the language is figurative.

A second voice urges God's people to flee from her allurements. Here the vision has clearly switched back to the state of affairs before the fall of Babylon, since God's people are informed there is still time to do something about it. The voice continues to exhort vengeance upon the harlot by those whose task it is (the vision does not specify the agency). Clearly judgment comes from the Lord God, who is seen as supreme over all the forces of Satan.

John now with eloquence describes the lament by the kings and merchants over the fall of Babylon. The kings look on from a distance in fear. The merchants who had become wealthy with trade now weep because no one will buy from their piled up stocks. There can be few more eloquent condemnations of mere materialism than this. The merchants affected stand back and helplessly watch. The gold, the jewels, the fine apparel are meaningless in the hour of judgment. Others who mourned over the destruction of the city were the sailors whose livelihood was jeopardized through the slump in trade. They were more demonstrative, as they lamented with ashes on their heads, the traditional method of indicating public mourning. Each of the three groups have the same cry and each stresses the hour of judgment as having come.

The occupants of heaven are called upon to rejoice over God's action on their behalf. The conviction that God will in the end judge justly is a constant assurance to God's people in times of great persecution. John knew that this would mean much to any of his readers who were then suffering.

With a dramatic symbolic gesture an angel in John's vision casts a millstone into the sea, followed by a poet's picture of all that will cease with the fall of Babylon. Arts and crafts and the joys of marriage are singled out, as darkness and desolation descend on the once great city.

The message is clear. Babylon, the epitome of evil, in spite of her material magnificence, is doomed. A far greater spiritual power will ensure its overthrow.

181. *Worship and Judgment*
(Rev. 19 and 20)

It is characteristic of John's visions that scenes of judgment on earth are interspersed with scenes of worship in heaven. After the lament of those who had been beguiled by the doomed harlot, it is a refreshing relief to look at her destruction from the viewpoint of those in heaven. First, a loud anthem of praise is heard, praising God for the justness of His judgments, especially in the condemnation of the harlot.

The act of homage on the part of the twenty-four elders and of the living creatures echoes the earlier scenes of worship. It is, however, a development when a voice comes from the throne itself calling on men to worship God. Another great chorus of praise comes in response. John is again at a loss for words to describe it — the rushing together of water and the pealing of thunderclaps is the nearest he can get. The theme of this chorus changes to an exultation of God and an announcement of the marriage of the Lamb. For the first time in his visions, John sees the Church as a bride, dressed in the symbolic white clothes of purity. The idea is not unique to this book, for it is found in the Pauline epistles. Moreover, Jesus spoke of Himself as the Bridegroom.

The marriage supper of the Lamb is announced by the angel to John who is to write the invitations. He is so overwhelmed that he offers homage to the angel, who at once reminds him that worship belongs to God. At this climax of human history, no creature, however exalted, is permitted to come between the humblest believer and God. John sees that the same Spirit who dwelt in Jesus has commanded him through the angel. The imagery of a marriage feast marking the climax of the age is found in the Old Testament (cf. Ps. 45:9-15; Isa. 54:5; Hos. 2:19). Among the men of the Jewish sect at Qumran the idea of a feast to mark the coming of the Messiah was also prevalent. The marriage of the Lamb and His bride marks the complete unity of Christ and His Church.

It is against this background of joyful announcement that the execution of final judgment upon the spiritual enemies of God's people is focused in the person of Satan, the beast and the false prophet. The drama begins with the appearance of the Warrior. His character is seen in His name — Faithful and True. Everything about Him speaks of judgment — the white horse, the flaming eyes, the bloodlike robe, the sword, and the rod of iron. His further name, Word of God, reveals His identity. John in writing his gospel used the same title, Word (or Logos), to describe Jesus Christ, and there is no doubt that the Warrior in this vision is none other than He. Moreover His royal robe bore the name of King of kings and Lord of lords, evidence of His Supreme sovereignty. John sees no incongruity between the Lamb and the warrior king. They speak of different aspects of His work, the one of mercy and redemption, the other of judgment and triumph.

The stage is set for battle. There is no doubt about the outcome. What John first sees is an angel announcing the victory supper. The certainty of victory is expressed poetically in a scene of destruction in which birds of prey swoop on the victims of battle. It is as devastating and conclusive as that.

The battle itself is described in the briefest terms. The defeat of the beast and the false prophet, the spiritual driving forces behind the harlot and her adoring dupes, was swift. The poet implies, but does not specifically state, that the warrior overcame by the power of His word, since a sharp sword proceeded from His mouth. He judges with a word of command which none of His enemies can withstand. A lake of fire as a figure of judgment would not have been unfamiliar in John's world. It is, moreover, in line with various statements of Jesus about hell.

The judgment on the arch-enemy, Satan, which follows, takes place in two stages. The seized enemy is confined in a bottomless pit for the space of 1,000 years after which he is loosed for "a little while." There is difference of opinion on the meaning here. Are the 1,000 years intended literally or symbolically? To what period do they refer? Many suppose a millenium for the Church after the close of the present age and before the final consummation. But others take the number as symbolic, because numbers are generally used symbolically in this book. In this case it merely indicates an allotted span. The first stage of binding could in fact begin at the beginning of the Christian era, in which case John is being shown an event near to his own time. This interpretation has the advantage of avoiding a double judgment on Satan at the end of the age. But there are difficulties. During the Church age, Satan has certainly been deceiving the nations. Moreover John writes of a first and second resurrection, which seems to belong most naturally to the end time unless the first is regarded as spiritual. Again it is difficult to relate the reigning with Christ to the Church age. It seems best to treat the 1,000 years symbolically and spiritually, but the literal view is by no means impossible.

A recap on the activities of Satan in the Church age reaches its climax in a battle, as the result of which Satan's allies are destroyed by fire and Satan himself is eternally condemned. The message to Christians is clear, i.e., that God will have the last word.

This part of the visions ends with the Great White Throne, where men's deeds are judged and where reference is made to those whose names are in the Book of Life. Although so much is said in this book on judgment, there is throughout a strong thread of mercy. The readers are not allowed to forget the provision of God for the salvation of His people.

182. *All Things New*

(*Rev. 21 and 22*)

The vision switches from scenes of judgment to scenes of renewal. The heaven and earth are renewed. The sea, possibly symbolic for the masses of unregenerate people, is no longer in existence. Attention focuses on the new Jerusalem, which is mentioned first and fully described later. John hears a voice from the throne announcing the benefits of God dwelling among His people, especially the banishment of sorrow — a great encouragement to John's hard-pressed readers.

The further announcement of the renewal of all things is accompanied by an assurance of tenderness for those thirsty for true life and an announcement of severe judgment on evil deeds. There is an echo from earlier in the book as God announces Himself as Alpha and Omega (see 1:8).

Then comes the description of the New Jerusalem. In vision John is transported to a vantage point from which he could see the descending city. At first sight it is strange to find the Lamb's bride (i.e., the Church) described as a city. The imagery seems particularly impersonal, especially compared with the personal description of that other city Babylon in the figure of the harlot. Yet the identification of the Church with a new kind of Jerusalem would be highly significant to a Jewish mind, especially after the destruction of the old city. The description is symbolic. It was certainly a glorious sight, glittering like a most precious jewel. It was moreover perfectly symmetrical with three gates on each side of its square perimeter. Indeed, it is described as a cube, a symbol of perfection. The number twelve comes into the description several times and is connected with the number of tribes among the Israelites and the number of apostles in the Church. John must have seen the significance of this number, particularly as the angelic surveyor announced the size of the cube as 12,000 furlongs (1,500 miles). There was no possibility of taking this in any way other than as symbolic. Again the surrounding wall (an important characteristic of the old Jerusalem) was twelve times twelve cubits high. The precious materials used throughout in the construction of the symbolic city, even in its foundations, gates, and streets, speak eloquently of its value. Moreover, the city is not dominated, as the old Jerusalem was, by the Temple. It is no longer necessary. God and the Lamb replace the Temple, as they also replace the light of sun and moon. The poet sees God as the ultimate source of all light. This is why night is banished, which must be understood as spiritual not physical darkness. The whole place is aglow with glory, and impurity finds no place there. The sheer beauty and purity of the description comes through the limitation of words to describe the indescribably glorious. The vision appears to relate to the future, but John's contemporaries would have seen its relevance to their immediate situation. The "Jerusalem" to which they belonged has been ideally glorious in every age.

Focus next falls on the environment of the city and in this John sees a river, reminiscent of the river which appeared in Paradise. It is not insignificant that the first book in the Old Testament and the last in the New Testament both show a scene of Paradise, the one lost, the other restored. Moreover, inside the new city is perfect worship of the Lamb and the absolute sovereignty of God. It is as if the pages of revelation could not close until the complete rectification of all the ruin wrought by sin had been effected.

The book closes with an epilogue which at many points links with the introductory section. The words of prophecy which John has received are declared to be true by the same angel mentioned in Revelation 1:1. Moreover the assurance of the imminent coming of Jesus Christ echoes the statement of Revelation 1:7, only here it is more personal. John's overawing obeisance in Revelation 1:17 comes out again here, although he mistakenly offers homage to the angel and has to be corrected. In Revelation 1:10 he is commanded to write what he sees in a book, whereas here blessing is promised to those who keep its words. There is a similar use of the names Alpha and Omega, but with a difference, for in Revelation 1:8 they are applied to God, but here to Jesus Christ. Moreover in both passages there is reference to the churches, showing clearly that the entire book, visions as well as epistles, was intended for general circulation.

In a mysterious command to John not to seal up the book, we find the opposite to the command given to Daniel, because now the time of revelation has come. The prophetic words are intended to make clear the distinction between the evil and the righteous, which is never blurred in Scripture. John hears a guarantee of just rewards in view of Christ's second coming.

It is remarkable that Jesus speaks directly through the prophet (22:16), and introduces Himself as the "offspring of David," a clear reference to His humanity. After this comes from both the Spirit and Bride the invitation, addressed particularly to the thirsty, i.e., those with a deep sense of need.

John closes his book with a note of warning. He seems to be conscious that his words are those of Another and must therefore be treated as sacrosanct. It is appropriate that a warning not to add to or subtract from the book should not only close this book, but also the collection of Christian books. What John says here would apply equally to all the apostolic writings. The apostles passed on, but their words remain to provide inspiration to all who believe in Jesus Christ. The final prayer, "Come, Lord Jesus," is still not obsolete in spite of the passing of nineteen centuries.

Select Bibliography

GENERAL WORKS OF INTRODUCTION AND BACKGROUND

Conybeare, W. J., and Howson, J. S. *The Life and Letters of St. Paul.* London: Longmans, 1853.

Gundry, R. H. *A Survey of the New Testament.* Grand Rapids: Zondervan; Exeter: Paternoster, 1970.

Guthrie, D. *New Testament Introduction.* Chicago and London: Inter-varsity Press, 1970.

Harrison, E. F. *Introduction to the New Testament.* Grand Rapids: Eerdmans, 1964.

Kümmel, W. G. *Introduction to the New Testament.* Translated by A. J. Mattill. London: SCM; New York: Abingdon, 1966.

Martin, R. P. *Worship in the Early Church.* London: Marshall, Morgan and Scott, 1964.

Moule, C. F. D. *The Birth of the New Testament.* London: SCM; New York: Harper and Row, ²1966.

Tenney, M. C. *New Testament Survey.* Grand Rapids: Eerdmans; London: Inter-varsity Press, ²1961.

Unnick, W. C. van. *Tarsus or Jerusalem, the City of Paul's Youth?* Naperville, Ill.: Allenson, 1962.

WORKS ON THE APOSTLES

Barclay, W. *The Mind of St. Paul.* London: Collins, 1958.

Chadwick, H. *The Enigma of St. Paul.* London: Athlone, 1969.

Cullmann, O. *Peter: Disciple, Apostle and Martyr.* London: SCM, ²1962.

Davies, W. J. *Paul and Rabbinic Judaism.* London: SPCK, 1955.

Deissmann, A. *Paul: A Study in Social and Religious History.* Translated by W. E. Wilson. London: Hodder and Stoughton, 1926.

Dibelius, M., and Kümmel, W. G. *Paul.* Translated by F. Clarke. New York: Longmans, 1953.

Dodd, C. H. *The Mind of Paul: A Psychological Approach.* Manchester: John Ryland Library, 1934.

Ellis, E. E. *Paul's Use of the Old Testament.* Edinburgh: Oliver and Boyd, 1957.

——. *Paul and His Recent Interpreters.* Grand Rapids: Eerdmans, 1961.

Foakes-Jackson, F. J. *The Life of Saint Paul.* London: Jonathan Cape, 1927.

Glover, T. R. *Paul of Tarsus.* London: SCM, 1925.

Headlam, A. C. *St. Paul and Christianity.* London: Murray, 1913.

Holden, J. S. *The Master and His Men.* London: Marshall, Morgan and Scott, 1953.

Hudson, D. F. *The Life and Letters of St. Paul.* Madras: Christian Literature Society, 1962.

Hunt, E. W. *Portrait of Paul.* London: Mowbrays, 1968.

Hunter, A. M. *Paul and His Predecessors.* London: SCM, 1961.

——. *Interpreting Paul's Gospel.* London: SCM, 1954.

Karrer, O. *Peter and the Church: An Examination of Cullmann's Thesis.* Edinburgh and London: Herders, 1963.

413

Kennedy, H. A. A. *The Theology of the Epistles.* London: Duckworth, 1919.
Knox, W. L. *St. Paul.* Edinburgh: Davies, 1932.
Longenecker, R. N. *Paul, Apostle of Liberty.* New York: Harper and Row, 1964.
————. *The Ministry and Message of Paul.* Grand Rapids: Zondervan, 1971.
Lowe, J. *Saint Peter.* Oxford: Clarendon, 1956.
Machen, J. G. *The Origin of Paul's Religion.* London: Hodder and Stoughton, 1921.
McNeile, A. H. *St. Paul: His Life, Letters and Christian Doctrine.* Cambridge University Press, 1932.
Munck, J. *Paul and the Salvation of Mankind.* Translated by F. Clarke. London: SCM; Richmond, Va.: John Knox Press, 1959.
Ogg, G. *The Odyssey of Paul: A Chronology.* Old Tappan, N.J.: Revell, 1968.
Pollock, J. *The Apostle: A Life of Paul.* Garden City, N.Y.: Doubleday, 1969.
Ramsay, W. M. *The Cities of St. Paul: Their Influence on His Life and Thought.* London: Hodder and Stoughton, 1907.
————. *St. Paul, the Traveller and the Roman Citizen.* London: Hodder and Stoughton, 1908.
Ridderbos, H. *Paul and Jesus.* Translated by D. H. Freeman. Philadelphia: Presbyterian and Reformed, 1958.
Scott, C. A. A. *Saint Paul, the Man and Teacher.* Cambridge University Press, 1936.
Simon, M. *St. Stephen and the Hellenists in the Primitive Church.* London: Longmans, 1958.
Smith, D. *The Life and Letters of St. Paul.* New York: Doran, 1920.
Stalker, J. *The Life of St. Paul.* New York: Revell, 1900.
Stewart, J. S. *A Man in Christ.* London: Hodder and Stoughton, 1935.
Thomas, W. H. G. *The Apostle Peter.* Grand Rapids: Eerdmans, 1946.
————. *The Apostle John.* Grand Rapids: Eerdmans, 1948.
Von Loewenich, W. *Paul, His Life and Work.* Translated by G. E. Harris. Edinburg: Oliver and Boyd, 1960.
White, R. E. O. *Apostle Extraordinary: A Modern Portrait of St. Paul.* Grand Rapids: Eerdmans, 1962.
Whitely, D. E. H. *The Theology of St. Paul.* Philadelphia: Fortress, 1964.

SELECTED COMMENTARIES

ACTS

Blaiklock, E. M. *The Acts of the Apostles.* London: Tyndale; Grand Rapids: Eerdmans, 1959.
Blunt, A. W. F. *The Acts of the Apostles.* Oxford: Clarendon, 1923.
Bruce, F. F. *Commentary on the Book of Acts.* Grand Rapids: Eerdmans; London: Marshall, Morgan and Scott, 1954.
Rackham, R. B. *The Acts of the Apostles.* London: Methuen, 1964.

GALATIANS

Bring, R. *Commentary on Galatians.* Translated by E. Wahlstrom. Philadelphia: Muhlenberg Press, 1958.
Cole, A. *Commentary on the Epistle of Paul to the Galatians.* Grand Rapids: Eerdmans; London: Tyndale, 1965.
Guthrie, D. *Galatians.* London: Oliphants, 1969.
Hendriksen, W. *Galatians.* London: Banner of Truth, 1969.
Ridderbos, H. N. *The Epistle of Paul to the Churches of Galatia.* Grand Rapids: Eerdmans; London: Marshall, Morgan and Scott, 1953.

THESSALONIANS

Morris, L. *The Epistles of Paul to the Thessalonians.* London: Tyndale, 1956.
————. *The First and Second Epistles to the Thessalonians.* Grand Rapids: Eerdmans, 1959.
Neil, W. *The Epistles of Paul to the Thessalonians.* London: Hodder and Stoughton, 1950.

CORINTHIANS

Barrett, C. K. *The First Epistle to the Corinthians.* London: A. & C. Black, 1968.
Grosheide, F. W. *Commentary on the First Epistle to the Corinthians.* Grand Rapids: Eerdmans; London: Marshall, Morgan and Scott, 1953.
Hughes, P. E. *Paul's Second Epistle to the Corinthians.* Grand Rapids: Eerdmans; London: Marshall, Morgan and Scott, 1962.
Morris, L. *The First Epistle of Paul to the Corinthians.* Grand Rapids: Eerdmans; London: Marshall, Morgan and Scott, 1958.
Tasker, R. V. G. *The Second Epistle of Paul to the Corinthians.* London: Tyndale, 1958.
Thrall, M. E. *The First and Second Letters of Paul to the Corinthians.* Cambridge University Press, 1965.

ROMANS

Barrett, C. K. *The Epistle to the Romans.* London: A. & C. Black, 1958.
Bruce, F. F. *The Epistle of Paul to the Romans.* London: Tyndale, 1963.
Murray, J. *The Epistle to the Romans.* 2 vols. Grand Rapids: Eerdmans; London: Marshall, Morgan and Scott, 1959-60.
Nygren, A. *Commentary on Romans.* London: SCM, 1952.

COLOSSIANS AND PHILEMON

Bruce, F. F. *The Epistle to the Ephesians.* London: Pickering and Inglis, 1961.
Carson, H. M. *The Epistles of Paul to the Colossians and Philemon.* London: Tyndale, 1961.
Lightfoot, J. B. *St. Paul's Epistles to the Colossians and to Philemon.* London: Macmillan, 1879.
Moule, C. F. D. *The Epistles of Paul the Apostle to the Colossians and to Philemon.* Cambridge University Press, 1958.

EPHESIANS

Bruce, F. F. *The Epistle to the Ephesians.* London: Pickering and Inglis, 1961.
Foulkes, F. *The Epistle of Paul to the Ephesians.* London: Tyndale, 1963.
Simpson, E. K., and Bruce, F. F. *Commentary on the Epistles to the Ephesians and Colossians.* Grand Rapids: Eerdmans; London: Marshall, Morgan, and Scott, 1957.

PHILIPPIANS

Blaiklock, E. M. *From Prison in Rome.* Grand Rapids: Eerdmans, 1964.
Martin, R. P. *The Epistle of Paul to the Philippians.* London: Tyndale, 1959.
Muller, J. J. *The Epistles to the Philippians and to Philemon.* Grand Rapids: Eerdmans; London: Marshall, Morgan and Scott, 1955.

THE PASTORALS

Barrett, C. K. *The Pastoral Epistles.* Oxford: Clarendon, 1963.
Guthrie, D. *The Pastoral Epistles.* London: Tyndale, 1957.
Hanson, A. T. *The Pastoral Epistles.* Cambridge University Press, 1966.

Kelly, J. N. D. *A Commentary on the Pastoral Epistles.* London: A. & C. Black, 1963.

HEBREWS

Bruce, F. F. *The Epistle to the Hebrews.* Grand Rapids: Eerdmans; London: Marshall, Morgan and Scott, 1964.

Filson, F. V. *"Yesterday": A Study of Hebrews in the Light of Chapter 13.* London: SCM, 1967.

Hewitt, T. *The Epistle to the Hebrews.* London: Hodder and Stoughton, 1951.

Tasker, R. V. G. *The Gospel in the Epistle to the Hebrews.* London: Tyndale, 1950.

Westcott, B. F. *The Epistle to the Hebrews.* Greek text. London: Macmillan, 1889.

JAMES

Mitton, C. L. *The Epistle of James.* London: Marshall, Morgan and Scott; Grand Rapids: Eerdmans, 1966.

Robertson, A. F., and Peacock, H. F. *Studies in the Epistle of James.* New York: Doran, ²1959.

Ross, A. *The Epistles of James and John.* Grand Rapids: Eerdmans, 1954.

Tasker, R. V. G. *A Commentary on the General Epistle of James.* London: Tyndale, 1957.

PETER AND JUDE

Cranfield, C. E. B. *The First Epistle of Peter.* London: SCM, 1950.

Green, E. M. B. *The Second Epistle General of Peter and the General Epistle of Jude.* London: Tyndale, 1968.

Kelly, J. N. D. *The Epistles of Peter and Jude.* London: A. & C. Black, 1969.

Selwyn, E. G. *The First Epistle of St. Peter.* Greek text. London: Macmillan, 1946.

Stibbs, A. M., and Walls, A. F. *The First Epistle General of Peter.* London: Tyndale, 1959.

THE JOHANNINE EPISTLES

Findlay, G. G. *Fellowship in the Life Eternal.* London: Hodder and Stoughton, 1909.

Law, R. *The Tests of Life.* Edinburgh: T. & T. Clark, 1909.

Scott, J. R. W. *The Epistles of John.* London: Tyndale, 1966.

Westcott, B. F. *The Epistles of John.* 1892. Reprint with additions by F. F. Bruce. London: Macmillan, 1966.

REVELATION

Caird, G. B. *The Revelation of St. John the Divine.* London: A. & C. Black, 1966.

Hendriksen, W. *More Than Conquerers.* London: Tyndale, 1962.

Kiddle, M. *The Revelation of St. John.* London; Hodder & Stoughton, 1940.

Milligan, W. *The Book of Revelation.* London: Hodder & Stoughton, 1898.

Morris, L. *The Revelation of St. John.* London: Tyndale, 1969.

Subject Index

Abraham 119ff., 132, 237f., 357
Adam 239ff.
Agabus 89, 265
Agrippa 282ff., 285f.
Ananias 73ff., 270f.
Ananias and Sapphira 47ff.
Angels 51, 69, 80, 92, 307, 346f., 365, 374, 393ff.
Antichrist 380, 382
Antioch church 47, 87ff., 90, 96f., 98, 108, 109, 113
Apollos 172ff., 180f., 204
Apostolic office 21, 23, 115, 190
Artemis 170, 205ff.
Athens 149ff.

"Babylon" 371, 406f.
Baalam 374
Baptism 31, 70, 85, 139, 143, 174f., 240, 307, 369
Baptism of the dead 201
Baptism with the Holy Spirit 16, 85f., 175
Barnabas 48, 76, 88, 97f., 114
Beroean church 148f.

Casting lots 23
Church Council at Jerusalem 108f., 112, 117
Church officers 55f., 107, 331f.
Circumcision 86, 108f., 115, 117, 118, 124, 136, 237, 307
Claudius Lysias 277
Colossian church 304ff.
Communal living 34f., 46f.
Corinth 154
Corinthian church 156, 174, 180ff.
Cornelius 80f., 83, 84
Crucifixion 20, 29, 30, 40, 298

Damascus church 73ff.
David 22
Demon possession 64, 139f.
Diaspora 26, 87, 100
Doctrine 33, 34, 56, 251f., 338, 343

Early Church 15ff., 23, 25, 34, 36, 56, 64, 79, 90, 112, 137, 168, 237, 253f., 337
Elymas 98f.
Ephesian church 389
Ephesus 179, 205ff.
Eutychus 259f.

Faith 31, 36, 120, 124, 132f., 237, 341, 348, 358
Felix 277, 279f.
Festus 280ff., 285f.
Filling with the Spirit 25

Gaius 385f.
Gallio 168f.
Gamaliel 53f., 59
Gifts of the Holy Spirit 25, 67, 85, 196ff.
Gospel 16, 18, 19, 25, 106, 115f., 144, 167, 208, 231, 232, 305, 311
Grace 237, 316
Great Commission 18

Healing 35ff., 50f., 64, 78f., 105, 134, 176
Heaven 392f.
Holy Spirit 16, 19, 20f., 23, 24, 26f., 31, 32, 40, 45, 56, 66, 85, 86, 96, 112, 124ff., 137, 173, 175, 181, 196, 211, 238, 245, 316f., 319, 321, 322, 339, 373, 382
Hymns 142f., 304, 309f., 325

Israel 18, 21, 30, 39, 111, 249ff., 348

James 91
James (the Lord's brother) 94, 110ff., 129, 134
Jerusalem Appeal Fund 203, 217
Jerusalem church 62f., 85f., 88, 111, 112, 118, 266f.
Jesus as Head of the Church 305
Jesus as high priest 348ff., 353, 356
Jesus as Messiah 30, 38, 44, 101f., 146, 285, 372, 393
Jesus, ascension of 16, 19

417

Scripture Index